The Selected Letters of Ralph Waldo Emerson

The Selected Letters of
Ralph Waldo Emerson

Edited by Joel Myerson

 Columbia University Press   NEW YORK

The Press acknowledges with thanks a Centennial gift from Betsy Carter and Paul Carter, Emeritus Trustee of the Press, toward the costs of publishing this book.

Columbia University Press
Publishers Since 1893
New York   Chichester, West Sussex
Copyright © 1997 Ralph Waldo Emerson Memorial Association
All rights reserved

For Greta

Contents

Introduction

> Ah you always ask me for that unwritten letter always due, it seems, always
> unwritten, from year to year, by me to you, dear Lidian,—I fear too more widely
> true than you mean,—always due & unwritten by me to every sister & brother of
> the human race. I have only to say that I also bemoan myself daily for the same
> cause—that I cannot write this letter, that I have not stamina & constitution
> enough to mind the two functions of seraph & cherub, oh no, let me not use such
> great words,—rather say that a photometer cannot be a stove. . . . Besides am I
> not, O best Lidian, a most foolish affectionate goodman & papa, with a weak side
> toward apples & sugar and all domesticities, when I am once in Concord?[1]

Ralph Waldo Emerson did not feel comfortable writing letters. The excerpt
above from a letter to his wife addresses the problems he had in fully
expressing his feelings to her as well as to "every sister & brother of the
human race." As a well-known author and lecturer, who was often referred to
as "the Sage of Concord," Emerson had a firmly established public persona
behind which he could take refuge. Whether he faced the public in print or
on the lecture platform, he was able to be separated from them and their
questions; but the medium of correspondence did not offer the same type of
defensive barrier. Emerson was able to stave off those who wished access to
the private man until 1939, when Ralph L. Rusk published his magisterial six-
volume edition of *The Letters of Ralph Waldo Emerson*.

Earlier editions of Emerson's letters had been controlled by his family,
friends, or literary executors. Besides a few scattered letters published in the
typical nineteenth-century "life and letters" biographies of his friends and
acquaintances or in newspaper and magazine articles (the most extensive
being his correspondence with Henry David Thoreau), the only significant
collections of Emerson's letters published before Rusk's edition were the ones
that appeared in James Elliot Cabot's two-volume *Memoir of Ralph Waldo
Emerson* (1887) and in the book-length collections of his correspondence with
Thomas Carlyle (3 vols.; 1883, 1886), the German writer Herman Grimm
(1903), and his childhood friend William Henry Furness (1917), as well as his
letters to the British poet John Sterling (1897) and his long-time friend
Samuel Gray Ward (1899).[2] In each case, the published letters presented a
sanitized Emerson, a public portrait suitable for veneration. To accomplish

this, the editorial policies were appropriately lax; just as the makeup artist covers or eliminates the physical blemishes of the subject, these editors covered Emerson's spelling and grammatical lapses, and eliminated references they considered too personally revealing according to the standards of the time or the picture of him that they were trying to present. Accordingly, the man who defined evil as "merely privative, not absolute" in his "Divinity School Address," stood before the admiring pubiic as a smiling and beneficent Boston Brahmin incarnation of his own essay on "Self-Reliance." This filio-pietistic editing may have satisfied the concerns of the family, but it did not present an Emerson in touch with the global wars and other concerns of the early twentieth century.

Rusk's edition changed forever the way in which we view Emerson. In nearly 2,800 pages, Rusk presents 2,313 letters never before published and 271 hitherto published only in part, as well as references to 509 letters already printed[3] and another 1,281 that were probably written. Rusk's editorial policy is straightforward: he prints the letters as they were written with only a few, minor editorial interventions.[4] Finally, the private Emerson is allowed to speak for himself directly to his public, and the results are impressive. Odell Shepard heralds the publication of the *Letters* with a front-page review in the *New York Times Book Review,* announcing that "[n]ot many events in the history of American literature have been more important than the publication of these long-awaited volumes," for here is "a performance boldly planned and triumphantly achieved, of which America has every reason to be proud."[5] Reviewers praise Rusk for his editorial work and for giving us the unvarnished Emerson, one whom we could now reassess in light of this important new addition to his canon. Shepard feels that "those who know how he suffered throughout life with an almost total inability to heave his thought and feeling into spontaneously spoken words will be glad to know that he often made himself amends with a racing, garrulous, and somewhat slovenly pen." Thus, the "effect of the many letters in which he thus lets himself go, oblivious of the points of punctuation and scornful of capital letters, is like that of a log-jam suddenly broken." In addition to this new vitality, Van Wyck Brooks notices "an impression of Emerson that is new and unexpected in its concrete-ness. . . . It is the social and mundane Emerson who chiefly appears in these letters, and it will surprise many readers to find out how much of his life was social and mundane"; or, as Townsend Scudder III phrases it, the "casual explorer may get something of a shock to learn how much the brain of a great intellectual can be stuffed with the customary events of existence."[6]

But on the other side of the Atlantic, the man who embodied so many aspects of American intellectual and literary history was not receiving such a positive reception. The reviewer in the *Times Literary Supplement* dismisses the letters because "as a whole they do little to illuminate that deeper side of him," and the reviewer in the *Manchester Guardian,* after describing the six volumes as having "a massive dignity befitting the last rites of an inevitable canonisation," goes on to complain that "Emerson was more concerned with what he said than with his way of saying it; and if, in fact, he had not much to say he had an irresistible impulse to go on saying it."[7]

These and many other reviews show that while everyone agrees that Rusk's editorial work is superb, there is much less consensus about what the letters themselves demonstrate. Typical of this lack of agreement is the reviewer in *Time,* who, while positively commenting on Emerson's letters, raises questions about letter writing in general: "The best letters are brief, direct, factual. The best letter writers are usually women and soldiers, who observe closely, state simply. Worst letter writers are usually writers—who philosophize."[8] Part of the reason for this simultaneous praise of and resistance to Emerson's letters may have been the fact that they were the first private documents of his to be released without serious editorial intervention and thus were a univocal presentation of a man whose private writings are truly multivocal.

The only other edition of Emerson's private writings published before Rusk's *Letters* was *The Journals of Ralph Waldo Emerson,* edited by Emerson's son, Edward Waldo Emerson, and grandson, Waldo Emerson Forbes, in ten volumes between 1909 and 1914. Just as in the various editions of letters edited by family members, the *Journals,* too, presented the "Sage of Concord" to the public. As the editors of the modern edition of Emerson's journals characterize their predecessor, the editors of that earlier edition believed "[e]ssential privacy was not to be invaded, no one was to be embarrassed, texts were to be made grammatical and 'correct,' 'trivia' were to be eliminated," resulting in a portrait of "what his chief editor felt impelled to make him, still more the mystic than the Yankee, and always, from beginning to end of the five thousand well printed pages, 'Mr.' Emerson."[9] Rusk's edition literally breaks this mold by allowing readers to form their own versions of Emerson through enabling them to read his texts without mediation.

Twenty years later, this task of reading the private Emerson was made considerably easier as four decades of intense (and highly professional) editorial work began. The mere six volumes of Emerson's letters were soon joined by three volumes of his early lectures (1959–1972), sixteen volumes of journals and miscellaneous notebooks (1960–1982), a new edition of the correspondence with Carlyle (1964), one volume of poetry notebooks (1986), four volumes of his complete sermons (1989–1992), three volumes of topical notebooks (1990–1994), and four additional volumes of letters (1990–1995).[10] Both Joseph Slater, editor of the Carlyle correspondence, and Eleanor M. Tilton, editor of the supplement to Rusk (which printed another 2,000 letters), maintained the high editorial standards of the earlier edition, as did the editors of the other editions. The result, though, is a decidedly mixed blessing: scholars have thirty-eight volumes of Emerson's lectures, letters, journals, and notebooks to mine for their studies of Emerson, but the general reader has few collections that, like anthologies of the published writings, enable them to peruse a "representative" Emerson in one volume.[11] The present volume will, I hope, offer a good, representative selection of Emerson's letters for the modern reader.

Emerson was born in 1803, and much of his early literary training was in the works of the seventeenth and eighteenth centuries. One might also assume that his letter-writing skills were honed by the practitioners of these earlier ages, about whom one recent critic has written: "The universal dictum, which pervades all levels of discourse about letter writing, is that letters should sound like conversation; that they are in fact simply substitutes for conversation with an absent person."[12] As Barbara Packer characterizes Transcendentalist letter writing, "In these intimate reflections and exchanges the Transcendentalists could write with an exuberance their sense of decorum kept out of their published works; in letters particularly they could be witty, malicious, and seductive as well as high-minded and devoted to truth."[13] We can see all of these characteristics in Emerson's letters, but we must also remember that Emerson, like all people, spoke in different voices to different people (and, as I will discuss below, he disliked conversation). The Emerson who asks Carlyle about the mysteries of the universe must have used a different vocabulary and tone than the Emerson who asks a fellow townsman to buy a cow for him; similarly, the Emerson who corresponds with Carlyle does not write in the same fashion as the Emerson who buys a cow. And not only did Emerson assume different postures with different people, he assumed various personae at different stages of his career: the Emerson who writes a tortured letter to George Ripley declining to join the Brook Farm community is simply not the same man who jots perfunctory epistles to Nathaniel Hawthorne or Henry Wadsworth Longfellow or James Russell Lowell a decade and a half later inviting them to a dinner at the Saturday Club.

Another problem in reading someone's published letters is the feeling that we are violating their privacy, for, in the words of a recent critic of the genre, the published letter "carries with it the cachet of violated boundaries and revealed secrets simply by virtue of circulating in print what was once (or is alleged to have been) written for an audience of one."[14] But Emerson's circle of friends regularly circulated their journals and letters among themselves. Bronson Alcott, for example, consistently gave his journal to Margaret Fuller to read during the late 1830s. In 1837 he copies into his journal a note from Fuller, who is returning his journal, beginning "I thank you for the look you have esteemed me worthy to take into your views and feelings, and trust you will never have reason to repent your confidence, as I shall always rejoice in the intercourse which has been permitted me with so fair a soul."[15] Alcott also recognizes the ways in which nominally private documents have a public purpose when he enters in his journal that it "more than any other means, shall best apprize her [Fuller] of the intents of her friend. It is the best substitute for epistolary correspondence."[16] Likewise, Fuller and Emerson read each other's journals.

Emerson knew that many of his letters would be read by people other than their recipient. For example, during his long career as a lecturer in America and Britain, he sent home long, detailed letters of his travels (usually to his wife), fully expecting them to be shared with his extended family and circle of friends; after all, the alternative was to write the same letter to each of them. Or, as he wrote Lidian in 1847 from England, "[f]or letters, do as you will with them, only not print them" (*L*, 3:461). So, in reading these letters, we must be aware that Emerson often envisioned a wider audience for them than one person.

Emerson himself recognized at a young age the multivocal requirement that his correspondence placed upon him. Writing to his brother Edward in 1818, he begins:

> now to tell you the truth there are three or four different moods in which I write to three or four different persons; & in the following order. When I think I should like to write a letter & yet feel sufficiently sober to keep all my nonsense down, then I begin my letter with "My dear Mother" but when I think I can write a grammatically correct epistle or any thing that I am sure can raise the risible muscles of gravity itself, *then* I address my fastidious brother—Bachelor—When in a very *compositorial rhetorical*

mood, I send to an uncle in the Alibama—and last of all when I want to scribble I know not why, & care not what, & moreover have leisure & rhyme at command, and peradventure want to amuse myself, *then* as *now* the pen flies over the lines to my semi-Andover semi-Boston brother Ned. In short I write to you when I am in a serio-ludrico tragico-comico miscellany of feelings. (*L,* 1:70)

Likewise, he early on showed his recognition and understanding of the nonprivate nature of his letters, as he writes Edward in the same letter that "I must sober & season my letters with moral scientifick economical &c sentiments; especially when I am as sure that they will be shown to all my friends as that you will get them" (*L,* 1:71).

Still, while accepting the rules of letter writing ("Mother says that our letters should be improving to both, that we ought to write what strikes us in our reading particularly thereby improving each with the reading of the other"), Emerson felt uncomfortable in the medium ("[t]his letter as almost all mine contains little else than nonsense" [1816; *L,* 1:21]). He complains that "My letters in general you see are a strange medley of every thing and any thing" (1816; *L,* 1:27). Very often he feels about himself the way he describes his friend Sarah Clarke as "a very true person but with the right New England frost in her nature forbidding the streams to flow" (1840; *L,* 2:330). As late as 1841 he complains to Fuller "But how to reply to your fine eastern pearls with chuckstones of granite and slate" (*L,* 2:384). Moreover, his natural disposition not to enter into arguments curtailed his use of the letter as a vehicle for such discussions; as he writes Henry Ware, Jr., who had inquired about what Emerson had *really* meant in the "Divinity School Address," "I thought I would not pay the nobleness of my friends so mean a compliment as to suppress any opposition to their supposed views out of fear of offence. I would rather say to them These things look so to me; to you otherwise: let us say out our uttermost word, & let the all prevailing Truth, as it surely will, judge between us" (1838; *L,* 2:150).

Emerson partially overcame his reluctance to write by adopting different voices at various stages of his life and career, as well as with various correspondents. Although many of his roles in life overlapped, we can discern in his letters Emerson the youth and Harvard student (through 1821), teacher (1821–1825), divinity student and minister (1825–1832), resident of Concord (from 1834 on), lecturer (from 1835 on), Transcendentalist (primarily from 1836 to 1844), professional author (from 1836 on), traveler (from the late 1830s on in America and in 1832–1833, 1847–1848, and 1872–1873 in Britain and Europe), supporter and editor of the *Dial* (1840–1844), and, above all, family man: from 1829 to 1831 with Ellen, from 1835 to his death with Lidian (and their children), and with his mother (d. 1853) and brothers Edward (d. 1834), Charles (d. 1836), Bulkeley (d. 1859), William (d. 1868). Each persona wrote a different type of letter; each correspondent who penetrated to Emerson's inner circle of friends drew forth a different voice.

The early deaths of Emerson's brothers Edward and Charles deprived him of correspondents with whom he felt completely at ease. As their older brother, Waldo could act freely with his younger siblings in ways that he could not with his own elder brother, William. Indeed, the tone of his correspondence with William, while always warm, turns somehow less personal after the latter leaves the ministry and takes up law in New York; most of their correspondence deals with business matters, of which Waldo, as the family banker, was in charge. One assumes that his youthful and romantic letters to Ellen Tucker Emerson were also unguarded, but we cannot know because none of them have come down to us. In the 1830s and 1840s he again breaks down his customary reserve in writing about the topic of friendship with Fuller, Caroline Sturgis (Tappan), and Anna Barker (Ward); these letters show an emotionalness rare in the other letters as he grapples with his feelings, as when he writes Barker "if you grow so fast on my love & reverence that I can dare believe that this dear style we are learning to use to each other is to become very fact then we can drop our words-of-course & can afford the luxury of sincerity" (1840; *L,* 2:339). The correspondence with Fuller is also revealing, with Emerson endorsing one of her first letters to him with "what shocking familiarity!" but concluding, in a memoir of her, that "it was impossible long to hold out against such urgent assault." [17]

But most correspondents received letters tailored to their own needs: his Aunt Mary Moody Emerson was part of an ongoing discussion of theology; Carlyle was approached with carefully written letters about business matters (Emerson helped publish the latter's books in America) and philosophical areas in which they could agree; Abel Adams, Emerson's Concord banker, received business letters; and, as Emerson's public career continued, there were many, many business letters to publishers about his books and to lyceums about his lectures. As the man of Concord becomes a man of the world, his correspondence increases accordingly, if grudgingly, for, as he tells Lidian, it begins to interfere with his writing: "I have got into a pretty good way of reading & writing at last, and so rather grudge to write letters" (1841; *L,* 2:427).

When Emerson finds someone he likes, or a topic he wants to expound upon, his letters rise to greatness. He always preferred letters to conversation; as he writes his brother William, their brother Charles "was born with a tongue[,] you & I with a pen" (1831; *L,* 1:333). When he hears people say "they had rather have ten words vide voce from a man than volumes of letters for getting at his opinion," Emerson thinks "I had rather converse with them by the interpreter." To him, "[p]oliteness ruins conversation" because we "get nothing but the scum & surface of opinions when men are afraid of being unintelligible in their metaphysical distinctions" (1827; *L,* 1:191). To Fuller he suggests "I think you should read the letters & diaries of people[:] you would infer a better conversation than we ever find" (1841; *L,* 2:441).

Emerson was always uneasy in conversational groups and much preferred the written to the spoken word for the communicative act (lectures being an uneasy compromise between the two mediums). As he describes his situation to Sturgis, "I am so born & qualified for solitude that as a spoonful of wine makes some people drunk so a little society, one person whom I cherish turns my head with too much excitement, and no doubt I make compliments and fatuities not a few" (1843; *L,* 7:570). And in writing to a former student of his in 1835 about why he has not answered a letter, Emerson makes this summary statement about conversation in contrast to correspondence: "It was not because it [the student's letter] was neglected for to my habits of intercourse a written page always comes more welcome than much conversation: the pen is a more faithful index than the tongue of those qualities in my fellow man that most excite my curiosity & whatever the proverbs may say of the untrustworthiness of words I know more of all my friends by them than by their acts" (*L,* 1:431).[18]

One thought in the last letter that runs throughout Emerson's correspondence is what he calls "my chronic & constitutional reluctance to write a letter" (1869; *L,* 9:338). Again, he formed his judgment on this subject very early, as we see in this letter from 1823 to a former classmate:

I dislike cordially an exact correspondence which makes it binding on the conscience of the receiver of a letter to write his answer by the next post. I rather choose to claim the liberty of writing when I am in the humour, and in what dialect of the nations I will. If to write twice without waiting for an answer, please my despotic whims, I shall write twice; or if I should let my pen rot a whole year, unwet, I should feel no qualms. Claiming so large a charter for myself, I must needs allow the same to those who honour me with their epistles, and if my lord would not always wait for my tardy letter, but would sometimes vouchsafe a gratuitous sheet—I should be exceedingly grateful. (*L*, 7:120)

Or, as he writes his brother Charles, "A few sincere & entire communications are all we can expect in a lifetime. They are they which make the earth memorable to the speakers and perhaps measure the spiritual years. For the rest we dodge one another on our diverse pursuits[,] waste time in the ado of meeting & parting or usurp it with our pompous business" (1834; *L*, 1:427). But as the years went on, Emerson found it harder and harder to write these kinds of communications; by 1853 he informs Caroline Sturgis Tappan "I believe, my slowness to write letters has grown from the experience, that some of my friends have been very impatient of my generalizings, as we weary of any trick, whilst theirs are still sweet to me. So I hesitate to write, except to the assessors, or to the man that is to slate my house" (*L*, 8:374) [19]

Emerson's complaint to Tappan that he is reduced to writing run-of-the-mill letters is echoed elsewhere in his correspondence. As he complains to Carlyle in 1856, "we do not write letters to the gods or to our friends, but only to attorneys landlords & tenants," [20] or to Aunt Mary in 1857, "the oppressive miscellany of my *business-letter*,—so to call them, has long ago destroyed almost any inclination to write" (*L*, 5:91). By the 1860s he explains to a correspondent inquiring about an unanswered letter that "my correspondence is large, larger than I can meet as it requires, & I at almost all times indisposed to write any letter that is not indispensable. Tis only at intervals that I dare take up my sheaves of letters to see what has been neglected" (1868; *L*, 6:22). [21]

Also, by the late 1860s Emerson's mental powers are beginning to decline, a situation exacerbated by a fire that severely damaged his Concord house in 1872. While it was being repaired Emerson and his daughter Ellen went abroad, during which time she wrote most of the couple's letters home while he suffered from a "long idleness—say incapacity to write anything . . . not a line in my diary, not any syllable that I remember unless a word or two to the bankers, or unavoidable billets in reply to notes of invitation here or there has been written" (1873; *L*, 6:234). As his mental decline continues into the 1870s, he is reduced to confessing to Emma Lazarus that he rarely goes abroad to see his friends because he is not "willing to distress [them] with his perpetual forgetfulness of the right word for the name of the book or fact or person he is eager to recall, but which refuses to come." "I have grown silent to my own household under this vexation," he adds, "& cannot afflict dear friends with my tied tongue" (1876; *L*, 6:296). Letter writing, too, is painful: his mental ability is diminished, what energies he has left are spent on business correspondence, and he has outlived most of his friends. Lacking vitality, and thus reflective of his own diminished physical and mental abilities, the letters from the last decade of Emerson's life are pale reflections of his earlier letters.

The Selected Letters of Ralph Waldo Emerson prints 350 letters written between 1813 and 1880, and includes some to all of his major correspondents. I have tried, as much as possible, to present a "representative" Emerson, one who corresponded with the famous and the unknown, who wrote on interesting and also mundane subjects, who soared in philosophical speculation but also came down to earth to discuss financial matters, whose letters provide the germs for some of his publications (most notably "Friendship") yet deal with the nitty-gritty of the profession of authorship, who can write eloquent letters of condolence to others yet strip his soul bare in grief himself, and who, above all, refashioned himself according to the needs of the moment and the correspondent.

We see Emerson writing about family and other matters to his brothers Bulkeley, Charles, Edward, and William; his Aunt Mary Moody Emerson; his step-grandfather Ezra Ripley; his "adopted sister," Elizabeth Hoar, who had been engaged to Charles Emerson and was called "Aunt Lizzie" by the family; and his wife Lidian and their children. Here, too, are the major participants in the Transcendentalist movement: Bronson Alcott, Ellery Channing, James Freeman Clarke, Christopher Pearse Cranch, John Sullivan Dwight, Fuller, Frederic Henry Hedge, Theodore Parker, Elizabeth Palmer Peabody, George Ripley, and Thoreau, as well as such second-generation converts as Moncure Daniel Conway and Thomas Wentworth Higginson. I have tried to be especially generous in selecting from the revealing correspondence with Fuller, Caroline Sturgis Tappan, Anna Barker Ward, and Samuel Gray Ward. The letters to Carlyle provide interesting glimpses into their book dealings, as well as discussions of theological and philosophical issues. Other famous literary and historical figures are also represented, including George Bancroft, Horatio Greenough, William Dean Howells, Emma Lazarus, Henry Wadsworth Longfellow, James Russell Lowell, John Muir, Wendell Phillips, Charles Summer, and Walt Whitman.

While Emerson's letters to his family and to his better-known contemporaries are usually the most revealing, many other letters help us to see the multifaceted personality of their writer. There are, for example, his evaluations of the prose and poetry of his friends and of strangers, which present in miniature Emerson's theories of writing and literature. There is his lifelong correspondence with such people as his childhood friend William Henry Furness or Benjamin Peter Hunt, a former student of his, that gives us in passing Emerson's views on friendship. The 1850s witness a number of strong letters speaking out against slavery. His letters of condolence provide fascinating character sketches that help to define what Emerson looked for in his own representative men and women.

Some of these letters stand out vividly on their own as gems of the art of letter writing (such as those to Carlyle or Fuller) or as signposts in Emerson's life. Printed here are letters accepting—and then resigning—his post with Boston's Second Church and Society; announcing with joy his marriage to Ellen Tucker, and then with grief her death; giving vivid descriptions of his travels across America and in Britain, France, and Egypt; supporting Alcott in the Boston newspapers against his critics (and then telling him how to write plainly); recommending both Thoreau and Whitman for positions (and saluting the latter upon the publication of *Leaves of Grass*); greeting the birth of his children and revealing his anguish and his inability to grieve at the death of his young son Waldo; rejecting an offer to join the Brook Farm community; trying to get his nephew an army post (here published for the first time); and engaging in the business of writing, both for himself and for others, with numerous publishers.

Emerson's sermons and lectures, while unpublished until recently, nevertheless represent a public face that he wore when dealing with an audience, just as the works he published himself were to stand alone without reference to the personality behind them. His journals and notebooks provide many personal revelations, but they served primarily as the raw material out of which he formed his writings, what he called his "savings bank."[22] It is in his letters that Emerson shares with us his likes and dislikes, praises and blames, highs and lows, griefs and joys, loves and deaths, empyrean heights and down-to-earth matters, and it is through the letters that we gain a unique insight into the mind of this seminal figure in American literary and intellectual history.

EDITORIAL POLICY

This selected edition of Emerson's letters reprints the texts from the earlier editions by Rusk, Slater, and Tilton with few changes. Because matters of styling differ among these three editors, I have imposed uniformity in such matters by placing all date and place lines, and closing salutations and signatures flush right; placing all opening salutations flush left; indenting all paragraphs the same distance; setting words underlined by Emerson in italics; and lowering all superscript letters to the line. I have also not reported any of Emerson's revisions, such as insertions and cancellations, choosing instead to present the final layer of text. Nor have I reported ellipses used to indicate missing material from printed texts for which no manuscript source exists. Like the earlier editors, I have not modernized or regularized Emerson's spelling, punctuation, or capitalization practices, except in a few cases.[23]

Square brackets in the texts of letters indicate my interpolations. The wax seal used on many of Emerson's letters often tore the manuscript when removed. When words are missing because of such damage, I have indicated this by "[manuscript mutilated]"; Rusk and Tilton often supplied missing words in brackets for these cases, and I have printed their surmises here without brackets. Emerson's signature has been cut away from some letters (probably for autograph collectors), a fact I do not report.

Because the annotations in the earlier editions are models of thoroughness, I have kept annotations here to a minimum, knowing that readers may return to the originals for more information. I have provided a chronology to present the outline of Emerson's life for reference, and biographies to help introduce his major correspondents. Further information may be easily obtained from Albert J. Von Frank, *An Emerson Chronology* (New York: G. K. Hall, 1994), and *Biographical Dictionary of Transcendentalism* and *Encyclopedia of Transcendentalism,* both edited by Wesley T. Mott (Westport, Conn.: Greenwood, 1996).

I have, in general, attempted to create readable texts for this edition, while retaining as much of Emerson's original style as possible; full textual information is, of course, available in the Rusk, Slater, and Tilton editions.

Ralph L. Rusk, Joseph Slater, and Eleanor M. Tilton all produced editions of Emerson's letters that will stand the tests of time and scholarly usage. Without their work, this edition—and much of the scholarship on Emerson over the past fifty-plus years—would not have been possible.

In preparing this edition I am grateful to the University of South Carolina, and especially Robert Newman, chair of the English department, for support. Michael McLoughlin assisted in seeing the work through press. Scott Gwara graciously provided translations. Ronald A. Bosco, Lawrence Buell, and Robert D. Richardson Jr. all made valuable suggestions about the introduction. Jerome Loving helped with information on Whitman.

Jennifer Crewe supported this book from the start and made it possible for me to enjoy putting it together.

All manuscripts are quoted by permission of the Ralph Waldo Emerson Memorial Association. The *RWEMA* has, ever since it was formed in the 1930s, supported scholarly work on Emerson, and the public is much in its debt for both preserving and making available the great treasure trove of papers in its collection, now at the Houghton Library of Harvard University.

Greta has put up with Emersoniana spreading throughout our house and lives for more than twenty years, and has brought me, as Emerson says (1866; *L*, 5:451) of one of Ellen's letters, "an otto of roses." This book is important; so naturally it is for her.

Joel Myerson
Edisto Beach, South Carolina

Notes

1. Letter to Lidian Jackson Emerson, 8–10 March 1848, *The Letters of Ralph Waldo Emerson,* ed. Ralph L. Rusk and Eleanor M. Tilton (New York: Columbia University Press, 1939; 1990–1995), 4:33. Further references to this edition will be cited parenthetically in the text by year of the letter and volume and page number.

2. Full citations for these and other works by Emerson may be found in my *Ralph Waldo Emerson: A Descriptive Bibliography* (Pittsburgh: University of Pittsburgh Press, 1982). Rusk's edition of Emerson's correspondence with Arthur Hugh Clough (1934) is the exception to my general statements about editorial policy in this paragraph.

3. Because of limited space, Rusk did not print any letter that had been previously published (but he did list the place of publication in his edition). This resulted in a skewed picture of Emerson in his edition, for such correspondences as those with Carlyle, Furness, Thoreau, and Ward were omitted. Tilton printed all these in her edition, plus the letters to Tappan and Anna Ward, which had not been available to Rusk.

4. Rusk did not report cancellations or insertions in the manuscripts. He also left out a few personal references at the request of the Emerson family; these were later restored by Tilton (and can be identified through using the "Calendar" at the end of the tenth volume). Tilton reports insertions and cancellations in the manuscripts.

5. "Emerson's Collected Letters," *New York Times Book Review,* 28 May 1939, pp. 1, 15.

6. Brooks, "Emerson in His Time," *New Republic* 90 (23 August 1939): 78–80; Scudder, "The Human Emerson," *Saturday Review of Literature* 20 (10 June 1939): 3, 4, 15.

7. Anon., "The Essential Democrat," *Times Literary Supplement,* 1 July 1939, pp. 388, 390; H. B. Charlton, "Emerson's Letters," *Manchester Guardian,* 27 June 1939, p. 7.

8. Anon., "Waldo," *Time,* 29 May 1939, p. 82.

9. *The Journals and Miscellaneous Notebooks of Ralph Waldo Emerson,* ed. William H. Gilman, Ralph H. Orth, et al., 16 vols. (Cambridge: Harvard University Press, 1960–1982), 1:xiii–xiv.

10. An edition of Emerson's later lectures is underway by Ronald A. Bosco and me for publication by the University of Georgia Press. Bosco and I are also editing the correspondence of the Emerson brothers.

11. See *Young Emerson Speaks: Unpublished Discourses on Many Subjects,* ed. Arthur Cushman McGiffert Jr. (1938); *The Heart of Emerson's Journals,* ed. Bliss Perry (1926); *The Journals of Ralph Waldo Emerson,* ed. Robert N. Linscott (1960); and *Emerson in His Journals,* ed. Joel Porte (Cambridge: Harvard University Press, 1982).

12. Rosemarie Bodenheimer, *The Real Life of Mary Ann Evans: George Eliot, Her Letters and Fiction* (Ithaca: Cornell University Press, 1994), p. 8.

13. Barbara L. Packer, "The Transcendentalists," in *The Cambridge History of American Literature,* vol. 2 (*Prose Writing 1820–1865*), ed. Sacvan Bercovitch (New York: Cambridge University Press, 1995), p. 425.

14. Bodenheimer, *The Real Life of Mary Ann Evans,* p. 3.

15. Larry A. Carlson, "Bronson Alcott's 'Journal for 1837' (Part Two)," in *Studies in the American Renaissance 1982,* ed. Joel Myerson (Boston: Twayne, 1982), p. 80.

16. Larry A. Carlson, "Bronson Alcott's 'Journal for 1838' (Part One)," in *Studies in the American Renaissance 1993,* ed. Joel Myerson (Charlottesville: University Press of Virginia, 1993), p. 216.

17. Emerson's endorsement on Fuller's letter to him of 30 May 1837, *The Letters of Margaret Fuller,* ed. Robert N. Hudspeth, 6 vols. (Ithaca: Cornell University Press, 1983–1994), 1:277; [William Henry Channing, James Freeman Clarke, and Ralph Waldo Emerson], *Memoirs of Margaret Fuller Ossoli,* 2 vols. (Boston: Phillips, Sampson, 1852), 1:203.

18. Despite Emerson's strictures on conversation, the paucity of letters to his Concord family and friends suggests that he did indeed talk freely with the people whom he liked. Most of his surviving letters to Lidian and to Henry David Thoreau are written during his travels. Elizabeth Hoar, whom he treated like a sister after the death of her fiancé Charles Emerson, barely figures in his correspondence, partly because she lived nearby in Concord, and partly because his public letters to Lidian during his travels were also meant for her to read.

19. In a similar fashion, he writes Carlyle about his "slowness to write" and that "I

believe the reason for this recusancy is, the fear of disgusting my friends, as with a book open always at the same page" (1853, in *The Correspondence of Emerson and Carlyle*, ed. Joseph Slater [New York: Columbia University Press, 1964], p. 491).

20. *Correspondence of Emerson and Carlyle*, p. 508.

21. Emerson gives an unusual reason why he has let drop one segment of his letter-writing audience in replying to a friend wishing a letter of introduction to someone in England: "I have let fall all my English correspondence . . . This state of things is not owing solely to my indolence, but partly to the fact that my friends abroad very seldom sent friends to me, so that I could not well request kind offices of them" (1862; *L, 5:277*).

22. He also copied letters—most notably those written to Aunt Mary—in his journal. One brief letter to Thoreau in his journal ("My dear Henry, / A frog was made to live in a swamp, but a man was not made to live in a swamp. Yours ever. R.") is included by Tilton, even though she confesses it is "probably not to be taken as a genuine letter" (1858; *L, 8:562*).

23. I have silently emended punctuation that is confusing, such as redundant periods; changed Emerson's elongated equal signs into one-em dashes; and emended Emerson's brackets to parentheses in his letters of 25 June 1840 and 30 December 1844. I have also silently corrected Tilton's erroneous transcription of the fourth sentence in Emerson's letter to Whitman of 21 July 1855.

Chronology

1796
25 October   Reverend William Emerson marries Ruth Haskins

1798
9 February   Phebe Ripley Emerson born

1799
28 November   John Clarke Emerson born

1800
28 September   Phebe Ripley Emerson dies

1801
31 July   William Emerson born

1802
20 September   Lydia Jackson born

1803
25 May   Ralph Waldo Emerson born

1805
17 April   Edward Bliss Emerson born

1807
11 April   Robert Bulkeley Emerson born
26 April   John Clarke Emerson dies

1808
27 November   Charles Chauncy Emerson born

1811
26 February   Mary Caroline Emerson born
12 May   Reverend William Emerson dies

1812
Spring?   Enters Boston Latin School

1814
14 April   Mary Caroline Emerson dies

1817
October   Enters Harvard College

1818
January   Begins occasional school-teaching at Waltham

1821
29 August   Graduates from Harvard College
October   Assists William in a school for young ladies

1822
November   "Thoughts on the Religion of the Middle Ages," RWE's first publication, appears in the *Christian Disciple* and *Theological Review*

1823
5 December   Takes over William's school when he leaves for Germany

1824
April   Begins formally studying religion
31 December   Closes school

1825
11 February   Registers as a student of divinity at Harvard
12 September   Opens school at Chelmsford (closes it at end of year)

1826
3 January   Takes over Edward's school in Roxbury when he leaves for Europe (closes it on 28 March)
1 April   Opens school in Cambridge (closes it on 23 October)
10 October   Approbated by American Unitarian Association to preach
25 November   Sails to Charleston, S.C., and St. Augustine, Fla., to improve health

1827
3 June   Returns to Boston

25 December	Meets Ellen Louisa Tucker in Concord, N.H.

1828

2 July	Edward is committed to McLean Asylum (released in the fall)
17 December	Engaged to Ellen Tucker

1829

30 January	Becomes colleague pastor at Second Church, Boston
11 March	Ordained at Second Church
1 July	Promoted to pastor
30 September	Marries Ellen Tucker

1830

12 December	Edward goes to Puerto Rico for his health (returns August 1832)

1831

8 February	Ellen Louisa Tucker Emerson dies of tuberculosis
7 December	Charles goes to Puerto Rico for his health (returns 1 May 1832)

1832

6 October	Edward returns to Puerto Rico for his health
22 December	Sends farewell letter to Second Church resigning his position
25 December	Sails for Europe

1833

26 August	Meets Jane and Thomas Carlyle
7 October	Returns to America
5 November	Delivers his first public lecture, "The Uses of Natural History," in Boston
3 December	William Emerson marries Susan Woodward Haven

1834

March	Meets Lydia Jackson of Plymouth
13 May	Receives partial inheritance of $11,600 from Ellen Emerson's estate
1 October	Edward dies of tuberculosis in Puerto Rico
9 October	Moves to Concord, Mass.

1835

24 January	Proposes to Lydia Jackson (engagement announcement at end of month)
29 January	Begins first lecture series, "Biography," in Boston
12 September	Delivers discourse on Concord's history (published in November)
14 September	Marries Lydia Jackson (whom he calls "Lidian")

1836

9 May	Charles dies suddenly in New York
9 September	*Nature* published
19 September	First meeting of the Transcendental Club
30 October	Waldo Emerson born
8 December	Begins "Philosophy of History" lecture series in Boston

1837

late July	Receives remainder of inheritance (another $11,675) from Ellen Emerson's estate
31 August	Delivers address on the "American Scholar" at Harvard (published 23 September)
6 December	Begins "Human Culture" lecture series in Boston

1838

14 July	Carlyle's *Critical and Miscellaneous Essays* published, edited by RWE
15 July	Delivers address at the Harvard Divinity School (published 21 August)
24 July	Delivers address on "Literary Ethics" at Dartmouth College (published 8 September)

1839

24 February	Ellen Tucker Emerson born
7 September	Jones Very's *Essays and Poems* published, edited by RWE
4 December	Begins "Present Age" lecture series in Boston

1840

1 July	First issue of *Dial* appears
20 March	Begins "Human Life" lecture series in Providence
2 September	Attends the last meeting of the Transcendental Club

1841

19 March	*Essays [First Series]* published (and in England on 21 August)
11 August	Delivers "The Method of Nature" at Waterville College, Maine (published 21 October)
22 November	Edith Emerson born

1842

27 January	Waldo Emerson dies of scarlatina
March	Margaret Fuller resigns as editor of *Dial;* Emerson becomes editor

1843

10 January	Begins "New England" lecture series in Baltimore
May	Carlyle's *Past and Present* published, edited by RWE

1844

8 April	Last issue of *Dial* appears
10 July	Edward Waldo Emerson born
1 August	Delivers address on "Emancipation of the Negroes in the British West Indies" at Concord Court House (published 9 September and in England in October)
19 October	*Essays: Second Series* published (and in England on 9 November)

1845

2 December	Purchases forty-one acres at Walden Pond
31 December	Begins "Representative Men" lecture series in Concord

1846

12 December	*Poems* published in England (and in America on 25 December)

1847

5 October	Sails for England

1848

7 May	Arrives in Paris
2 June	Returns to England
6 June	Begins "Mind and Manners in the Nineteenth-Century" lecture series in London

    27 July   Returns to America

    1849
    1 February   Begins "English Traits" lecture series in Chelmsford, Mass.
    20 March   First meeting of Town and Country Club
    11 September   *Nature: Addresses, and Lectures* published

    1850
    1 January   *Representative Men* published (and in England on 5 January)
    13 May   Begins midwestern lecture tour (returns 28 June)
    19 July   Margaret Fuller dies

    1851
    22 December   Begins "The Conduct of Life" lecture series in Boston

    1852
    14 February   *Memoirs of Margaret Fuller Ossoli* published, co-edited by RWE
    April   Lectures in Montreal
    24 November   Begins midwestern lecture tour (returns mid-February 1853)

    1853
    16 November   Ruth Haskins Emerson dies

    1854
    2 January   Begins midwestern lecture tour (returns 20 February)
    3 January   Begins "Topics of Modern Times" lecture series in Philadelphia
    16 December   First meeting of the Saturday Club

    1855
    ca. 27 December   Begins midwestern lecture tour (returns late January 1856)

    1856
    6 August   *English Traits* published (and in England on 6 September)

    1857
    8 January   Begins midwestern lecture tour (returns 10 February)

1859

27 May   Robert Bulkeley Emerson dies

1860

16 January   Begins midwestern lecture tour (returns 25 February)

8 December   *The Conduct of Life* published (and in England on 8 December)

1861

2 April   Begins "Life and Literature" lecture series in Boston

16 July   Edward Waldo Emerson admitted to Harvard

1862

6 May   Henry David Thoreau dies

August   "Thoreau" appears in *Atlantic Monthly*

1863

2 January   Begins midwestern lecture tour (returns 7 February)

1 May   Mary Moody Emerson dies

10 October   Thoreau's *Excursions* published, edited by RWE

27 November   Begins "American Life" lecture series in Boston

1865

11 January   Begins midwestern lecture tour (returns 10 February)

22 July   Thoreau's *Letters to Various Persons* published, edited by RWE

3 October   Edith Emerson marries William Hathaway Forbes

1866

9 January   Begins midwestern lecture tour (returns 20 February)

23 June   *Complete Works* published in two volumes in England

10 July   Ralph Emerson Forbes, RWE's first grandchild, born

18 July   Awarded LL.D. degree by Harvard

1867

8 January   Begins midwestern lecture tour (returns 22 or 23 March)

29 April   *May-Day and Other Pieces* published (and in England on 8 June)

17 July   Appointed Overseer of Harvard University

2 December   Begins midwestern lecture tour (returns 2 January)

1868

13 September   William Emerson dies

1869

27 October   *Prose Works* published in two volumes in America

1870

5 March   *Society and Solitude* published (and in England on 5
        March)

26 April   Begins "Natural History of Intellect" series at Harvard

1871

11 April   Begins trip to California (returns 30 May)

25 November   Begins midwestern lecture tour (returns 14 December)

1872

24 July   RWE's house severely damaged by fire

23 October   Goes to Europe with Ellen

25 December   Arrives in Egypt

1873

19 February   Returns to Europe

27 April   Sees Carlyle for the last time

26 May   Returns to America

1 October   Delivers address at the opening of the Concord Free
        Public Library

1874

19 September   Edward Waldo Emerson marries Annie Shepard Keyes

19 December   *Parnassus* published, a poetry collection edited by RWE

1875

15 December   *Letters and Social Aims* published (and in England on 8
        January 1876)

1876

24 June   The "Little Classic Edition" of RWE's works is
        published in nine volumes

1878

25 February   Delivers address on "Fortune of the Republic" in
        Boston (published 10 August)

7 April	Elizabeth Hoar dies	25

1880

4 February   Delivers one hundredth lecture before the Concord Lyceum

1882

20 April   Catches cold

27 April   Ralph Waldo Emerson dies in Concord, Mass.

30 April   Buried in Sleepy Hollow Cemetery, Concord

Biographies

Adams, Abel (1792–1867). A lifelong friend of Emerson and neighbor of his in Concord, who advised the family on financial matters.

Agassiz, Jean Louis (1807–1873). A Swiss-born natural scientist, who founded the Museum of Comparative Zoology at Harvard University. He was a friend of Thoreau's and often visited Concord. He was also a member of the Saturday Club.

Alcott, Amos Bronson (1799–1888). A teacher at the Temple School in Boston (1834–1838), whose progressive educational views brought him to Emerson's attention. Emerson defended Alcott against his critics when the Temple School was in trouble, read his manuscript on the development of his daughters ("Psyche") many times without being able to get Alcott to revise it successfully, helped him to attend Transcendental Club meetings, and published his writings in the *Dial.* Alcott moved to Concord in 1840, visited a group in England interested in his ideas in 1842, and (with one of the Englishmen, Charles Lane) worked at the Fruitlands community in Harvard, Massachusetts, during the last half of 1843. After the failure of Fruitlands, the Alcotts moved about a good deal before permanently settling in Concord in 1857.

Bancroft, George (1800–1891). An historian and member of the Saturday Club, Bancroft had earlier trained for the ministry, studying theology in Germany and teaching at Harvard College.

Blake, Harrison Gray Otis (1816–1898). One of the students who had invited Emerson to deliver his "Divinity School Address," Blake was a lifelong admirer of Emerson and a disciple of Thoreau. He later edited four volumes of selections from Thoreau's journal. After the death of Thoreau's sister Sophia, he was left all Thoreau's manuscripts.

Bradford, George Partridge (1807–1890). A Harvard Divinity School graduate, who was the brother of Sarah Alden Bradford Ripley, a member of the Brook Farm community, and a good friend of Alcott, Emerson, and Thoreau.

Brisbane, Albert (1809–1890). A major spokesperson for the communitarian philosophy of Charles Fourier in the 1840s, he wrote a regular column on the subject in the *New York Tribune* and also edited the *Phalanx* (1843–1845), the predecessor of the Brook Farm journal, the *Harbinger.*

Brook Farm (1841–1847). A social experiment begun by George Ripley and his wife, Sophia, in West Roxbury, near Boston, to see if there was an alternative to an ever-increasing materialistic way of life. Begun as the Brook Farm Institute for Agriculture and Education, in 1845 it adapted to the more structured ideas of the French socialist Charles Fourier and was renamed the Brook Farm Phalanx. In 1845 it began publishing a journal, the *Harbinger.* Brook Farm failed when an uninsured new central building, then under construction, burned down.

Cabot, James Elliot (1821–1903). A contributor to the last number of the *Dial,* who became Emerson's literary executor. As Emerson's mental and literary powers began to fail, Cabot, often with the help of Ellen Tucker Emerson, assisted Emerson in preparing material for publication. He later wrote *Memoir of Ralph Waldo Emerson* (2 vols., 1887) and edited Emerson's *Complete Works* (11 vols., 1883–1893), for which he compiled three new volumes.

Carlyle, Thomas (1795–1881). A Scottish essayist and biographer, whose meeting with Emerson in August 1833 began a lifelong friendship and correspondence (published separately in 1964). Emerson was instrumental in getting his *Sartor Resartus* (1836), *The French Revolution* (1837), and *Critical and Miscellaneous Essays* (4 vols., 1838–1839) published in America. Their friendship grew strained in later years as Carlyle became more critical of American democracy and what he considered Emerson's impractical idealism.

Channing, William Ellery (1780–1842). An influential Boston minister, whose sermon on "Unitarian Christianity" (1819) helped to define that religion. His sermon on "Likeness to God" (1828) greatly influenced the Transcendentalists by proposing a type of human perfectibility, and his *Slavery* (1835) was an important abolitionist document.

Channing, William Ellery the Younger ("Ellery") (1817–1901). A nephew of the Reverend William Ellery Channing, who became a poet and longtime resident of Concord and friend of Emerson's. He married Margaret Fuller's sister, Ellen, in 1842. Emerson helped him publish his poems (to which Emerson had been introduced by Samuel Gray Ward) in the *Dial*—even writing an article about them ("New Poetry," October 1840)—and wrote the preface to his *Wanderer* (1871). Channing wrote the first biography of his friend Thoreau in 1873 (*Thoreau: The Poet-Naturalist.*)

Channing, William Henry (1810–1884). A nephew of the Reverend William Ellery Channing, he was called the "evil time's sole patriot" in Emerson's "Ode" inscribed to him. He was a co-editor of the Transcendentalist journal in the midwest, the *Western Messenger* (1839–1841), contributor to the *Dial*, and editor of the reform journal, the *Present* (1843–1844). Channing was also a frequent visitor to the Brook Farm community. He co-edited, with Emerson and James Freeman Clarke, *Memoirs of Margaret Fuller Ossoli* (2 vols., 1852).

Clarke, James Freeman (1810–1888). A Harvard Divinity School graduate, he helped edit the *Western Messenger* (1836–1839), was a member of the Transcendental Club, and was a contributor to the *Dial*. He began his own congregation, the Church of the Disciples, in Boston in 1841. With Emerson and William Henry Channing, he co-edited *Memoirs of Margaret Fuller Ossoli* (2 vols., 1852).

Clough, Arthur Hugh (1819–1861). Emerson met this poet when he visited Oxford University in 1847. When Clough visited America in 1852–1853, Emerson tried unsuccessfully to help him find permanent employment. Their correspondence was published separately in 1934.

Conway, Moncure Daniel (1832–1907). A Virginia-born Harvard Divinity School graduate, who became an abolitionist, historian, and biographer, Conway was one of the second-generation Transcendentalists who were in-fluenced by Emerson. In 1860 he began the *Dial*, named in homage of the Boston journal, but it lasted for only one year.

Cranch, Christopher Pearse (1813–1892). A Harvard Divinity School graduate, co-editor of the *Western Messenger* (1837–1839), *Dial* contributor, and painter in the Hudson River School tradition, who is best known today for his caricatures based on passages from Emerson's writings.

Dial (1840–1844). The periodical of the Transcendentalists, this journal ap-peared quarterly for four volumes. Margaret Fuller served as editor for its first two years, Emerson for the last two, while George Ripley served as business manager and Elizabeth Palmer Peabody as publisher. Thoreau helped to edit one number. The *Dial* failed because the public did not buy it and because Emerson had no more time to give to its editorial demands.

Duyckinck, Evert Augustus (1816–1878). An important New York literary figure, who helped edit Wiley and Putnam's Library of American Books, the
Literary World (1847–1853), and the *Cyclopædia of American Literature* (2 vols.,
1855).

Dwight, John Sullivan (1813–1893). A Harvard Divinity School graduate, who
went on to contribute to the *Dial,* join the Brook Farm community and help
edit the *Harbinger,* and found *Dwight's Journal of Music* (1852–1881).

Emerson, Charles Chauncy (1808–1836). Emerson's younger, and probably
favorite, brother, who was less successful at Harvard than Edward but more
accomplished than Waldo. He studied law and became engaged to Elizabeth
Hoar in 1835. He suffered from tuberculosis, which he tried unsuccessfully to
cure by a visit to Puerto Rico in 1831–1832. Emerson published selections
from his journals in three issues of the *Dial.*

Emerson, Edward Bliss (1805–1834). With William, the best student of the
Emerson brothers. He studied law, but was committed to the McLean
Asylum in July 1828 after suffering a complete breakdown. After his release
that fall he was plagued by tuberculosis and tried to restore his health by
going in 1830 to Puerto Rico, where he became a merchant. Emerson published a poem of his in the *Dial.*

Emerson, Edward Waldo (1844–1930). Emerson's son, who became a physician
in Concord, author of *Emerson in Concord* (1889), editor of the Centenary
Edition of his father's *Complete Works* (12 vols., 1903–1904), and co-editor of
his father's *Journals* (10 vols., 1909–1914). He married Annie Shepard Keyes in
1874 and they had seven children.

Emerson, Ellen Louisa Tucker (1811–1831). Emerson's first wife, whom he
married in 1829. Her death from tuberculosis helped shape Emerson's
thoughts on such subjects as compensation. The income from her estate
helped to give Emerson some financial independence.

Emerson, Ellen Tucker (1839–1909). Emerson's daughter, named after his first
wife, became companion to her mother and father as they grew older. She
accompanied her father on his 1872–1873 trip to Britain, Europe, and Egypt.
She helped James Elliot Cabot to edit her father's writings after his literary
and mental powers began their decline.

Emerson, Lidian Jackson (1802–1892). A native of Plymouth, Massachusetts,
she became Emerson's second wife in 1835. Emerson considered their marriage

less romantic, more practical than his first, and Lidian's religiosity occasionally put him off, but their relationship was a good one, producing four children.

Emerson, Mary Moody (1774–1863). The sister of Emerson's father, she helped in the education of the Emersons' children. Her Calvinistic upbringing and beliefs were an important early influence on Emerson's thought.

Emerson, Robert Bulkeley (1807–1859). Emerson provided important financial support for his mentally impaired younger brother, who was institutionalized or boarded out for nearly all of his adult life.

Emerson, Ruth Haskins (1768–1853). Emerson's mother married his father, William Emerson, in 1796. After her husband's death, she took on boarders and made her most important goal the education of her sons. She stayed with Emerson in his house in Concord for the last twenty years of her life.

Emerson, Waldo (1836–1842). Emerson's first child, whose sudden death from scarlatina greatly affected Emerson (and is memorialized in his poem "Threnody").

Emerson, William (1801–1868). As the oldest Emerson brother, William was supposed to be a minster like his father, but exposure to German biblical criticism while he was studying in Göttingen (1824–1825) shook his faith, and he returned to New York, later becoming a lawyer and judge. He married Susan Woodward Haven in 1833, and three of their children lived to adulthood: William, Jr. (1835–1864), John Haven (1840–1913), and Charles (1841–1916). Susan died in 1868, a few months before her husband.

Fields, James Thomas (1817–1881). An influential member of the firm Ticknor and Fields (which later evolved into Houghton Mifflin), he became Emerson's publisher in 1860 and later helped arrange for Emerson to give the private lecture series in Boston that was among his most financially successful. James and his wife, Annie Adams Fields (1834–1915), ran a popular literary salon in Boston.

Forbes, Edith Emerson (1841–1929). Emerson's second daughter. She married William Hathaway Forbes in 1865 and they had eight children.

Francis, Convers (1795–1863). The brother of the reformer Lydia Maria Child, he was the oldest member of the Transcendental Club. He was seen as becoming more conservative after taking up a professorship at Harvard University in 1842.

Fuller, Sarah Margaret (1810–1850). Educated by her father as if she were a son, Fuller could hold her own in intellectual discussions with the Transcendentalists and was invited to attend meetings of the Transcendental Club. She edited the *Dial* for two years, contributing many articles to it, but had to resign when none of her salary was paid. She was an occasional visitor to the Brook Farm community, and one of the cottages there was named after her. She left Boston for New York in 1844, serving as a columnist and literary critic on the *New York Tribune. Summer on the Lakes, in 1843* (1844) chronicles her trip to the midwest, and *Woman in the Nineteenth Century* (1845) became an important feminist work. In 1846 she left for Europe, where she participated in the Roman Revolution. There she became involved with Giovanni Ossoli and possibly married him. The Ossolis and their child, Angelo, died when their ship was wrecked off Fire Island, N.Y.

Furness, William Henry (1802–1896). Emerson's oldest friend, he and Emerson attended the Boston Latin School together. Furness studied divinity at Harvard and in 1825 went to preach in Philadelphia, where he spent his life. His influential *Remarks on the Four Gospels* (1836) argued for a natural, as opposed to supernatural, religion. His correspondence with Emerson was published separately in 1910.

Godwin, Parke (1816–1904). An enthusiastic supporter of Charles Fourier's communitarian ideas, he published books on the subject in the 1840s and, as a frequent visitor to Brook Farm, assisted that community in moving from being an "association" to becoming a Fourierist "phalanx."

Greeley, Horace (1811–1872). An enthusiastic supporter of Emerson, Transcendentalism, and Fourierism, he founded the *New York Tribune* in 1841 and later employed Margaret Fuller and George Ripley on the paper.

Greenough, Horatio (1805–1852). A sculptor, who was attracted to Emerson because they shared a belief in the concept of organic theory, in which forms are adapted to functions.

Griswold, Rufus Wilmot (1815–1857). The most prolific anthologist of the period, beginning with *Poets and Poetry of America* (1842), who often included writings by the Transcendentalists in his volumes. He later served as Edgar Allan Poe's literary executor.

Hawthorne, Nathaniel (1804–1864). A neighbor of Emerson's in Concord in the early 1840s, 1850s, and 1860s, whose personal friendship was stronger than their literary relationship. Hawthorne thought Emerson's writings entirely too optimistic, while Emerson, who did not as a rule like fiction, never really became a champion of Hawthorne's work.

Hawthorne, Sophia Peabody (1809–1871). One of the famous Peabody sisters of Salem (along with Mary, who married Horace Mann, and Elizabeth), she moved to Concord with Nathaniel after their marriage in 1842. Unlike her husband, she was very fond of Emerson—both the man and his writings.

Hedge, Frederic Henry (1805–1890). A Harvard Divinity School graduate, his article on Coleridge in the March 1833 *Christian Examiner* is acknowledged as one of the first documents in the Transcendentalist controversy. His removal to Bangor, Maine, in 1835 restricted his involvement with the movement and its participants, although the Transcendental Club was originally called the "Hedge Club" because it first met during his trips back to Boston from Maine.

Higginson, Thomas Wentworth (1823–1911). A second-generation Transcendentalist, he attended Harvard Divinity School and later became an active abolitionist. Higginson was the colonel of a black regiment during the Civil War, corresponded with Emily Dickinson and later edited her poems, and wrote a number of books containing his recollections of the period.

Hoar, Elizabeth (1814–1878) When Charles Emerson died in 1836, only a year after their engagement, Emerson treated Elizabeth Hoar as his sister. The whole family treated her as a member, and the Emerson children considered her their "aunt."

Holmes, Oliver Wendell (1809–1894). This doctor, poet, and satirist (*The Autocrat of the Breakfast Table*) was a conservative supporter of abolitionism, a member of the Saturday Club, an editor of the *Atlantic Monthly*, and the author of a biography of Emerson (1885).

Howells, William Dean (1837–1920). A midwesterner, who made a pilgrimage to visit Emerson in Concord when he first went east in 1860. He became a major magazine editor and novelist.

Hunt, Benjamin Peter (1808–1877). Emerson maintained a lifelong correspondence with Hunt, who had been a student of his in Chelmsford in 1825. Three of Hunt's articles on the West Indies, where he lived, were published by Emerson in the *Dial*.

James, Henry, Sr. (1811–1884). A social and religious writer (and the father of Alice, William, and Henry, Jr.), he felt that Transcendentalism was too loosely organized and not focused strongly enough on the concept of evil.

Lane, Charles (1800–1870). Influenced in part by Alcott's educational ideas, he helped found Alcott House outside London. After Alcott visited there in 1842, Lane and his son William returned with him to America. In the summer of 1843 Lane purchased land in Harvard, Massachusetts, near Concord, for a community he would begin with the Alcott family and a few other followers. The project barely lasted a year before failing from ineptitude. Lane published in the *Dial* before returning to England in 1846.

Lazarus, Emma (1849–1887). The publication in 1867 of a volume of her poems caught Emerson's attention, and he invited her to Concord, beginning a long friendship and correspondence. She dedicated *Admetus and Other Poems* (1871) to him.

Longfellow, Henry Wadsworth (1807–1882). The most popular poet in mid-nineteenth-century America, Longfellow moved in the same social circles as did Emerson. In 1845 he had included Emerson's "Each in All" in his anthology *The Waif.*

Lowell, James Russell (1819–1891). He first became acquainted with Emerson while being rusticated to Concord from Harvard in his senior year, and later contributed poems to the *Dial.* Later, as editor of the *Atlantic Monthly* (1857–1861) and *North American Review* (1863–1872), he published Emerson's writings.

Mann, Horace (1796–1859). A strong proponent of public schooling, his ideas about human perfectibility greatly influenced the direction of American education. He married Mary Peabody in 1843.

Martineau, Harriet (1802–1876). A British abolitionist, who visited America in 1834–1836, during which time she stayed in Concord with Emerson. She described her trip in *Society in America* (1837) and *Retrospect of Western Travel* (1838).

Muir, John (1838–1914). Emerson visited this influential naturalist in Yosemite in May 1871, after which they struck up a correspondence.

Newcomb, Charles King (1820–1894). Another of the youths whom Emerson championed but was eventually disappointed by, Newcomb stayed at Brook

Farm and published a story in the *Dial* (based in part on Emerson's son, Waldo) that was his only literary work.

Parker, Theodore (1810–1860). A Harvard Divinity School graduate and member of the Transcendental Club, whose South Boston sermon on "The Transient and Permanent in Christianity" (1841) created more controversy than Emerson's "Divinity School Address." This sermon, as well as the elaboration of its ideas in *A Discourse of Matters Pertaining to Religion* (1842), resulted in Parker's being virtually banned from exchanging pulpits with his fellow ministers in Boston. He contributed to the *Dial* and, as minister in West Roxbury (1837–1846), was a frequent visitor to Brook Farm. In 1846 he began to organize his own congregation in Boston and preached to large crowds at the Boston Melodeon. He edited the *Massachusetts Quarterly Review* (1847–1850) before becoming very involved in abolitionist activities. His *Ten Sermons of Religion* (1853) was dedicated to Emerson.

Peabody, Elizabeth Palmer (1804–1894). An educational and social reformer, she assisted Alcott in the Temple School, contributed articles to the *Dial* on such subjects as Brook Farm, published the *Dial*, operated a book store and circulating library in Boston, and helped begin the kindergarten movement in America. She helped to get Emerson interested in Jones Very.

Phillips, Wendell (1811–1884). An abolitionist and women's right advocate, who was a frequent visitor to Concord.

Ripley, Ezra (1751–1841). A Congregationalist minister, who, two years after he moved to Concord, married Phebe Bliss Emerson, widow of Emerson's grandfather William Emerson. He owned the Old Manse, where both Emerson and the Hawthornes lived at different times.

Ripley, George (1802–1880). A Harvard Divinity School graduate, member of the Transcendental Club, contributor to the *Dial*, and its business manager for the first few years. Ripley and his wife Sophia founded the Brook Farm community in 1841 (where he also helped to edit the *Harbinger*). When Brook Farm failed in 1847, he turned to journalism, most notably as literary critic of the *New York Tribune*.

Ripley, Sophia Alden Bradford (1793–1867). The sister of George Partridge Bradford, she was mentored by Mary Moody Emerson, whose half-brother Samuel Ripley she married in 1818. Considered one of the best-read and most intelligent women of her day, she tutored students for admission to Harvard and was invited to meetings of the Transcendental Club.

Sanborn, Franklin Benjamin (1831–1917). A second-generation Transcendentalist, he first met Emerson in 1853. He taught school in Concord after being graduated from Harvard, was a member of John Brown's "secret six," and later became an indefatigable chronicler of the Transcendental period in numerous articles and books.

Saturday Club (begun 1854). Many of Boston's intellectual and social elite were in this club, which met at the Parker House on the last Saturday of the month because, as legend has it, this was when Emerson made his regular visit to the Old Corner Bookstore.

Sterling, John (1806–1844). A British poet championed by Carlyle (who later wrote his biography), who carried on a good correspondence with Emerson (published as a book in 1897).

Sumner, Charles (1811–1874). A United States Senator from Massachusetts, widely regarded as a man of honor, who opposed slavery and its spread into the new territories and states. After Sumner was caned on the floor of Congress by a South Carolina congressman in 1856, Emerson delivered a speech protesting the action.

Tappan, Caroline Sturgis (1819–1888). The daughter of a well-to-do merchant, she first met Emerson in Concord in 1836 and formed a lifelong friendship with him. She was also one of Margaret Fuller's closest friends. Nearly two dozen of her poems appeared in the *Dial.* She married William Aspinwall Tappan (to whom Emerson had introduced her) in 1847.

Thayer, James Bradley (1831–1902). A lawyer, who accompanied Emerson on his trip to California in 1871, he published his account of it as *A Western Journey with Mr. Emerson* (1884).

Thoreau, Henry David (1817–1862). Emerson's neighbor in Concord, Thoreau in the 1840s stayed a number of years with the Emerson family as a type of handyman; he later squatted on Emerson's land at Walden Pond while effecting his social experiment. Emerson actively helped Thoreau's literary career by trying to get his articles in print (some appeared in the *Dial*) and to have his *A Week on the Concord and Merrimack Rivers* (1849) and *Walden*

(1854) published. After Thoreau's death, Emerson published a memorial sketch of him in the August 1862 *Atlantic Monthly,* and edited his *Excursions* (1863) and *Letters to Various Persons* (1865).

Town and Country Club (1849–1850). A short-lived social club that failed because it was financially insolvent and because debates over its constitution (as, for example, whether to admit women, which Emerson opposed) were divisive.

Transcendental Club (1836–1840). Beginning in September 1836, when Frederic Henry Hedge returned from Bangor for a visit and when Harvard held its bicentennial celebration, this group of mostly Unitarian ministers (Alcott and women such as Margaret Fuller were invited to attend later) was the most notable social activity of the Transcendentalists. Plans for the *Dial* were made at these meetings, which served nearly thirty times as an opportunity for much vigorous intellectual, religious, and literary discussion.

Very, Jones (1813–1880). In 1838 this Harvard Divinity School student announced that the Holy Spirit was speaking through him; he was dismissed from Harvard and sent to the McLean Asylum. Elizabeth Peabody brought him to Emerson's attention, and in 1839 Emerson edited Very's *Essays and Poems.* By 1840 Very's spirit had left him and he thereafter spent a quiet life in Salem.

Ward, Anna Hazard Barker (1813–1907). Her beauty and personality made a great impression on Emerson, who counted her in his circle of close friends in the late 1830s and early 1840s. She married Samuel Gray Ward in 1840.

Ward, Samuel Gray (1817–1907). Although he had initially wished to pursue a career in art or letters (some of his poetry and prose appeared in the *Dial*), he turned to banking soon after his marriage to Anna Hazard Barker in 1840. Margaret Fuller, who had been emotionally attached to Ward earlier, was disappointed in his marriage and his career choice. Ward had attended Round Hill school with Ellery Channing and introduced Channing's poems to Emerson.

Ware, Henry, Jr. (1794–1843). Emerson's predecessor at the Second Church, Ware reacted to Emerson's "Divinity School Address" (which he felt ignored the concept of a personal God) by writing the pamphlet *The Personality of the Deity* (1838).

Whitman, Walt (1819–1892). "I was simmering, simmering, simmering," Whitman is supposed to have said, "Emerson brought me to a boil." After receiving a copy of the 1855 edition of *Leaves of Grass* from Whitman, Emerson wrote him an enthusiastic letter, which Whitman then (to Emerson's embarrassment) published in a newspaper and in the 1856 edition of his book (even stamping the phrase "I greet you at beginning of a great career" in gold on the spine). The two remained friendly, with Emerson visiting Whitman in Boston while he was seeing the 1860 edition of *Leaves of Grass* through the press and later helping Whitman in obtaining jobs in Washington.

Concord, 21 July
Mass.ts } 1855

Dear Sir,

I am not
blind to the worth of
the wonderful gift of
Leaves of Grass." I find
it the most extraordi-
nary piece of wit & wisdom

R.W. Emerson

To Mary Moody Emerson, April 16 and May 11, 1813

Boston April 16th 1813

Dear Aunt

I lately heard of our cousin Caspers death you don't know how affected cousin Rebecca was. I am much obliged to you for your kind letter. I mean now to give you an account of what I do commonly in one day if that is what you meant by giving an account of one single day in my life Friday 9th I choose for the day of telling what I did. In the Morning I rose as I do commonly about 5 minutes before 6 I then help Wm in making the fire after which set the table for Prayers. I then call mamma about quarter after 6. We spell as we did before you went away I confess I often feel an angry passion start in one corner of my heart when one of my Brothers get above me which I think sometimes they do by unfair means after which we eat our breakfast then I have from about quater after 7 till 8 to play or read I think I am rather inclined to the former. I then go to school where I hope I can say I study more than I did a little while ago. I am in another book called Virgil & our class are even with another which came to the Latin School one year before us. After attending this school I go to Mr Webbs private school where I write & cipher I go to this place at 11 and stay till one oclock. After this, when I come home I eat my dinner & at 2 oclock I resume my studies at the Latin School where I do the same except in studying grammar after I come home. I do mamma her little errands if she has any then I bring in my wood to supply the break-fast room, I then have some time to play & eat my supper after that we say our hymns or chapters & then take our turns in reading Rollin as we did before you went. We retire to bed at different times I go at a little after 8 & retire to my private devotions & then close my eyes in sleep & there ends the toils of the day. May 11 Samuel Bradford went yesterday to Hingham to go to Mr. Colman's School. Your little pensioner Eliza Twist if you remember her is now established in a Charity School and doing pretty well. Cousin John sends his love to you & is well. I have sent a letter to you in a Packet bound to Portland which I suppose you have not received as you made no mention of it in your letter to mamma. Give my love to Aunt Haskins & Aunt Rypley with Robert & Charles & all my cousins & I hope you will send me an answer to this the first opportunity & beleive me I remain your most dutiful Nephew

R. *Waldo Emerson*

M M Emerson

To Edward Bliss Emerson, October *c.* 23, 1816

Dear brother

Perhaps you have not received any letter from home so soon as you had a right to expect but it has not been from any neglect on our part; I began a letter to you the same evening mother came home and finished it the next morning; but no chance came till Sunday evening by Dr Woods I hope you have not been homesick. If you remember when you was at home you boasted and "knew" you should not be: you now can tell best and I hope will soon tell us by letter how you like Andover "the seat of the Muses, Knowledge," and so forth.

Andover, I fear, with all its attractions in gloomy weather as it has been does not look as pleasant as home to you not accustomed to the voices or house of Strangers—

In my last if you remember I drew you off in great style as E. B. E. the great, entering the town of Andover but now begging your honor's pardon I will point out (be not offended) one of your honor's failings—viz—sometime before you went I believe it was while you expected to go to Exeter you told me that I was to have the whole museum while you was gone but when you was just going you resigned your whole part to Charles which did not please me much I confess as I am not willing to keep a Museum with him and the handsomest things are "in common" and furthermore I think I had some little right to be consulted and therefore I cannot that half the museum is legally the Property of aforesaid Charles—but enough—we must leave it to some Arbiter at another time—thus I have finished the Law business.

Mother wishes you to ask some gentleman whether it be as cheap for you to buy your quills and other Stationary at Andover as it would be for her to buy it here and send it you.

The day I wrote to you Dr Warren called here and told Mother I must have a blister on for ten days; that time has not expired yet and therefore I am kept home (as the Irishman said) sick ten days after I was well.

This letter as almost all mine contains little else than nonsense; I hope no more will be like it in that respect. Mother says that our letters should be improving to both, that we ought to write what strikes us in our reading particularly thereby improving each with the reading of the other. During my stay at home I have read "Whelpeley's Historical Compend" that Mary Ladd has lent me—I have finished that and Joan of Arc and the "Vision of Don Roderick" which book William bought me at auction. "Joan of Arc" is a poem by Southey This woman was famous in the time of one of the Henry's of England (I beleive the 5th) when he invaded France he obtained several victories over Charles King of France and took many of the towns and laid seige to Orleans—This woman beleiving herself inspired to be the savior of France went to Chinon where Charles was obtained from him an army and immediately went to Orleans where she conquered the English army in several battles and continuing her course went to Rheims where she crowned Charles before assembled France—On this the Poem is [manuscript mutilated] though of course he exaggerates and makes her really inspired—She afterwards fell into the hands of the English who murdered her—but the Poet takes good care not to have his heroine degraded so much as that and therefore closes it at the coronation of Charles.

The vision of Don Roderick is a short poem of W. Scott's but not any thing great. Whelepeley's History is a brief survey of the history of every nation on earth; and as you now know what I have been reading I beleive I must close as the paper shortens. Dr Moody (self stiled) is very anxious about the health of Ned Bliss: all send love

Yrs &c
Ralph

P.S. William promised to write to you; perhaps you have received his letter— when you write tell what hours the Academy keeps &c

Ralph W Emerson

To Edward Bliss Emerson, November 17, 1816

Boston—Sunday even. Nov 17

Dear Edward,

I cannot begin with that sublime expression "I now take this opportunity" because I do not know of any and besides I have another letter a week old, to send to you which as it contains no news may be as good when old as new— I expect, however, that Mrs Cooper will know of some opportunity—4 minutes after—Thomas has just come to say that Dr Woods has come to preach the Park Street Lecture therefore I must write my letter so that he can bring it to you—We have in the house Jebb's Sermons which are a new book from England—I like them very much indeed. There are two Sermons on the Sabbath from this text Isaiah 58–13, 14. "If thou turn away thy foot from the sabbath, from doing thy pleasure on my holy day; and call the Sabbath a delight, the holy of the Lord, honourable; and shalt honour him, not doing thine own ways, nor finding thine own Pleasure, nor speaking thine own words; then shall thou delight thyself in the Lord." I think it a most beautiful text and wonder I have not seen it before and I mean to read the Volume through—Mr. Frothingham on the Sunday before last requested the assembly to stand during singing as being a more proper position—but left it to themselves to judge—and now the generality of the audience stand during singing Today Mr. Frothingham read the Governour's Proclamation and I liked it very much

At Latin School your classmates Withington, Paine, Hubbard, and Winslow still remain but are in the same class with Child &c studying Greek Testament—You are (according to your account) very busy in your *lectiones;* but there I can sympathise with you because that long morning lessons, with French besides fill up my time—

Yesterday I went down upon Long Wharf and was surprised to see how changed the Central or New Wharf appeared to be in so short a time—It was but a little time ago, you remember, when there was nothing but water to be seen there; and now, a long block of about 30 stores fill up the place. New Cornhill is much the same: one of the Stores is already occupied—

Do you know why a tallow-chandler is the most wretched of all beings? because that he deals in *wicked* works and his wicked works are brought to *light!*—My letters in general you see are a strange medley of every thing and any thing—Whatever comes first I put in, if I think it will interest or amuse you at all: and when I have exhausted my brain I then go and end it with flattery or rhyme sometimes with both—(oh mirabile dictu!) But I have worn both of those threadbare and therefore dare not try them again. So you must excuse me from writing any more or *Poetice* from writing any more excuse

Your
Waldo

All send love to
  To E. B. Emerson—A. B. C. D. E. F.
  N. B. No Postscript this time!!

TO EDWARD BLISS EMERSON, JULY 3, 1817

Boston July 3d 1817

Dear Edward

I suppose you have wondered why I have not written for so long a time; I believe, the want of news, and natural indolence, must be the only excuses I can plead, but now I *must* write since neither of these, I believe, can prove valid. I am very sorry on your account, that you cannot see the President, [James Monroe] but I suppose you *know* every thing that I *see* relative to him. We have been expecting him for a great while till at last he arrived *yesterday:* Then at sunrise, the American flag was raised at Liberty pole at the Gunhouses and on the top of the State House: at nine the cavalcade met and begun their march to meet his—*Excellency* shall I say or *Presidency?* At the same hour the members of the B. P. L. G. S. met at their *Hall* in School St. drest in blue coats and white trousers and forming two and two according to height, after recicving as a badge of the school an artificial *rose,* half red and half white we attended to the directions of Mr Gould. This rose each of us wore in the left buttonhole of the coat. We then marched off under the direction of the Hon. Marshals, Leverett, Curtis, Loring, and Gardner, who each carried the *scroll* of *office,* tied with red and white ribbands, in conformity to the red and white roses. We then went to the *common* where on one side all the boys of the other schools were arranged, in general drest alike, and we took the *Place* of *Honor* appointed for our school, by the Committee of Arrangements, by the gunhouse with police Officers and Constables behind and side of us. Opposite to the line of boys, (which reached from the Sea Fencible's Gunhouse, to the other end of the Common by Park Street Church) was a line of Girls though not so many most people thought it improper to have girls but there were only the girls of the town schools and one or two private. After being thus arranged we waited *two or three hours* standing up all the time, till after one, when we heard the cannon of the 74 and of the forts giving the signal that the "long expected had come at last" no! not quite *come* but had crossed the line between Boston and Roxbury— The bells rung and having waited some time longer we saw to our great joy the plume of the Captain of the Hussars! While the Hussars and Light Horse, at the head of the Cavalcade, entered the Common the Artillery fired their salute of 18 guns from the hill. When the two horse Companies had entered the common the President and Suite halted and one of the Gentlemen a Marshal I believe, said something to him after which he took off his hat and made a bow which the ladies in the windows and piazzas around answered by curtsies, waving their handkerchiefs &c and the crowd by waving their hats huzzaing &c &c Then they entered the Common and the President made his first bow to our school who all took off their hats and cheered with the [manuscript mutilated] He was mounted on an elegant horse which belo[nged to the] Circus sent to him by the Committee of Arr[angements]. An immense cavalcade followed with chaise and carriages behind. He went through the Com. to the Exchange where after the addresses were delivered the company dined at *six*—People are not so pleased with J. Munroe as they expected but you will be tired if I scrawl any longer so I must bid you good bye with love from all. Yrs with affection

Ralph.

E. B. Emerson Esq

To Edward Bliss Emerson, October *c.* 24, 1817

Cambridge October 24th or 5 or 6

Dear Edward,

I have but a few moments to write since C Jarvis has just come in to tell me that there is a person going from his room immediately after Commons and now, we have been to prayers and I am only waiting for the Recitation bell to go in to Prof. Brazer. My studies, (of which you know I promised not to be as silent as some folks, and am now going to plague you with the rehearsal hot & heavy) are in Latin Livy, Grotius, &c in Greek, Majora, and in English, History and Rhetorick. The College day seems about the fifth part of a Boston day! because it is so cut up in parcels—at six in the morning the bell rings for prayers. (at which, by the way, I did not get up this morng till after the second bell had begun to toll,) then about half an hour after prayers the bell rings for Recitation, which bell I am now expecting then Commons and the bearer goes directly after so I must cut short by telling you Uncle Kast boards with Mother all are well I have read. the Grammar and will write again soon as sure as my name is Ralph—

To William Emerson, February 6? 1818

Waltham, Feb. 7th, 1818

Well, my dear brother, I am *here* safe & sound as yet unmuzzled & unsnow-balled—It is Friday night and I have just recieved verbal message from mother that if I can get a letter to her, before Monday, she will send it to you—desirable object!—Boys are gone to bed—I am tired—let this be my excuse for sending thin half sheet again—When in Boston I begun a long letter to you, but came here before I could finish it. Thank you for your kind, scolding, long, letter—thank you kindly—to pay you in some weak measure for which I am "setting *to*" head & foot, heart & hand to fill up my three pages with——no matter what, if not nonsense Since I have been here I have learned to skate, rhymed, written & read, besides my staple commod-ity—schoolkeeping & have earned me a new coat! Ah my boy! that's the dasher!!! wear it tomorrow to Mr Gore's to dinner by invitation from King—

his birthday—Oh Wm what makes you grin now?—have not I guessed right? Now I'll be sober on the next page—

I did hope to have my "merces" in cash—envied you bringing your 5 Doll. Bills to mother; but Mr R said I needed a coat & sent me to the tailor's though I should rather have worn my old coat out first & had the *money*—mean-minded me!—Just before I came from Boston Mr Frothingham sent Mother a note containing 20 Dolls. given him by a *"common friend"* for her with a promise of continuing to her 10$ Quarterly for the use of her sons in College; not stipulating the *time* of continuance. At this time this assistance was peculiarly acceptable, you know. It is in this manner, from the charity of others, Mother never *has,*—& from our future exertions I hope never *will be in want.*—It appears to me the happiest earthly moment my most sanguine hopes can picture, if it should ever arrive, to have a home, comfortable & pleasant, to offer to mother, in some feeble degree to repay her the cares & woes & inconveniences she has so often been subject to on our account alone. In this you *doubtless* sympathize as I often have heard you express your *intentions* on that subject though I think more & better than you will find realized.

I think your present adventure would have been far more profitable if you had a less expensive distance to go. To be sure, after talking at this rate I have done nothing myself—but then I've less faculty and age than most poor collegians—But when I am out of College I will (Deo volente) study divinity & keep school at the same time try to be a minister & have a house (I'll promise no further—)—

People are watching for the intended bride of their minister in the good town of Waltham—He appears in a hurry for he has workmen in his house night as well as day & advises people to go to church early rainy sundays to hear—

But my hands are so cold I cannot scribble any longer with ease & must therefore, since my paper is short, say Finis—

Your brother
Ralph

Wm Emerson

Waltham May 19th 1818

Dear William,

A long preliminary discourse to a letter, as to my health, situation, &c is I suppose wholly unnecessary, since every thing is as it should be.

My motive for writing *you* first is merely to renew my request and entreaty that you would devote your time & talents to that Miltonian Dissertation.— Perhaps you will laugh at me for asking so urgently & so often; but you *must* know it is of some importance as well to yourself as to Mother & friends. Only weigh in an even balance, its advantages & obstacles & it is evident which side will preponderate; in the first place, Your improvement in that accomplishment, which you must acknowledge you possess in some degree— fine writing—besides the unacquired learning of the Poet that you gain to qualify yourself for an Essayist & which in a humbler degree your poor brother is gaining in another branch & then the last & brilliant prospect of the fame & *money* that attend success. And success you must have if you will but afford to the subject a few hours where Labour will answer the purpose of Genius & Inspiration. As to the obstacles, all that you can reasonably present are Indolence & self-stiled Inability which one vigorous effort would easily sacrifice at the altar of literary distinction. Foster, you remember, says "A resolute mind is omnipotent," which thought it be an expression scarcely admissible within the bounds of truth, only believe it, & reconcile it to your mind by some metaphysical argument and *dissertative* ability will not be wanting. Consider too the character of Milton as Johnson gives it, at the conclusion of his life "Milton was born for all that was great & arduous; Difficulty retired at his touch." I do not know that I have the words exactly it is the sense however. But if your breast be callous to all desire of fame & your heart hard to all the calls of literary Glory, then I would appeal to your natural *affections* & there you cannot be *null & void*. If you gain a prize only consider how much honour it would reflect on mother & with what pleasure a purse so earned would be recieved. And as probably a long period will elapse before our family will be independent of the assistance of Society our Benefactors might encouraged by a gleam of hope darted *from underneath the locks of the "Scrof'lous"* and thus inclined to assist the "other brother" by some faint expectations, never alas to be realized that he would be enabled at some future time to *dissert* like his predecessor in favour. But this low motive instead of natural affection is an appeal to the family purse.

You like the Edinburgh Reviews; by only reading one solid dissertation there, where the finest ideas are ornamented with the utmost polish & refinement of language you will feel some enthusiasm to turn your own steps into a *new* path of the field of belles lettres—Believe me I had rather you would get a prize than myself if I try, since it is of more importance to you as it is your last & my first chance.

I will not trouble you with details of my own progress as it may be uninteresting & is unimportant in comparison with yours—Please to give & recieve love & my best wishes for your success in poetical pursuits.

Your affectionate brother
Ralph

W Emerson.

To Edward Bliss Emerson, June 2, 1818

Cambridge June 2 1818

Dear Edward,

In a very sentimental mood, with a warm evening in a cool room, I suppose I may venture to address a few prosaic lines to my dearly beloved brother, wrapt probably in philosophick meditation on the grandeur, beauty and magnificence of Nature as displayed in the woodland scenery of Andover. Unreproved by the urgency of lessons & unoccupied by the pressure of business, a summer evening like this, is one of the pleasantest enjoyments of the Cambridge Student. If his pen is good and his inclination thitherward, he may amuse himself like *me,* by endeavouring to impart some of his agreeable sensations to his literary brothers in Andover and like me write a letter just long enough not to tire himself or his reader. Your next letter— pray let it be a flashy sentimental—Gaze on the stars, till you get asleep and then dash off a letter about "vast concave" &c in ten minutes or so! Tell how they glare, with unremitting stare, on the sons of wickedness & sloth; then turn your address to Jupiter, (who has been sick lately as I understand,) or

some other bright luminary & ask him if he will be kind enough to guard
your slumbers & don't forget to ask him about your brother Ralph—

Uncle Ripley is engaged to S[arah]. A[lden]. B[radford]. "by the way."

To Edward Bliss Emerson, June 12 and 17, 1818

Cambridge, June 12th 1818—

Dear Edward,

If long letters suit your taste, I believe I can gratify it now; for I just recieved
this paper as a present, and have one of those ruled papers under it. Let me
see—I believe it was you that I asked to find me a motto, but I recieved
none. You need not trouble yourself now, for I am not in want; I mentioned
it to season my kindness in giving you a whole sheet of Letter-paper—oh
present unprecedented in the annals of nations! the 6 last words are so often
found in the Essay that I have just *finished* that I cannot resist their frequent
repetition. I am engaged in copying off my work at present—I was going to
say for the press but I fear for the *fire*, so that if it turns out prizeless, I will
say it was unjust, for the flame of human genius never *blazed brighter*. Nor
shall I become a love-lorn, disconsolate, solitary eremite, even if the Government think fit to light their cigars with my *elaborate* production. "Nil
desperandum" I will say, and then go immediately to work—to prepare
another somniferous dissertation for next year, & if that succeeds no better
than its elder brother, I'll put them to sleep each succeeding year with one,[1]
till they, tired out by my Morphean draughts, give me the long-expected
prize. "Oh how sweet is revenge" but thus it shall be, if I live &c But you
must never whisper a syllable about it to any person or admit any one to my
arcana & to that end please burn up this letter after perusal. I don't write
poetry when at Cambridge or I would give a specimen of it since you like to
have my letters bring the muse with them as you said.

Were it my fortune to be in a situation like Lord Byron & some other
British Poets, I think I would cultivate Poetry & endeavour to propitiate the

---

*1. There are several references in later letters to Emerson's interest in the Bowdoin prizes,
and he was successful in his junior and senior years. [Rusk]*

muses To have nothing to do but mount the heights of Parnassus & enjoy the feasts of polite literature must necessarily be a very pleasing employment. But in this country where every one is obliged to study his profession for assistance in living & where so little encouragement is given to Poets &c it is a pretty poor trade. Yes I believe both epithets are true in their literal sense, so that I have not the least thought of determination to follow it. I am going some night to the top of Parnassus—(any other hill will do·as well) & there I will bid them farewell in some tender elegiac stanza and so pathetick that I shall hear some voice issuing out of a blasted oak, or dark cavern, that will perhaps utter those words of enchantment, on the mystick seal of Solomon,—"Dont go"—and I, warm with enthusiasm, will respond—"I must" & then awestruck will commence my departure, yet still "will cast one longing, ling'ring look behind." But you are wearied, per adventure, by my poetick powers of description, wherefore, I will cease, howsomdoever, I cease with regret, for you know I am one of those that love to wander "Round the vast top of some gigantick height." &c

Boston—June 17th

Here I am at home having got my name out for sickness; I have about me an unpleasant friend named a Sore Throat, but I am fast getting well. I recieved yesterday morning your pleasant letter and am now proceeding to answer it. As to your present happiness, I congratulate you, as to your love of Solitude, I sympathize with you, as to your prospects of diligence, I wish you well. You are going to write many letters, and ask me for subjects. Can you "walk forth to meditate at even tide" and want a subject? can you absorb yourself in contemplation of classick lore, in the Works of Homer Virgil & Cicero and yet want a subject for epistolary correspondence? or nearer home can you read a letter of Aunt Mary's, an enthusiast in rural pleasures, and yet want a subject.

There is a theme, which has been the subject of many college Orations, which would wake you to the pen I think since you love study so well, I mean "Senectute literis ornata" "Otium dignitatis"[2] &c You might write a long letter embellished with all the ornaments of Rhetorick on the Age of the American Scholar. Imagine to yourself all the gratifications of taste and riches

---

2. *"In old age, which is adorned with learning"; "ease of dignity."*

to form his library, philosophy room &c and take what is excellent out of Mr. Gore, Mr. Vaughan, Thos. Jefferson, and others of our distinguished countrymen. Perhaps the muses enraptured by the beauty of your prose ideas will fly to your assistance and give you a friendly hand to help you to the summit of Parnassus; but prose suits your taste better so why cannot you write me a theme-letter on this or some other equally refined subject? and if you like it you may write in Latin, the language of Literature, or Greek the tongue of Herodotus &c or Gallic the language of Voltaire or vernacular the language of ourselves. I am fast getting well by the enlivening air & scenery of the town. Mother and brothers are well & send love.

Ralph.
Send Sarah's French book, with Goldsmith. R W E—

Edward B. Emerson.—

To William Emerson, July 20 and 21, 1818

Cambridge, July 20th 1818

Dear William,

My motives for writing to you now, are rather selfish, as I am scribbling to fill up some leisure time, as well as to draw some lines from *you* before a great while. I sent your Kennebunk letter, & mother as well as myself are quite anxious to know its contents.— —Has St. Cecilia descended yet from "the seventh Heaven" to help your pen over the smoothly white expanse of writing paper? You must go & see Miss Lowell & whilst her ladyship is singing to you, imagine that it is St. C. & then go home on the strength of it & write about "Musick of the Spheres" &c. &c. & tell your audience at Commencement of some lay more sweetly melancholy than that which echoes from the mountain harp of Scotland, tuned by the unearthly maiden that warns, the ill-fated traveller who passes her impenetrable grove, of approaching dissolution, singing sadly & melodiously!—Imitate in some degree Everett's "fabled spirit of the North, who is fairer than all the daughters of the Earth, & the rose is in her cheek, & the fire in her eye—but that rose was never crimsoned by a blush & a heart never throbbed beneath that marble bosom to the sounds of icy coldness["]—I will not go any further for

I cannot give his own expressions & since I heard it I have been constantly wishing—sometimes for his memory to recall his words and at others, for the exalted genius that could compose such exalted language & sentiments— "And now, my classmates, the bark is ready, the masts are up, the sails are spread—and away to the dark blue sea!"—I never was better pleased in my life & never expect to be—I wish however in this particular my expectations might be agreeably disappointed at Commencement when the *First Confer-ence* is announced. In six weeks, moderate talents might effect a great deal; and your subject is very poetical—you may tell them some strange tale about Memnon's Harp—or read Walter Scotts superstitious innumerables—& con-jure up

The fishers have heard the water-sprite—into some heavenly harmony more delightful to the pensive Soul than the blast of expiring Autumnus reechoed through the leafless forest.* July 21st We have begun Lowth's Gram-mar; and consequently I have much more leisure than usual, having just finished my first lesson, and therefore continue to scribble, but with a better pen.

I shall chum next year with Dorr, and he appears to be perfectly disposed to study hard. But, to tell the truth, I do not think it necessary to understand Mathematicks & Greek thoroughly, to be a good, useful, or even *great* man. Aunt Mary would certainly tell you so, and I think you yourself believe it, if you did not think it a dangerous doctrine to tell a Freshman. But do not be afraid, for I do mean to study them, though not with an equal interest to the other studies. Apropos, you owe Dorr 50 Cts—On Saturday I saw Edward at home. He had come in the morning and went away while I was there; was well and in as high spirits as usual.

I believe you do not love walking as well as I, but if you do, I think the walk to Mr Lovejoy's Factory was the most beautiful that I found in Waltham; but perhaps, far more congenial to your benevolent feelings is the employ-ment of *teaching the young idea how to shoot,* and you are contemplating in your little band, the future statesmen & heroes who are to elevate Columbian glory! Success to you in your endeavours to that end. But now that I have seen my third page, and have exhibited specimens of various kinds of writ-ing—viz. poetical scribble—stiff regularity, & a mixture of both, you will be as willing as myself to view the close. After you have given my respects to Mr Ripley and my "desired to be remembered" to Mrs Upham & family you may sit down & write a long letter to your brother

Ralph.

Mr William Emerson

    The Seniors remaining here, mope about, as soberly and steadily as the Graduates themselves, not excepting even Hathaway himself.

This you see is a mere repetition of the sentimentality on the first page of this harping epistle.

To Edward Bliss Emerson, September *c.* 6, 1818

Waltham, September 1818—

Dear & honoured brother Edward,

You have written me for the sole purpose, it seems of enforcing on my negligent pen the obligation of writing to you; now to tell you the truth there are three or four different moods in which I write to three or four different persons; & in the following order. When I think I should like to write a letter & yet feel sufficiently sober to keep all my nonsense down, then I begin my letter with "My dear Mother" but when I think I can write a grammatically correct epistle or any thing that I am sure can raise the risible muscles of gravity itself, *then* I address my fastidious brother—Bachelor When in a very *compositorial rhetorical* mood, I send to an uncle in the Alibama—and last of all when I want to scribble I know not why, & care not what, & moreover have leisure & rhyme at command, and per-adventure want to amuse myself, *then* as *now* the pen flies over the lines to my semi-Andover semi-Boston brother Ned. In short I write to you when I am in a serio-ludrico tragico-comico miscellany of feelings. If the paper is filled it matters not how. The old proverb is Circumstances alter cases; & now that your horizon is so essentially changed; from the dark murky clouds of misanthropy, fanaticism, & error that encircle Andover to the careless noisy scenes of Boston (two equally dreaded extremes) I suppose I must begin to vary my epistolary efforts—for more than once, whilst you have been at Andover, genuine compassion (I do not know if you will thank me for it) has dictated my letter; but now you are in the very centre of the frolicsome lively busy town you must impart some of its gaiety to your out-of-town friends whilst I must sober & season my letters with moral scientifick economical &c sentiments; especially when I am as sure that they will be shown to all my friends as that you will get them. Put your secret-keeping power to the test by shutting up this in your own pocketbook or in the flames—'tis immaterial which—but unseen by all eyes save your own. I suppose when you left Andover, on the principle that "habit is a second nature" you made some pathetick "loud lament," perhaps addressing its fields as Farewell my own dear land! or the like—I hope you did not get naturalized. By the way I have transcribed the enclosed from the Edinburgh Review. Ugolino describes the starvation of his family to the last line but three; his own actions there related is most horrid of all. This is translation from the Italian I believe.

> With love to all
> Your affectionate brother
> Ralph.

Edw. B. Emerson Esqr.

To William Emerson, April 1 and 10, 1819

Cambridge, April 1st 1819.

Dear William,

I cannot possibly find those books for sale, which I am trying to get for you; it has become very fashionable indeed to study French so that there are very few books for sale. I have advertised but cannot get them yet—April 10th 1819—Still my search is vain, so that I think I must send a letter unaccompanied by books. You must not think me negligent in writing for I should have written a long time ago had I not waited to make my purchase. I shall still, however, endeavour to obtain them unless you send me word, *not*—You do not know how much Aunt Mary has enriched us in intelligence from you; she appears to have been very much pleased with her visit—has imparted all the opinions of the Kennebunkians with regard to *the Preceptor*—viz—a profound scholar, a *small eater* &c &c. I rather think you have raised yourself considerably in Aunt's opinion, for formerly, if you recollect, you did not always agree, and now I don't know of any think she likes to talk of better than Wm's modesty & Wm's—but I see you blush, I will have regard to your delicacy—

But I forgot a determination I made when I saw your *fat* letter a little while since; for I resolved that as a *trait* of such singular excellence in character required the highest strains of panegyrick I must write an eulogy to

Ken[nebunk, Me.]. That letter made several faces shine and when I came humbly plodding home Saturday and carried a sum to the bank to change I believe I held up my head 6 inches higher than before—Mother and Aunt were afraid you had not left yourself enough to subsist upon. Have you?

I told you I was waiter last quarter, and now I am this—You wonder why I was not appointed in the first quarter—it was because I did not petition, which was owing to ignorance when to go—I went a little while since to get my name out & the Pres[iden]t was very gracious—told me I had grown & said he hoped *intellectually* as well as *physically* & told me (better than all) when my next bill comes out to bring it to him as I had never recieved the Saltonstall benefit [i.e., scholarship] promised me before I entered College. My next bill has not come out yet but I think I shall be inclined to remember *that.* My criticism (a theme) on Guillaume le Conqurant had two marks on the back, which distinction only six of the class obtained. Mathematics I hate—In Greek I have been taken up every time but one this week (now Saturday) and have only been corrected in ἐπειτοι,[3] which for me is doing well. And now as to Bowdoin I am very doubtful about writing this year for though reading Boswell I have not read half of Johnson's works; & probably a great many will try for it. Do you not think I should do better to be a year writing the Character of Socrates? I have not yet begun anything. Your chum boards at Mr Wyeth's where you did; & has been to my room lately. Dickinson has a private school in Cambridgeport of 30 scholars; boards at Dr Chaplin's; has been to see me too & asks after you as also does Mr James Farnsworth—I do not know whether I have told you that Farnsworth is engaged to a Cambridge old maid named Munroe. "I have done." I have nothing more to say that I can think of except apologies for scrawling which are cheap. I will carry this letter to Boston & if I have any thing further to add will add it there. Your second North American [Review] has been sent.

All well.—Ralph—

Boston Apr 10th

All are well & send love Charles particularly & has got into Greek Grammar You did not comply with a request I formerly made that you would name when you sent for books a price which you think reasonable for the whole.

---

3. *That is, Emerson had confused the adjectival form of this word with its adverbial form* ("thereafter").

Tell me when you write again what books you are likely to need & I will purchase them at Auctions—Mother desires you to write as quick as possible.

Ralph

To Willliam Emerson, June 14, 17, and 20

Cambridge, June 14th 1819.

Dear Wm,

I have nothing to interest you, no news to tell, no business to transact, no sentiment or poetry to communicate, no important questions to ask, & yet with all these negatives I am presumptuous enough to put so much trust in the workings of my own barren brain as to sit down with the intention of writing a letter of respectable length to your most serene sobriety. But, (to use a vulgar but expressive phrase) I shall take it fair & easy, and as usual shall not regard a month or two's difference in the commencing & concluding dates; only you will remember it was begun Monday June 14th in the year of our Lord 1819.

But let me not forget to record in the first article of my gazette that the Sophomore Class & their unworthy member your very humble servt have commenced the notorious & important study of Logic. I am getting and am intending to get *my* "lessons *verbatim* and the rest word for word" Spirit of Metaphysicks![4] (my pen trembles with reverential awe while I write) oh smile on thy pupil & graciously hear his petitions for preeminence among thy sons! Oh by the way Ticknor has got home and Everett is expected in August and therefore they will most probably have an inauguration next term—What a noble address Everett will make! so much is expected of him & he has had so long time to prepare, that I think expectation will not be disappointed. A very fine subject—Grecian Literature, (I'm soliloquizing now) why yes! I dont know but I would like it myself.—

You know there was one of the Faculty in Boston, one Dr Kast & family who boarded with mother; well they go today to housekeeping unless they

---

4. *Young Emerson made the most of his jest by writing this word in a trembling hand. [Rusk]*

lied last Saturday when I visited the family; this you see puts us out of order again & brings toil on trouble for us to procure a *boarding* reinforcement. I shall have to save my ink now by using blacking when I write to you & keep the ink to write advertisements & other similar state papers. Moreover to descend to the rules of economy still further I must let my nails grow long to make pens of and—but that is going far enough to shew you how necessity would give acumen to my already well-known-admirable powers.

It is contemplated to build the new Episcopal Church in Boston of *white marble* like the city hall in New York since some proprietor or proprietors of a quarry have offered to supply them with materials at reduced prices, out of pure love to the Episcopal cause. You know its site is to be opposite the old Mall between Washington Gardens & Winter St.

June 17th I went into Boston last night & heard that the Kasts had removed yesterday & while I was there Mr & Mrs Whitman made an agreement with Mother; they are to come Friday or Saturday so that Mother is not to be two days without some boarders; at present she wants two more persons & then she will be full, & certainly with a dozen more she could not feel more anxiety than she did with four by whom the house has been— blessed, (I was going to say *infested*).

June 20th

Mr Emerson has told our class to furnish ourselves with Enfield tomorrow when we shall finish Legendre—What think you? Sophomore class such a fine one that they have Enfield put into their hands two terms sooner than other classes, besides their loss of a full fortnight sometime since, as you may recollect—The other day I was chosen into the Pythologian Club which has been formed since you graduated—It contains the fifteen smartest fellows in each of the two classes Junior & Soph. its object, extemporaneous discussion—Some of its members in the Junior are--Bowie, Gannett, Davis, Tucker 1st, Hall 1st, Stewart, Deering, &c, in our class Otis first, King, Gourdin, Lyon, &c—and a very fine set they are—It is a publick club & patronized by Government though I believe its objects are meant to be secret—

Lord Byron has published a new tale in prose called the Vampyre about 44 little pages—he is [manuscript mutilated] of course who walks in the tombs, gnaws sculls, & other equally delicious viands; but perhaps you have read it—which is more than I have though some one told me about it.

I have written a poetical theme about fancy & fairy land & enthusiasm & the like—an eccentrick though *inspired* medley of such matters.

June 20th.

I have just come to Boston & found your letters to *me* & the rest & have to say in answer to the Library Businesses that I will renew what you desire at one, but cannot send "Cours" &c from the other by Mr McKulloch since he goes home today

But by the way, I am &c
Ralph W Emerson

To Mary Moody Emerson, April 7, 1821

Boston Saturday Apr. 7th 1821

My dear Aunt

Mother directed me to write a note to you signifying the utter discrepancy of opinion which exists between you & herself with regard to Waldo's Exhibition, & my object is to convert you to our views. Now you must be aware that if all reasoned like you the luckless performers would speak their well-conned exercises to bare walls. And if I may be allowed to be impudent I shall suggest the fact that not twenty present will know that your proud ladyship is related to the despised & ragged poet. You are wont to say that the spectacle of this world's splendour amuses you and if it will gratify you I am very confident the company of the day will be the leaders of the fashion as the sons of senators &c have parts on that day. Furthermore if you would wish your bashful nephew to do well & claim the ground his own vanity aims to reach, you must encourage him with your presence on Tuesday, 24th April—My room is No 9 Hollis. Should you come from Hamilton you must not ask for Waldo the Poet—he is better known by the name of Emerson the Senior—

Mother says she cannot write herself for Bulkeley is sick but insists upon your coming to Boston & thence to Cambridge with her & agrees with you that a refusal would be a whim engendered of *Solitude.* I could say more in scandal of this last dame were I not her sworn defender, by my oath to the muses. Professor Everett has preached a fine Fast Sermon at Mr Frothingham's church & elsewhere. You must recollect your large promises of correspondence to your mostc affectionate

Waldo

Miss M. M. Emerson.
      Inhabitant of Hamilton, (or rather the World.)

To Mary Moody Emerson and Robert Bulkeley Emerson, November 8, 1821[5]

Boston, Nov 8th 1821

My dear Aunt,

The winds and rains have combined to wet your delightful ramble and to disappoint the schemes which the love of nature planned. I hardly think you have wandered in wood or grove by lake or lawn through the three dismal days last past. Nature willing to atone for your wretched entertainment has hung out the moon in this transparent sky to cheer you with its brilliant beams. But to a dull mortal like myself whom the fates have condemned to school-keeping, it is entirely indifferent what planet rules—Venus or dogstar the warm solar Mercury, or cold and solitary Mars who shone on me all last winter in my little loghouse on the mountains. Notwithstanding my abhorrence of midnight or morning vigils I did once think that there was something lofty something sublime in the watchfulness which claimed to itself the shining host in their solemn and silent revolution & something honourable in the solitude which mingled with such pure society. The Assyrian shepherds have inherited a spotless fame who have written their names and fancies in the stars to be read as long as language lasts. I suppose you are tired of the stars but I am one who mourn the destruction of Astrology.

    Mother sends her love and wishes to hear; also of the boy Bulkeley Is he not a great deal of trouble?—but I ask pardon; that would implicate the wisdom and skill of your ladyships administration. If you stay longer I must

---

5. *This letter is remarkable as an example of the new mastery of style and the new maturity of mind that now begin to make themselves felt.* [Rusk]

beg the favour of letters. I am not yet in the fatal *Gehenna* and will not alarm you by by naming the doleful day. *The drama* crawls on but clamours for inspiration. Dr Sam. Clarke is read; indeed I have nothing in the world to tell you and must close. Desolate hall hath grown doubly desolate and Charles complains of your absence. Though we have not the slightest apprehension of any real intention on your part to withdraw in earnest from the town, yet we are willing to tell you what a blank is percieved. Theological controversy is all over; brilliant repartee hath vanished also;—we all wish to see you none more so than

Your nephew
Waldo

Miss M M Emerson
    Dear Bulkeley, I hope you are a very good boy and very happy in the country. Mother and all send their love to you. Give our love to Grandmother Grandfather Aunt Sarah and Aunt Mary.

Your affectionate brother
Waldo

R Bulkeley

To Mary Moody Emerson, November? 1821?

The Muse ceases to own her name when she is not prone & fond to assert her rectitude assailed. Were it only to hear herself talk she must reply. Ever since the fatal entrance to Gehenna she hath been awake—"But there was a pride" True, there was a pride, but it was kindled elsewhere than is supposed. Friend, thou thinkst mine hour is passed, the waters of self-annihilation and contempt are already settling calmly over me and expanding their muddy sheet between my name, and *light* forever. The child's dream was blest by some faint glimpses of strange light & strange worlds,—but the child looked at his bauble and played again with his bauble and the light was withdrawn. Now if such light had been imparted, there was *one* of whom the boy was taught the nature and advantage of the visions but when his weak nature & strong fates began to darken them—will instructer & friend alike forsake him? Joy brightens, they say, the edge of the cloud where is grief; but joy is not mine for I dislike events; grief is not mine for the spirits & the blood will circulate in some so that they shall be too silly to be sad. Pride works a little but cannot supply the place of encouragement, and the being on whom you throw your gentle execrations would rejoice to find in himself a little more of the lion for a recoil—upon a long train of woes mustered by thy predictions. Will the Nine be shamed by the company of their sex? Did they shun Corinna and abhor de Stael Have such things shed dreary clouds about the Aonian hill and put far away the templed heights of Parnassus and the silver fountain of the Pierides. These were rich thoughts which have been nourished as long and as ardently as a weak & unpoetical temperament could keep them and I do not yet know that the second sight of Cassandra or the robes of later prophecy shall shroud them all behind its dark drapery. But you speak of holier Muse. Thy stern spirit would, I presume, refuse the pages of Clarke to so humble and unworthy hands; but if I am in the very jaws of peril I need a shield more. Then perhaps it will be profanation to look further; to read what Clarke hath written is wholesome but to dare hereafter to write myself—you think it wrong, while I think it to be a just & sublime employment. I do not understand the grounds of your reason and we can therefore speak no more upon it—

Your letter is as Cassandra's should be, dark, and not entirely intelligible. I write not because it was necessary but that it is a pleasure. You will say I *prove nothing*—I know it but it was in reply to a letter of *sentiment*. Thy kinsman, Waldo.

To William Withington, April 27, 1822

Boston, 27 April, 1822

My dear lord Withington,

A tall cousin of mine (Mr Shepard) hath informed me that you have lately descended upon them at Andover, to learn their good ways—from the miserable school of heterodoxy at Cambridge. Now I determined forthwith to write to my right scholarly classmate—for several distinct reasons—to congratulate you upon your singular exemption from the general misery of your compeers who have rushed into the tutor's desks of every Minerva's temple in the country; then, to claim the *honour* of corresponding with one scholar in the land,—and to enjoin it upon you as a primal duty to write a letter from your seat of science to a desponding schoolmaster. I am delighted to hear there is such a profound studying of German and Hebrew, Parkhurst & Jahn and such other names as the memory aches to think of, on foot at Andover. Meantime Unitarianism will not hide her honours;—as many hard names are taken, and as much theological mischief planned at Cambridge, as at Andover. By the time this generation gets upon the stage, if the controversy will not have ceased, it will run such a tide, that we shall hardly be able to speak to one another, and there will be a Guelf & Ghibelin quarrel, which cannot tell where the differences lie. Here was a "Christian Disciple" came out with its meek motto—"Speaking the truth in love,"—and a most bitter christian sarcasm, & terrible christian contempt launched out against poor Dr Mason for his equally apostolic exhortation.

I have a high respect for Professor Stuart, but have never seen him. I want you to write me a description of his mind, body, & outward estate. The good people abroad, who are Calvinists up to the chin, do not treat him well. He watches upon their outposts, and recieves all the weapons of the enemy,—and those within the pale, his brethren of Connecticutt, accuse him of apostacy. They should know, that the opposite party humbly judge that if they lose him they lose all, and that any party can boast few such redeeming Palladiums.

What are you studying *beside* Bibles? Do you let suns and moons, eclipses & comets pass without calculation or account? Is there not time for Trigonometry, no, not for a logarithm? Or if all these are forgotten, I hope you have not sacrificed Johnson & Burke, Shakspeare & Scott altogether. Books are not so numerous at Andover, but that you will want the Cambridge library,—which, by the way, grows rich rapidly & bids fair to load its shelves to the breaking point, under the care of such an eloquent beggar as Professor Cogswell. He has already won away to the library most of the splendid European books in Boston and obliged Mr Thorndike to *cover* the Ebeling library which he presented—But whatever may be your pursuits, your designs, or your advantages, this is to remind you that I expect a very literary letter which may unfold them all to my admiration. You can form no conception how much one grovelling in the city, needs the excitement & impulse of literary example. The sight of broad vellum-bound quartos—the very mention of Greek & German names, the glimpse of a dusty tugging scholar will wake you up to emulation for a month.

You will excuse the liberty I have taken in addressing myself to you unasked, to solicit a correspondence, but I am aweary of myself, and Mr Frye told me he could send a letter to you any time so I thought proper to gratify myself by writing. I suppose you may know opportunities to send to Frye, if not pray drop a letter into the post Office the first time you pass by it to

Your friend & classmate
R. Waldo Emerson.

W. Withington, A. B.

To John Boynton Hill, May 11, 1822

Boston May 11th 1822.

My dear Hill,

I am infinitely obliged for the last letter, but as to writing sentiment & common sense &c—you sha'n't do it. I've a kind of despotic little caprice in my head, that ordains, and will not have its ordinances disputed. You shall hear what it saith—By the help of the stars I spy a man walking in Garrison Forest—a short man and a thick—but with a long head, & long sighted in the ways of this world both before & behind, and in a score of years he hath read books & men.—I determine & declare that such an one hath no business to write a good, amusing, epistolary kind of a letter; it is fit that such an one be *oracular,*—I ordain that he write a letter, which shall be no letter at all, but a treatise; which shall embody his most profound views of Plato, of Greece, of Rome; of national or local condition; of philosophy, of (even) statistics; of books, measures, men.—'Fol de rol,' saith Mr. Hill, 'and what have you to balance these extravagant demands?' Why, saith Caprice, we will contrive to scrape up somewhat of special entertainment for Mr H's literary appetite; we can steal perhaps an odd paragraph from the North American, &c. &c. A man of expedients will always thrive.

Now, by way of trying my pen, I am going to give you an insight into our city-politics, which must be vastly interesting to you—no matter—when Ive got something better, you shall have it. The inhabitants divide themselves here, as every where else, into three great classes; first, the aristocracy of wealth & talents; next, the great classes; first, the aristocracy of wealth & talent; next, the great multitude of mechanics & merchants and the good sort of people who are for the most part content to be governed without aspiring to have a share of power; lastly, the lowest order of day labourers & outcasts of every description, including schoolmasters. In this goodly assemblage, until the union of parties, at the election of Prest Monroe, there was no division of factions, except the giant ones of Federalist & Democrat. But when these died away, the town became so tiresomely quiet, peaceful, & prosperous that it became necessary at once, for decent variety, to introduce some new distinctions, some semblance of discord. A parcel of demagogues, ambitious, I suppose, of being known, or hoping for places as *partisans* which they could never attain as citizens—set themselves down to devise mischief. Hence it has followed, that, within a twelvemonth, the words "Aristocracy," "Nabob," &c have begun to be muttered. The very natural circumstance, that the very best men should be uniformly chosen to represent them in the legislature, is begun to be called a formal conspiracy to deprive them of their rights & to keep the power entirely in the hands of a few. Lately, this band of murmurers have actually become an organized party calling themselves "the Middling Interest," & have made themselves conspicuous by two or three troublesome ebullitions of a bad spirit at the town meetings. For the purpose of looking into their neighbours' concerns, they called a Town Meeting where they appeared in sufficient numbers to secure a majority, and there voted to publish & distribute a kind of Doomsday Book, to wit, a statement of every mans property & tax from the assessor's books. This you may easily conceive, in a money getting town, where every one conceals his coppers, must be a very obnoxious measure. Another more important proceeding at the same meeting was the vote that the Selectmen be directed to instruct the Representatives to obtain from the Legislature leave to erect Wooden Buildings, which has long been against law. You know, nobody ever goes to a town meeting who is not personally interested; these votes, therefore, though easily passed, excited a general indignation when known, and a remonstrance was sent to the legislature by the whole respectable portion of the town, and the Bill was in consequence rejected. By dint of management, the other party have contrived to persuade the Mechanics & most of the Second Class, that it is their interest to have Wooden Buildings, & part of a plan to deny them, & that they are oppressed &c &c, and they have succeeded in obtaining 26 hundred subscribers to a second petition to legislature, which will be offered at the next session. In a new Senatorial ticket they interfered, but did not succeed; and lastly they have been very pernicious to our interests in the election of Mayor. (By the way, did you ever see a live Mayor?) Mr Otis was nominated, and is, you know, our first citizen; his was the only public nomination and it was considered certain that he would succeed; but the Mid-Interest fixed upon Quincy, and on the day of Election, no choice was made, & both Candidates then withdrew their names. By this ingenious device the parties were reduced to take the third best, & acquiesce in the appointment of our present sublime Mayor, with the mortifying reflection that, Boston had many a worthier son than he. Such is our party history, and among our staid countrymen, we shall scarcely have a Guelf & Ghibelin controversy, though this be an ill-managed, poor-spirited party, and promises little good to our civil welfare. A *mob* is a thing which could hardly take place here; —I wish I could say as much for Baltimore. And as to your sparing me the description of the City, it is the very thing you should not have spared; I wait a full & ample history of it, outside & inside, although legendary relics from Garrison forest, would I confess please the poetic vein better, & tickle the inner poetic man. Thank you much for your description of life & manners there; it is quite comprehensive, but vastly too sketchy. You recollect Marot, the "tyrant of words & syllables,"—be it known to you I have constituted myself—no matter by what right—an awful Censor upon the epistles of all who any word dare write to me. In the elation of my dignity I trample upon the silly insinuation that my reforming labours will be limited to a little correspondence. What! will not all nations flock to obtain a share in the advantages of my transcendant instructions? I shall have letters from Germany, Greece, China, Iceland & Siam—from the King of Hayti, & from the poet Ung—who singeth on the banks of the Yellow Sea. And even on the desperate supposition, that unforeseen obstacles should prevent their arrival— I shall still write resolutely on—at such sleepy length as this same letter of mine. Here I can favour you with a beautiful morsel—from the very pen, perhaps of the Oriental poet last named.——Ding dong, ding dong, said the bells of St Giles, as the poor Madge Groateon was carried by in a cart for to be hanged. And she cried, "Ring on, ye kind bells, for nobody has mourned for me, but you." And the bells St Giles answered —Ding dong, ding dong.

I think, Mr Hill, we rather improve in the book line. Washington Irving is just about to publish a book called "Bracebridge hall" which he has sold to a London bookseller for 1000 guineas. Alexander Everett's Europe is a popular book in England. N.A. Review grows better, & travels further. Wm Tudor, who wrote Letters on Eastern States is going to publish here, in the summer, a Life of James Otis of which great hope is entertained; and though we are inundated with silly poetry, we [manuscript mutilated] to improve. Then, books are growing *cheaper* because they are imported from France. I bought a Quintilian in 3 Vols, quite a handsome book for 2.50; La Fontaine, in 2 Vols, for 62 cts. &c &c Here too I may add as testimony of our liberal spirit that the Town voted 2500 dollars to George B Emerson to procure a philosophical apparatus for the Classical School. He has just recieved part of his instruments which are the most beautiful in the country.—Bancroft is expected to return from Europe in July and it is supposed that he will become the successor of Mr Greenwood in the New South Church. And now I believe I have exhausted all & more than will be interesting to you of news, jests, criticism, &c; and, Soul of Caesar! upon looking back, this is what I call a *vasty* letter. Tell me, when you write, how long you propose to honour Maryland with your instructions. Sit down & write a long letter to

> *Your friend & Classmate*
> *R. Waldo Emerson*

Recollect that I have altered my name from Ralph to Waldo, so be sure & drop the first—It is quite a marrying time among our ministers; if it were not for postage, I would send you a piece of Everett's Wedding Cake.—

To Mary Moody Emerson, October 16, 1823

> *Roxbury, Oct. 16th 1823.*

The satirist of women claimed the love of being sought as a prerogative of the sex, & the design of being followed as the reason of retiring. I will not insinuate that my dear Aunt is liable to these frailties or that aught but motives which I respect restored her to her mountains. But the consequence follows as a thing of course, & I have a catalogue of curious questions that have been long accumulating to ask you. You have been no indifferent spectator of the connexions existing between this world & the next & of all the marvellous moral phenomena which are daily exhibiting. Every day (that is, every day of the few & seldom visitations of my coy & coquettish muse,) I ramble among doubts to which my reason offers no solution. Books are old & dull & unsatisfactory the pen of a living witness & faithful lover of these mysteries of Providence is worth all the volumes of all the centuries. Now what is the good end answered in making these mysteries to puzzle all analysis? What is the ordinary effect of an inexplicable enigma? Is it not to create opposition, ridicule, & bigoted skepticism? Does the Universe great &

glorious in its operation aim at the slight of a mountebank who produces a wonder among the ignorant by concealing the causes of unexpected effects. All my questions are usually started in the infancy of inquiry; but are also I fear the longest stumblingblocks in philosophy's Way. So please tell me what reply your active meditations have forged in metaphysical armoury to What is the Origin of Evil? And what becomes of the poor Slave born in chains living in stripes & toil, who has never heard of Virtue & never practised it & dies cursing God & man? It cannot be but that in the frightful variety of human misery the counterpart of this picture is often found. Must he die in Eternal Darkness because it has been his lot to *live* in the Shadow of death?—A majority of the living generation, & of every past generation known in history, is worldly & impure. or, at best, do not come up to the Strictness of the Rule enjoined upon human virtue. These then cannot expect to find favour in the Spiritual region whither they travel. How is it, then, that a Benevolent Spirit persists in introducing onto the Stage of existence millions of new beings, in incessant series, to pursue the same wrong road, & consummate the same tremendous fate? And yet if you waver towards the clement side here, you incur a perilous responsibility of preaching *smooth* things. And, as to the old knot of human liberty, our Alexanders must still *cut* its Gordian twines. Next comes the Scotch Goliath, David Hurne; but where is the accomplished stripling who can cut off his most metaphysical head? Who is he that can stand up before him & prove the existence of the Universe, & of its Founder? He hath an adroiter wit than all his forefathers in philosophy if he will confound this Uncircumcised. The long & dull procession of Reasoners that have followed since, have challenged the awful shade to duel, & struck the air with their puissant arguments. But as each new comer blazons 'Mr Hume's objections' on his pages, it is plain they are not satisfied the victory is gained. Now though every one is daily referred to his own feelings as a triumphant confutation of the glozed lies of this Deciever, yet, it assuredly would make us feel safer & prouder, to have our victorious answer set down in impregnable propositions. You will readily find a reason for my putting down this old A, B, C, of moral studies, to wit, to get a letter upon these threadbare enigmas. You have not thought precisely as others think & you have heretofore celebrated the benevolence of De Stael who thought for her son. Some revelation of nature you may not be loath to impart & a hint which solves one of my problems, would satisfy me more, with my human lot. Dr Channing is preaching sublime sermons every Sunday morning in Federal St. one of which I heard last Sunday, & which infinitely surpassed Everett's eloquence. It was a full view of the subject of the light of Revelation compared with Nature & to shew the insufficiency of the latter alone. Revelation was as much a part of the order of things as any other event in the Universe. Give my love & respect where they are due. Your affectionate & obliged nephew

R. Waldo E

To Sarah Ripley, August 1, 1824

Canterbury, 1 August. 1824

My dear Aunt

I have found in my Geometry a certain problem that I never read there before, couched in words of great kindness, & containing gold, & demonstrating certain *moral* truths with the force of mathematical. Every body loves to be the object of kind & partial feelings, & I more than any. But nevertheless I wish my Aunt were less open-handed; for, in the first place, there was nothing to reward, the debt being on our side; &, in the next, if there had been, you thereby strip us of our poor merit of goodwill; for goodwill that is to be recompensed in this world, it seems to me, has got, among the moralists, an ignoble name. Besides, you & your house have already laid us under so many obligations that you put it out of our power to pay our just debts; which an honest man always counts a calamity. I shall keep this pledge of your kindness which it were churlish to reject, but I shall keep it as a pledge, which I ought to restore. If you wish to know about us,—the whole Archbishopric of them are well. Edward broods over the Oration; Charles over the School Dissertation; Mother keeps them in order; and Old Mortality in his cell smiles, admires, & moralizes. Time & Chance hold on their old way & we shape ourselves to them as well as we can. Young men & old soon find that these ancient principles, whether they shall call them fates or providences are the lords of life, to whose ordinations they must conform themselves & despite all the big looks of ambition & all the declamations of poets concerning the majesty of man, must yield up their plans & their pride. The seed may be the best that ever was planted, but if it fall on stony ground it will not grow. The man & his project, the most plausible in the world, but out of tune with his times, & cannot prosper. Like all the rest, we at home strut in a straight line to the end of our string & then, must needs, like all the rest, turn or stop. Proud & poor spirits are not very far divided in this world, and with all the difference of their pretensions may end in a like event. Men cheat each other & themselves with ostentatious distinctions of Master & disciple, of Monarch & Slave but in those hours of each mans life when the truth comes out he finds (excepting moral distinctions) not the choice of a hair's breadth among the multitude of his fellows; they are all the disciples & slaves, & your only true Masters & Emperors are Time & Chance.

After this long homily I have only to add that I have sent my letter to Uncle Daniel & Mother has sent your ribbon to Concord by Stage. Mother & Edward send their love & respects to Grandfather, & Grandmother & much love to yourself. How does your cough? As soon as it troubles you, you must try Canterbury again Edward begs you & Grandfather to remember how much he depends on your Company at Holworthy, No 4, by 9 o'clock A.M. Commencement Morng.

Your affectionate nephew
Waldo

To Elizabeth B. Francis, February 18, 1825

Cambridge, Feb. 18, 1825.

Your kindness must excuse me for my long delay in sending you the note I promised. Nor do I know inclose the list of books which I mentioned to your mother, since I have already given your friend Miss Wainwright a copy of it, & Miss Parsons, a summary of the same. but I use the opportunity to say a word or two of those studies which are to form the best entertainment of your leisure hours. And in the first place I think you will pardon me, tho' I recommend with peculiar emphasis, the old bugbear,—*Writing.* Because in your ambition you cannot write epics & philosophy at once, you are disgusted with ill success & desist from further trial. Now, since we are born to many heavy hours, it is not wise to slight an art which makes solitude pleasing, without abridging the joys of society; an art, which, perhaps, more than any other, increases the strength of the intellectual faculties, by the demand it makes on them all. When pen & paper were before me, if my memory furnished me with no observations on books or characters, I would, at the least, recount in a diary the events of a day. Our eyes and ears assuredly are rich enough in facts even when our judgments & imaginations are torpid, and my journal should take the risk of being frivolous this week, in the hope of being wiser the next.

It is not because of the skill in letter writing this habit will teach, (tho' next to powers of conversation, I know no more agreeable talent among the gifts of common life,) but on account of the indirect advantage which springs from it in the habit of drawing subjects of thought out of ordinary occurrences—and also, the sharpening of our desire of reading, & the better ability we gain of judging of books, from being petty bookmakers ourselves.

As for Latin, I confide to your interest in the fortunes of pious Aeneas, for keeping your Virgil open,—and when this is finished to your curiosity about the greatest name in Rome, for leading you to Cicero's orations against Catiline. If, in connexion with the Orations, you read Middleton's Life of Cicero, you will find both books interesting.

In English, you must have resolution enough to read the whole of Stewart's first Volume,—if it require any resolution to read a book so beautiful and wise. As to Locke, I think I can excuse you from his instructions. But in History, it will be easy to continue Hume, without other interruption than Shakespear's historical plays in connexion with each reign, down to Henry VIII, where Robertson's Charles V. comes in. The first vol. contains a sketch of the state of Europe which you can skip if you choose.

For the books that lie on your shelf, you will always find Johnson's Lives of the Poets, & Rambler, &c entertaining. and for poetry, Miltons Paradise, & Minor Poems, are above praise. I am glad to know you study Italian & hope you will not leave it till you have read Tasso and that other greater bard whose works you have given me in so beautiful a dress.

I know not but my letter may come a day too late; for, when stated lessons are exchanged for voluntary ones, it is hard to observe our appointed hours; and, with all your habits of diligence, perhaps, you have already found how much resolution it costs. So if bachelor's balls & Lionel Lincoln have quite driven the books into corners & cobwebs,—you must forgive this prosing of a college recluse which grows, no doubt, out of inveterate habits of keeping school.—With my respects to your father & mother, I remain your sincere friend.

R. W. Emerson.

To William Emerson, December *c.* 20? 1825

Dear Wm,

In obedience to your letter I am about to close my school here & to migrate to your latitudes. One thing is unlucky—that same lame hip of mine which I have been magnifying into a scarecrow, maugre Dr Dalton's opinions who nicknames it rheumatism. But for safety's sake I insist on its being dandled and hunted as the worst form of hip complaint, whereat he laugheth. Obsta principiis[6] I make much of the matter because said malady hath crippled its hundreds & slain its tens. Please tell Uncle Ralph I will God willing keep school here till 1st of January & hope then or 2 or 3 days after to drive & clinch the nails of instruction into at least 30 brains of the State's good town of Roxburgh. For 20 is not enow. I shall probably bring boarding scholars 3 or four if room cd. be readily found. But don't take a house till I come Better begin moderately by boarding teacher & taught with some resident family. They are pleased to say in Chelmsford that they are in the gall of bitterness. If you send me a letter again put it into that old odd Vol of Montaigne & send it bundlewise by stage. If you can find an old Liber Primus to spare put it in also. The first I must have before I leave C. I use my eyes to write. Bulkeley is perfectly deranged & has been ever since I have been here. I shall try to leave him here.

I enclose a letter writ without great expense of eye at 3 sittings which transmit if you please.

Love to mother & tell her not to look grave at the beginning of my letter for I wrote such a horrible story to shew how careful an old lady I am

R. W. E.
Geo is very well

---

6. *"Stand against principles."*

To Mary Moody Emerson, April 6, 1826

Cambridge, April 6, 1826.

My dear Aunt,

Epicurus said to his fellow men 'We are a sufficient spectacle to each other'; and he said truly; for it is the business & pleasure of life to make the best acquaintance we can with the individuals of the enormous crowd of the living & the dead. They so press on each other in the innumerable procession that tis little we can learn distinctly of each yet we can distinguish here & there a man clad with the purple of empire, & another with the motley of prejudice, a third disfigured with the dust of libraries & a fourth with the blood of his brethren. But altho we are by the distance necessarily made strangers to infinite numbers the same distance helps us to group them together and to trace the general direction & many windings of the march. And who are the guides & where the encampments whither the progress & when the period of this tragic journey of humanity thro' the champaign of the world? Nation travels after nation some in chains, & some in mail, of diverse complexions of diverse tongues, some in weeds of peace singing paeans to every muse in accents of noble harmony and some stumbling onward with heavy step & downcast eyes, the ensigns of former honor dragging—in the dust whilst now and then bursts of bitter lamentation answer to each other from space to space in this funeral Congregation of mourners.

Let us draw nearer & make the most of our vantage-ground to satisfy our curiosity respecting the intents & condition of those we are favourably situated to observe. They are banded into companies in the outset of their array for better defence against the wolf & the lion, against famine & storm. They are organized under governments for the convenience & protection of the individuals But who leads the leaders & instructs the instructor? I behold along the line men of reverend pretension who have waited on mountains or slept in caverns to receive from unseen Intelligence a chart of the unexplored country a register of what is to come. But, wo is me! as they proceeded the gods of the nations became no gods, the facts belied the prophecies, & the advancing journey betrayed the falsehood of their guides. Goodness was not found with the servants of the Supremely Good, nor Wisdom with those who had seen the all Wise.—But still, on they went—the stately procession by tribes & kindreds & nations, substituting experience of the past for

knowledge of the future, advancing with courageous heart into the unexplored wilderness, tho' with many delays & many retrograde wanderings,
thro' sunshine & storm whilst many a day of beauty lighted their march, &
many a halcyon sign of hope & knowledge illuminated the future.

At the last an obscure man in an obscure crowd bro't forward a new
Scripture of promise & instruction. But the rich & the great leaned to their
ancient holdings & the wise distrusted this teacher for they had been often
misled before. But the banner inscribed with his Cross has been erected and
it has been to some a cloud & to some a pillar of fire.

We too have taken our places in the immeasurable train & must choose
our standard & our guide. Is there no venerable tradition whose genuineness & authority we can establish, or must we too hurry onward inglorious
in ignorance & misery we know not whence, we know not whither. Perhaps
you are tired of my metaphors but I write to get answers not to please
myself—and cannot tell how much I was disappointed to find my long
expected letter nothing but an envelope.

My eyes are well comparatively, my limbs are diseased with rheumatism.

I beseech you again to write. Samuel Gilman of Charleston, S. Carolina
writes the Brown Reviews. Norton wrote the last review of Byron, & Alex.
Everett the one before. Edward writes that he mends daily.

Your affectionate nephew
R. Waldo E.

Mother hopes a favourable opportunity will occur by which Hannah can
come.

Why so anxious about C[harles].—He stands we suppose first in his class;
he loves letters, he loves goodness; But goodness is an abstraction & we cannot
always be goodhumoured even tho' we love to madness. He will be eloquent, & will *write* but comes not up to the force & nobleness of the transat-
lantic boy—certainly not to my cherished image of the same.

To Mary Moody Emerson, June 30, 1826

Cambridge June 30 1826.

In all the vagaries I have troubled you with not much has been said of poetry
tho a subject near to us both. I shd. be glad to see your tho'ts on its general
nature & value. Does the continuation of your own speculations shew its

fairy web to be superficial or wrot into the grain of man. Is it left behind as we advance or is it perfect in the Archangel than in the child? And for the professors of the art can they not err by excess of relish for the same? It wd seem that the genuine bard must be one in whom the extremes of human genius meet; that is his judgment must be as exact & level with life as his imagination is discursive & incalculable. It would seem as if abundant erudition foreign travel & gymnastic exercises must be annexed to his awful imagination & fervent piety to finish Milton. That the boisterous childhood, careless of criticism & & poetry the association of vulgar & unclean companions were necessary to balance the towering spirit of Shakspear and that Mr Wordsworth has failed of pleasing by being too much a *poet*. A man may pursue a course of exercises designed to strengthen his arm with such indiscreet zeal as to paralyze it. A boy enamoured of the beauty of a butterfly chases & clutches it with such eagerness that he finds his hand full of dirt & blood. I cant read this poets mystic & unmeaning verses without feeling that if had cultivated poetry less & learning & society more he wd have gained more favor at the hands of the muses who must be courted not taken by violence. Tis sufficient proof of a mans aberration to know that he is writing verses on a theory; that he has agreed with two or three antics more to bring the public over to a new taste in poetry. It would seem there was some kindred between the new philosophy of poetry & the undisciplined enterprizes of intellect in the middle age. The geniuses of that era all on fire with that curiosity which is in every age inextinguishable to break the marble silence of nature & open some intercourse between man & that divinity with which it seems instinct, struggled to grasp the principles of things, to extort from the spheres in the firmament some intimations of the present or some commentary on the past. They were impatient of their straitened dominion over nature, & were eager to explore the secrets of her own laboratory that they might refine clay & iron into gold might lengthen life & deduce formulas for the solution of all those mysteries that besiege the human adventurer. Not otherwise this modern poet, by natural humour a lover of all the enchantments of wood & river, & seduced by an overweening confidence in the force of his own genius has discarded that modesty under whose influence all his great precursors have resorted to external nature sparingly for illustration & ornament, & have forborne to tamper with the secret & metaphysical nature of what they borrowed. He has been foolishly inquisitive about the essence & body of what pleased him, of what all sensible men feel to be in its nature evanescent. He cant be satisfied with feeling the general beauty of a moonlight evening or of a rose. He wd pick them to pieces &

pounce on the pleasurable element he is sure is in them, like the little boy who cut open his drum to see what made the noise. The worthy gentleman gloats over a bulrush moralizes on the irregularity of one of its fibres & suspects a connexion between an excrescence of the plant & his own immortality. Is it not much more conformable to that golden middle line in which all that is good & wise of life lies, to let what Heaven made small & casual remain the objects of a notice small & casual, & husband our admiration for images of grandeur in matter or in mind? But I shd not worry myself with abusing Mr Wordsworth, not even for his serene egotism whereby he seems at every turn thunderstruck to see what a prodigious height human genius has headed up in *him,* but that he has occasionally written lines wh I think truly noble. He wd be unworthy your notice but that now & then comes from him a flash of divine light & makes you uneasy that he shd be such an earthen vessel. He has nobly embodied a sentiment wh. I know not why has always seemed congenial to humanity that the soul has come to us from a preexistence in God; that we have a property in the past wh. we do not ourselves recognize, & a title to the future of wh. we shd be little thankful. Wait a little says this venerable faith & this feverish being for which you are so anxious will be whelmed in a vaster being to wh. it is only subsidiary; but let the glory & virtue of other worlds be as they may, in parting with our identity we part with happiness.

Every age, as it augments the number of the successful experiments of genius whilst it shd, seem to furnish that large induction from whence we can ascertain the true extent & nature of poetry has rather appeared to carry its title into new empires & annex an import yet more vague & universal of the word. What is Poetry? It is philosophy, it is humour it is a chime of two or three syllables, it is a relation of thot to things or of language to tho't. It converses with all science & all imagination with all accidents & objects from the grandest that are accessible to the senses & grander than those to the coarsest parts of life. And I wd. go to the farthest verge of ye green earth to learn what it was or was not. If the spirit of him who paced the academe & had this virtue in his soul tho he feigned to disparage it in his philosophy or ye laurelled lovers of ye British muse harp in hand sit on your misty mount or soothe their majesties by the margin of your lakes, conjure them I beseech you to announce this secret that the wit of humanity has been so long in vain toiling to unriddle. It shall be reverently received & cautiously dispensed & shall add a rich item to the scanty stock of truth of which your friend is the humble master.

TO MARY MOODY EMERSON, SEPTEMBER 23, 1826

Cambridge, Sept 23d, 1826

My dear Aunt,

I need small persuasion to send you pretty long letters of which fact you have already had some sad experience. But I am so pleased to get rid of my mean cares a little & sculk into the lobbies that lead into the heaven of philosophy and listen when the door is open if perchance some fragment some word of power from the colloquy sublime may fall on mine ear—Such words purify poor humanity. They clear my perceptions for my duties.

Is it not true that modern philosophy by a stout reaction has got to be very conversant with feelings? Bare reason, cold as cucumber, was all that was tolerated in aforetime, till men grew disgusted at the skeleton & have now given him in ward into the hands of his sister, blushing shining changing Sentiment. And under this guardian of public opinion, it is respectfully submitted that public opinion will be apt to run to & fro, a little. Be that as it may, it is one of the *feelings* of modern philosophy, that it is wrong to regard ourselves so much in a *historical* light as we do, putting Time between God & us; and that it were fitter to account every moment of the existence of the Universe as a new Creation, and *all* as a revelation proceeding each moment from the Divinity to the mind of the observer. If this position have a foundation as it would seem in genuine Sentiment, another remark of a parallel tendency may hold also. It is certain that the moral world as it exists to the man within the breast is illustrated, interpreted, defined by the positive institutions that exist in the world; that in the aspect that is disclosed to a mind at this hour opening in these parts of the earth, Christianity appears the Priest, the expounder of God's moral law. It is plainly a fit representative of the Lawgiver. It speaks the voice God might speak. We ought not therefore to have this mighty regard to the long antiquity of its growth, and to the genuineness or fallacy of pretensions on which the dust of 16 or 18 centuries has gathered, but to consider its present condition as a thing entirely independent of the ways & means whereby it came into that condition & neither seeing what it was nor hearing what it said to past generations, examine what it is & hear what saith to *us*.

This is probably the most plausible statement of the doctrine of relative and absolute truth. That it *is absolutely* true is perhaps capable of evidence.

That it is relatively true is certain, and thus it may procure for us all the eternal good it ever pretended to offer Such reasoning we know is admitted in law. The subject is never required to know whether the prince on the throne (de facto) is the prince of right (de jure) and cannot afterward be challenged for this allegiance at any time to a successful usurper.

There is a sort of truth in all this but it will never bear a statement. The understanding recoils as insulted from an attempt to disguise a sophistry and is less pliant in the lesson, than she is in the world. This is called sophistry, but it is precisely this reasoning which under one or another colour men use, when they unite Mysticism to the profession of Christianity. It has always the apology that we hold truth by a tenure so subtle that the most grave speculation carried many steps from our first principles, loses itself in irrecoverable cloud. Despise nothing was the old saw, and this ambiguous light in wh. we live is authority for the rule. To grow wise is to grow doubtful; and it ill becomes that man to pronounce an opinion absurd who feels in the consciousness of the changes his mind has already undergone, that before another sun the truth of that exploded dogma may be dearest to his mind. How does Aunt Sarah? Mother sends with mine her best love. And respects to Grandfather & to Mrs R. I depend on the letter for wh. I have waited by G. R.

Yr affectionate nephew
Waldo.

To Charles Chauncy Emerson and Edward Bliss Emerson, December 30, 1826.

Dec 30, 1826.
Charleston, S.C.

Dear Charles

I am very glad to get a letter from you. Its fault was that it came alone. It shd. have been 'e pluribus unum.' It comes however at a convenient time to get answered, and I am glad to have that work to do. It cannot be a new matter of speculation to you,—the effect of science on the bulk of mankind. That the effect of successful abstruse inquiries is minute &, for long periods, inappreciable is the burthen of many a sigh. But that in the event Jack &

Gill are the better for the painful speculations of Leibnitz & Kant is equally undeniable. The search after truth is always by approximation. The wise man begins a train of tho't whose farthest results he does not live to see, nor perhaps do his children's children. We have an instinctive perception of the value of certain ideas, which are the seeds of great conclusions, which all our efforts often are unable to unfold. The clown sees these beginnings, these first gropings of the intellect after something which he does not see and which he is satisfied are very far removed from any vulgar interest & scoffs of course at "studies which end in new studies, & do not tend to lessen the price of bread." Whenever a new truth results, it is readily made known to many more minds than were acquainted with the inquiry; for truth is attractive; and it enlightens many more subjects than the one in whose discussion it was ascertained; for all truth is correlated. Whatever therefore be the indifference with which the majority of men regard the ordinary *studies* of the philosopher, the moment he arrives at any signal discovery, the good contagion of truth is propagated from the higher circles of society to the lower and all men are in some manner affected by it. Conspicuously in our day has science become practical when the seas are navigated by Bowditch's book & by the Nautical Ephemeris annually issued by the philosophers of the Royal Soc. at Greenwich, and when the government of England, France, America takes lessons from the Political Economist. But tis shame to write so dully about what mt. be triumphantly represented with a little labour. Besides the subject has another face, to wit, That the distinctions of society were intended, and there is a fine saying of Voltaire's which is something like this, "le triomphe de la raison, c'est de bien vivre avec ceux qui n'en ont pas."[7] Amid all the distinctions, there is a wonderful equality, & however distinctly a man of genius, may perceive his advantage when he walks in a crowd, he can hardly encounter any one individual of the crowd in a casual conversation, without a disposition to doubt his own pretensions. As to what you say respecting universal genius I am not satisfied that your latest opinion was the truest. There have been unquestionably men whose genius was equally excellent in grand & minute performances. And Cato you know seemed born only for that one thing he was at any moment doing. Nevertheless, it cannot be denied, there are trifles, & they are to be valued as trifles. But much I doubt if the blood & temperament you were born to will let you spurn

---

7. *"The triumph of Reason is to live well among those who do not have any."*

names manners & compliments in your way to great distinctions which I know they will not deny.

This letter I see is open to great exceptions, but I shd. be shamed to withhold it after having written so far, so let it lie as quietly on the shelf as may be. By the way, it is strange you shd. be so incorrect a writer, when so scholarly,—"landlegs" for sea legs—'day of a port' for *in*, &c. besides unfinished sentences. It raised the gall of Holofernes in me tho' I cd. almost cry for joy at the letter. Tell them all I love them & am a little better. As to Aunt Marys advice, & your question, I add my solemn Yea.

Y. a. brother Waldo

Edward Edward why dont you write. Why one wd. think I was in the same country with you & not as I am beyond the farthest islands mountains swamps in these offscourings of the world. I think of going to the W. Indies, for greater heat. If I do, I shall first write to Waltham.

To William Emerson, January 6 and 9, 1827

Charleston S. C. 6 Jan. 1827.

Dear William,

I received with great joy a letter from you a few days since & suppose that before this time you have received mine, written a fortnight ago & sent by I know not what ship. I believe I recounted in that letter the plagues which had fallen upon me & which appear to have excited your kind curiosity. The cold has been so considerable here as to prevent me from deriving any signal benefit from the change of climate. Indeed I am scared out & tis more than probable that I shall take passage for St. Augustine, where I am promised the most balmy air in the world, in the sloop William next Tuesday or Wednesday. I beseech you however not to be in any particular alarm on my account. I am not sick; I am not well; but luke-sick—and as in my other complaints, so in this, have no symptom that any physician extant can recognize or understand. I have my maladies all to myself. I have but a single complaint,— a certain stricture on the right side of the chest, which always makes itself felt when the air is cold or damp, & the attempt to preach or the like exertion of the lungs is followed by an aching. The worst part of it is the deferring of hopes—& who can help being heart sick? Moreover it makes me dependant inasmuch as my excellent friend in Waltham undertakes to supply me with funds without appointing the pay day. I have books & pens enough here to keep me from being desperately homesick but have not succeeded in overcoming certain physical & metaphysical difficulties sufficiently to accomplish any thing in the way of grave composition, as I had hoped. There are here scarce any materials for "Letters from S. Carolina," if I were ambitious.

But I wish you the happiest of years and do rejoice you have got something to eat, & do particularly hope & pray that you eat it. We are not cameleons we are not anchorets but being born to the roast beef of New England must eat it or smart for it. You say nothing of *law,* What is your expectation with regard to the term of study prescribed to you? Have you any definite prospects of any kind which I do not know? Do you really mean to abide by the City of N.Y. As to what you say about 2d Unit. Ch. I am very glad. Shd. be glad if H. Ware wd go. they can better spare him in Boston than there. For myself, I had rather be a doorkeeper at home than bishop to aliens. tho' I confess it mends the matter that there is such a huge fraction of Yankee blood.

I have always intended to return by land & if possible to preach for Furness in Phil. & to you in N.Y. but do not expect to get out till April. I want to make a visit at Alexandria. Your room is better than your company O January February & March! Am sincerely obliged for your good will in the money matter but shall be your debtor fast enough, if my ails last. I scribble on in my bluebooks & remind Edward that Müller left his MSS. to public auction to pay his debts.

Tuesday 9 Jan. I have been compelled to leave my letter till this time unfinished, & have now to say that I have engaged my passage to St Augustine, for very cold, & shall sail probably tomorrow in the sloop William. There I intend to pass 7 or 8 weeks on air & oranges said to be all that the city affords except fish. Any vessel bound thither from N. York must bring me letters. Otherwise send by water to Charleston to the Care of S. Davenport & Co & they will send them by water to me, as I have requested. I am pretty well, tho not as you see particularly brilliant. Yr affectionate brother

Waldo—

I saw Wm Geo Reed the other day who was first scholar in class before mine, & who is recently become a flaming Roman Catholic. He is a lawyer settled in Baltimore, & did once run away with the daughter of a wealthy Mr Howard of that city.

To Charles Chauncy Emerson, January 27, 1827

St Augustine, E. Florida—
27 Jan. 1827.

Dear Charles,

In these remote outskirts of civilization the idea of home grows vivid, & grave men like me are sometimes pestered with a curiosity, very unbecoming doubtless, & very keen, to know what is done & said by certain beardless aspirants who are giving their days to philosophy & virtue. Whosoever is in St Augustine resembles what may be also seen in St A. the barnacles on a ledge of rocks which the tide has deserted; move they cannot; very uncomfortable they surely are,—but they can hear from afar the roaring of the waters & imagine the joy of the barnacles that are bathed thereby. The entertainments of the place are two,—billiards & the sea beach; but those whose cloth abhors the billiards—why, theirs is the sea beach. Here therefore day by day do I parade, and think of my brother barnacles at a distance as aforesaid. I place before my eye a youth well born & well bred moving in colleges with the assured step of one at home in learned societies, commencing a pure noviciate not to vain superstitions, or transitory sciences but to Truth, serene, immutable, divine Truth. I see him conscious of the dignity of the vows that are on him, measuring with impatient eye the sin & ignorance of the world and hailing the tokens that glimmer in the horizon, of a better era to come. I behold him with industry, with vigils, & with prayers, arming himself in the cause of humanity reconciling a lowly mind with the high ambition to be fellow worker with God in the regeneration of man. May good angels accomplish him in his preparation, & send him out conquering & to conquer. Let him disdain the fading echoes of vulgar renown whilst he remembers that praise is the reflection of virtue. Let him blush to rest satisfied with partial attainments, adjusting a petty balance of venial faults with compensating merits but hew out to himself a great & perfect character which the world present & to come may behold & take pleasure in—the spectacle.—

Thus you see the poorest of us hath his ideal; a small greycoated gnat is wagoner to the Queen of Fairies, and we who walk on the beach are seers of prodigious events & prophets of noble natures. Let us make the ordinary claims of our class—'It is not us, it is not us; we are but pipes on which *another finger* plays what stop it pleases.'

It is not to be denied that the agency of an individual may be immense. The nature of man or the face of society is wonderfully plastic, and tho' it be conceded that it requires certain rare combinations of events to create the greatness of Washington, yet every hour that passes may contribute to open the genius of Milton, of Newton, of Rousseau, engines of forces that can never be computed for the production of good & of evil. I do not therefore, exaggerate, I use no unauthorised language when I figure to myself the youthful glory of such an one whose vein of genius leads him to literature and whose taste has received its bias from Everlasting beauty. You will pardon therefore the preceding page & not imagine that your exhorting brothers use you as the whetstone on which to sharpen their wits, but believe me to be in very truth your fond & loving brother

Waldo

If the vessel stays another day, I shall write to Waltham.

To Charles Chauncy Emerson, February 23, 1827

St Augustine, E. F. 23 Feb. 1827.

Dear Charles,

How is it with the ambitious youth? he of the sometime melancholy temperament, he that was called the ardent, eloquent, irresistible scholar, he who loved great men & defied fair women, he who adored virtue on a great scale, but was squeamish at viewing it on a small one, he who had enthusiasm from nature, but it was almost all evaporated in the kneading, he whose taste would be correct were it more manly, & whose form would be good, if it were more stout—thyself. I am prone to mercy or I would draw your character to the life, so that your own eye shd acknowledge the fidelity of the portraiture. The memory is sharp when home is distant and the dim congregation which my fancy nightly & daily visits, always appear in costume,— each in his virtues & vices. So beware, & bid Edward beware of provoking me or I will use my vantage ground to set him down in black & white putting him in sore peril if he remember the story of Archilochus.

I have not yet recd. your letters of which I heard in Edw.'s letter Write half a dozen. The world is before you for topics & when sense is not to be had, nonsense is a thousandfold better than nothing. You are in the heyday of youth when time is marked not by numbering days but by the intervals of mentality the flux & reflux of the soul. One day has a solemn complexion the next is cheerful, the south wind makes a third poetic, and another is 'sicklied oer with a pale cast of thought,' but all are redolent of knowledge & joy. The river of life with you is yet in its mountain sources bounding & shouting on its way & has not settled down into the monotony of the deep & silent stream. Vouchsafe then to give to your poor patriarchal exhorting brother some of these sweet waters. Write. write. I have heard men say (heaven help their poor wits,) they had rather have ten words viva voce from a man than volumes of letters for getting at his opinion.—I had rather converse with them by the interpreter. Politeness ruins conversation. You get nothing but the scum & surface of opinions when men are afraid of being unintelligible in their metaphysical distinctions, or that the subtlety & gravity of what they want to say will draw too largely on the extemporaneous attention of their company. Men's spoken notions are thus nothing but outlines & generally uninviting outlines of a subject, & so general, as to have no traits appropriate & peculiar to the individual. But when a man writes, he divests himself of his manners & all physical imperfections & it is the pure intellect that speaks. There can be no deception here. You get the measure of his soul. Instead of the old verse, "Speak that I may know thee," I write 'Speak, that I may suspect thee; write, that I may *know* thee.' Brandish your pen therefore, & give me the secret history of that sanctuary you call *yourself;* what new lights illuminate, what fragrant affections perfume it; what litanies are sung, what work is daily done in its mysterious recesses and to what god it is consecrated. And if you have any inclination to retort & play the La Bruyere on me, I defy you. It will give me extreme pleasure to see you miss your mark, & more if you hit it. Any thing sent as late as 1st April I suppose will reach me in Charleston; Afterward tis doubtful. I am going to write to Alexandria to advertise them of my purpose of spending a few weeks there if no objection exist—& expect to get home about Election. They say here I am fatter than when I came, I know not. I weigh 141½ pounds. Possibly Edward may remember what I weighed in Cambridge. I forget. My love & honour to Mother & she is welcome to see all my letters when she comes to town, but it is scarce worth while to send much trash so far. And love to all from your affectionate brother Waldo.

I have just recd. a letter from Edward without date out of some diplomacy I suppose & one from Aunt Mary both which were abundantly grateful. Say to E. that I know nothing about Barrow or Dante. Edward speaks of your oration at Hasty pudding. Take in time a just resolution Be proud & honest, & let it be *original* to the word & to the letter.

To Ezra Stiles Gannett, July 29, 1827

Sunday Evg 29 July

Dear Sir,

I received last evening the note containing the vote of the Association,[8] & have to express my obligations to the society for the kindness manifested in the appointment. But I believe I better consult my health by remaining in the country, & preaching only half days in Boston. I shall not therefore accept the appointment. I designed to have called upon you tomorrow, not knowing of your absence & promise myself that pleasure the next time I am in town.

With great regard Your friend & servt
R. Waldo Emerson.

To William Emerson, August 31, 1827

Aug 31, 1827.
Cambridge.

Dear William,

The channels of intercourse are obstructed a little but I have heard by casual travellers of your health, & I hope the announcement of an article in the Am. Qu. Rev on Germ. literature means yours.—I heard Charles's oration & day before yesterday, Edward's. Of the first, I gave you, thro another hand, some account. Of the last, voici. The matter was excellent & illuminated all

---

8. *On 25 July 1827 Emerson was appointed to serve for three months as a missionary in western Massachusetts, under the direction of the Franklin Association. [Rusk]*

along with fine & in one passage sublime ornaments of the imagination. It was spoken in a manly graceful significant manner & with a fine voice. But it was spoken with so much deliberation, that in my poor tho't, very much of the effect was lost. I anticipated a flaming excitement in mine & in the popular mind, and if the oration which occupied 30 minutes had been delivered in 15, I think it would have answered this purpose. As it was, people were pleased & called it the finest of orations &c &c—no lack of praise— but I meant they should be electrified. *and too* much astounded to be complimentary. I am going to preach at Northampton, in the service of the Unitarian Assoc., for Mr Hall, a few weeks, whilst he goes into the adjoining towns to missionize His church is a small one, & I shall be able to preach all day I suppose without inconvenience. Afterward I am at liberty to do the same for Mr Williard of Deerfield & send him on the same errand. But that shall be as health & circumstances may be. Meantime be pleased to rejoice, that I have in my trunk eleven entire sermons all which I have preached at First Ch. Mr Frothingham has come home in excellent health & spirits & would not exchange his recollections of the Capitoline hill for any possessions. The President's illness cast a sadness over Commencement day, & every body is sincerely sorry for him. & the more because it is tho't the chair which he will probably resign, will not be easily worthily filled. Yet Mr Eben. Francis told Furness a few days ago, that he had not any doubt that if Everett were elected he would accept the place. And Mr F. is one of the corporation in virtue of being treasurer, & no gossip. Mr Walker did decently but disappointed any one that expected much, at Φ. B. K. Dr Bradford delivered a poem abounding in jokes good & evil. Greenwood was elected into the Society, & Charles Sprague black balled. The new class that has entered contains about 70, which has much refreshed the courage of the friends of the college. And the President is to be married on Sunday night. And now I have finished the gossip floating in Cambridge that may interest you. I have no news of home Mother returned to Concord, Wednesday evg. Charles begins now his term. Edw. continues with Webster. George Ripley was married a week since, & Stetson of Medford the same day.

Prithee, dear William send me some topics for sermons or if it please you better the whole model 'wrought to the nail.' For much of my time is lost in choosing a subject & much more in wishing to write. Everett in his early discourses used great plainness & simplicity. I have by me seven of them in MSS. I aspire always to the production of present effect thinking that if I succeed in that, I succeed wholly. For a strong present effect is a permanent impression. Perhaps sooner than I wish I may come & repeat my sermons to you in N. Y. My health has mended with the weather, heat being my best medicine. I am not so well but that the cold may make another Southern winter expedient. I hope not. What of Scott's Napoleon? A real Gazetteer in appearance. I have not read it. But I like Everett's America very well, & eagerly expect the Quarterly Review & am your

Affectionate brother Waldo

I preach in Northampton the 2d Sunday in Sept. & shall stay 4 weeks I believe.

You will say to Edward if you say anything that you have heard from Waldo of his success for, I have heard today that "it was the perfection of speaking" & he looks sad under the suspicion that it was not. I send you with the Orders a ridiculous jeu d'esprit that was stuck up one morning about College. A previous one had promised the tragedy of Job. Job—Mr Noyes—&c

I shall try send this by my friend Rev Mr Motte who is to preach in N.Y. & afterwards in Washington.

To Ezra Ripley, October 7, 1827

Deerfield 7 Oct. 1827

My dear Sir,

I have led such a roving life since I left your hospitable roof, that it has not always been easy for me to write when I have been disposed, or I should sooner have consulted my inclination as well as my duty in sending you some account of my motions It was, you know, my expectation in coming here, to spend four successive weeks at Northampton, and then I was to be at liberty to do the same at Deerfield or perhaps at Greenfield, whilst the clergyman whose pulpit I supplied, should preach in the waste places. This plan I acceded to very readily, when proposed by Mr Gannett, in obedience, as he said, to the wishes of the Franklin Association. It promised me retirement, leisure for increasing my stock of sermons, and such advantage to my health as this inland mountain air might bring me. But wo to him that trusts to the frailty of human plans. . broken reeds. The second Sunday it was found convenient to send me to Greenfield; the third to Deerfield; on the Tuesday following, the association met at Northampton, & could not make their mutual plans tally without Mr Emerson would go to Greenfield again for the following Sabbath, & to Deerfield on the next after. Now, Sir, as it would not do for a missionary to set up his Ebenezer & be stiffnecked I must needs comply with what grace I could. So I carried my scrip & my doctrines to the courthouse at Greenfield last Sunday & am to give my testimony here tomorrow. Then, as I told the association I was not engaged until November, I shall probably supply Mr Hall's pulpit for three Sabbaths,—unless new emergencies shall again turn out of doors the wayfaring divine. All this, Sir, as you will readily perceive, is not a little unfavourable to my purposes of study. One of the plots of the reverend gentlemen against my peace was to send me into Conway hoping that my name & consanguinity to the last minister might peradventure take captive the confidence of some of his parishioners in that stronghold of Calvinism. But owing to some unforeseen circumstances this project miscarried. Mr Henry Ware wrote to me lately to engage me to supply Mr Deweys pulpit during the three first weeks of November, which I consented to do, much against my will, for I wanted to go to Concord for a little time. On my journey thither I promise myself the pleasure of a day or two at your house.

I do not find orthodoxy so strongly rooted as I had imagined. At elections in this Country Unitarians almost always get majorities. Intelligent men are of opinion that the majority of this Country is unitarian. I had supposed it must be so, from my acquaintance with the human mind, but feared to be contradicted by acquaintance with the Country.

Please to give my affectionate respects to my mother. I trust this will find you, Sir, in as vigorous health as you enjoyed in the summer That God may long preserve it to you, & enrich it with blessings is the prayer of

Dear Sir, Your affectionate Grandson

To Edward Bliss Emerson, *c.* November? 1827

Concord Tuesday Evg

Dear Edward,

Why hesitate? The way is clear to the Temple of fame thro' the Mechanics Institutes. or the converse. Carve your way thro' the objections which you will first magnify & then demolish It would on any arena of Controversy be gravely urged yt the scheme of universal education was fanciful inasmuch as neither laws nor customs but sovran Nature alone distributes the lights of the mind. There is no entail of Genius. No court probate to secure to the heir of Pindar the inheritance of Song. The son of Cicero may be a prolix talker; the Child of Chesterfield a wrong-headed clown. Now the same power that expands at the birth the native force of a few individuals in a generation far, beyond the common mark, fired the desires of those individuals to reach their proper ends. It was not then the education of Pericles that gave him the controul of the Peloponnesian War but the inward craving of a great intellect that drove him on from height to height of knowledge till his education was the institution of a perfect hero. The same fiery soul & not peculiar fortunes enlisted him in the service of the state & in the sequel made his opinion the preponderant opinion of Attica & Greece—In like manner the lowest of men, the drudges that worm along thro the mud & bottom of society—it is not for want of cultivation of their powers but the want of powers themselves. Hence tis vain to attempt to regenerate mankind by a patent education whilst the evil we would cure is out of the reach of education viz. the original inequality of intellect.

Now this reasoning would be wonderfully conclusive if applied to the brute creation; would serve in a world of lions; in a prairie of buffaloes. Would serve wherever instinct supplied the place of reason. But in the world of forecasting reasoning men, of men advancing on themselves, drawing daily accessions of light from the innumerable objects about them & depending for their character on the series of circumsts into which they are thrown,—it will not do. I am no fanatic disciple of Mr Owen; I nourish no predilection for the exploded experiments of New Harmony—I do not adopt the cant of the *pupilage* of *circumstances* Yet I must venture on the repetition of an ancient truism that every man's character depends in great part upon the scope & occasions that have been afforded him for its development. That the Mind is something to be unfolded & will disclose some faculties more & some less just in proportion to the room & excitements for action that are furnished it. Is it not known to you on the great scale of nations as well as in the history of individuals. Is it not remembered hath it not been told you how in past times the exigences of the state have evoked as with a clarion voice men of war & men of council, armed & wise equal to her need altho' till that moment their existence had not been surmised. Is the age of the Revolution forgotten so soon when the volley of a rustic militia line at

Concord was a signal note whose thundering echoes were heard in every glen of the Alleganies calling out the farmer from the tillage of his few paternal acres to take his post in the loading platoon; reading backward the mighty prophecy of peace to turn his scythe into a sword & his pruning hook into a spear; & Liberty sat on the mountain tops astonished at the multitude of her armed sons, who flocked by scores of thousands to her holy side.

To Charles Chauncy Emerson, January 1, 1828

Concord, N.H. 1 Jan. 1828

A happy new year to my dear brother & many blessings may it bring vigour to the intellect & charity to the soul golden dispositions & happiness their fatal fruit. May it bring the desert of honours & under its wing may it find a snug corner wherein to tuck a particular honour a mere appendix to your merits but a balm to the fretted expectations of one of your ancients. I am in no hurry I wait the leisure of the Year—Lay it up in the later constellations; near Lyra, for example, which ascends in August. And how did the new comer from eternity find you employed Did it ever come to your sharpened ear—that rumor once rife among the immortals, that Saturn & Nemesis were at league together—the wary witness & the implacable retributor and according to the the work of the mortal when Saturn came in, should Nemesis deal with you as Saturn went out? It is an idle fashion of your College to let the new year commence in vacation. But I will generously trust that ardent virtue shall be guard for itself.

I would give more than I now own to find a convenient acquaintance such as I have read of & heard of & thought of times without number that would answer anyhow to the fabulous descriptions of a friend—yours for instance in the [Harvard] Register. I would not be difficult; he should rub & go.

The creature must have at least as much sense as God has given me, which, malice might say was an easy condition of the advertisement, & then his condition must be cleanly; that is, not a vile mechanical person, but having education & manners, a decent slovenly gentleman who believes in the resurrection of the dead. Now these are not hard terms; there are many such in the community looking, doubtless, after just such a person (I contemn your mirth) as I myself. And yet no tongue can tell how much inconvenience & loss of time I suffer for the want of this useful person. Here in the snows, and at Cambridge in the chambers, I want him. A thousand smart things I have to say which born in silence die in silence for lack of his ear. A thousand goodly plans of thoughts or things to be farther unfolded that perish untimely; & hours of idleness & pain that might by his help be crowded with action & virtue. Brothers, even if I had decent ones, can never in any manner answer this purpose. Their education is so uniform & their habits of tho't so similar that they make insipid society; & furthermore my stars! they take such liberties, that literally a man can hardly say his soul is his own; if the soul is not very quiet if she say any thing above her breath it will be cabbaged & leave the poor soul nothing but her wrath. If you could see me as I uncomfortably draw my pen thro this sheet bent over my knee with a stranger by my side you would guess how great must be the inconveniences which send me for refuge to such idle employment how sincere is the want I have exposed.

My quarrel is with my race which will not give me what I want, either in the shape of man or woman. I look out impatient for the next stage of my existence that is the bodiless & expect there to ride my ray (you have read Tucker's vision) in this quest with more diligence than Diogenes bare his lanthorn Behold my resentment was kindled & my wrath said unto men ye are an insect race. But the historian Gibbon said I, remarks—The historian Gibbon, interrupted anger, is a learned pismire. Newton was a calculating pismire Voltaire an unbelieving pismire and your poor idol Everett is—a delightful pismire, added I. Nay said relenting wrath there is ichor in *his* veins. It is worth all the blood of all the pismires.

I am going if the day be fair tomorrow to the Shaker Society, at Canterbury with a sleighing party, & perhaps I will put on the drab cowl. Among the earliest institutions to be invented, if I read the stars right, is a protestant monastery, a place of elegant seclusion where melancholy gentlemen & ladies may go to spend the advanced season of single life in drinking milk, walking the woods & reading the Bible & the poets. I have a treatise on this subject in preparation. How is my brother Edward? I am impatient to hear him at the bar. When you next declaim you shall find a noble passage or selection from the last article in the XCI number of Ed[inburgh]. Review & I hope soon to see you & am yours.

Concord, 2 June, 1828

My dear brother,

Edward is a great deal better.[9] We were all thoroughly scared, & I was hastened hither from New Concord. He had fainting fits, & delirium, & had been affected strangely in his mind for a fortnight. He is now restored to his former habits of thinking which I cannot help saying were always perverse enough. Dr Jackson however said to me what I think is true that he will never be cured of a notion that he had that he was suddenly & totally recovered from his old disease a fortnight before he came here. Dr J. recommends that he should not touch a book for a year but as the imperious patient is up & dressed this morning, the doctor's dominion will shrink back into an advisory council, & come in, I doubt not, for a due share of contempt.

Tho' tis but yesterday he was very weak on his bed & tho' mother perhaps expects to keep him here a month, yet I believe he will be in Boston before a great while & attend to your business, if business you have, with usual precision.

I confess I watch him with painful interest. I fear that any future disorder may again affect his nerves. Still he reasons on business & affairs with force & rapidity & for aught I know his health may be really recovering. I shall presently I know not how soon go to N. Concord for a few weeks. Write to Charles at Cambridge.

Yours entirely
Waldo

by mail of course if you write concerning Edward.

---

9. *Edward's health, though apparently better for brief periods, was fast approaching a crisis after years of overstudy and nervous strain during a brilliant college career. Charles Emerson told William, 29 May, that Edward had been seized with fainting fits the preceding Sunday and had been almost stupefied since. [Rusk]*

To William Emerson, July 3, 1828

Divinity Hall—3 July—

Dear William,

I have just returned from Concord from a desolate house—Yesterday we brought Edward down to Charlestown—Horrible as is the bare idea it was the least of the two evils—for poor mother was almost down, with distress & attendance. He has been now for one week thoroughly deranged & a great deal of the time violent so as to make it necessary to have two men in the room all the time. Concord people were very kind The Shattucks, & Stone & Mellen law students & Mr Keyes & especially Jarvis & Dr Bartlett have staid with him. His frenzy took all forms sometimes he was very gay & bantered every body, & then it was only necessary to humour him & walk the room with him Afterward would come on a peevish or angry state & he would throw down every thing in the room & throw his clothes &c out of the window; then perhaps on being restrained wd. follow a paroxysm of perfect frenzy & he wd. roll & twist on the floor with his eyes shut for half an hour.—But whats the need of relating these—there he lay—Edward—the admired learned eloquent thriving boy—a maniac. Poor Charles dismayed at these tidings asks what good it is to be a scholar? Edward did not sleep—that is—hardly ever—Yesterday we procured a hack & Dr Bartlett & Jarvis came down with me & him. Dr Wyman objected very strongly to taking him saying it was a very peculiar & important case & ought to be dealt with alone under private care & of course tho't Dr Haskins & Bulkeley serious objections—But we had obtained leave of the Board & we made him see the impossibility of doing anything else & he grants the only great privilege they can that of entire seclusion from all other patients.—We returned in the afternoon to Concord & carried up Mrs Ripley—for mother had no woman to lean upon or comfort her. It was dreadful to hear her moans.—She is now suffering from a swollen foot the consequence of debility & constant going up & down stairs & Mrs Ripley thinks the care of it will be an useful occupation & diversion to her. Mrs Ripley will stay with her till Friday afternoon. Grandfather has been incessant in his kindness & attention. But the calamity is as great as any I ever heard of. For I cannot persuade myself to hope. But God can do all things. I have very little doubt but he will again be restored to reason. But I fear he will now always hold it on the precarious tenure of the state of stomach. And I do not know that it is desireable for him to come to a sense of his tremendous loss.—

But now for his business. He owes he told me about $700. I suppose he included in that his debts to me after his return, & excluded those before. I am responsible for his $100 note to Mr Francis, $150 to Mrs Cook $75. to Kasts. He has a small debt due him from a scholar but no money in his pocket books & tho' his mind was unsettled, seemed to think his drawer had been opened at his boarding house whilst he lay sick at Concord first time.—

He is admitted to the Asylum at $3.00 per week. I am principal. Dr Bartlett in the hurry gave his name as surety. But you will be here in August to advise. Charles's debts end now & if God is merciful to him, he will be in a condition to help us. On Bulkeley's notes, my name stands as principal tho' I have paid nothing hitherto except by lending Edw. a small sum. Write to me here at Cambridge. I will call at Munroe & Francis for letters. Yours affectionately Waldo

Charles, as if in a kind of mockery, has a first prize for dissertation.

To Charles Chauncy Emerson, July 15, 1828

15 July, 1828.

This day I heard Mr C. C. Emerson deliver a valedictory oration to his Class. This young man's performance deserves particular notice. He is a beautiful orator but never eloquent. His advantages for speaking both natural & acquired are very great. His voice his person & his action are (to that end) excellent. But the vice of his oratory lies here—he is a *spectacle* instead of being an *engine;* a fine show at which we look, instead of an agent that moves us. There is very good management of the voice, fine tones, varied & delicate sounds—some that are music to hear; there is very elegant and very nervous gesture; and these are used to convey beautiful & forcible periods indeed a very finished oration—to all who have a mind to hear it. Theres the rub—you may hear it or not as you choose. The orator leaves you to your option. He does not address you. He has chalked around him a circle on the floor & within that he exhibits these various excellences to all the curious. I happened to see the Manuscript before it was pronounced, & noticed a particular passage which was a sudden & touching appeal to the audience with the remark that Mr E. would not speak it well. It was even so. Though he uttered the words, *he did not appeal* to the audience. And so that moving passage passed with no more effect than if the same elegant speaker had said Butterfly, butterfly butterfly.—In short during this very pleasing performance I was many times reminded of Mr Everett's remark upon the ancients that they made the greatest advances in arts & commerce & politics & yet in each, thro' some strange mischance fell short of the last advance. So Mr E. with noble elements for eloquence, was all but eloquent. I felt that that voice should have thrilled me as a trumpet. I only heard it with pleasure. I felt that he should have made me laugh & cry at his will. He never touched me.

The cause of this peculiarity in this gentleman's harangue appeared to me to be that he came with a wrong feeling to the rostrum. His rank in College is very high. He has long enjoyed a considerable reputation for talents & acquirements & particularly as a speaker. The whole audience were known to him & were drawn together by the expectation of witnessing his powers. Mr E. was fully aware of all this, and aware, that, whatever he said would be eagerly & favorably listened to. Instead, therefore, of feeling that the audience was an object of attention from him, he felt that he was an object of attention to the audience. This of course is the reverse of what should be. Instead of finding his audience—like other orators—an angry master who is to be pacified, or a sturdy master who is to be cajoled,—&, in any case, one whose difficult regard is to be won,—he takes it for granted that he has the command. He makes a *King's Speech;* condescendingly drops very fine things, which, if you listen with all your might, will pay you.

As Revolutions take place in Colleges as well as monarchies, it appears that Mr E's situation is changed. He has been removed with some violence from the first to the second place. I suppose this event will do more than all masters or instructions, to mend the great error I have remarked—to push him out of his enchanted circle. He no longer claims deference by an unbroken prescription. His best title has been formally denied. At his next public appearance, he is to struggle uphill; he is to vindicate a right which has been set aside. Let him feel his situation. Let him remember that the true orator must not wrap himself in himself, but must wholly abandon himself to the sentiment he utters, & to the multitude he addresses;—must become their property, to the end that *they may become his.* Like Pericles, let him "thunder & lighten." Let him for a moment forget himself, & then, assuredly, he will not be forgotten.—

Waltham, 4 August, 1828.

Dear Charles,

Whilst I sit here whither I came to preach yesterday I can better acknowledge your letter than look at my fingers till breakfast time. I am glad you are in such good spirits, but you are a wicked lad to sharpen your pen against your kind cousins at Amherst You would be worth your weight in gold if you wd. fulfil the law of love as well as they. But tis good ground for the depravity men, that simple goodness, merum vinum,[10] without the alcohol of wit, is apt to disgust the young madcaps of the world. But the wheel goes round— the black hours come to them as to others; they become the greybeards in their turn; virtue loses its vulgarity in their eye & they learn to feel that one plain look or act of honest benevolence is worth all the frolic, fashion, & pride.

But there's no use of preaching You must like all your race eat your own pill of experience—so I'll save my sermon for another occasion

I hope you are not so sinful in what you very well understand as to leave your work unattempted till you return. When I told some of your friends that you had not written your oration, but were loitering in the temptations of the best company in the world, they said, yes, but the boy's trick was to work under the show of idleness; so, I hope you will have the grace to be guilty of thus much hypocrisy.

I am going to Concord today if it don't rain, & to Cambridge tomorrow. From what I heard of your chance for scholars in Boston I judge it would be best to go forward by all means. But I only heard my particulars thro' a byway.

You must present my particular respects to Mrs Lyman. It would give me the greatest pleasure to see Northampton again but have no reason to promise myself that gratification at present.

Edward is altered again, though hardly for the better. I saw him Saturday & Friday. His present idea is that he is suffering punishment for great offences. It was consoling however that for the first time he exhibits great interest in my visits & great affection for me, & begs me to stay with him all

---

10. *"Pure wine."*

the time. I shall see him tomorrow probably. Right or wrong, I got more hope of him from my last visit than ever before. He stands in need of nothing but God's aid.

Your affectionate brother,
Waldo.

To Charles Chauncy Emerson, August, 1828

Divinity Hall

Dear C

Suppose you should try your pen upon the subject of *Public Opinion*—a topic on which we have been a good deal dinged lately & which therefore must have some real foundation in present interests. What makes the value of any one man as precise & as well known as the stamp on a coin? Public opinion. What is a throne? What is a legislature? What is a Congress? What is a Constitution? Mere pipes, mere mouth-pieces for the expression of public opinion. The moment they cease to give it vent, the moment they resist & set up for original powers that moment they shrivel to cinders as cords in a flame. In fact there can be no resistance & there is no exception. For observe this is not a local doctrine—a limitary Genius dwelling only in the unfenced soil of a republic—with an ear too noble & hands too restless to bear the sound or to wear the shackles of monopolies, of privileges, of birthrights; No; for these also are founded upon *it*. And the czar of Russia sits on his iron throne over fifty millions of human souls in the old continent by precisely the same power that would crush him in attempting the same supremacy in the New.

Of course this part of the subject the general view will admit of very varied & splendid illustration.

Nations furnish sublime spectacles sometimes of horror sometimes of happiness when public opinion changes. When it quits its ancient bed & bursts thro' the mounds & levées that dammed it up, & strikes terror into ancient societies & institutions, that lie peacefully over the land, by the roar of the inundation. The outbreak of the French Revolution; the second expulsion of the Bourbons by Bonaparte; the triumphal progress of Lafayette thro' the States; The Restoration of the English Stuarts in 1688, are all fine commonplaces, & a thousand more.

In the next place where is the origin of Public Opinion?—In individual character & opinion. Each great national feeling, wave after wave, has been first the opinion of a few, the opinion of one. And is it not a better inquiry than hunting new minerals or dissecting spiders or counting lobes & petals of flowers to explore observe the obscure birth of a sentiment at the frugal board perhaps of a poor wise man & see how slowly it struggles into fame— to mark the earliest inadequate efforts that are made to propagate it; to note when it bands its friends into a sect—small misrepresented despised—till it waxes formidable enough to be persecuted—count its martyrs & see how truth makes men brave; then observe the reaction the impulse it derives from oppression—it scatters like wildfire it beats down resistance it annihilates prejudice & attains at last to omnipotent force,—Sometimes this *opinion* has been wrong sometimes it has been right but will not the history of the world be my warrant when I say it has been always strong? What were the Crusades those renowned emigrations that turned back the old current of population from Europe the colony to Asia the parent—What were those extravagant enterprizes but proofs that the opinion of of one had become the opinion of many that a fanatic voice saying 'It is the voice of God'—was able to bring an echo, a tremendous echo of a million voices to that shrill & evil sound? What was the Reformation but as you yourself said did you not? the opinion of one become the opinion of many—the feeling of a lonely monk become the sentiment of armed & angry nations? &c &c &c

What of all this? Cui Bono? Why—infinite good to be sure. An invaluable fact. What! is *public opinion* so strong that it will do its merry will, how grand or hideous soever, & never fail a hair? And then is *private opinion* so much stronger, that tho' it wont face this hippopotamus, it will yet get on its grand elephant back, & lead it with a word or a goose quill over land & sea? As Peter Hermit & Dean Swift & Mirabeau, & Burke can attest? Why, then, what a clean Damascus blade of an inference can you not draw, about the value of a brave lad in the world, that knoweth how to keep his hands clean & heart pure & then write a tract or speak a speech?

To William Emerson, December 4, 1828

Cambridge, 4 Dec 1828.

Dear William,

All that I hear of you is good but it has all the value that rarity can bestow. My mother lately bade me tell you that she had looked (I think) three months, with impatience for a letter from you, but had received none. I received & transmitted the letters containing cards which you sent. Had you not better send me half a dozen cards, without direction, to exercise my worldly wisdom in distribution? I am a great professor of that art, within these few months past, that I have meddled with Edward's matters. Did I not tell you that Peter C. Brooks sent me $100.00 for him? I paid thereof $50. to Mrs Cook on E.'s note of $150. The other $50, I paid to Mr Francis, on his note of $100. & he gave me the note therefor. A generous gentleman. Edward is quite well—it seems. He is going with me day after tomorrow to Concord. N. H. to spend three Sundays & then returns to Concord Ms. But to finish my detail of business for tis better since I act without counsel I should at least have a confidante & the better that he is learned in the law—I found that it was Mr Frothingham who had intercepted Bulkeleys bill at the Asylum & told them it shd. be paid otherwise. On receiving therefore this donation to Edwd, I told Dr Wyman, they had done what they intended & I paid the debt which was $47.57.—something more than one quarter. I have since been to Chelmsford & saw Bulkeley in beautiful health & frame of mind. Mr Putnam said he had earned his board for some time back, &, that for the first 6 weeks of his residence there, he shd charge him 6 dollars. There were some other matters making a dollar or two, &, I gladly gave him $10.00. You understand this is all the charge from the middle of July till the first of December, at least for board: something for clothes. I have furthermore settled fully with Charlotte Farnham on Edwds a/c & paid his interest to Mrs Cook; to Φ B K; & settled Marshalls a/c—a note travelling with comp. int. Did I tell you one of those beautiful angels the 'unknown benefactors,' which are in the universe the correlative terms of the 'silent poor' had given G. B. E. $50. to give me for E B E's behoof? This has enabled me to do as I have said. Edward will find himself on 1st Jan. '29 in much better fiscal state than in '28.—I also find it in my ledger (for I keep accounts) that in July & August I received from Mrs R. E. 21.50 pd. by you to her for R. B. E's use. I am myself meantime not the ower of any considerable debts excepting about $300 to Mr S. Ripley something of which, I hope to discharge in Feb. when its anniversary comes, not a penny to C. & H. once dire initials! not a penny to Whitmarsh, & little to Hall—Now for my professional affairs. I have preached a good while at Mr Ware's. I was on no definite agreement as to time. It is well understood Mr Ware wd. shortly resign & go to Cambridge. I did not think it very delicate to hang on longer; if the parish was to be regarded as open for candidates I was monopolizing. So having spoken with Dr Ripley I told them I wd. come away at the end of November. They made a fuss & sent me word that if they heard candidates there wd. be a division & therefore the best people in the society wanted me by all means to stay I told them if there was a chance they wd like any body better than I, t'was a reason why I should leave them forthwith, for if I am settled, I choose it should be on my own merits & not because I have kept a better man from being heard. So I have left them. All this in confidence, about the committee coming to me, & Mr Ware's leaving. Why I should come away is in plain daylight. Now I have told you my whole story & my body is very well & I love you.

Waldo Emerson.

To William Emerson, December 24, 1828

Divinity Hall, Cambridge—
Dec. 24, 1828

My dear brother,

I have the happiness to inform you that I have been now for one week engaged to Ellen Louisa Tucker a young lady who if you will trust my account is the fairest & best of her kind. Not to drive you to skepticism by any extravagances, I will tell you a simple story. She is the youngest daughter of the late Beza Tucker a merchant of Boston of whose children you may remember William Sewall was guardian. When we were at Roxbury they lived in the Sumner house on the Dedham turnpike. The mother has been now three or four years the wife of Col W. A. Kent of Concord, N. H. It is now just a year since I became acquainted with Ellen at the house—but I thought I had got over my blushes & wishes when now I determined to go into that dangerous neighborhood again on Edward's account. But the presumptuous man was overthrown by the eye & the ear & surrendered at discretion. He is now as happy as it is safe in life to be in the affection of the lady & the approbation of the friends. She is 17 years old, & very beautiful by universal consent. Her feelings are exceedingly delicate & noble—and I only want you to see her. Edward is very highly gratified.

I shall have time soon to say much more upon this matter and am your affectionate

Waldo E.

To William Emerson, January 28, 1829

Boston, 28 January, 1829

Dear William,

I received a letter from you yesterday for which I am much obliged to you But since I wrote before my beautiful friend has made me very sorry by being very ill & with that dangerous complaint [tuberculosis] which so often attacks the fairest in our stern climate. She has raised blood a week ago & I have been one of her nurses most unskilful but most interested & am writing my letter in her chamber. Beauty has to go better & so I am better & now though in such a place I fear you will put no credit in my account, yet am I sorely tempted to give you her character. Well then she is perfectly simple though very elegant in her manners; then she has common sense; then she has imagination & knows the difference between good poetry & bad; then she makes fine verses herself, then she is good,—& has character enough to be religious. then she is beautiful, & finally I love her. If my story is short, it is true.

I have abstained in much hesitation & perplexity from giving any answer to the call at the Old North. thinking that perhaps the doctors might tell Ellen she ought to go away; & then—

But now that I have talked with Dr Jackson & talked with the committee men I believe next Sunday I shall say Yes. As to going to New York in the Spring, I believe not. I shall probably be ordained the second or third week in March & until that time I must find supply for the pulpit which I do by exchanges.

I do not know that there is any chance of rescuing Edward from the Law nor do I know that it were desireable. If his talents look any way, it is that way. And his health certainly appears more firmly established than any one cd. have believed possible a year ago. It is strange. I wish you could see Ellen. Why can't you come to my ordination (if such thing shall be) & see the queen of Sheba & of me. You shall say as she said.—

Charles is very well. In these times of tribulation I am living at house of T. W. Haskins Sumner St. Charles is very well & doing finely. Mother is very well & I am your affectionate brother

Waldo

I told Charles to enclose to you $5.00. It was because Hilliard & Brown paid themselves some time ago by transferring the balance of my debt to your account, & it was I believe a little more than that sum. When I can think of it I will find the exact account.

The vote at 2d Church was 74 for me out of 79 total. 4 for Dr Follen; 1 for John Lothrop—that means S. K. L. Three given for Dr F were by one person holding 3 pews who declares himself no wise unfriendly to Mr E but wants to wait a little. Every thing in reference to this call is in ye highest degree gratifying as far as a decided & strong good will can be so.

To the Second Church and Society in Boston, Cambidge, January 30, 1829

To the Second Church & Society in Boston.
Cambridge, 30 January, 1829.

Christian brethren & friends,

I have received the communication transmitted to me by your committee inviting me to the office of junior pastor in your church & society. I accept the invitation.

If my own feelings could have been consulted, I should have desired to postpone, at least, for several months, my entrance into this solemn office. I do not now approach it with any sanguine confidence in my abilities, or in my prospects. I come to you in weakness, and not in strength. In a short life, I have yet had abundant experience of the uncertainty of human hopes. I have learned the lesson of my utter dependency; and it is in a devout reliance upon other strength than my own, in a humble trust on God to sustain me, that I put forth my hand to his great work.

But, brethren, whilst I distrust my powers, I must speak firmly of my purposes. I well know what are the claims, on your part, to my best exertions, and I shall meet them, as far as in me lies, by a faithful performance of duty. I shun no labour. I shall do all that I can.

In approaching these duties, I am encouraged by the strong expression of confidence & goodwill, I have received from you. I am encouraged by the hope of enjoying the counsel and aid of the distinguished servant of God who has so long laboured among you. I look to the example of our Lord, in all my hopes of advancing the influence of his holy religion, and I implore the blessing of God upon this connexion to be formed between you and myself.

I am your affectionate friend & servant,

Ralph Waldo Emerson.

To Charles Chauncy Emerson, June 19, 1829

Concord N. H 19 June

Dear Charles,

Yesterday Ellen was taken sick in the old way,—very suddenly, & suffered in the night great distress, but the quantity of blood raised has not been much & some symptoms her mother says are much less unfavorable than at former times—but tis bad enough at the best & has wonderfully changed my visit. I was perfectly happy now I am watching & fearing & pitied.—We have no physicians here in whom any kind of confidence can be reposed & so I write today to Dr Jackson a letter which will come in the same mail with this & if he is not in town please ask James J. to forward it to him at once.

I may write to Mr Adams tomorrow or next day but please go there & tell him I am disappointed once more but rejoiced that since this was ordained I am here at the time. It wd have been unspeakable trouble to me if I had been in Boston. Ellen has an angel's soul & tho very skeptical about the length of her own life hath a faith as clear & strong as those do that have Gods kingdom within them.

The moment the queen of me gets relief from one of her ill turns her spirits return also & she is playful & social as ever tho' her sociability is imprisoned in whispers. And now I write in her room & she sends you her love & I am yours affectionately

Waldo E.

Is Edward in town Tell him to be in no hurry to return for Mr Thomas will not probably go down till Thursday of next week. & tell him human happiness is very unstable & I am sorry I have no better letter to send you.

To William and Edward Emerson, January 4, 1830

Boston, 4 Jan. 1830—

Excellent men, I hope you will not be afflicted with Charles's caricature of a New York letter—He says he is determined to give as good as he gets. If you scold, I send herewith the antidote, oil for the sore from a sisters flagon. Did not somebody ask me what books I read? I heard it in my sleep or waking. Coleridge's Friend—with great interest; Coleridges "Aids to reflection" with yet deeper; Degerando Hist. Comparée des Systemes de Philosophie, I am beginning on the best recommendation. & one more book—the best Sermon I have read for some time, to wit, Combe's Constitution of Man. You see the present is too mighty for me, I cannot get away to do homage to the mighty past. Yet what commands me in the present is its relation to the future. & so with sincere wishes that the New Year may be your best year & yet only seed of good to come I remain your affectionate brother

Waldo—

To Charles Chauncy Emerson and Margaret Tucker Kent, March 19, 1830

New York, 19 March, 1830.

Dear Charles,

We had a very stormy passage through the Sound from New Haven. We got on board the boat at 6 A.M. & expected to be at N.Y. at 4 P.M. But a gale came up from the Southwest which we cd. not weather & so at 12 o'clock we made into Norwalk roads as well as we could & came to anchor. There we lay pouting & snuffing the insufferable mephitis of the cabin, & hearing the rain patter & looking at each other grimly, forty stout passengers, (though fortunately only two beside E. & M. in the ladies cabin) & lastly sleeping or trying to sleep in an air that wd doubtless have put out a lamp on the floor. But morning came, the wind abated, & the steam chimney began once more to puff. The clouds broke, & we were repaid for our troubles by a noble passage up the Sound—fine sun mild air, swift vessels, beautiful shores, noble seats—& through all—got to this long London town—to the American Hotel at 2 o'clock yesterday. You may imagine I bit my lips with mortification to find I had got the queen into this bad navigable box. She bore it very well—all but the impossibility of sleep. Glad we were to get to this house & shall stay here today, & tomorrow take the Phila. boat—another sort of thing & on other sort of waters viz inland instead of outland.

Friday p.m. Ellen is quite weak today, & though she insists upon our going tomorrow—as we shall probably try—yet I fear that she will not be so well at Philad. as to suffer me to leave her for a few days. I therefore think it probable I shall not be able to get home to preach as soon as the third Sunday. Of course I shall compass it if possible but you must engage somebody to supply the desk that day positively, & then if I get home I will preach half the day. If you can, engage a young man from C[ambridge]. with the request from me that he will be so good as to exchange with Mr Ripley of Waltham (who promised to gratify me on such an occasion recently) or with Dr Ware or any of the Boston ministers half or the whole day, he will gratify our people's love for old preach. This you can forbear doing or saying if you judge expedient in the particular case. But see that good word is dispensed on that day from Sec Ch pulpit on the 28th instant. as you love your loving brother

Waldo.

To Mrs. Kent—

My dear Mother,

Ellen is troubled today as yesterday with her "red wheezers" as we call them & considerable fulness in the head. Still she has walked out twice, tho' weak. On the whole, we think it prudent to hasten southward and are in every particular so cautious that you must rely on Margaret & me as yourself. I shall write again speedily.—

Philadelphia 26 March 1830.

I enjoyed highly the company of my dear Aunt & the pleasure of making her acquainted with my faery queen who wrote verses about you which perhaps she will send you some day. And since we arrived here we have been delighted with a letter. I am getting to be sadly impatient of my life here, which has petty engagements which tear time into slivers, and are singularly unfavorable to any thing like intellectual progress. Oh fie that we—no—that I should be so enthralled to small accidents, that the first derangement of my domestic routine should put a chain on the wheels of the spirit—& the old trains of thot are broken up—the landmarks are gone—the favorite speculations grow faint & dim, and when I come back to my arm chair, I shall be recreated not enriched. Some indirect advantage roaming certainly furnishes, some side glances at other minds some comparative observations that if they do not lead to new conclusions keep you from making premature conclusions on human nature as all of us are prone to do. What stone walls of incommunicability do exist between mind & mind. I converse with a man whose faculties are active & healthy enough yet I find his horizon is limited in some place where mine is extended; yet can I not, (with the clearest perception that he does not see far enow) for the life of me tell him what is the difference between us. Linnaeus classified plants by their stamens Another botanist by their fruit. What feature or fact shall be assumed to classify the immortal plant man? Each of the professions underrates the other, each science, each art, each habit of life. Dr Channing thinks the *Reformer* the first mind; the great mob think the *Conqueror,* the smaller mob the *poet.* I think respectfully enough of Statesmen,—yet I have been reading Jefferson & can't but think that he & his great mates look little already, from this short distance where we stand, & he would be sorry to know my feelings about their ambition.— Not by their objects then can they be measured for the naturalists are ridiculous when they so often forget their end in their means & learn nothing but the anatomy of a leaf or a fly—& not less ridiculous though far worse are the polemic theologians when they are only polemics. But *virtue* is always venerable, & the *attention* which seems proper to the condition of humanity set in this world to learn whatever lesson God chuses to teach—surprized at nothing—greedy of all knowledge & arranging all upon the vast conception of God's being. The seeker the seeker is your only philosopher after all.

Christianity teaches him to seek better but there is no absolute finder in this world. The first moment of consciousness after we have shot the great Gulf we shall cry Found with an infinite [manuscript mutilated] again. I shall [manuscript mutilated]

Do write to Ellen again here, & write to the care of Mr George Merrill, Philadelphia.

New York. 1 April. I have boldly left Ellen in Philad. ramparted round with troops of friends. She seems better, & there is a good physician, and *there is a good Physician.* I shall be in Boston tomorrow & will see W. H. presently. Write me very soon.

To Benjamin Peter Hunt, September 6, 1830

Boston, 6 Sept. 1830—

My dear Sir,

When I was lately at Chelmsford Dr Dalton showed me a letter he had received from you, which interested me very much. It contained expressions of great kindness toward me, which except that they overestimated a very little kindness were very grateful to me. Then it contained an account of yourself which looked very much like an old acquaintance for some time past lost to me in a cloud. It has been one of the puzzles that outran the skill of my philosophy how any one of that small class of persons who love goodness & truth for their beauty simply should choose an oblique course instead of a straight one. I never learned any particulars but knew you had not made your residence in College pleasant & had gone suddenly without leaving that respect for your powers & feelings which I had felt, & tho't all good people wd. feel. I am quite sorry I did not borrow the letter & bring it home. But certainly your account of yourself was interesting & relieved me as it put a better than reputable face on the matter by suggesting the principles on which you acted. They are good & I honour them. I see far less independence of character, & scorn of patronage than I could wish in the world, & your *Soul* cannot have better friends. But, my dear Sir, I cannot bring myself to believe that the times are so out of joint that these virtues are proscribed & must damn the possessor's worldly interests. Johnson was as proud, yet strode shod or barefoot through Oxford & took his degrees. It seems to me that a generous mind goes naturally to the highest places in society & not to obscure resorts & has that nobleness to assert its own title to all such advantages in spite of poverty or opposition. Go to Cambridge & eat bread & water & live to *think. Think* your way up to your true place among men,—no doubt it will be accorded. I believe the world is far more just than is often said & that every man will have in it every inch of his merits allowed him, & that not by its pleasure or displeasure but by God's order.

I was glad to see you mean to go to Yale. If you do not return to Cambridge, do not fail to go there. But do try to work—intellectually I mean. Force yourself to something regular & methodical if only for the experiment & for vir [manuscript mutilated] humdrum maxims about industry & order are apt to prove stronger than we, when we are wayward.

But I had almost forgot to say what first set me on writing now, & that is, that I never pretended to have done anything for you that shd. give me a right to feel angry or cold on your going away, as your letter seemed to charge me. My recommendation to the College Gov't was what I wd. have done for a stranger, & I only *promised* more. So you are free of me.—I will not plague you with offers of service now (yet you may command me) but I will say that if you have the valour to borrow money I can procure you probably one or two hundred dollars at the usual interest to be paid when your convenience serves. You will deeply gratify me if you will write me any news of your inner self what you purpose, what you think, what you doubt, what you know; what progress you make in developing the great Idea which Time develops the idea of God. May his blessing guard & direct you. Your friend

R. Waldo Emerson.

To William Emerson, December 5, 1830

Boston Sunday night 5 Dec

Dear William,

I have just recd your letter of yesterday. Mother would go to N. Y. if a boat went tomorrow, but now she fears lest Edwd sail on Tuesday & she mt. miss of him. We have talked over the matter a good deal & are all pretty strongly of one mind—that he ought to come here rather than go alone to sea. It was his very decided conviction when he came home from Europe that it was a great mistake to send him as he was sent for his health. He suffered every thing at sea & much on shore. I am afraid his chance cannot be much better now. It wd. be adviseable if anybody could go with him; but as no one can it seems best he should not undergo so much certain exposure for uncertain advantage. Better far it seems to me roll him up in hot blankets & send him here to hybernate in a chamber by a coal fire & the first of March when the east winds blow we will send him to Carolina if need be. Charles & Mother & Mr Adams all concur strongly in this view of the matter. Had he not better let Capt Lotman go alone & wait for Mothers careful counsel. Perhaps she will set out Tuesday morng. We all feel for your embarrassments which must be very great. Much love to Edward & tell him we have seen six troubles & shall be carried thro' the seventh by the same hand which will yet lead us when we quit this sickening planet.

Yours affectionately
Waldo.

Please write immediately on recg this mother says what your conclusion is. but I think mother will go Tuesday.

To Edward Bliss Emerson, December 24? 1830

I find wifeys letter[11] here unfinished & so to prevent her destroying it which is always a strong probability until it has got into the postmasters fingers I will put thus much insurance hereon. I have mislaid a letter I had half written, & wonder what shd come of it. The only fact there stated of importance was that G B E has pd. the remaining $50. due to you & $10 interest.

How are you. We all sympathize with & pray for you. Follow Ellens advice about inquisitiveness. Pray make *written minutes* of places & prices & persons & climate that may be of use to any of us hereafter.

Carried you any books? If not, stick to the stout principle of both the

---

11. *Ellen, in her part of the letter, here omitted, congratulates Edward on his escape from the northern winter and tells of a recent visit from Mary Moody Emerson, who seemed to her "not of the earthy nor altogether of the heavenly—to be wondered at and in some sort admired." [Rusk]*

wise & the ignorant 'the fewer the better.' No other man's thot's can be comparable in value to my own whenever my experience or reason will deign to utter a conclusion of theirs. But the long & often intervals,—question comes how to use them, whether in hoeing the proper ownty spot or getting a graft from a better soil. But perhaps sickness & homesickness may lead your tho'ts more directly to the Source of Being & the hope of living with him & owing to him directly & to no second source your knowledge & your morals. I saw a man yesterday to wit, Sampson Reed, who told me that it was now ten years since he had known the fear of death: His new faith teaches him not to regard it as a *punishment,* he says. I trust in Heavens care of you & that we shall yet pass pleasant days of health together but let us rejoice in the New Testament which makes sickness & distance safe to us. Yours dear Edward with all my heart.

Waldo.—

Be sure not deny yourself any necessary or comfortable accommodation.—

To Mary Moody Emerson, February 8, 1831

Tuesday 11 o'clock Feb. 8th

Dear Aunt

My angel is gone to heaven this morning & I am alone in the world & strangely happy. Her lungs shall no more be torn nor her head scalded by her blood nor her whole life suffer from the warfare between the force & delicacy of her soul & the weakness of her frame. I said this morn & I do not know but it is true that I have never known a person in the world in whose separate existence as a soul I could so readily & fully believe & she is present with me now beaming joyfully upon me, in her deliverance & the entireness of her love for your poor nephew. I see it plainly that things & duties will look coarse & vulgar enough to me when I find the romance of her presence (& romance is a beggarly word) withdrawn from them all. But now the fulness of joy occasioned by things said by her in the last week & by this eternal deliverance is in my heart. She has a great deal to say always about Aunt Mary & would gladly have seen you when Grandfather came, & said then she should like now a letter from you.

But the past days the most eventful of my life are all a dim confusion & now the pall is drawn over them, yet do they shine brilliantly in my spiritual world. Say, dear Aunt, if I am not rich in her memory?

Respectful love to Grandfather & tell him Ellen blessed him for his prayer—of which her lips repeated every word.

Your nephew
Waldo E

To Mary Moody Emerson, August 19, 1832

Boston, 19 August, 1832

My dear Aunt,

I have been shut up almost ever since I returned home with the meanest complaint & though I came home stronger & fatter than for years it has stripped me to bones. The air is poisoned here to every person who is only slightly imprudent. It is high time I was well but I have been put back several times But what cares your sphered spirit for stomach aches If I had others, I would tell you; but I have not yet come to any point with my people, my explanation being postponed by my ails, and have not come to any new point with myself. I remain of the same mind not prepared to eat or drink religiously, tho' it seem a small thing, & seeing no middle way, I apprehend a separation. This, tho' good nature & prudence condemn & possibly something else better than both, yet promises me much contentment & not the less opportunity of usefulness in the very partial & peculiar channel by which I must be useful if at all.—The farthing candle was not made for nothing— the least leaf must ope & grow after the fashion of *its own* lobes & veins & not after that of the oak or the rose, and I can only do my work well by abjuring the opinions & customs of all others & adhering strictly to the divine plan a few dim inches of whose outline I faintly discern in my breast. Is that not German enow? It is true. How gay & glorious the prospect looks. In the darkest event the human fancy can portend is nothing very black, for if we hasted to nothing, what signifies whether the clean swept cobwebs were well or ill spun? And if we are to be what the constitution of the mind predicts, every change is instruction & every misfortune is a trifle & it is the being we are to build up, & not situation & influence that import. So I will sing the hymn of hope in light or gloom for a time or forever as pleases Heaven. Ellen is beyond misfortune, & I will not invite any others to penury & disappointment if I am doomed. I am entering into acquaintance with Goethe who has just died. The Germans think there have been but three men of genius—Homer, Shakspear, & Goethe. If I go into the country to books, I shall know him well, & you will come & board with Mother & me, & we will try him whether he deserves his niche. S. A. R[ipley]. grieved he shd. die because he & Mme de Stael were suited to this world. The Germans regard him as the restorer of Faith & Love after the desolations of Hume & the French. that he married Faith & Reason, for the world. In the Wilhelm Meister he leads a child of Nature up from the period of 'Apprenticeship' to that of 'Self production' & leaves him, Schiller says, assured on the way to infinite perfection. But the *form* of the book is for us so foreign that it long repels,—full of theatricals, green room, &c

How is my friend Stone? Quicken him to write me what he promised, an account of Mackintosh's Ethics. William & Edward are both here. William has just come from Portsmouth where he has engaged himself to Susan W. Haven daughter of John H. & his mother & his brothers are mightily pleased. Edward has come to spend a month & then returns to P[uerto]. R[ico]. He is very well & in fine spirits. Charles is disposed to go to Concord when he opens his office in October. Much better on some accounts—health, reason, & comfort. but he has not decided. I have suggested so many topics that I ardently hope to have a letter on some one. Do Write Give my respects & love to both families. Your affectionate nephew

Waldo.

To the Proprietors of the Second Church, September 11, 1832

To the Proprietors of the Second Church.

Boston, 11 September, 1832.

Christian Friends,

In the discourse delivered from the pulpit last Sabbath, I explained the circumstances which have seemed to me to make it my duty to resign my office as your minister.[12] I now request a dismission from the pastoral charge. On this occasion, I cannot help adding a few words.

I am very far from regarding my relation to you with indifference. I am bound to you, as a society, by the experience of uninterrupted kindness; by the feelings of respect & love I entertain for you all, as my tried friends; by ties of personal attachment to many individuals among you, which I account the happiness of my life; by the hope I had entertained of living always with you, and of contributing, if possible, in some small degree, to your welfare.

Nor do I think less of the office of a Christian minister. I am pained at the situation in which I find myself, that compels me to make a difference of opinion of no greater importance, the occasion of surrendering so many & so valuable functions as belong to that office. I have the same respect for the great objects of the Christian ministry, & the same faith in their gradual accomplishment through the use of human means, which, at first, led me to enter it. I should be unfaithful to myself, if any change of circumstances could diminish my devotion to the cause of divine truth.

And so, friends, let me hope, that whilst I resign my official relation to you I shall not lose your kindness, & that a difference of opinion as to the value of an ordinance, will be overlooked by us in our common devotion to what is real & eternal.

Ralph Waldo Emerson.

12. *Emerson resigned his pulpit because he refused to administer the sacrament of the Lord's Supper, which he felt represented a supernatural rather than a natural religion. The sermon Emerson refers to, wherein he explains his position, is in* The Complete Sermons of Ralph Waldo Emerson, *ed. Albert J. von Frank et al., 4 vols. (Columbia: University of Missouri Press, 1989–1992), 4:185–194.*

To the Second Church and Society, December 22, 1832

Boston, 22d December, 1832.[13]

To the Second Church and Society.

Christian Friends,—Since the formal resignation of my official relation to you in my communication to the proprietors in September, I had waited anxiously for an opportunity of addressing you once more from the pulpit, though it were only to say, Let us part in peace and in the love of God. The state of my health has prevented and continues to prevent me from so doing. I am now advised to seek the benefit of a sea-voyage. I cannot go away without a brief parting word to friends who have shown me so much kindness, and to whom I have felt myself so dearly bound.

Our connexion has been very short. I had only begun my work. It is now brought to a sudden close, and I look back, I own, with a painful sense of weakness, to the little service I have been able to render, after so much expectation on my part,—to the chequered space of time, which domestic affliction and personal infirmities have made yet shorter and more unprofitable.

As long as he remains in the same place, every man flatters himself, however keen may be his sense of his failures and unworthiness, that he shall yet accomplish much; that the future shall made amends for the past; that his very errors shall prove his instructors,—and what limit is there to hope? But a separation from our place, the close of a particular career of duty, shuts the books, bereaves us of this hope, and leaves us only to lament how little has been done.

Yet, my friends, our faith in the great truths of the New Testament makes the change of places and circumstances, of less account to us, by fixing our attention upon that which is unalterable. I find great consolation in the thought, that the resignation of my present relations makes so little change to myself. I am no longer your minister, but am not the less engaged, I hope, to the love and service of the same external cause, the advancement, namely,

---

13. *Because no manuscript exists for this letter, the text printed here is that of the 1832 pamphlet printing, which is styled with large and small capitals in the date, salutation, and signature lines.*

of the kingdom of God in the hearts of men. The tie that binds each of us to that cause is not created by our connexion, and can not be hurt by our separation. To me, as one disciple, is the ministry of truth, as far as I can discern and declare it, committed, and I desire to live no where and no longer than that grace of God is imparted to me—the liberty to seek and the liberty to utter it.

And, more than this, I rejoice to believe, that my ceasing to exercise the pastoral office among you, does not make any real change in our spiritual relation to each other. Whatever is most desireable and excellent therein, remains to us. For, truly speaking, whoever provokes me to a good act or thought, has given me a pledge of his fidelity to virtue,—he has come under bonds to adhere to that cause to which we are jointly attached. And so I say to all you, who have been my counsellors and co-operators in our Christian walk, that I am wont to see in your faces, the seals and certificates of our mutual obligations. If we have conspired from week to week, in the sympathy and expression of devout sentiments; if we have received together the un-speakable gift of God's truth; if we have studied together the sense of any divine word; or striven in any charity; or conferred together for the relief or instruction of any brother; if together we have laid down the dead in pious hope; or held up the babe into the baptism of Christianity; above all if we have shared in any habitual acknowledgment of that benignant God, whose omnipresence raises and glorifies the meanest offices and the lowest ability, and opens heaven in every heart that worships him,—then indeed are we united, we are mutually debtors to each other of faith and hope, engaged to persist and confirm each other's hearts in obedience to the Gospel. We shall not feel that the nominal changes and little separations of this world, can release us from the strong cordage of this spiritual bond. And I entreat you to consider how truly blessed will have been our connexion, if in this manner, the memory of it shall serve to bind each one of us more strictly to the practice of our several duties.

It remains to thank you for the goodness you have uniformly extended towards me, for your forgiveness of many defects, and your patient and even partial acceptance of every endeavor to serve you; for the liberal provision you have ever made for my maintenance; and for a thousand acts of kindness, which have comforted and assisted me.

To the proprietors, I owe a particular acknowledgment, for their recent generous vote for the continuance of my salary, and hereby ask their leave to relinquish this emolument at the end of the present month.

And now, brethren and friends, having returned into your hands the trust you have honored me with—the charge of public and private instruction in this religious society, I pray God, that whatever seed of truth and virtue we have sown and watered together, may bear fruit unto eternal life. I commend you to the Divine Providence. May He grant you, in your ancient sanctuary, the service of able and faithful teachers. May He multiply to your families and to your persons, every genuine blessing; and whatever discipline may be appointed to you in this world, may the blessed hope of the resurrection, which He has planted in the constitution of the human soul, and confirmed and manifested by Jesus Christ, be made good to you beyond the grave. In this faith and hope, I bid you farewell.

> *Your affectionate servant,*
> *RALPH WALDO EMERSON.*

To Susan Woodward Haven, March 22, 1833

Naples, 22 March, 1833.

I promised my brother William to write a letter from this city to my dear sister that shall be.[14] I regretted my sickness last summer the more because it prevented me from seeing you. But Time, they say, brings roses, & makes acquaintances, & so, I trust, we shall be good friends yet. But what can I tell you of this famous town now that I am here? It takes some time for a peaceable person who for the first time has strayed away some thousand miles from his armchair & inkstand into this monstrous hurlyburly—to recover himself & walk with his eyes straight before him. However having had my pockets picked twice in the course of the same day, I have learned to behave on the Toledo with tolerable composure. Naples is set down in all the books for a Paradise, & I suppose with reason, but it rains every day & my first impressions are that it is a very large boisterous disagreeable city. Now do not think the fault is mine. I am very easy to please. Since I landed at Malta I hardly pass a monastery but I ask them on what terms they will receive me for life; and in Sicily when I saw them taking cicinelli in their sunny bays I

---

14. *Susan Woodward Haven had become engaged to William Emerson in mid-August 1832; they would marry on 3 December 1833.*

had half a mind to be a fisherman & draw my net at Taormina the rest of my days. The hymn says "Man wants but little."—Calm civil people, warm weather, a fine prospect, a few books & a little coffee will content my philosophy but here in Naples I am lonely & a-'cold & my chamber is dark, & who can go to Vesuvius or Paestum or the Villa of Cicero when the rain pours? However, to be just, when the sun shines, it does seem a decent place, yea, its Chiaia (as they call the range of palaces on the margin of the bay,) its islands, & surrounding mountain country, marvellously beautiful. I crawled out the other day between the drops to Baiae, & since, have been to Pompeii & Herculaneum, & I could not help thinking I was paid for my pains. Baiae was 2000 years ago a sort of Nahant—a pleasure ground where the Roman senators & Emperors built beautiful villas on the edge of the bay. Time & earthquake & volcano have made sad work with the palaces. The whole soil is made of broken brick & marble, & dig where they will, they open chambers & cellars & baths. But the natural beauties of the spot which recommended it to the taste of the Romans still remained to charm my poor eyes the day before yesterday. But I am not going to pester you with descriptions of this unrivalled landscape. I leave it to the painters. One day, tis likely, you will come hither yourself. And though a hermit such as I, may find his profit now & then in going alone to these old places, yet the true way for profit & delight doubtless is, to come & see them with those whose society is our daily food. So one of these days as I said, when the courts of New York are closed in the summer heats—I wish you a very pleasant excursion.

In a few days I go to Rome, where I hope I may find your brother George, who I am glad to know is in these parts. Every body is crowding to Rome just now, for the Holy Week begins on the 1st April & that is the season of the great annual pomp of the Catholic Church. I follow the multitude & yet without much curiosity. I go to see old Rome, not new, & if I were not satisfied with seeing Naples, I would remain here till the Show was over. Perhaps I shall think differently when I see the purple & gold, & hear the Pope & his monks chaunt the "Miserere" in St Peters.

And so I greet you well, my fair sister, till I have the pleasure of seeing you, which I hope I shall have some time in the next autumn. I do not feel as if I was writing in the dark in addressing a letter to a lady I have not seen, for an earnest good will unites people more than neighborhood, and with sincere desires for your present & future happiness, I am your affectionate servant, R. Waldo Emerson.

To George Adams Sampson, March 23, 1833

Naples, 23 March, 1833.

My dear friend,

What is the reason I have not written to you all this time? I cannot tell but shall please myself with writing now. How go the days & the months with you & yours? How fares the soul under the wear & tear of vulgar events? What new thoughts? What brighter hope? I long to have a good talk with you which the rolling moons may soon grant. I am so much indebted to your manly friendship, specially in the last year, that I miss my counsellor much in this vast Babel too where there is so much argument for conversation always occurring. Time which brings roses, will bring us topics, I trust, less sombre than the old ones. I have regretted the vexation they gave you. It looks now to me as it always did,—only Dr Kirklands opinion a more just bon mot.—I am moving about here in much noise & myriads of people & see much grandeur & much poverty, but am not very sure that I grow much wiser or any better for my travels. We put very different matters into the scales but the balance never varies much. An hour in Boston or an hour in Naples have about equal value to the same person; the pains of travelling are as real and about as vivid as the pleasures. Besides a thousand petty annoyances that are always fretting an inexperienced traveller, he is perpetually disappointed—his plans of study his hopes of good society, above all, his covenants with himself—the heroism, the wisdom, he is to make his own— are always flying before him—never realized. Still, though travelling is a poor profession—bad food, it may be good medicine. It is good, like seasickness, to break up a morbid habit, & I sometimes fancy it is a very wholesome shaking for me. One thing however I rejoice at. It furnishes the student with a perpetual answer to the little people that are always hinting that your faith & hope belong to your village or your country, & that a knowledge of the world would open your eyes. He who thinks for himself knows better, & yet is glad to have his most retired & unuttered thought confirmed & echoed back to him by his observation of new men & strange institutions. I am glad to recognize the same man under a thousand different masks & hear the same commandment spoken to me in Italian, I was wont to hear in English. But the new discipline is only begun, & I can give you a maturer opinion by & bye. My greatest want is the very one I apprehended when at home, that I never meet with men that are great or interesting. There are such everywhere, & here no doubt, a just proportion; but a traveller, for the most part, never learns even their names, whilst he sees in every city a good deal of its very worst population. That is why we ought not to travel too young. If you know the language your chance of acquaintance is very much increased; if you are yourself great & good, why I think your chance would be best of all.

I have been now to Vesuvius & was almost suffocated with the hot vapors of the Crater. Tis a fearful place. I have been also to Pompeii & Hercula-neum & seen the handiwork of the volcano. This whole country is an unrivalled picture. The Bay is a beauty look from whatever side you will. But I will not pester you with descriptions which you may find better in all the books.

Where shall I find a letter from you? At Rome or Florence? And surely another at Paris. I have some letters from home, but they say not a word of the Second Church. Tell me of it—particularly. But chiefly tell me of yourself. I hope this finds your wife in health, & the little household of my nephews. Remember me with much kindness to Mrs S. & so to all your friends & mine. Monday I am going to Rome, & there & everywhere am your affectionately

Waldo Emerson

To Mary Moody Emerson, April 18 and May? *c.* 17? 1833

Rome, 18 April, 1833.

My dear Aunt

The sights & names of this wonderful town remind me much of my gifted correspondent, for the spiritual affinities transcend the limits of space and a soul so Roman should have its honor here. How glad should I be of a letter to make the image livelier. I trust I shall find one at Florence where I hope to receive a large pacquet. Did they tell you that I went away from home a wasted peevish invalid. Well I have been mending ever since & am now in better health than I remember to have enjoyed since I was in college. How should one be sick at Rome? It is a wonderful town. Yet I strive to possess my soul in patience, &, escaping both giddiness & pedantry, to feel truly & think wisely. 'Here is matter for all feeling,' said Byron and yet how evanescent & superficial is most of that emotion which names & places, which Art or magnificence can awaken. It yields in me to the interest the most ordinary companion inspires. I never get used to men. They always awaken expectations in me which they always disappoint, and I am a poor asteroid in the great system subject to disturbances in my orbit not only from all the planets but from all their moons. The wise man—the true friend—the finished character—we seek everywhere & only find in fragments Yet I cannot persuade myself that all the beautiful souls are fled out of the planet or that always I shall be excluded from good company & yoked with green dull pitiful persons. After being cabined up by sea & by land since I left home with various little people, all better to be sure & much wiser than me but still such as did not help me—I cannot tell you how refreshing it was to fall in with two or three sensible persons with whom I could eat my bread & take my walk & feel myself a freeman once more of Gods Universe. Yet were these last not instructers & I want instructers. God's greatest gift is a Teacher & when will he send me one, full of truth & of boundless benevolence & heroic sentiments. I can describe the man, & have already in prose & verse. I know the idea well, but where is its real blood warm counterpart. I know whilst I write thus that the creature is never to dawn upon me like a sun-burst I know too well how slowly we edge along sideways to every thing good & brilliant in our lives & how casually & unobservedly we make all our most valued acquaintances. And yet I saw Ellen at once in all her beauty & she never disappointed me except in her death. And why may not the Master which the soul anticipates, so appear. You are so far off that I shall scarce get your answers very soon, so I may as well set down what our stern experience replies with the tongue of all its days. Son of man, it saith, all giving & receiving is reciprocal; you entertain angels unawares but they cannot impart more or higher things than you are in a state to receive But every step of your progress affects the intercourse you hold with all others; elevates its tone, deepens its meaning, sanctifies its spirit, and when time & suffering & selfdenial shall have transfigured & glorified this spotted self you shall find your fellows also transformed & their faces shall shine upon you with the light of wisdom & the beauty of holiness.—You who cling with both hands to the literal Word & to venerable traditions will find in my complaints a confession & a self accusation no doubt. You will say I do not receive what Heaven gives. But you must not say any such thing. For I am, you see, speaking truly as to my Maker. That excellent Teacher whom He sent who has done so much to raise & comfort human life & who prized sincerity more than sacrifice, cannot exist to me as he did to John. My brothers my mother my companions must be much more to me in all respects of friendship than he can be.

I began this letter at Rome, I am finishing it at Florence close by the tombs of Galileo, of Michel Angelo, of Machiavel, & the empty urn of Dante. My letter sheet has got sadly soiled & so I give the history of its places.—I get no letters from home here as I hoped & have heard very little from any one there since I came hither. Let me dear Aunt find a letter from you in Paris & believe me most affectionately your nephew

Waldo

To Samuel Ripley and Sarah Bradford Ripley, July 9, 1833

Paris, 9 July, 1833.

To Mr & Mrs Ripley
My dear friends,

I have been looking round me to see if I could not pick up some facts in the great town that would interest you but it is such a vulgar superficial unspiritual marketing community or I so bad or so ill conditioned an observer that I am much at a loss. To be sure if the splendid soirées where Fontenelle or Madame de Stael might talk, existed, the traveller in his fortnight would not find them but he might hear the fame of them & some effect would go out from them into this immense extemporaneous literature, so called, with which the press groans here from day to day. But Politicks have spoiled conversation & men in France. Cousin has quit Plato & M. Arago his magnet & galvanic battery since those unlucky 3 days. And to such paltry purpose. The press to be sure is free & says the sauciest things every day but otherwise the government has very much the character of the old government & exiles shoots or imprisons whom it pleases.

The charm of Paris to so many people seems to consist in the boundless domestic liberty which releases each man from the fear of the eyes & ears of all his neighbors, opens a public parlour for him to take his coffee & read his newspaper, in every street; go where his business may lead him he can always find an ice, a bath, a dinner, & good company, at the next corner; and next in the ample provision for what the newspapers call 'nos besoins recreatifs.'[15] From 15 to 20 theatres open their doors to him at a small price every evening—the best of them splendid beyond a Yankee's belief. I saw at Malta a masqued ball given by the English Governor in the ancient Palace of the Grand Masters. Yet it did not compare for good taste & imposing effect with a masqued ball introduced by way of ballet into the Opera of Gustave on the stage of the French Opera. Yet the Englishman had half a dozen grand saloons each of which seemed half as big as Fanueil hall Ah they understand here the powers of the lookingglass; and all Paris is a perpetual puzzle to the eye to know what is object & what is reflection. By this expedient reading rooms & cafés have all a bewildering extent & the wealth of the shops is multiplied. Even on the dessert service at the dinner table they set mirrors into the fruit-stands to multiply whips cherries & sugar plums, so that when I took one, I found two were gone. Then the poorest Frenchman may walk in the kings garden every day; he may go read if he chuse, in the kings library—wide open—the largest in the world, or in the Mazarine library, or in several more. He may go hear lectures on every branch of science literature at the Sorbonne, or the College of France, or the College of Law, or the Garden of Plants. If he love botany he may go to this last place & find not-quite-all plants growing up together in their scientifick classes; then by a public placard, Jussieu gives notice that next Sunday he goes out on a botanical excursion & invites all & sundry to go with him naming the village of the rendezvous. But if the Frenchman prefer natural history of animals he has only to turn down a green lane of this garden of Eden, & he shall find all manner of lions bisons elephants & hyenas the giraffe 17 feet high and all other things that are in the dictionary but he did not know were in the world—large & small ostriches white peacocks golden pheasants & the like—not to mention the museums & cabinets which in this garden & elsewhere on certain days of every week are thrown open. So the Louvre, so is the Luxembourg. What strikes a stranger most of all is the splendour of the shops—such endless profusion of costly goods of every sort that it is a constant wonder where they find purchasers. This is accounted for by the idolatrous love which Frenchmen all over the earth have for Paris. The

---

15. *"Our recreational needs."*

merchant in Montreal & the planter in Louisiana are toiling patiently, they say, in the expectation of coming to Paris to spend their gains. Mr Horace Gray told me of an acquaintance of his in Florence who as often as he earns a hundred louis goes to Paris to spend them. He is a French teacher & now 76 years old. "He did not think that this year he should be quite able to make the sum complete, but next winter he should." Yesterday I went to the Institute & saw Biot, Arago, Gay Lussac; Jussieu, Thenard—

But whilst I see the advantages of Paris they are not very great to me. Now that I have been here fifteen days I find I spend most of my time in the reading room & that I can do at home. So I promise myself soon the pleasure of seeing you & earnestly hope to find you both in the best health. I send my love to all my little grandchildren & flatter myself that I shall have an iliad of stories for them that will rival Peter Parley. At least I have had the honor of travelling with this last gentleman.—I saw Lewis Stackpole at Rome. Very respectfully & affectionately yours, Waldo E.

To Alexander Ireland, August 30, 1833

Liverpool, 30 August, 1833.

My dear Sir,

A shower of rain which hinders my visiting gives me an opportunity of fulfilling my promise to send you an account of my visits to Mr Carlyle & to Mr Wordsworth. I was fortunate enough to find both of them at home. Mr C. lives among some desolate hills in the parish of Dunscore 15 or 16 miles from Dumfries. He had heard of my purpose from his friend who gave me my letter & insisted on dismissing my gig which went back to Dumfries to return for me the next day in time to secure my seat in the evening coach for the south. So I spent near 24 hours with him. He lives with his wife, a most agreeable accomplished woman, in perfect solitude There is not a person to speak to within 7 miles. He is the most simple frank amiable person—I became acquainted with him at once, we walked over several miles of hills & talked upon all the great questions that interest us most. The comfort of meeting a man of genius is that he speaks sincerely that he feels himself to be so rich that he is above the meanness of pretending to knowledge which he has not & Carlyle does not pretend to have solved the great

problems but rather to be an observer of their solution as it goes forward in
the world. I asked him at what religious development the concluding passage
in his piece in the Edin. Review upon German Literature (say 5 years ago) &
some passages in the piece called Characteristics, pointed? he replied, that he
was not competent to state it even to himself—he waited rather to see.—My
own feeling was that I had met with men of far less power who had yet
greater insight into religious truth.—He is as you might guess from his papers
the most catholic of philosophers—he forgives & loves everybody & wishes
each to struggle on in his own place & arrive at his own ends, but his respect
for eminent men or rather his scale of eminence is almost the reverse of the
popular scale; Scott, Mackintosh,—Jeffrey;—Gibbon;—even Bacon are no
heroes of his; stranger yet he hardly admires Socrates, the glory of the Greek
world—but Burns & Samuel Johnson; Mirabeau he said, interested him, & I
suppose whoever else has given himself with all his heart to a leading
instinct & has not *calculated* too much. But I cannot think of sketching even
his opinions or repeating his conversation here. I will cheerfully do it when
you visit me in America. He talks finely, seems to love the broad Scotch, & I
loved him very much, at once. I am afraid he finds his entire solitude tedious,
but I could not help congratulating him upon his treasure in his wife & I
hope they will not leave the moors. tis so much better for a man of letters to
nurse himself in seclusion than to be filed down to the common level by the
compliances & imitations of city society—And you have found out the
virtues of solitude I remember with much pleasure.

The third day afterwards, I called upon Mr Wordsworth at Rydal Mount.
He received me with much kindness & remembered up all his American
acquaintance. He had very much to say about the evils of superficial educa
tion both in this country & in mine. He thinks the intellectual tuition of
society is going on out of all proportion faster than its moral training, which
last is essential to all *education* He don't wish to hear of schools, of tuition,—
it is the education of circumstances which he values & much more to this
point. He says that he is not in haste to publish more poetry, for many
reasons but that what he has written will be at some time given to the world.
He led me out into a walk in his grounds where he said many thousands of
his lines were composed, & repeated to me three beautiful sonnets which he
has just finished, upon the occasion of his recent visit to Fingal's Cave at
Staffa. I hope he will print them speedily—the third is a gem. He was so
benevolently anxious to impress upon me my social duties as an American
citizen that he accompanied me near a mile from his house talking vehe-

mently & ever & anon stopping short to imprint his words. I noted down some of his words when I got home & you may see them in Boston, Massachusetts, when you will. I enjoyed both my visits highly & shall always esteem your Britain very highly in love for its wise & good mens' sake.

I remember with much pleasure my visit to Edinburgh & my short acquaintance with yourself. It will give me very great pleasure to hear from you, to know your thoughts. Every man that ever was born has some that are peculiar. Address to me "Care of Barnard, Adams, & Co., Boston." I left the letter at Stirling & the other here. Present my respects to your father & family

Your friend & servant
R. Waldo Emerson.

To Abby Larkin Adams, December 2, 1833

New Bedford, 2 December, 1833

My dear Abby,[16]

Am I to stay here till I get a letter from you. Write soon, for I cannot stay much longer. And yet I live very pleasantly among kind people. The lady with whom I board, is a Quaker, and I suppose you know the Quakers use what they call 'plain speech.' When she helps me at the table, she says "Waldo, shall I give thee bread?" and she never calls the days of the week by their common names, but 'first day,' 'second day,' & so on, to 'seventh day.' This is because the old Saxons, whose descendants we are, called the days from the names of their gods, as the Sun's day, the Moons day, Thor's day, Woden's day, Saturn's day, & the Quakers disapprove of pagan names. But many of them are excellent people, and I have a long story to tell you of the goodness of this old lady on a particular occasion; & whenever she comes to Boston I want to introduce you to Mrs Deborah Brayton.

I hope the French comes on beautifully. I attended a French examination here, the other day, of class of girls who spoke in French throughout the whole recitation; & then presented themes in French as candidates for a

---

16. *Abby Adams was about ten years old when Emerson wrote this letter.*

prize. I was one of the judges, and there were so many good ones that there was much difficulty in deciding on the best. Do you know where New Bedford lies on the map? It is worth knowing, for though it is a small town it has more ships than any other town in the United States except New York & Boston. At least they say so here. All these vessels are employed in chasing the poor whale wherever he swims all round the globe, that they may tear off his warm jacket of blubber & melt it down into oil for your lamp, & to steal from him his bone to make stays & parasols for ladies. If you get the volume of Harper's Family Library called 'Polar Seas & Regions' which is a very interesting book you will find a good account of this fishery. Wait till I come home & I will lend it to you. Meantime give my love & respect to your Uncle & Aunt & to Aunt Mary also.

Your affectionate Uncle,—
R Waldo Emerson.

To Edward Bliss Emerson, December 22, 1833

Boston, 22 December, 1833.

Dear Edward,

Thank you heartily for your kind remembrances of me in two letters I have lately read. I rejoice to see a more cheerful tone in your recent letters than in those of the early summer. I hope I augur rightly therefrom your better health & greater ease of mind. You are in the same situation with hundreds of our enterprizing nation who eat the bitter bread of exile in their youth, that they may eat sweeter bread on their return. What has reconciled me to your expatriation is the belief that you had found a climate where you could live, when your own threatened to kill you & I have hoped & do hope that months & years are producing though slowly such a revolution in your constitution as will enable you to live in health through many Massachusetts Decembers. Meantime you are always dearly prized by those you have left & will find your place waiting for you whenever you seek it. But who are they that are at home? Mother has been living at Newton. I have just returned to this city from New Bedford where I have been for a month & am shortly to return thither. Charles sleeps in Washington St, boards with Geo. B. E[merson]., & spends the day in Court St. So that in truth you are about as much at home as any of us. One of these days if we may believe the lawyers I am to be the richer for Ellen's estate & whenever that day arrives I hope it will enable me to buy a hearth somewhere to which we pious Æneases may return with our household gods from all the quarters of our dispersion. If you wish to know what I do—I preach at New Bedford, sometimes in Boston; I have written a lecture upon Natural History & am now preparing another for next Tuesday evg. & have promised one to the Mechanics Institute. I meditate something more seriously than ever before, the adventure of a periodical paper which shall speak truth without fear or favor to all who desire to hear it, with such persuasion as shall compel them to speak it also. Henry Hedge is an unfolding man who has just now written the best pieces that have appeared in the Examiner and one especially was a living leaping Logos, & he may help me.

Charles & I went to Concord a few days ago. He delivered a fine lecture upon Socrates; But Charles looks often despondent & finds his fate as hard as you yours. Indeed that property belongs to the race man rather than to any individual. How come on the adventures. I was sorry to hear of any disappointments. Pray rein in that sanguine genius of yours that risks & projects so magnificently & which I can well remember from Latin School & Andover upward, & make him trot tame & safe for a year or two, for nothing is so important as your health to which the anxieties of indebtedness will never contribute. We can get used to being poor for the first men & happiest men of the earth have been but we can't away with pain & disease so easily. & whatever loss you suffer by following this bad advice set down to my account & it shall be cheerfully & affectionately honoured by your brother Waldo.

I regretted much not seeing Mr. Mason. I called at his house in Myrtle St the day after he left town. Before that I was at Newton, & did not know of his whereabout.

To James Freeman Clarke, March 12, 1834

Plymouth, Mass. March 12, 1834.

My dear Sir,

As the day approaches when Mr Lewis should leave Boston I seize a few moments in a friend's house in the first of towns to thank you heartily for your kindness in lending me the valued Mss which I return. The translations excited me much & who can estimate the value of a good thought? I trust I am to learn much more from you hereafter of your German studies & much I hope of your own. You asked in your note concerning Carlyle. My recollections of him are most pleasant & I feel great confidence in his character. He understands & recognizes his mission. He is perfectly simple & affectionate in his manners & frank, as he can well afford to be, in his communications. He expressed some impatience of his total solitude & talked of Paris as a residence. I told him I hoped not for I should always remember him with respect meditating in the mountains of Nithsdale. He was cheered, as he ought to be by learning that his papers were read with interest by young men unknown to him in this continent & when I specified a piece which had attracted warm commendations from the New Jerusalem people here his wife said, That is always the way; whatever piece he has writ that he thinks has fallen dead, he hears of two or three years afterward.—He has many many tokens of Goethes regard, miniatures medals books & many letters. If you should go to Scotland one day you would gratify him yourself & me by your visit to Craigenputtock, in the parish of Dunscore near Dumfries. He told me that he had a book which he had thot to publish but was now in the purpose of dividing into a series of articles for Fraser's Magazine. I therefore subscribed for that book which he calls *the Mud magazine* but have seen nothing of his workmanship in the two last numbers.

The mail is going, so I shall finish my letter another time.

Your obliged friend & servant
R. Waldo Emerson.

To Thomas Carlyle, May 14, 1834

Boston, Massachusetts
14 May, 1834

My dear Sir,

There are some purposes we delay long to execute simply because we have them more at heart than others, & such an one has been for many weeks I may say months my design of writing you an Epistle.

Some chance wind of Fame blew your name to me perhaps two years ago as the author of papers which I had already distinguished, (as indeed it was very easy to do,) from the mass of English periodical Criticism as by far the most original & profound essays of the day the works of a man of Faith as well as Intellect sportive as well as learned & who belonging to the despairing & deriding class of philosophers was not ashamed to hope & to speak sincerely. Like somebody in Wilhelm Meister, I said, this person has come under obligations to me & to all whom he has enlightened. He knows not how deeply I should grieve at his fall if in that exposed England where genius always hears the devil's whisper "All these kingdoms will I give thee,—" his virtue also should be an initial growth put off with age. When therefore I found myself in Europe I went to your house only to say "Faint not—the word you utter is heard though in the ends of the earth & by humblest men; it works, prevails." Drawn by strong regard to one of my teachers I went to see his person & as he might say his environment at Craigenputtock. Yet it was to fulfil my duty, to finish my mission, not with much hope of gratifying him; in the Spirit of "If I love you what is that to you?" Well, it happened to me that I was delighted with my visit, justified to myself in my respect, & many a time upon the Sea in my homeward voyage I remembered with joy the favored condition of my lonely philosopher,—his happiest wedlock, his fortunate temper, his steadfast simplicity, his all means of happiness not that I had the remotest hope he should so far depart from his theories as to expect happiness. On my arrival at home I rehearsed to several attentive ears what I had seen & heard, & they with joy received it.

In Liverpool I wrote to Mr Fraser to send me his Magazine & I have now received four numbers of the Sartor Resartus for whose light, thanks evermore. I am glad that one living scholar is self-centred & will be true to himself though none ever were before; who, as Montaigne says, "puts his ear close by himself, & holds his breath, & listens" And none can be offended with the self subsistency of one so catholic & jocund. And 'tis good to have a new eye inspect our mouldy social forms, our politics, & schools, & religion. I say *our,* for it cannot have escaped you that a lecture upon these topics written for England may be read to America. Evermore thanks for the brave stand you have made for Spiritualism in these writings. But has literature any parallel to the oddity of the vehicle chosen to convey this treasure. I delight in the contents, the form which my defective apprehension for a joke makes me not appreciate I leave to your merry discretion. And yet did ever wise & philanthropic author use so defying a diction? As if society were not sufficiently shy of truth without providing it beforehand with an objection to the form. Can it be that this humour proceeds from a despair of finding a contemporary audience & so the Prophet feels at liberty to utter his message in droll sounds. Did you not tell me, Mr Thomas Carlyle, sitting upon one of your broad hills, that it was Jesus Christ built Dunscore kirk yonder. If you love such sequences, then admit, as you will, that no poet is sent into the world before his time; that all the departed thinkers & actors have paved your way; that (at least, when you surrender yourself) nations & ages do guide your pen, yes & common goose-quills as well as your diamond graver. Believe then that harp & ear are formed by one revolution of the wheel; that men are waiting to hear your Epical Song; and so be pleased to skip those excursive involved glees, and give us the simple air, without the volley of variations. At least in some of your prefaces you should give us the theory of your rhetoric. I comprehend not why you should lavish in that spendthrift style of yours Celestial truths. Bacon & Plato have something too solid to say than that they can afford to be humorists. You are dispensing that which is rarest, namely, the simplest truths—truths which lie next to Consciousness & which only the Platos & Goethes perceive. I look for the hour with impatience when the vehicle will be worthy of the spirit when the word will be as simple & so as resistless as the thought, & in short when your words will be one with things. I have no hope that you will find suddenly a large audience. Says not the sarcasm "Truth hath the plague in his house." Yet all men are *potentially* (as Mr Coleridge would say) your audience & if you will not in very Mephistophelism repel & defy them; shall be actually & whatever the great or the small may say about the charm of diabolism a true & majestic genius can afford to despise it.

I venture to amuse you with this homiletic criticism because it is the sense of uncritical truth seekers to whom you are no more than Hecuba, whose instincts assure them that there is Wisdom in this grotesque teutonic apocalyptic strain of yours, but that tis hence hindered in its effect. And though with all my heart I would stand well with my Poet, yet if I offend, I shall quietly retreat into my Universal relations wherefrom I affectionately espy you as a man, myself as another.

And yet before I come to the end of my letter I may repent of my temerity & unsay my charge. For are not all our circlets of will as so many little eddies rounded in by the great circle of Necessity & *could* the Truth-Speaker perhaps now the best Thinker of the Saxon race, have written otherwise? And must not we say that Drunkenness is a virtue rather than that Cato has erred.

I wish I could gratify you with any pleasing news of the regeneration, education, prospects of man in this Continent. But your philanthropy is so patient so farsighted that present evils give you less solicitude. In the last six years Government in the United States has been fast becoming a job, like great Charities. A most unfit person in the Presidency [Andrew Jackson] has been doing the worst things & the worse he grew the more popular. Now things seem to mend. Webster, a good man & as strong as if he were a sinner, begins to find himself the Centre of a great & enlarging party & his eloquence incarnated & enacted by them. Yet men have not hope that the Majority shall be suddenly unseated. I send herewith a volume of Websters that you may see his Speech on Foots Resolutions, a speech which the Americans have never done praising. I have great doubts whether the book reaches you, as I know not my agents. I shall put with it the little book of my Sweden-borgian druggist, of whom I told you.[17] And if, which is hardly to be hoped, any good book should be thrown out of our vortex of trade & politics, I shall not fail to give it the same direction.

I need not tell you, my dear Sir, what pleasure a letter from you would give me when you have a few moments to spare to so remote a friend. If any word in my letter should provoke you to a reply I shall rejoice in my sauciness. I am spending the summer in the country, but my address is "Boston, care of Barnard, Adams, & Co." Care of O. Rich London. Please to make my affectionate respects to Mrs Carlyle whose kindness I shall always gratefully remember. I depend upon her intercession to insure your writing to me. May God grant you both his best blessing. Your friend,

R. Waldo Emerson

To Edward Bliss Emerson, May 31, 1834

Newton, 31 May, 1834

My dear brother,

Your last letter to mother postpones to a pretty distance our prospect of seeing you but as some of our feet were shod with quicksilver when we came into the world there is still an even chance that you may slip in upon us in

---

17. *Sampson Reed's* Observations on the Growth of the Mind *(1826).*

some of these revolutions of Night & Morn. Here sit Mother & I among the pine trees still almost as we shall lie by & by under them. Here we sit always learning & never coming to the knowledge of.—The greatest part of my virtue—that mustard seedlet that no man wots of—is Hope. I am ever of good cheer & if the heaven asks no service at my hands am reconciled to my insignificance yet keeping my eye open upon the brave & the beautiful. Philosophy affirms that the outward world is only phenomenal & the whole concern of dinners of tailors of gigs of balls whereof men make such account is a quite relative & temporary one—an intricate dream—the exhalation of the present state of the Soul—wherein the Understanding works incessantly as if it were real but the eternal Reason when now & then he is allowed to speak declares it is an accident a smoke nowise related to his permanent attributes. Now that I have used the words, let me ask you do you draw the distinction of Milton Coleridge & the Germans between Reason & Understanding. I think it a philosophy itself. & like all truth very practical. So now lay away the letter & take up the following dissertation on Sunday. Reason is the highest faculty of the soul—what we mean often by the soul itself; it never *reasons*, never proves, it simply perceives; it is vision. The Understanding toils all the time, compares, contrives, adds, argues, near sighted but strong-sighted, dwelling in the present the expedient the custom-ary. Beasts have some understanding but no Reason. Reason is potentially perfect in every man—Understanding in very different degrees of strength. The thoughts of youth, & 'first thoughts,' are the revelations of Reason. the love of the beautiful & of Goodness as the highest beauty the belief in the absolute & universal superiority of the Right & the True But understanding that wrinkled calculator the steward of our house to whom is committed the support of our animal life contradicts evermore these affirmations of Rea-son & points at Custom & Interest & persuades one man that the declara-tions of Reason are false & another that they are at least impracticable. Yet by & by after having denied our Master we come back to see at the end of years or of life that he was the Truth. 'Tell him,' was the word sent by Posa to the Spanish prince 'when he is a man to reverence the dreams of his youth.' And it is observed that 'our first & third thoughts usually coincide.' Religion Poetry Honor belong to the Reason; to the real the absolute. These the Understanding sticks to it are chimaeras he can prove it. Can he, dear? The blind men in Rome said the streets were dark. Finally to end my quotations, Fenelon said, 'O Reason! Reason! art not thou He whom I seek.'—The manifold applications of the distinction to Literature to the

Church to Life will show how good a key it is. So hallelujah to the Reason forevermore.

But glad should I be to hold academical questions with you here at Newton. Whenever you are tired of working at Porto Rico & want a vacation or whenever your strength or your weakness shall commend to you the high countenances of the Muses, come & live with me. The Tucker estate is so far settled that I am made sure of an income of about $1200.[18] wherewith the Reason of Mother & you & I might defy the Understanding upon his own ground, for the rest of the few years in which we shall be subject to his insults. I need not say that what I speak in play I speak in earnest. If you will come we will retreat into Berkshire & make a little world of other stuff. Your brother

Waldo

To Ezra Ripley, September 20, 1834

Newton, Sept 20, 1834.

My dear Sir,

After much conversation with the New Bedford people & Mr Dewey I have declined going there for the coming winter & therefore I return with pleasure to our former prospect of spending the winter at Concord. We are not confined in our present quarters by any fixed term, yet I think it will not be convenient to us to go to Concord until the second week in October, say on the 10th. I wish to carry my books which are in Boston & some pieces of furniture & baggage which are here & I think I had better engage Mr Buttrick or some other person in Concord to transport them as Mr Allen has not horses. I suppose a large horse cart would carry all we have here;—A

---

18. *Charles wrote William on 13 May that Emerson had then received one half of his inheritance from Pliny Cutler, the executor, by order of the court—67 shares of City Bank stock, 19 of the Atlantic Bank, and 31 of the Boston and Roxbury Mill Dam, together with cash amounting to between $3,000 and $4,000, making altogether about $11,600. The second "half" paid in July 1837 was $11,674.49, so that the total amount he received from Ellen Tucker's estate seems to have been $23,274.49, or approximately that. [Rusk]*

bureau; a small table; 2 bookcases containing each 2 shelves; 2 armchairs; a trunk & 2 beds;—& some small articles. I think it would need two horses. Mother & I will go to Boston & go up in the stage from thence. My books from Boston can go afterwards. May I ask you to engage Mr Buttrick to come here with his wagon, & I will write to you again to name the day. Aunt Mary is here, & is desirous of boarding somewhere in Concord. Mother thought perhaps Mr Prescott's would be a good place, if they would accommodate her.

With kind regards to Miss Ripley, believe me, dear Sir, Your affectionate grandson

R. Waldo Emerson

To Thomas Carlyle, November 20, 1834

Concord, Mass
20 November 1834

My dear Sir,

Your letter, which I received last week, made a bright light in a solitary & saddened place. I had quite recently received the news of the death of a brother [Edward] in the island of Porto Rico, whose loss to me will be a life-long sorrow. As he passes out of sight, come to me visible as well as spiritual tokens of a fraternal friendliness which by its own law, transcends the tedious barriers of Custom & nation, & opens its way to the heart. This is a true consolation, & I thanked my jealous Δαιμων ["demon"] for the godsend so significantly timed. It, for the moment, realizes the hope to which I have clung with both hands, through each disappointment, that I might converse with a man whose ear of faith was not stopped, and whose argument I could not predict. May I use the word, "I thank my God whenever I call you to remembrance."

I receive with great pleasure the wonderful Professor now that first the decent limbs of Osiris are collected. We greet him well to Cape Cod & Boston Bay. The rigid laws of matter prohibit that the soul imprisoned within the strait edges of these types should add one syllable thereto, or we had adjured the Sage by every name of veneration to take possession by so much as a Salve! of his Western World, but he remained inexorable for any new communications.

I feel like congratulating you upon the cold welcome which, you say, Teufelsdroch [i.e., *Sartor Resartus*] has met. As it is not earthly happy, it is marked of a high sacred sort. I like it a great deal better than ever, & before it was all published, I had eaten nearly all my words of objection. But do not think it shall lack a present popularity. That it should not be known seems possible, for if a memoir from Laplace had been thrown into that muckheap of Frasers Magazine, who would be the wiser? But this has too much wit & imagination not to strike a class who would not care for it as a faithful Mirror of this very Hour. But you know the proverb "To be fortunate, be not too wise." The great men of the day are on a plane so low as to be thoroughly intelligible to the vulgar. Nevertheless, as God maketh the world forevermore, whatever the devils may seem to do, so the thoughts of the best minds always become the last opinion of Society. Truth is ever born in a manger, but is compensated by living till it has all souls for its Kingdom. Far far better seems to me the unpopularity of this Philosophical Poem (shall I call it?) than the adulation that followed your eminent friend Goethe. With him I am becoming better acquainted, but mine must be a qualified admiration. It is a singular piece of good nature in you to apotheosize him. I cannot but regard it as his misfortune with conspicuous bad influence on his genius,—that velvet life he led. What incongruity for genius whose fit ornaments & reliefs are poverty & hatred, to repose fifty years in chairs of state; & what pity that his Duke did not cut off his head to save him from the mean end (forgive) of retiring from the municipal incense "to arrange tastefully his gifts & medals." Then the Puritan in me accepts no apology for bad morals in such as *he*. We can tolerate vice in a splendid nature whilst that nature is battling with the brute majority in defence of some human principle. The sympathy his manhood & his misfortunes call out, adopts even his faults, but genius pampered—acknowledged—crowned—can only retain our sympathy by turning the same force once expended against outward enemies, now against inward, & carrying forward & planting the standard of Oromasdes so many leagues farther on into the envious Dark. Failing this, it loses its nature & becomes talent, according to the definition—more skill in attaining the vulgar ends. A certain wonderful friend of mine said, that "a false priest is the falsest of false things" But what makes the priest? A cassock? O Diogenes! or, the power (& thence the call) to teach man's duties as they flow from the Superhuman. Is not he who perceives & proclaims the superhumanities, he who has once intelligently pronounced the words "Self Renouncement" "Invisible Leader," "Heavenly Powers of Sorrow" & so on, forever the liege of the same?

Then to write luxuriously is not the same thing as to live so, but a new & worse offence. It implies an intellectual defect also, the not perceiving that the present corrupt condition of human nature (which condition this harlot muse helps to perpetuate) is a temporary or superficial state. The good word lasts forever: the impure word can only buoy itself in the gross gas that now envelopes us, & will sink altogether to ground as that works itself clear in the everlasting effort of God. May I not call it temporary? for when I ascend into the pure region of truth, (or, under my undermost garment, as Epictetus & Teufelsdroch would say,) I see that to abide inviolate though all men fall away from it; yea though the whole generation of Adam should be healed as a sore off the face of the creation. So, my friend, live Socrates & Milton, those stanch puritans, forevermore! Strange is it to me that you should not yet sympathize (yet so you said) with Socrates, so ironical, so true, & who "tramped in the mire with wooden shoes whenever they would force him into the clouds." I seem to see him offering the hand to you across the ages which sometime you will grasp.

I am glad you like Sampson Reed & that he has inspired some curiosity respecting his church. Swedenborgianism, if you should be fortunate in your first meetings, has many points of attraction for you: for instance this article "The Poetry of the Old Church is the reality of the New"; which is to be literally understood, for they esteem, in common with all the Trismegisti; the Natural World as strictly the symbol or exponent of the Spiritual, & part for part; the animals to be incarnations of certain affections; & scarce a popular expression esteemed figurative, but they affirm to be the simplest statement of fact. Then is their whole theory of social relations—both in & out of the body—most philosophical, & tho' at variance with the popular theology, selfevident. It is only when they come to their descriptive theism, if I may say so, & then to their drollest heaven, & to some autocratic not moral decrees of God that the mythus loses me. In general, too, they receive the fable instead of the moral of their Aesop. They are to me however deeply interesting as a sect which I think must contribute more than all other sects to the new faith which must arise from out of all.

You express a desire to know something of myself. Account me "a drop in the ocean seeking another drop," or God-ward, striving to keep so true a sphericity as to receive the due ray from every point of the concave heaven.

Since my return home, I have been left very much at leisure. It were long to tell all my speculations upon my profession & my doings thereon; but, possessing my liberty, I am determined to keep it at the risk of uselessness, (which risk God can very well abide,) until such duties offer themslves as I can with integrity discharge. One thing I believe,—that, Utterance is place enough: & should I attain through any inward revelation to a more clear perception of my assigned task, I shall embrace it with joy & praise. I shall not esteem it a low place, for instance, if I could strengthen your hands by true expressions of the pleasure & hope which your writings communicate to me & to some of my countrymen. Yet the best poem of the poet is his own mind & more even than in any of the works I rejoice in the promise of the workman.—Now I am only reading & musing & when I have any news to tell of myself you shall hear them.

Now as to the welcome hint that you might come to America, it shall be to me a joyful hope. Come & found a new Academy that shall be church & school & parnassus, as a true Poet's house should be. I dare not say that wit has better chance here than in England of winning world-wages, but it can always live, and it can scarce find competition. Indeed, indeed, you shall have the continent to yourself, were it only as Crusoe was King. If you cared to read literary lectures, our people have vast curiosity & the apparatus is very easy to set agoing. Such "pulpit" as you pleased to erect would at least find no hindrance in the building. A friend of mine & of yours remarked, when I expressed the wish that you would come here, "that people were not here as in England sacramented to organized schools of opinion, but were a far more convertible audience." If at all you can think of coming here, I would send you any & all particulars of information with cheerfullest speed.

I have written a very long letter, yet have said nothing of much that I would say upon chapters of the Sartor. I must keep that, & the thoughts I had upon "poetry in history," for another letter, or (might it be!) for a dialogue face to face. Let me not fail of the Diamond Necklace. I found three greedy receivers of Teufelsdroch, who also radiate its light. For the sake of your knowing what manner of men you move I send you two pieces writ by one of them, Frederic Henry Hedge, the article on Swedenborg & that on Phrenology. And as you like Sampson Reed, here are two more of his papers. *Do* read them. And since you study French History, do not fail to look at our Yankee portrait of Lafayette. Present my best remembrances to Mrs Carlyle,—whom that stern & blessed solitude has armed & sublimed out of all reach of the littleness & unreason of London. If I thought we could win her to the American shore, I would send her the story of those godly women, the contemporaries of John Knox's daughter who came out hither to enjoy the worship of God amidst wild men & wild beasts.

Your friend & servant,
R. Waldo Emerson.

To Benjamin Peter Hunt, January 23, 1835

Concord, Mass. 23 Jan. 1835.

My dear Sir,

I have just been reading an old letter from you dated Sept. 1830 & which I believe was never answered. It was not because it was neglected for to my habits of intercourse a written page always comes more welcome than much conversation: the pen is a more faithful index than the tongue of those qualities in my fellow man that most excite my curiosity & whatever the proverbs may say of the untrustworthiness of words I know more of all my friends by them than by their acts. "Action is less near to vital truth than description" And your letter interested me much by exhibiting the same consciousness of principles—the inward vision—which had attracted me before & which is the basis of all that is noble in the character. You have doubtless forgotten the letter but may remember its tenor. I write now to beg you to write me again & inform me of your manner of life, or better yet, your manner of thought. As we saunter along in the world we are soon apprized that the number of those in whose genius & faith we can take any strong interest is small, & we can ill afford to lose one.

What are your books? Have you fallen in with the writings of Thomas Carlyle? In Scotland eighteen months ago I sought & made the acquaintance of this gentleman author of the pieces "Burns" "Characteristics" "Corn Law Rhymes—Review," &c. in the Edinburgh, & of many singular papers in the Foreign Review, & Frasers Magazine,—all alive—& all true. My friends think I exaggerate his merit but he seems to me one of the best, & since Coleridge is dead, I think, the best thinker of the age. His last Essay is a series of papers in Frasers Magazine called Sartor Resartus ending about Nov. 1834. If you have not seen it pray make inquiry after it. Very early in your reading I remember you had discrimination enough to appreciate Sampson Reed. So does Carlyle, to whom I sent Reed's Tract, & in very different costume they are of one faith. You used to talk of Self-Reverence That word indeed contains the whole of Philosophy & the whole of Religion. I would gladly know how profoundly you have pierced it. Did you ever meet a *wise Quaker?* They are few, but a sublime class of speculators. They have been perhaps the most explicit teachers of the highest article to which human faith soars the strict union of the willing soul to God & so the souls access at all times to a verdict upon every question which the opinion of all mankind cannot shake & which the opinion of all mankind cannot confirm. Or I wonder if quitting this thin air & alpine ground you rather borne by the tide of the time that sets so strong to natural Science amaze yourself with those laws of terrible beauty which took the soul of Newton & Laplace & Humboldt Yet is to me far the best charm of Natural laws their correspondence with Spiritual laws of which they seem but symbols & prophecies. But I will not fatigue you with guessing any longer in the dark at your inclinations & pursuits. Explain them yourself. They cannot be uninteresting to me. Most of all would it please me if you would take the occasion of your first liberty (I know not your occupation if you have withdrawn from the school) in paying me a visit in old Concord here. My mother & myself are boarding with Dr Ripley & have a capital spare chamber for prophet or scholar. Fail not to acquaint me with your doing & being. Your old friend & servant

R. *Waldo Emerson.*

To Lydia Jackson, January 24, 1835

Concord 24 January 1835

To Miss Lydia Jackson

I obey my highest impulses in declaring to you the feeling of deep and tender respect with which you have inspired me. I am rejoiced in my Reason as well as in my Understanding by finding an earnest and noble mind whose presence quickens in mine all that is good and shames and repels from me my own weakness. Can I resist the impulse to beseech you to love me? The strict limits of the intercourse I have enjoyed, have certainly not permitted the manifestation of that tenderness which is the first sentiment in the common kindness between man and woman. But I am not less in love, after a new and higher way. I have immense desire that you should love me, and that I might live with you alway. My own assurance of the truth and fitness of the alliance—the union I desire, is so perfect, that it will not admit the thought of hesitation—never of refusal on your part. I could scratch out the word. I am persuaded that I address one so in love with what I love, so conscious with me of the everlasting principles, and seeking the presence of the common Father through means so like, that no remoteness of condition could much separate us, and that an affection founded on such a basis, cannot alter.

I will not embarrass this expression of my heart and mind with any second considerations. I am not therefore blind to them. They touch the past and the future—our friends as well as ourselves, & even the Departed. But I see clearly how your consent shall resolve them all.

And think it not strange, as you will not, that I write rather than speak. In the gravest acts of my life I more willingly trust my pen than my tongue. It is as true. And yet had I been master of my time at this moment. I should bring my letter in my own hand. But I had no leave to wait a day after my mind was made up. Say to me therefore anything but NO. Demand any time for conversation, for consideration, and I will come to Plymouth with a joyful heart. And so God bless you, dear and blessed Maiden. and incline you to love your true friend,

Ralph Waldo Emerson.

My address is Concord, Mass.

To Lydia Jackson, January 28, 1835

Concord 28 Jan. 1835

My dear friend,

I have your letter & will have, please God, for it cannot be a sudden gift, your heart.—The foolish lecture which having promised for Thursday eve. I staid to write has been most strangely writ as on rack & pincers which I had wisely prepared for myself by writing instead of going to you. So join the great & the little in our web. Friday I shall come to Plymouth & we will compare notes & you shall judge of the risques you incur. But with me now is peace. I said nothing touching the announcing of this matter to friends not having a wish to abridge your liberty. If nothing is yet said pray say nothing till I come. But if, (as from my mode of communication is almost unavoidable) it is already known, why then may it rejoice all as much as me. Your friend

Waldo E.

To Lydia Jackson, February 1, 1835

Concord, 1 February—

One of my wise masters, Edmund Burke, said, 'A wise man will speak the truth with temperance that he may speak it the longer.' In this new sentiment that you awaken in me, my Lydian Queen, what might scare others pleases me, its quietness, which I accept as a pledge of permanence. I delighted myself on Friday with my quite domesticated position & the good understanding that grew all the time, yet I went & came without one vehement word—or one passionate sign. In this was nothing of design, I merely surrendered myself to the hour & to the facts. I find a sort of grandeur in the modulated expressions of a love in which the individuals, & what might seem even reasonable personal expectations, are steadily postponed to a regard for truth & the universal love. Do not think me a metaphysical lover. I am a man & hate & suspect the over refiners, & do sympathize with the homeliest pleasures & attractions by which our good foster mother Nature draws her children together. Yet am I well pleased that between us the most permanent ties should be the first formed & thereon should grow whatever others human nature will.

My Mother rejoices very much & asks me all manner of questions about you, many of which I cannot answer. I dont know whether you sing, or read French, or Latin, or where you have lived, & much more. So you see there is nothing for it but that you should come here & on the Battle-Ground stand the fire of her catechism.

Under this morning's severe but beautiful light I thought dear friend that hardly should I get away from Concord. I must win you to love it. I am born a poet, of a low class without doubt yet a poet. That is my nature & vocation. My singing be sure is very 'husky,' & is for the most part in prose. Still am I a poet in the sense of a perceiver & dear lover of the harmonies that are in the soul & in matter, & specially of the correspondences between these & those. A sunset, a forest, a snow storm, a certain river-view, are more to me than many friends & do ordinarily divide my day with my books. Wherever I go therefore I guard & study my rambling propensities with a care that is ridiculous to people, but to me is the care of my high calling. Now Concord is only one of a hundred towns in which I could find these necessary objects but Plymouth I fear is not one. Plymouth is streets; I live in the wide champaign.

Time enough for this however. If I succeed in preparing my lecture on Michel Angelo Buonaroti this week for Thursday, I will come to Plymouth on Friday. If I do not succeed—do not attain unto the Idea of that man—I shall read of Luther, Thursday & then I know not when I shall steal a visit.—

Dearest forgive the egotism of all this letter Say they not 'The more love the more egotism.' Repay it by as much & more. Write, write to me. And please dear Lidian take that same low counsel & leave thinking for the present & let the winds of heaven blow away your dyspepsia.

Waldo E.

To William Emerson, February 5, 1835

Boston, 5 February, 1835

Dear William,

May not my tardiness make me a teller of stale news & may not my news be strange or unwelcome if I say that I am engaged to marry Miss Lydia Jackson of Plymouth. I announce this fact in a very different feeling from that with which I entered my first connexion This is a very sober joy. This lady is a person of noble character whom to see is to respect. I find in her a quite unexpected community of sentiment & speculation, & in Plymouth she is dearly prized for her love & good works. So be glad with & for me & as soon as possible let me make you & Susan personally acquainted with her. Love to Susan. Yours affectionately

Waldo E

TO LYDIA JACKSON, FEBRUARY 13, 1835

Concord 13 Feb

Dear Lidian, Days have I not to give, I heartily wish I had. Pride as well as love tell me that none but I should bring my betrothed into Boston but the spirit by which we live is despotic or at least I am yet far from that discipline of my powers or powerules that shall enable me to control by my will what we call (fondly) the moment of inspiration. O no I am its reverent slave. I watch & watch & hail its aurora from afar. Great words you will think for little works. Be it so. We must make much of our all, be it ever so little. And the knowledge of very unfit preparation for my three last Lectures made me say at Plymouth that I could not come again till they were done. Then as to your deliberate visit to Concord could you not most wise Lidian defer it until December! I deny that it will take any horse from the first of March to the first of May to go from Plymouth to Concord. Really my dear friend we live several miles *on this side* the Ohio.

Ah Lidian Lidian go to bed betimes! Do you sit up writing letters till three in the morn? So shall I never have that brave Spartan wife I pray for. This is a poor sign of that philosophy of action that was to be commenced.

And then the dark eyes could not read clearly the sentence about recent love wounds. That word *recent* only respected the long past, it did not touch the present. And whatever I said, referred to some page or pages of my Day Book where is most pompously recorded the homage its author paid to bright village eyes. Will you not honor me, my sibyl, by visiting my lowly study & reading the page. Right welcome shall you be & it is the only way I can think of to reconcile this divided empire which you & my inkstand both claim in me. O if you could hear Inkstand's silent reproaches addressed to me touching you. Inkstand says he will not budge one foot asks how I dare imagine the thing asks me if I have not the eye to see his roots in this paternal soil whether I know not the voice "There where thou art, there where thou remainest, work." In fine Inkstand concludes that unless Lidian can trundle Plymouth rock a score of miles northward, she must even quit it & come & sit down by Concord Battle-Bridge. In reward of that grace, Inkstand is full of promises of verses & histories writ in & by her love.

Now must I tell Lidian why I play with this question? I never incline to make influence the measure of the fitness of actions. For me to measure my influence would be to deal with infinitesimal quantities & I might commit suicide. God who makes the influence of the great, little, & of the little, great, takes care of that cattle. I seek rather to act simply; to live where I can possess my soul, & considering that where I am put, there I am due, I do not forsake my native corners without manifest reason. For me to go to Plymouth would be to cripple me of some important resources & not so far as I see to do any work I cannot do here. And you, my dear friend, have paid much of your debt there & when you see some souls here that are now "unwillingly deprived of truth" will thirst to come. So do love

Waldo E.

To Lydia Jackson, March *c.* 4, 1835

Concord

I hope our poor town whose name I duly superscribe to my epistles will not come to read Discord through Lidians lenses gray. The innocent river flows through the flats under my eye yet unknowing that his friends friend loves the surly sea's roar better than his childish murmuring. Ah he would look me pathetically in the face, did he imagine, that I his almost sole votary, (for I fear he hath not on his banks another watcher of his poetical aspects,) meditated a desertion of his gentle side. I have promised him a song too, whenever the tardy, callow muse shall new moult her feathers. River large & inkstand little, deep & deep would blend their voices.

Magical fitting of our eye to nature, that a few square miles of rocks bushes & water should present us under the changing light with such resplendent pictures & ever new transformations. Is n't it, Lidian? Why, Plymouth's but a seabeach. What can you say for it? Let me hear let me read your sea song.

I send Carlyles letter for Mrs Bliss, & Charles will bring her the 3d Vol. of the Friend. Lidian what have you done with my Plymouth sermon. I forgot twice to take it away. All that is important is to keep it out of sight. If you have left it at P. do not let it be lent again & if you have it in Boston seal it up for me. I have a copy of it that I shall presently finish & bring it to more connected & luminous conclusions, I hope, than when at P. I cannot stay next Friday O magnet mine, for, Saturday night I am to lecture at Waltham & Sunday preach there on an old agreement, which abridges my brief week. One thing more among the facts,—please never write my name with that prefix *Rev.* Have I not told you, dear Lidian, that I meet much more reverence than I know what to do with? I never asked this of any before, yet Charles & most of my particular friends as if by consent write me simple Mr—And so having despatched this budget of most momentous trifles I pray to be commended to your friends—to Miss Russell first, as my oldest friend, & next to Mrs Bliss, with sad regret that I must lose the kind society she had designed for me. My mother taxed me for not carrying her love to you as she had enjoined me. Your lover,

Waldo E.

To Thomas Carlyle, March 12, 1835

Concord,
12 March 1835.

My Dear Sir,—I am glad of the opportunity of Mr. Barnard's visit to say health and peace be with you. I esteem it the best sign that has shone in my little section of space for many days, that some thirty or more intelligent persons understand and highly appreciate the *Sartor.* Dr. Channing sent to me for it the other day, and I have since heard that he had read it with great interest. As soon as I go into town I shall see him and measure his love. I know his genius does not and cannot engage your attention much. He possesses the mysterious endowment of natural eloquence, whose effect, however intense, is limited, of course, to personal communication. I can see myself that his writings, without his voice, may be meagre and feeble. But please love his catholicism, that at his age can relish the *Sartor,* born and inveterated as he is in old books. Moreover, he lay awake all night, he told my friend last week, because he had learned in the evening that some young men proposed to issue a journal, to be called *The Transcendentalist,* as the organ of a spiritual philosophy. So much for our gossip of to-day.

But my errand is yet to tell. Some friends here are very desirous that Mr. Fraser should send out to a bookseller here fifty or a hundred copies of the *Sartor.* So many we want very much; they would be sold at once. If we knew that two or three hundred would be taken up, we should reprint it now. But we think it better to satisfy the known inquirers for the book first, and when they have extended the demand for it, then to reproduce it, a naturalized

Yankee. The lovers of Teufelsdröckh here are sufficiently enthusiastic. I am an icicle to them. They think England must be blind and deaf if the Professor makes no more impression there than yet appears. I, with the most affectionate wishes for Thomas Carlyle's fame, am mainly bent on securing the medicinal virtues of his book for my young neighbors. The good people think he overpraises Goethe. There I give him up to their wrath. But I bid them mark his unsleeping moral sentiment; that every other moralist occasionally nods, becomes complaisant and traditional; but this man is without interval on the side of equity and humanity! I am grieved for you, O wise friend, that you cannot put in your own contemptuous disclaimer of such puritanical pleas as are set up for you; but each creature and Levite must do after his kind.

Yet do not imagine that I will hurt you in this unseen domain of yours by any Boswellism. Every suffrage you get here is fairly your own. Nobody is coaxed to admire you, and you have won friends whom I should be proud to show you, and honorable women not a few. And cannot you renew and confirm your suggestion touching your appearance in this continent? Ah, if I could give your intimation the binding force of an oracular word!—in a few months, please God, at most, I shall have wife, house, and home wherewith and wherein to return your former hospitality. And if I could draw my prophet and his prophetess to brighten and immortalize my lodge, and make it the window through which for a summer you should look out on a field which Columbus and Berkeley and Lafayette did not scorn to sow, my sun should shine clearer and life would promise something better than peace. There is a part of ethics, or in Schleiermacher's distribution it might be physics, which possesses all attraction for me; to wit, the compensations of the Universe, the equality and the coexistence of action and reaction, that all prayers are granted, that every debt is paid. And the skill with which the great All maketh clean work as it goes along, leaves no rag, consumes its smoke,—will I hope make a chapter in your thesis.

I intimated above that we aspire to have a work on the First Philosophy in Boston. I hope, or wish rather. Those that are forward in it debate upon the name. I doubt not in the least its reception if the material that should fill it existed. Through the thickest understanding will the reason throw itself instantly into relation with the truth that is its object, whenever that appears. But how seldom is the pure loadstone produced! Faith and love are apt to be spasmodic in the best minds. Men live on the brink of mysteries and harmonies into which yet they never enter, and with their hand on the doorlatch they die outside. Always excepting my wonderful Professor,[19] who among the living has thrown any memorable truths into circulation? So live and rejoice and work, my friend, and God you aid, for the profit of many more than your mortal eyes shall see. Especially seek with recruited and never-tired vision to bring back yet higher and truer report from your Mount of Communion of the Spirit that dwells there and creates all. Have you received a letter from me with a pamphlet sent in December? Fail not, I beg of you, to remember me to Mrs. Carlyle.

Can you not have some *Sartors* sent? Hilliard, Gray, & Co. are the best publishers in Boston. Or Mr. Rich has connections with Burdett in Boston.

> *Yours with respect and affection,*
> *R. Waldo Emerson*

To Thomas Carlyle, March 30, 1835

> *Concord,*
> *30 April, 1835.*

My Dear Sir,—I received your letter of the 3d of February on the 20th instant, and am sorry that hitherto we have not been able to command a more mercantile promptitude in the transmission of these light sheets. If desire of a letter before it arrived, or gladness when it came, could speed its journey, I should have it the day it was written. But, being come, it makes me sad and glad by turns. I admire at the alleged state of your English reading public without comprehending it, and with a hoping scepticism touching the facts. I hear my Prophet deplore, as his predecessors did, the deaf ear and the gross heart of his people, and threaten to shut his lips; but, happily, this he cannot do, any more than could they. The word of the Lord *will* be spoken. But I shall not much grieve that the English people and you are not of the same mind if that apathy or antipathy can by any means be the occasion of your visiting America. The hope of this is so pleasant to me, that I have thought of little else for the week past, and having conferred with some friends on the matter, I shall try, in obedience to your request, to give

---

19. *That is, Professor Teufelsdröckh of* Sartor Resartus.

you a statement of our capabilities, without indulging my *penchant* for the favorable side.

Your picture of America is faithful enough: yet Boston contains some genuine taste for literature, and a good deal of traditional reverence for it. For a few years past, we have had, every winter, several courses of lectures, scientific, political, miscellaneous, and even some purely literary, which were well attended. Some lectures on Shakespeare were crowded; and even I found much indulgence in reading, last winter, some Biographical Lectures, which were meant for theories or portraits of Luther, Michelangelo, Milton, George Fox, Burke. These courses are really given under the auspices of Societies, as "Natural History Society," "Mechanics' Institutes," "Diffusion of Useful Knowledge," &c., &c., and the fee to the lecturer is inconsiderable, usually $20 for each lecture. But in a few instances individuals have undertaken courses of lectures, and have been well paid. Dr. Spurzheim received probably $3,000 in the few months that he lived here. Mr. Silliman, a Professor of Yale College, has lately received something more than that for a course of fifteen or sixteen lectures on Geology. Private projects of this sort are, however, always attended with a degree of uncertainty. The favor of my townsmen is often sudden and spasmodic, and Mr. Silliman, who has had more success than ever any before him, might not find a handful of hearers another winter. But it is the opinion of many friends whose judgment I value, that a person of so many claims upon the ear and imagination of our fashionable populace as the "author of the *Life of Schiller*," "the reviewer of *Burns's Life*," the live "contributor to the *Edinburgh* and *Foreign* Reviews," nay, the "worshipful Teufelsdröckh," the "personal friend of Goethe," would, for at least one season, batter down opposition, and command all ears on whatever topic pleased him, and that, quite independently of the merit of his lectures, merely for so many names' sake.

But the subject, you say, does not yet define itself. Whilst it is "gathering to a god," we who wait will only say, that we know enough here of Goethe and Schiller to have some interest in German literature. A respectable German here, Dr. Follen, has given lectures to a good class upon Schiller. I am quite sure that Goethe's name would now stimulate the curiosity of scores of persons. On English literature, a much larger class would have some preparedness. But whatever topics you might choose, I need not say you must leave under them scope for your narrative and pictorial powers; yes, and space to let out all the length of all the reins of your eloquence of moral sentiment. What "Lay Sermons" might you not preach! or methinks "Lectures on

Europe" were a sea big enough for you to swim in. The only condition our adolescent ear insists upon is, that the English as it is spoken by the unlearned shall be the bridge between our teacher and our tympanum.

Income and Expenses.—All our lectures are usually delivered in the same hall, built for the purpose. It will hold 1,200 persons; 900 are thought a large assembly. The expenses of rent, lights, doorkeeper, &c. for this hall, would be $12 each lecture. The price of $3 is the least that might be demanded for a single ticket of admission to the course,—perhaps $4; $5 for a ticket admitting a gentleman and lady. So let us suppose we have 900 persons paying $3 each, or $2,700. If it should happen, as did in Prof. Silliman's case, that many more than 900 tickets were sold, it would be easy to give the course in the day *and* in the evening, an expedient sometimes practised to divide an audience, and because it is a great convenience to many to choose their time. If the lectures succeed in Boston, their success is insured at Salem, a town thirteen miles off, with a population of 15,000. They might, perhaps, be repeated at Cambridge, three miles from Boston, and probably at Philadelphia, thirty-six hours distant. At New York anything literary has hitherto had no favor. The lectures might be fifteen or sixteen in number, of about an hour each. They might be delivered, one or two in each week. And if they met with sudden success, it would be easy to carry on the course simultaneously at Salem, and Cambridge, and in the city. They must be delivered in the winter.

Another plan suggested in addition to this. A gentleman here is giving a course of lectures on English literature to a private class of ladies, at $10 to each subscriber. There is no doubt, were you so disposed, you might turn to account any writings in the bottom of your portfolio, by reading lectures to such a class, or, still better, by speaking.

Expense of Living.—You may travel in this country for $4 to $4.50 a day. You may board in Boston in a "gigmanic" style for $8 per week, including all domestic expenses. Eight dollars per week is the board paid by the permanent residents at the Tremont House,—probably the best hotel in North America. There, and at the best hotels in New York, the lodger for a few days pays at the rate of $1.50 per day. Twice eight dollars would provide a gentleman and lady with board, chamber, and private parlor, at a fashionable boardinghouse. In the country, of course, the expenses are two thirds less. These are rates of expense where economy is not studied. I think the Liverpool and New York packets demand $150 of the passenger, and their accommodations are perfect. (N.B.   I set down all sums in dollars. You may commonly reckon a pound sterling worth $4.80.)

"The man is certain of success," say those I talk with, "for one winter, but not afterwards." That supposes no extraordinary merit in the lectures, and only regards you in your leonine aspect. However, it was suggested that, if Mr. C. would undertake a Journal of which we have talked much, but which we have never yet produced, he would do us great service, and we feel some confidence that it could be made to secure him a support. It is that project which I mentioned to you in a letter by Mr. Barnard,—a book to be called *The Transcendentalist,* or *The Spiritual Inquirer,* or the like, and of which F. H. Hedge was to be editor. Those who are most interested in it designed to make gratuitous contributions to its pages, until its success could be assured. Hedge is just leaving our neighborhood to be settled as a minister two hundred and fifty miles off, in Maine, and entreats that you will edit the journal. He will write, and I please myself with thinking I shall be able to write under such auspices. Then you might (though I know not the laws respecting literary property) collect some of your own writings and reprint them here. I think the *Sartor* would now be sure of a sale. Your *Life of Schiller,* and *Wilhelm Meister,* have been long reprinted here. At worst, if you wholly disliked us, and preferred Old England to New, you can judge of the suggestion of a knowing man, that you might see Niagara, get a new stock of health, and pay all your expenses by printing in England a book of travels in America.

I wish you to know that we do not depend for your *éclat* on your being already known to rich men here. You are not. Nothing has ever been published here designating you by name. But Dr. Channing reads and respects you. That is a fact of importance to our project. Several clergymen, Messrs. Frothingham, Ripley, Francis, all of them scholars and Spiritualists, (some of them, unluckily, called Unitarian,) love you dearly, and will work heartily in your behalf. Mr. Frothingham, a worthy and accomplished man, more like Erasmus than Luther, said to me on parting, the other day, "You cannot express in terms too extravagant my desire that he should come." George Ripley, having heard, through your letter to me, that nobody in England had responded to the *Sartor,* had secretly written you a most reverential letter, which, by dint of coaxing, he read to me, though he said there was but one step from the sublime to the ridiculous. I prayed him, though I thought the letter did him no justice, save to his heart, to send you it or another; and he says he will. He is a very able young man, even if his letter should not show it. He said he could, and would, bring many persons to hear you, and you should be sure of his utmost aid. Dr. Bradford, a medical man, is of good courage. Mr. Loring, a lawyer, said, "Invite Mr. and Mrs. Carlyle to spend a couple of months at my house," (I assured him I was too selfish for that,) "and if our people," he said, "cannot find out his worth, I will subscribe, with others, to make him whole of any expense he shall incur in coming." Hedge promised more than he ought. There are several persons beside, known to me, who feel a warm interest in this thing. Mr. Furness, a popular and excellent minister in Philadelphia, at whose house Harriet Martineau was spending a few days, I learned the other day "was feeding Miss Martineau with the *Sartor.*" And here some of the best women I know are warm friends of yours, and are much of Mrs. Carlyle's opinion when she says, Your books shall prosper.

On the other hand, I make no doubt you shall be sure of some opposition. Andrews Norton, one of our best heads, once a theological professor, and a destroying critic, lives upon a rich estate at Cambridge, and frigidly excludes the Diderot paper from a *Select Journal* edited by him, with the remark, "Another paper of the Teufelsdröckh School." The University perhaps, and much that is conservative in literature and religion, I apprehend, will give you its cordial opposition, and what eccentricity can be collected from the Obituary Notice on Goethe, or from the *Sartor,* shall be mustered to demolish you. Nor yet do I feel quite certain of this. If we get a good tide with us, we shall sweep away the whole inertia, which is the whole force of these gentlemen, except Norton. That you do not like the Unitarians will never hurt you at all, if possibly you do like the Calvinists. If you have any friendly relations to your native Church, fail not to bring a letter from a Scottish Calvinist to a Calvinist here, and your fortune is made. But that were too good to happen.

Since things are so, can you not, my dear sir, finish your new work and cross the great water in September or October, and try the experiment of a winter in America? I cannot but think that if we do not make out a case strong enough to make you build your house, at least you should pitch your tent among us. The country is, as you say, worth visiting, and to give much pleasure to a few persons will be some inducement to you. I am afraid to press this matter. To me, as you can divine, it would be an unspeakable comfort; and the more, that I hope before that time so far to settle my own affairs as to have a wife and a house to receive you. Tell Mrs. Carlyle, with my affectionate regards, that some friends whom she does not yet know do hope with me to have her company for the next winter at our house, and shall not cease to hope it until you come.

I have many things to say upon the topics of your letter, but my letter is already so immeasurably long, it must stop. Long as it is, I regret I have not more facts. Dr. Channing is in New York, or I think, despite your negligence of him, I should have visited him on account of his interest in you. Could you see him you would like him. I shall write you immediately on learning anything new bearing on this business. I intended to have despatched this letter a day or two sooner, that it might go by the packet of the 1st of May from New York. Now it will go by that of the 8th, and ought to reach you in thirty days. Send me your thoughts upon it as soon as you can. I *jalouse* of that new book. I fear its success may mar my project.

> *Yours affectionately,*
> *R. Waldo Emerson.*

To William Joseph Loring, October 3, 1835

Concord, 3 October, 1835.

My dear Sir,

I think I shall be ready by the beginning of November to begin a course of eight lectures on English Literature. I shall probably fill two lectures with discussion of such general questions, as; the nature of literature; its intimate relation to the history of nations; the interest which not only scholars but all men have in it; leaving myself room to enlarge upon some doctrines, which, I think, ought to be urged upon our people, touching the *intellectual duties,* or the discipline of the mind. I propose to follow these with lectures upon the history of the English language & literature; upon the genius & writings of Chaucer; Spenser; Shakspear; Bacon; Ben Jonson, & some of his contemporaries; shorter notices of the later writers, & one lecture upon the literary character, in the present age, of the nations speaking the English tongue. Is it the desire of the Committee that I should deliver all my lectures consecutively? Mr Gould intimated some necessity of interrupting them to accommodate the other lecturer or lecturers. I shall be glad of immediate information, if you wish me to begin on the first Thursday of November, & give one every week till my course is completed. I had rather begin a week or two later, if it can be so.

Your obedient servant,
R. Waldo Emerson.

Mr W. J. Loring, Committee of
Soc. diff. Usef. Knowledge.

To Amos Bronson Alcott, February 27, 1836

Concord, Feb. 27, 1836

My dear Sir,

I am afraid you think me very remiss in failing to send back your MSS ["Psyche"] in so many weeks. But truly they were not easily dispatched; and my readings have been much interrupted. I have now read all the pages twice; some of them, many times; and have to return you hearty thanks for the privilege and the pleasure. As you were pleased to challenge my critical powers on this reading, I will endeavor to give you the results both in general & in particular.

I think the book original, and vital in all its parts; manifestly, the production of a man in earnest, & written to convince. I think it possesses, in certain passages, the rare power to awaken the highest faculties, to awaken the apprehension of the Absolute. I think it discovers, throughout, that delicate discrimination of the proprieties & felicities of expression which is an essential organ of literary genius. It is almost uniformly elegant; and contains many beautiful & some splendid passages.

These seem to me prominent merits of the book. Let me now tell you what, with some diffidence, I deem its defects. Its fault arises out of the subtlety & extent of its subject. I think it grapples with an Idea which it does not subdue & present in just method before us. It seems to me too much a book *of one idea,* somewhat deficient in variety of thought & illustration, and even sometimes pedantic from the wilfulness (shall I say) with which every thing is forced into the author's favorite aspects & forms of expression The book has a strong mannerism. (Much of this might be removed and I think the fastidious eye relieved by striking out the antiquated form of the verb as *"revealeth," "seeth,"* &c & writing *reveals, sees,* &c. and by a more frugal use of certain words, as "mirror forth", 'image,' 'shape forth,' & others of that character.) But its capital fault I think, is the want of compression; a fault almost unavoidable in treating such a subject, which not being easily apprehensible by the human faculties, we are tempted to linger around the Idea, in the hope, that what cannot be sharply stated in a few words, may yet chance to be suggested by many.

If you should publish this work, as it is, it would, I doubt not, find many readers, & discerning persons would discover that it contained fine gold. But it would please me still better, if you would do for it what I am now doing with some papers of my own; that is, to go through the work (chiefly by the memory) and take the *things* out, leaving the rest. That extract will be precious as the Sybils remaining scrolls. For example, I can tell you some of the parts which I would save as brands from the burning. The Chapter XI, first of all. The XXXIX Chapter, which yet I think would be much improved by condensation. Nursery maids p. 46 Immortality p 57–8 City influence p. 67 Culture of Imagination p. 76 Philosophy p 91–2; Chapter XIII; Lust p. 118–9 Punishment p 149 Dreams p 167 Loneliness, 161. Affluence of Spirit 223 Bivision p. Chap. XXXIII Signs of Spirit p 234 End of matter p 241–2 Chapter XXXVI Holidays p. 275–6–7 Chapter XVIII Counsels, p 182–3

I have read the whole book with great interest and I think the power of reflection & of expression exhibited is too great to leave you any liberty in our time and country wherein is such a dearth of both, to neglect or conceal your gifts. I may say what Burke said of Howard "Your plan is original & as full of genius as of humanity So do not let it sleep or stop a day.

Imagining I saw many verbal inaccuracies I ran over the first hundred pages this morn with a pen in my hand & I enclose you my sheet of spoils.

With great respect & affection
Your friend,
R. Waldo Emerson.

To Frederic Henry Hedge, March 14, 1836

Concord, 14 March, 1836.

My dear friend,

The East Lexington Committee referred to me yesterday your note to Mr Robbins respecting the supply of their pulpit for a part or the whole of May and told me to do as I pleased I did not at the moment nor until this morning remember that I have agreed to supply them only till 1 May, & therefore had nothing to do with it. I answered that the arrangement would be exactly what I wished; and they begged me to write you so, as it was very agreeable to them. So they will depend upon you the first Sunday in May.

I am glad to know that you will come hither and shall depend on a good visit from you here in Concord. Not a word from Carlyle, I think since I saw you. I am at a loss for the cause. I think I have written him twice since the date of his last letter. If I think of books that should interest you I am almost ashamed to find how little I have read this winter. To write a very little takes a great deal of time So that if one indulges in that species of dissipation he will have little to show for his solid days. And there are not many greater misfortunes to peace of mind than to have keen susceptibility to the beautiful in composition and just to lack that additional wit which suffices to create it. So shall a man weary himself and spend good oil in vain attempts to carve Apollos which all turn out scarecrows. My versification of this ancient lament is

Happy Bard or Dunce! but hard
Is it to be half a bard.

A man feels like one who has lost his way in the Universe when he discovers that he has aims which he has no faculties to satisfy. Yet in better hours we own that there is medicine for this disease. The sentiment of piety restores to us our property in the Universe, and so do some of our intellectual states which obscurely involve it. Indeed I do not know but the mere apprehension of the Absolute (whether this is attained for moments by books, or fine conversation, or by solitary thought) is a true & perfect balsam for all our literary maladies. Alas that the balsam is so hard to find! Yet I think at times I shall never be unhappy again. I shall heartily thank you however for any prescriptions your philosophy and faith can supply. I think the Scholar's Ascetic ought to be systematically and generally taught—

What do you write—what do you think at Bangor? Stimulate us to hope & emulation by telling us your projects. Certainly to the carnal and unrenewed mind no country or politics seemed ever less romantic than our own. The eye must be anointed that can decorate it with beauty and deify the men. Yet I hold fast with both hands to a cheerful man-respecting faith. Do you not owe me a letter already? Do give me the first epistolary hour.

Yours affectionately,
R. Waldo Emerson

To William Emerson, April 24, 1836

Springfield, Mass
Sunday Evg 24 Apr.

Dear William,

I have never told you that Charles & I meditate a present visit to you. Charles has been withered by a four or five weeks cold & racked by a cough until I became uneasy & insisted he should go & see you & bring mother home. When I went to Salem last Monday I left him strong injunctions to that effect but the next Thursday I found him in Boston too feeble to set out alone. So I excused myself at Salem & got him into the Worcester cars & we have come hither on the way to your house. Charles has certainly gained some vigor, though not yet much appetite. And his cough is relieved at least whilst he rides. Tomorrow morning if the weather is favorable we go down to Hartford—and at New Haven we mean to take the boat to N.Y. Dr Jackson does not find that anything is the matter with Charles but a catarrh & the bad effects of confinement & loss of appetite. His constutution has no power of resistance & therefore shut him up & starve him & he withers like a flower in the frost.

I can ill spare the time for this journey though I am to see you but I could worse spare Charles. So tell Mother we must get him well instantly & give my love to Susan & to my nephew whom I hope shortly to see. Yours hers his & Mother's

affectionate
Waldo E.

To Lidian Emerson, May 12, 1836

New York
Thursday 12 May

Dear Lidian,

Yesterday afternoon we attended Charles's funeral.[20] Mother & Elizabeth heard the prayers but did not go out. The remains are deposited for a time in a tomb of Mr Griswold a friend & connexion of Susan's.—Mother is very well & bears her sorrow like one made to bear it & to comfort others. Elizabeth is well and the strength & truth of her character appears under this bitter calamity. William & Susan are well & thoroughly kind to us as they have been tenderly faithful to Charles. I have told mother that I think it best, on every account, she should return immediately with me & end her painful visit at New York whither she came to spend a month of happiness in the new household of her son. It has been seven or eight months of much sickness anxiety & death. She will return with me & Elizabeth, & we take the boat tomorrow afternoon. We ought to arrive in Boston at 10 or 11 o'clock A.M. Saturday, & return to Concord, Saturday afternoon.

Now, my dear wife, shall I find you in Boston. or in Concord; do what you think best. You may think it necessary to go home on Friday, to make ready & receive us. or perhaps you can send sufficient word & go with us on Saturday. It is not of much importance any way. Trifles all. Only I wish Mother to sit down as gently & wontedly in her chamber in your house, as if she had never been in any other. I told her you would write but not just now & that you sent her all love. She begs me to write hers to you.

And so, Lidian, I can never bring you back my noble friend who was my ornament my wisdom & my pride.—A soul is gone so costly & so rare that few persons were capable of knowing its price and I shall have my sorrow to

20. *Elizabeth Peabody, who was allowed to read this letter—"a wonderful letter for the idea it gave of a friendship"—reported to her sister Mary what she could learn concerning Emerson at this time of crisis; and her narrative testifies to the terrible strain placed upon his habitual self-control. "And when I came home," she wrote, "I found a letter from Waterston who was in New York and at the funeral.—He said he stood at the grave with Waldo—& that when he turned away from it—compressed nature found its way in a laugh—and an ejaculation 'dear boy.' . . . 'When one has never had but little society— and all that society is taken away—what is there worth living for?' said he." [Rusk]*

myself for if I speak of him I shall be thought a fond exaggerator. He had the fourfold perfection of good sense, of genius, of grace, & of virtue, as I have never seen them combined. I determined to live in Concord, as you know, because he was there, and now that the immense promise of his maturity is destroyed, I feel not only unfastened there and adrift but a sort of shame at living at all.

I am thankful, dear Lidian, that you have seen & known him to that degree you have,—I should not have known how to forgive you an ignorance of him, had he been out of your sight. Thanks thanks for your kindest sympathy & appreciation of him. And you must be content henceforth with only a piece of your husband; for the best of his strength lay in the soul with which he must no more on earth take counsel. How much I saw through his eyes. I feel as if my own were very dim.

Yours affectionately
Waldo E.

I will inquire for you at Miss Lane's. I think Mother will stop at Front St with her sisters.

To Mary Moody Emerson, May 12, 1836

New York, 12 May, 1836.

My dear Aunt,

You have already heard that Elizabeth & I arrived too late to see Charles. He died on Monday afternoon immediately after returning from a ride with Mother. He got out of the coach alone, walked up the steps and into the house without assistance then sat down upon the stairs, fainted, and never recovered. Yesterday afternoon we attended his funeral. And that is the end, on this side heaven, of his extraordinary promise—the union of such shining gifts—grace and genius and sense and virtue. What a loss is this to us all—to Elizabeth, to Mother, to you and to me. In him I have lost all my society. I sought no other and formed my habits to live with him. I deferred to him on so many questions and trusted him more than myself that I feel as if I had lost the best part of myself. In him were the foundations of so solid a confidence and friendship that all the years to come of life leaned upon him. His genius too was a fountain inexhaustible of thoughts and kept me ever curious and expectant. Nothing was too great nothing too beautiful for his grasp or his expression and as brilliant as his power of illustration was he stuck like a mathematician to his truth and never added a syllable for display. I cannot tell you how much I valued his conversation for these last two or three years, and he has never stopped growing but has ripened from month to month. Indeed the weight of his thoughts and the fresh and various forms in which he instantly clothed them has made Shakspear more conceivable to me, as also Shakspear was almost the only genius whom he wholly loved.

His taste was unerring: What he called good, was good; but so severe was it, that very few works and very few men could satisfy him. And this because his standard was a pure ideal beauty and he never forgot himself so far as to accept any lower actual one in lieu of it. But I must not begin yet to enumerate his perfections—I shall not know where to stop, and what would be bare truth to me would read on paper like the fondest exaggeration.

I mourn for the Commonwealth which has lost, before yet it had learned his name, the promise of his eloquence and rare public gifts. He pleased himself that he had been bred from infancy, as it were, in the public eye; and he looked forward to the debates of the senate on great political questions as to his fit and native element. And with reason, for in extempore debate his speech was music, and the precision the flow and the elegance of his discourse equally excellent. Familiar as I was with his powers, when a year ago I first heard him take part in a debate, he surprised me with his success. He spoke so well that he was impatient of writing as not being a fit medium for him. I shall never hear such speaking as his, for his memory was a garden of immortal flowers and all his reading came up to him as he talked to clear and elevate and decorate the subject of his present thought. But I shall never have done describing as I see well I shall never cease grieving as long as I am in the earth that he has left it. It seems no longer worth living in, if whatever delights us in it, departs. He has quitted forever the apparent the partial. He has gone to make acquaintance with the real the good the divine and to find mates and cooperators such as we could not offer him.

I hope soon to see you and talk with you. Charles's last days have been comforted by the thorough kindness of William and Susan with Mother for his constant nurse. It is a great happiness. William and Mother bid me send you his watch which I shall do.

Yours affectionately
Waldo.

Concord, May 23, 1836.

My dear Sir,

I received the last week your kind letter, and the copy of your affectionate notice of Charles at Chauncey Place. I remember how little while ago you consoled us by your sympathy at Edward's departure,—a kind, elevating letter, which I have never acknowledged. I feel as if it was kind, even compassionate, to remember me now that these my claims to remembrance are gone.

Charles's mind was healthy, and had opened steadily (with a growth that never ceased from month to month) under favorable circumstances. His critical eye was so acute, his rest on himself so absolute, and his power of illustrating his thought by an endless procession of fine images so excellent, that his conversation came to be depended on at home as daily bread, and made a very large part of the value of life to me. His standard of action was heroic,—I believe he never had even temptations to anything mean or gross. With great value for the opinion of plain men, whose habits of life precluded compliment and made their verdict unquestionable, he held perhaps at too low a rate the praise of fashionable people,—so that he steadily withdrew from display, and I felt as if nobody knew my treasure. Meantime, like Aaron, "he could speak well." He had every gift for public debate, and I thought we had an orator in training for the necessities of the country, who should deserve the name and the rewards of eloquence. But it has pleased God not to use him here. The Commonwealth, if it be a loser, knows it not; but I feel as if bereaved of so much of my sight and hearing.

His judgement of men, his views of society, of politics, of religion, of books, of manners, were so original and wise and progressive, that I feel—of course nobody can think as I do—as if an oracle were silent.

I am very sorry that I cannot see you,—did not when we were both in Boston. My mother and brother rejoice in your success in New York, and I with them. They have had their part in the benefit. I hear nothing of the aching head, and hope it does not ache. Cannot I see you in Concord during some of your Boston visits? I will lay by every curious book or letter that I can think might interest you. My cousin Louisa, I know, would be glad to see this old town, and the old man at the parsonage whilst he is yet alive. My mother joins me in sending love to her.

Yours affectionately,
R. Waldo Emerson.

To Harriet Martineau, May 30, 1836

Concord, 30 May, 1836.

My dear friend,

I thank you heartily for your remembrance and sympathy. And you seem to have divined my brother for that which you say of him is altogether fit & worthy I am beginning to recover myself and after gazing at my calamity in the gross now to reckon the particulars of my loss. In Charles, I found society that indemnified me for almost total seclusion from all other. He was my philosopher, my poet, my hero, my Christian. Of so creative a mind that (tho' he wrote no verse) yet his conversation made Shakspear more conceivable to me; such an adorer of truth that he awed us, and a spirit of so much hilarity & elegancy that he actualized the heroic life to our eyes—partial, you must think, but I think only near. I cannot tell you how much I miss him I depended on him so much. His taste & its organs his acute senses were our domestic oracle. His judgment, his memory were always in request. Even his particular accomplishments, who shall replace to me? He was an excellent Greek scholar and has recently read with me, more properly, *to* me, a dialogue of Plato & the Electra of Sophocles. But why should I pore over my vanished treasures when I ought rather to remember the happiness whereof you remind me & in which light I certainly do regard his life even whilst I deplore him— viz as in the whole a Vision to me out of heaven and a perpetual argument for the reality & permanence of all that we aspire after But I cannot find with the best thought I can give it that I can attain to any thing beyond simple passion in relation to such events as this. Faith will become mere wonder and sad amazement. I can gather no hint from this terrible experience, respecting my own duties I grope in greater darkness & with less heed. Night rests on all sides upon the *facts* of our being, tho', we must own, our upper nature lies always in Day. But we can not stand still and Hope is behind all the changes even the last. We shall soon know all.

My wife thanks you for writing & would that she could see you. My mother is accustomed to disappointment and bears them well. Elizabeth Hoar is staying with us to compare notes of pleasure & pain and finds sincere comfort in the memory of her friends counsels & opinions & purposes.

To Frederic Henry Hedge, July 20, 1836

Concord, 20 July, 1836.

My dear friend,

I received your welcome letter a month ago,—as I see with much contrition. I ought to have testified my hearty good will to the project of the symposium,[21] which will certainly make the earth a more tolerable lodging even if it should not directly increase the wit of the compotators—rather say, cooperators. The men of strong understanding exercise an influence even baleful upon my power of conversation which is only sufficient to convey my meaning in calm times & quiet places when it is permitted to stretch out all its sloven length & by many fragments of thought to dot out the whole curve. The men of strong understanding are a menacing rapid trenchant race—they cut me short—they drive me into a corner—I must not suggest, I must define—& they hold me responsible for a demonstration of every sentiment I endorse. Whilst therefore I cannot sufficiently give thanks for the existence of this class, without whom there could not be either porridge or politics I do, for my particular, thoroughly avoid & defy them. But it happens that some individuals of the Reasonable class are endowed with Understanding; then again I am struck dumb & can scarcely give an intelligible sign of sympathy & respect. For this reason, I have never found that uplifting & enlargement from the conversation of many which I find in the society of one faithful person. However I confess the experiment you propose has never been fairly tried by us. And I will hope from it a pure pleasure. We must have a meeting at Commencement—Why not that evening? You must admit Mr Alcott over the professional limits, for he is a God-made priest. That man grows upon me every time I see him. He gave us some majestic

---

21. *This is the first mention of what would become the Transcendental Club.*

discourse at my house three weeks since He is a world builder—forever occupied with one problem—how spirit makes matter or how Be makes Seem This singleness is his strength & his weakness. He is so resolute to force all thoughts & things to become rays from his centre, that, for the most part, they come. Meantime Shakspeare, & all works of art, which require a surrender of the man to them in order to their full enjoyment, he suspects & disparages. But Coleridge he sets in the Zenith.

I had a letter from Carlyle a few weeks since He is still in London occupied on that book, and writes like a jaded man. He hardly deigns a word about his coming hither, so absorbed in his work—He speaks of A H. Everetts review of Sartor as either "a thrice plied quiz, or else opening on you a grandeur of still dulness rarely to be met with on earth." Meantime the book has sold very well & will shortly be out of print.

Did I tell you I had a Chapter which I call "Nature" in solid prose, & which I shall print I think presently, & send you. Then I wish to write another chapter called "Spirit" I have never had the pleasure of any conversation with your friend Miss Fuller. We expect her to come here tomorrow from Groton & make us a visit. I will tell you what society would please me; that you should be the minister of Concord & George P. B[radford] its school master & Carlyle a resident whilst he lectured in Boston and Mrs Ripley & Mr Alcott should be visiters. But my castles that stood have fallen, and these will never stand. But I shall rejoice in all your studies & writings for these are truly the things that bring us near. So forgive me this gossiping letter—I had company in the room so you must fill out its elliptical logic. Your friend,

R. W. Emerson.

To William Emerson, June 28, 1836

Concord, 28 June, 1836.

My dear brother,

I know I ought, according to all rules, to have answered your letter enclosing $65. which I duly received. But I tho't you would leave me more inches of line than a better merchant & of course I took some ells. Your account agrees perfectly with mine. If I should succeed in selling my Mill-dam shares, I can better wait your convenience in paying the balance. But Mr Adams whom I bade inquire & (if it could be) sell, sends me yet no word. Today I write to him & ask. I see how it is ever with me, thus far. I am never a dollar in advance of my wants & if it were not for an expedient once or twice in a twelve-month like Lecturing or an auction of my great *stock,* I should be flat on my back. But let me hope that my rotations are ended & that now I shall sit still & gather moss.

I have so far profited by your homily as to keep my Ledger very faithfully since May.

Mother says with her love that you must keep her informed of Susan & Willie's welfare for she has no means of greeting them & asking. I also would gladly know.

My little book is nearly done. Its title is "Nature." Its contents will not exceed in bulk S. Reed's Growth of the Mind. My design is to follow it by & by with another essay, "Spirit"; and the two shall make a decent volume.

Mr Alcott came hither last Saturday & spent Sunday & Monday. He is a great genius. So thoroughly original that he seems to subvert all you know & leave only his own theories. I would you could see him. He is a right preacher & gives one the rare satisfactions of being exercised & taught. Your affectionate brother

Waldo.

Mr Hoar returns next Friday. I have done nothing touching C's affairs, & now will wait for him. If I must have money, I will write you.

To Thomas Carlyle, September 17, 1836

Concord, Massachusetts,
17 September, 1836

My Dear Friend,—I hope you do not measure my love by the tardiness of my messages. I have few pleasures like that of receiving your kind and eloquent letters. I should be most impatient of the long interval between one and another, but that they savor always of Eternity, and promise me a friendship and friendly inspiration not reckoned or ended by days or years. Your last letter, dated in April, found me a mourner, as did your first. I have lost out of this world my brother Charles, of whom I have spoken to you,— the friend and companion of many years, the inmate of my house, a man of a beautiful genius, born to speak well, and whose conversation for these last years has treated every grave question of humanity, and has been my daily bread. I have put so much dependence on his gifts that we made but one man together; for I needed never to do what he could do by noble nature much better than I. He was to have been married in this month, and at the time of his sickness and sudden death I was adding apartments to my house for his permanent accommodation. I wish that you could have known him. At twenty-seven years the best life is only preparation. He built his foundation so large that it needed the full age of man to make evident the plan and proportions of his character. He postponed always a particular to a final and absolute success, so that his life was a silent appeal to the great and generous. But some time I shall see you and speak of him.

We want but two or three friends, but these we cannot do without, and they serve us in every thought we think. I find now I must hold faster the remaining jewels of my social belt. And of you I think much and anxiously since Mrs. Channing amidst her delight at what she calls the happiest hour of her absence, in her acquaintance with you and your family, expresses much uneasiness respecting your untempered devotion to study. I am the more disturbed by her fears, because your letters avow a self-devotion to your work, and I know there is no gentle dulness in your temperament to counteract the mischief. I fear Nature has not inlaid fat earth enough into your texture to keep the ethereal blade from whetting it through. I write to implore you to be careful of your health. You are the property of all whom you rejoice in heart and soul, and you must not deal with your body as your own. O my friend, if you would come here and let me nurse you and pasture you in my nook of this long continent, I will thank God and you therefor morning and evening, and doubt not to give you, in a quarter of a year, sound eyes, round cheeks, and joyful spirits. My wife has been lately an invalid, but she loves you thoroughly, and hardly stores a barrel of flour or lays her new carpet without some hopeful reference to Mrs. Carlyle. And in good earnest, why cannot you come here forthwith, and deliver in lectures to the solid men of Boston the *History of the French Revolution* before it is published,—or at least whilst it is publishing in England, and before it is published here. There is no doubt of the perfect success of such a course now that the *five hundred copies of the Sartor are all sold,* and read with great delight by many persons.

This I suggest if you too must feel the vulgar necessity of *doing;* but if you will be governed by your friend, you shall come into the meadows, and rest and talk with your friend in my country pasture. If you will come here like a noble brother, you shall have your solid day undisturbed, except at the hours of eating and walking; and as I will abstain from you myself, so I will defend you from others. I entreat Mrs. Carlyle, with my affectionate remembrances, to second me in this proposition, and not suffer the wayward man to think that in these space-destroying days a prayer from Boston, Massachusetts, is any less worthy of serious and prompt granting than one from Edinburgh or Oxford.

I send you a little book [*Nature*] I have just now published, as an entering wedge, I hope, for something more worthy and significant. This is only a naming of topics on which I would gladly speak and gladlier hear. I am mortified to learn the ill fate of my former packet containing the *Sartor* and Dr. Channing's work. My mercantile friend is vexed, for he says accurate orders were given to send it as a packet, not as a letter. I shall endeavor before despatching this sheet to obtain another copy of our American edition.

I wish I could come to you instead of sending this sheet of paper. I think I should persuade you to get into a ship this Autumn, quit all study for a time, and follow the setting sun. I have many, many things to learn of you. How melancholy to think how much we need confession! Yet the great truths are always at hand, and all the tragedy of individual life is separated how thinly from that universal nature which obliterates all ranks, all evils, all individualities. How little of you is in your *will!* Above your will how intimately are you related to all of us! In God we meet. Therein we *are*, thence we descend upon Time and these infinitesimal facts of Christendom, and Trade, and England Old and New. Make the soul now drunk with a sleep, and we overleap at a bound the obstructions, the griefs, the mistakes, of years, and the air we breathe is so vital that the Past serves to contribute nothing to the result.

I read Goethe, and now lately the posthumous volumes, with a great interest. A friend of mine who studies his life with care would gladly know what records there are of his first ten years after his settlement at Weimar, and what Books there are in Germany about him beside what Mrs. Austin has collected and Heine. Can you tell me?

Write me of your health, or else come.

Yours ever,
R. W. Emerson.

P. S.—I learn that an acquaintance is going to England, so send the packet by him.

TO WARREN BURTON, OCTOBER 23, 1836

In the newness of bereavement we are deaf to consolation the spirit being occupied with exploring the facts acquainting itself with the length & breadth of its disaster when a beloved person quits our society—What we are slow to learn we learn at last that this affliction has no acme & truly speaking no end. A passion of sorrow even though we seek it does not exhaust it but there stands the irreparable fact more grievous when all the mourners are gone than before that our being is henceforward the poorer by the loss of all the talents & affections of another soul. We may find many friends & other & noble gifts but this loss is never the less. My own faith teaches me that when one of these losses befals me it is because the hour is struck in my own constitution, a crisis has there taken place which makes it best for my whole being makes it necessary for my whole being that the influence be withdrawn. A purer vision an advanced state of the faculties shall hereafter inform you & me I doubt not of all those reasons & necessities which now transcend our faculties.

TO WILLIAM EMERSON, OCTOBER 31, 1836

Concord, Oct. 31, 1836

Dear William,

I have a son born last night at eleven o'clock, a large healthy looking boy. All the circumstances are favorable. Lidian is very comfortable, and we are all rejoiced & thankful. Mother & the bystanders all, pronounce favorable opinions upon the aspect form & demeanor of the bantling. He sucks his thumbs immediately as his grandmother says his father did, at his age, His eyes are of a color not ascertained, as he keeps them shut this morning, but it is thought they are dark blue. You shall have more particulars, shortly. Meantime with much love to Susan & Willie (to whom present greetings from his cousin) I am your affectionate brother

Waldo—

Concord 16 Dec. 1836

Dear William, I was at Boston yesterday & so did not receive your letter & its enclosure until this morng. $45.52—I am very sorry you shd. have the anxiety you speak of in money matters. To the amt you name, I have not the means of aiding you, but if there is time can I not help you by a part? I have 10 shares in the Commercial Bk. 19 in the Atlantic If they can be sold without loss they should pay 2900. which at least wd. cover the note you mention of Mr. Dodd.—(My City Bk. shares are in part pledged to the Savings Bk. for security) But as it always takes time to sell them, I see not how they can avail you at this distance & short period. I will however send this scrip (29 shares) to Abel Adams tomorrow morn. with instructions to sell it immediately on receiving orders from you to do so. I will not tell him to sell it at once, lest it should be too late even so, & I should lose an advantageous investment in vain. But my present thought is to offer you merely what facility you can make out of 29 shares lying subject to your order in hands of B, A, & Co. The terms are punctual payment of interest of $2900. at 6 percent. It is my living & I depend on this income 1 April, & 1 October. And for the sake of wife & child I should ask the landed security you offer.

P.M. I have been into the Concord Bank just now & learned that Bank stock does not command par values now, so that my offer is less good than I supposed & the sale of them now & the reconversion of the money into scrip again when the emergency is over cannot be effected without loss. I regret that in my great ignorance of business I know not how best to proceed & conclude to repeat my proposition on last page. I will put the scrip tomorrow with Barnard Adams & Co subject to your order. If it can help you, use it; & I shall rely on you to put me in as good condition as I am now, so soon as you can; i. e. in something which I consider as good as Boston Bk. stock. But you are a very naughty boy not to have informed me of this earlier that I mt. acquaint myself with the facts & whether I could not be of use.

We are all well. We received the letters of C[harles]. C. E[merson]. My Lectures are begun with as yet uncertain success—Next week I can tell you what. The boy Wallie well & sends love to Willie Love to Susan

Yours affectionately Waldo E

To Amos Bronson Alcott, March 24, 1837

Concord 24 March 1837

My dear friend,

I exceedingly regret the unfavorable notice of the book on the school in the Advertiser & that miserable paragraph of the Centinel. The latter contains its own antidote. The former might injure the school with the timid & inquiring. As soon as I came to town from Salem where I was, I endeavored to see Mr [Nathan] Hale, to ask if he would receive a paragraph of comment on his own, but he was not at his office all the forenoon. I have written him today & enclosed a plain paragraph such as I thot he could & would print Monday; but I do not know. I hate to have all the little dogs barking at you, for you have something better to do than to attend to them: but every beast must do after its kind, & why not these? And you will hold by yourself & presently forget them. Whatever you do at school or concerning the school, pray let not the pen halt, for that must be your last & longest lever to lift the world withal. And if you would compare chapters of accidents with celebrated men, go read the paper on Mirabeau by Carlyle in the new Westminster Review. It is all thunder & admonishes us of the might that in us lies, even in depression & under the frowns of the incapable. You are so deeply grounded in God that I shall not fear for you any loss of faith in your ends by opposition, but I do not want these people to hurt the school for the moment. But you will bide your time & with views so large & secular can better afford to wait than other men. Look at my Mirabeau again.

I talked with Dr Channing. I found him just to your character, wholly; but staggered by your opinions, & as I think not just to your powers. I told him so, & told him I was sure he had never heard you converse like yourself, that I was sure you two did not meet as men, but stood on uneven platforms. And he was very good natured & seemed willing to hear & know. I shall be in town Monday or Tuesday & mean to bring back your *astonishing* MSS & come & see you.

Yours affectionately,
R. W. Emerson.

To The Editor Of The *Boston Daily Courier,* APRIL 2 OR 3, 1837

To The Editor Of The Courier:

Sir,—I have seen in a Courier of last week, a severe notice of a book lately published in this city called, "Conversations on the Gospels." In that work, a passage or two occurs, which, separated from the connexion of the book, might give great uneasiness to many readers. Precisely these passages one of the daily papers selected, and dragging them out of the protection of all the philosophy and religion that hedged them round, held them up to pointed censure in its columns. These unlucky sentences,—innocent enough to the reader of the whole book,—were copied with horror into another paper, and now again have kindled the anger of your correspondent, and even your known urbanity has failed you, Sir, for a moment.

In behalf of this book, I have but one plea to make,—this, namely,—Let it be read: Any reasonable man will perceive that fragments out of a new theory of Christian instruction, are not quite in the best place for examination, betwixt the price current and the shipping list. Try the effect of a passage from Plato's Phaedo, or the Confessions of St. Augustine in the same place.

Mr. Alcott has given proof in the beautiful introduction to this work, as all who have read it know, to a strong mind and a pure heart. A practical teacher, he has dedicated, for years, his rare gifts to the science of education. These Conversations contain abundant evidence of extraordinary power of thought either in the teacher or in the pupils, or in both. He aims to make children think, and in every question of a moral nature, to sent them back on themselves for an answer. He aims to show children something holy in their own consciousness, thereby to make them really reverent, and to make the New Testament a living book to them.

Mr. Alcott's methods cannot be said to have had a fair trial. But he is making an experiment in which all the friends of education are interested. And I ask you, sir, whether it be wise or just, to add to the anxieties of his enterprise, a public clamor against some detached sentences of a book, which, as a whole is pervaded with original thought and sincere piety.

R.

TO WILLIAM EMERSON, JULY 10, 1837

Concord, 10 July, 1837—

Dear William,

On Saturday I stopped in Boston on my return from Plymouth and saw Mr Sohier who informed me that the final decree of the court on my claims on the Tucker estate was entered during the last week, and that in the course of a week probably a final distribution of the property to the several heirs might be made, save the annuties. But Mr Sohier had a great deal to say about your project of investing a portion of the principal. He took a deal of pains to impress me with the prudence (since I do not hope to increase my estate, and it is as he said only enough to live upon,) of not diminishing or risking the capital. Lend or give, he said, all your income, & live like an anchorite that you may, but do not touch the stock. He said you & he would probably differ entirely in opinion as to the judiciousness of the N. Y. investment. He apologised for volunteering his advice so strenuously but seemed to feel that what he had so kindly & laboriously gained for me he should be sorry to see slip away. He has indeed behaved very friendly to me, after a world of tedium & pains, charging me only $50.00 a fee wholly disproportionate to any other I have paid. Mr Sears, he said, he shd. charge three or four times so much, but absolutely refused to accept more. I therefore promised him that I would give so much weight to his counsel as to set it fairly before you. At the same time, I told him that the attitude in which he now saw you, was wholly unjust to your character & habits, for you were never before a speculator, & probably never would be again, but were the most discreet & honest of men. When I came home to Abel Adams, he expatiated on the same string.

I see, of course, the general propriety of their view. As I hope to put my leisure to high uses, I do not wish to put the good deodand which secures it, at hazard. I do not like so well the new relation of debtor & creditor as the old one brother; and in case of your death, I should not think it happy that I or my heirs should be drawing every thing that could be gotten from your wife & children. I should therefore be very glad rather to be made available to you for temporary aids or for sums within my income, than for any considerable & lasting investments.

But I have already intimated these facts & told you that if after you had considered them, you still adhered to your proposition, I would put myself in your hands. I am of the same mind still, only expecting that you will revise the matter in the new aspect which the new times have given it.

The amount of property to be paid me very soon is $11674.49. It is to be paid in stocks of the City, the Massachusetts, & the Atlantic Banks. All these stocks are now low, and, I heard on Saturday, all rising. Of course every thing we can scrape from income must be taken in preference before the necks of the good geese are wrung. Perhaps I can contrive to continue the loan for 1 July until October, or longer. But what I wish first, is to know exactly the sums you have yet to raise. Are the $2348. yet to be paid? When? & have you any means? Tell me what is the utmost you wish from me? What is the least? and then I will try the farthest that quiddling will do.

You will think I give the full importance to the affair, but such is the way of those who seldom trade.

I am getting well after being unusually weak & indisposed. We had a fine time at Plymouth where George Bradford loves his friends like an angel and follows them like their shadow. But Waldo [manuscript mutilated] caught cold & made the end of the visit & the return anxious by his coughing wheezing rattling lungs. He seems better & will escape fever we trust. Aunt Betsey is here. Mother & Lidian send abundant love to Susan Willie & you as doth your affectionate brother

Waldo.

To Margaret Fuller, August 17, 1837

Concord, 17 Aug. 1837—

My dear friend,

Mr Alcott & Mr Hedge have been here & only left me this morning or I should have written to you yesterday, at Providence. It will give Lidian & myself much pleasure if you will come back with us from Cambridge on Φ. B. K. day, & give us what time you can afford. Our plan now is to have a meeting here of Mr Hedges Club on the day after Φ. Beta—and who knows but the wise men in an hour more timid or more gracious may crave the aid of wise & blessed women at their session. I will not certainly engage for them to break down any rules or expectations, but you shall gentilize their dinner with Mrs Ripley if I can get her, and what can you not mould them into in an hour! My mother & Elizabeth Hoar are absent at Waterford: they will be home again soon. We will see you at Cambridge & there agree how we can return. Your affectionate servant,

R. W. Emerson.

To Thomas Carlyle, November 2, 1837

Concord,
2 November, 1837

My dear Friend,—Mr. Charles Sumner, a lawyer of high standing for his age, and editor or one editor of a journal called *The Jurist,* and withal a lover of your writings, tells me he is going to Paris and thence to London, and sets out in a few days. I cannot, of course, resist his request for a letter to you, nor let pass the occasion of a greeting. Health, Joy, and Peace be with you! I hope you sit still yet, and do not hastily meditate new labors. Phidias need not be always tinkering. Sit still like an Egyptian. Somebody told me the other day that your friends here might have made a sum for the author by publishing *Sartor* themselves, instead of leaving it with a bookseller. Instantly I wondered why I had never such a thought before, and went straight to Boston, and have made a bargain with a bookseller to print the *French Revolution.* It is to be printed in two volumes of the size of our American *Sartor,* one thousand copies, the estimate making the cost of the book say (in dollars and cents) $1.18 a copy, and the price $2.50. The bookseller contracts with me to sell the book at a commission of twenty per cent on that selling price, allowing me however to take at cost as many copies as I can find subscribers for. There is yet, I believe, no other copy in the country than mine: so I gave him the first volume, and the printing is begun. I shall take care that your friends here shall know my contract with the bookseller, and so shall give me their names. Then, if so good a book can have a tolerable sale, (almost contrary to the nature of a good book, I know,) I shall sustain with great glee the new relation of being your banker and attorney. They have had the wit in the London *Examiner,* I find, to praise at last; and I mean that our public shall have the entire benefit of that page. The *Westminster* they can read themselves. The printers think they can get the book out by Christmas. So it must be long before I can tell you what cheer. Meantime do you tell me, I entreat you, what speed it has had at home. The best, I hope, with the wise and good withal.

I have nothing to tell you and no thoughts. I have promised a course of Lectures for December, and am far from knowing what I am to say; but the way to make sure of fighting into the new continent is to burn your ships. The "tender ears," as George Fox said, of young men are always an effectual call to me ignorant to speak. I find myself so much more and freer on the platform of the lecture-room than in the pulpit, that I shall not much more use the last; and do now only in a little country chapel at the request of simple men to whom I sustain no other relation than that of preacher. But I preach in the Lecture-Room and then it tells, for there is no prescription. You may laugh, weep, reason, sing, sneer, or pray, according to your genius. It is the new pulpit, and very much in vogue with my northern countrymen. This winter, in Boston, we shall have more than ever: two or three every night of the week. When will you come and redeem your pledge? The day before yesterday my little boy was a year old,—no, the day before that,—and I cannot tell you what delight and what study I find in this little bud of God, which I heartily desire you also should see. Good, wise, kind friend, I shall see you one day. Let me hear, when you can write, that Mrs. Carlyle is well again.

R. Waldo Emerson

For Henry David Thoreau, May 2, 1838

I cordially recommend Mr Henry D. Thoreau, a graduate of Harvard University in August, 1837, to the confidence of such parents or guardians as may propose to employ him as an instructer. I have the highest confidence in Mr Thoreau's moral character and in his intellectual ability. He is an excellent scholar, a man of energy & kindness, & I shall esteem the town fortunate that secures his services.

R. Waldo Emerson.

Concord, May 2, 1838.

To Thomas Carlyle, May 10, 1838

Concord,
10 May, 1838.

My dear friend,

Yesterday I had your letter of March. It quickens my purpose (always all but ripe) to write to you. If it had come earlier, I should have been confirmed in my original purpose of publishing "Select Miscellanies of T.C." As it is, we are far on in the printing of the two first volumes (to make 900 pp.) of the papers as they stand in your list. And, now I find, we shall only get as far as the 17th or 18th article. I regret it, because this book will not embrace those papers I chiefly desire to provide people with; and it may be some time, in these years of bankruptcy & famine, before we shall think it prudent to publish two volumes more. But Loring is a good man & thinks that many desire to see the sources of Nile. I, for my part, fancy that to meet the taste of the readers we should publish *from the last,* backwards, beginning with the paper on Scott, which has had the best reception ever known. Carlyleism is becoming so fashionable that the most austere Seniors are glad to qualify their reprobation by applauding this review. I have agreed with the bookseller publishing the Miscellanies, that he is to guarantee to you on every copy he sells, $1.00; and you are to have the total profit on every copy subscribed for. The retail price to be $2.50; the cost of the work is not yet precisely ascertained. The work will probably appear in six or seven weeks. We print 1000 copies. So whenever it is sold, you shall have 1000 dollars.

The French Revolution continues to find friends & purchasers. It has gone to New Orleans, to Nashville, to Vicksburg. I have not been in Boston lately, but have determined that nearly or quite 800 copies should be gone. On the 1 July I shall make up accounts with the booksellers, & I hope to make you the most favorable returns. I shall use the advice of Barnard, Adams, & Co in regard to remittances.

When you publish your next book I think you must send it out to me in sheets, & let us print it here contemporaneously with the English Edition. The eclat of so new a book would help the sale very much. But a better device would be, that you should embark in the Victoria steamer, & come in a fortnight to New York, & in 24 hours more, to Concord. Your study armchair, fireplace & bed long vacant auguring expect you. Then you shall revise your proofs & dictate wit & learning to the New World. Think of it in good earnest. In aid of your friendliest purpose, I will set down some of the facts. I occupy or *improve,* as we Yankees say, two acres only of God's earth, on which is my house, my kitchen-garden, my orchard of thirty young trees, my empty barn. My house is now a very good one for comfort, & abounding in room. Besides my house, I have, I believe, $22 000. whose income in ordinary years is 6 per cent. I have no other tithe or glebe except the income of my winter lectures which was last winter 800 dollars. Well, with this income, here at home, I am a rich man. I stay at home and go abroad at my own instance. I have food, warmth, leisure, books, friends. Go away from home,—I am rich no longer. I never have a dollar to spend on a fancy. As no wise man, I suppose ever was rich in the sense of *freedom to spend,* because of the inundation of claims, so neither am I, who am not wise. But at home I am rich,—rich enough for ten brothers. My wife Lidian is an incarnation of Christianity,—I call her Asia—& keeps my philosophy from Antinomianism. My mother—whitest, mildest, most conservative of ladies, whose only exception to her universal preference of old things is her son; my boy, a piece of love & sunshine, well worth my watching from morning to night; these & three domestic women who cook & sew & run for us, make all my household. Here I sit & read & write with very little system & as far as regards composition with the most fragmentary result: paragraphs incompressible each sentence an infinitely repellent particle. In summer with the aid of a neighbor, I manage my garden; & a week ago I set out on the west side of my house forty young pine trees to protect me or my son from the wind of January. The ornament of the place is the occasional presence of some ten or twelve persons good & wise who visit us in the course of the year.—But my story is too long already. God grant that you will come & bring that blessed wife, whose protracted illness we heartily grieve to learn, & whom a voyage & my wifes & my mothers nursing would in less than a twelvemonth restore to blooming health. My wife sends to her this message; "Come, & I will be to you a sister." What have you to do with Italy? Your genius tendeth to the New, to the West. Come & live with me a year, & if you do not like New England well enough to stay, one of these years (when the History has passed its ten editions & been translated into as many languages) I will come & dwell with you.

I gladly hear what you say of [John] Sterling. I am foolish enough to be delighted with being an object of kindness to a man I have never seen & who has not seen me. I have not yet got the Blackwood for March, which I long to see, but the other three papers I have read with great satisfaction. They lie here on my table. But he must get well.

As to Miss Martineau I know not well what to say.[22] Meaning to do me a signal kindness (& a kindness quite out of all measure of justice) she does me a great annoyance—to take away from me my privacy & thrust me before my time, (if ever there be a time) into the arena of the gladiators, to be stared at. I was ashamed to read, & am ashamed to remember. Yet as you see her, I would not be wanting in gratitude to a gifted & generous lady who so liberally transfigures our demerits. So you shall tell her, if you please, that I read all her book with pleasure but that part, & if ever I shall travel west or south, I think she has furnished me with the eyes.—Farewell, dear wise man. I think your poverty honorable above the common brightness of that thorn crown of the great. It earns you the love of men & the praises of a thousand years. Yet I hope the angelical Beldame all-helping all-hated has given you her last lessons & finding you so striding a proficient will dismiss you to a hundred editions & the adoration of the booksellers.

R. W. Emerson

I have never heard from Rich who you wrote had sent his account to me. Let him direct to me at Concord.

A young engineer in Cambridge by name McKean volunteers his services in correcting the proofs of the Miscellanies & he has your Errata—for love of the reading. Shall we have anthracite coal or wood in your chamber? My old mother is glad you are coming.

To WILLIAM EMERSON, MAY 12, 1838

Concord, 12 May, 1838.

Dear William,

Your last letter troubled me somewhat because I supposed you had before fully understood the narrow limits of the aid I had just now offered; namely the use without interest of my private (say) 265.00 till *the first July only,*

---

22. Harriet Martineau, in her Retrospect of Western Travel, *praised the "American Scholar" address for its "philosophical reverence for humanity," and called Emerson a scholar who is neither narrow nor bookish and a thinker without being "solitary, abstracted, and unfitted for the time" ([London: Saunders and Otley, 1838], 2:106, 204).*

because it is my household purse for bread & meat & shoes—& of course, cannot be renewed: and secondly, the borrowing at the Concord Bk. for such short terms as banks lend. and which I supposed might give you time to borrow permanently elsewhere. Today it occurred to me that possibly the Savings Bank here might lend. Luckiest of thoughts. They answered that they could only lend in June & September and for June the existing applications would absorb all their funds. In September, they probably could lend me $500.00. Then I applied to the Bank to lend me 3, 4, or 500. until September telling them how I expected to pay them by borrowing of the Savings when the note is out; (The two institutions have one Cashier) and if the Savings cannot then lend why Bank must renew its loan until Savings can. Of course, I changed my Bank application from 200 to 500. Today being Saturday & not a discount day, the President preferred to give me 300. & on Monday refers to the Directors the request for 200. more. On this sheet is the draft for $300. on the Oriental Bank, which the Cashier told me would be worth a premium in New York. I lodge my Commercial Bank Scrip as security. Mr Biddle cannot be better pleased with his than I with my financiering. I will get two hundred on Monday if I can & when the Savings Bk. lends, I will borrow for one or two years. But you understand that on the 1 July accurately I need every dollar of my private loan. What a cross wind that is about the house assessment to come just now! Well brave men have ridden out rougher gales and if you can only keep your independence on the Messrs Haven, & your health what matters a little pinching & anxiety. Mother & Lidian send their love Yours affectionately,

Waldo

To Margaret Fuller, May 24, 1838

Concord, 24 May, 1838.

My dear friend,

I am today in such a ghostlike state all attempts at audible speech being frustrate that I am fain to flee from the remembrance of my hiant Stygian inarticulations by recurring to all the life & wit at a distance to cheer myself withal. I had your good letter which both gave us a holiday & promised us another. I am, further, maugre all my self-knowledge, all my humility, & all my other Christian virtues, delighted with being the object of so much good will & such memorable compliments If the givers could only remember them as long as the receivers! Since then, Henry Hedge has spent a couple of days with me, & left all kind messages. for you. [John S.] Dwight came with him & staid longer & we got as far as speech, this time. I think I told you once that between him & me, as chances so often with those we reckon intelligent, a good understanding was supposed not certified. But I find him now a very accurate mind active & genial with fine moral qualities though not of great reading or variously cultivated. What is a great satisfaction too, he has his own subject, Music. A man must never ask another for an aim. I was at Medford the other day at a meeting of Hedge's Club. I was unlucky in going after several nights of vigils & heard as though I heard not & among gifted men I had not one thought or aspiration. But Alcott acquitted himself well & made a due impression. So the meeting was good. I nevertheless read today with wicked pleasure the saying ascribed to Kant that "detestable was the society of mere literary men." It must be tasted sparingly to keep its gusto. If you do not quit the high chair, lie quite down, & roll on the ground a good deal, you become nervous & heavyhearted. The poverty of topics the very names of Carlyle Cambridge Dr Channing & the Reviews become presently insupportable. The dog that was fed on sugar died. So all this summer I shall talk of chenangoes. & my new garden spout that is to be. Have you heard of my pig? I have planted forty four pine trees. What do you think will my tax be this year?—and never a word more of Goethe or Tennyson.

Lidian is very well & my mother & Elizabeth. My boy defies your regrets at his departed beauty; he is as handsome as Walden pond at sunrise & the darling of the whole school house opposite my gate where he is shouldered & chaired every fine day at recess.

We are all specially pleased with the expectation of the coming of you & Caroline Sturgis a week from next Saturday for so it sings in our augury. I will get well tomorrow. Bring a portfolio full of journals letters & poems. And here I will not omit what was a main purpose of this letter to thank you heartily for the pleasure I found in reading your paper in the Western Messenger on Letters from Palmyra. Its superior tone its discrimination & its thought make it remarkable & indicate a golden pen apt for a higher service hereafter. Mr Dwight begged me to ask you to bring with you the letters of Bettina B[rentano]. to lend to him. Of course, you will not, if only by contingence needful to your studies. Lidian, though not present, loves you.

R. W. Emerson.

Of Waldo's Sanscrit, take this specimen; he has just bro't me a flower under the name of "liddel powup."

To Amos Bronson Alcott, June 28, 1838

Concord, 28 June, 1838

My dear Sir,

I have read Psyche twice through some pages thrice; and yet am scarcely able to make up my mind on the main question submitted to me—Shall it be published? It is good and it is bad; it is great, & it is little. If the book were mine, I would on no account print it; and the book being yours, I do not know but it behoves you to print it in defiance of all the critics.

The general design of the book as an affirmation of the spiritual nature to an unbelieving age, is good; the topics good; the form excellent, & of great convenience divided into natural chapters by the topics that arise. The ideas out of which the book originates are commanding; the book holy. There are in it happy & valuable thoughts; some good sentences; some happy expressions. It is the work of a man who has a more simple & steadfast belief in the soul, than any other man; and so it tends to inspire faith.

Yet with these merits, I read the book with a certain perplexity, arising, I think, from a want of unity of design in the book itself.

Is it a Gospel—a book of exhortation, & popular devotion?

Or, is it a book of thought addressed to cultivated men? Which of these two?

1. Is it a Gospel? It evinces on every page great elevation of character, & often assumes, in the thought & expression, the tone of a prophet. Well; let it preach, then, to the chidden world. There is sin & sorrow enough to make a call; & the preacher believes in his heart. And, in this view, I certainly would not criticise this scroll any more than that of Habbakuk or Jeremy; but would sit & take with docility my portion of reproof.—But, as I read, it

departs from that character. To the prophetic tone belongs simplicity, not variety, not taste, not criticism. As a book of practical holiness, this seems to me not effective. This is fanciful, playful, ambitious, has a periphrastic style & masquerades in the language of Scripture, *Thee & Thou, Hath & Doth.* The prophet should speak a clear discourse straight home to the conscience in the language of earnest conversation.

Such portions of the book, however, as are written in this vein, lead me to say, that, you only can be the judge whether the publication may be suspended.

But, as I have intimated, other passages come, & make the book amenable to other laws.

2. Is it a book of thought addressed to literary men? I looked for this; for the writing of a philosopher seeing things under a scientific point of view, & not for a book of popular ethics. But this it is not. In the first place, the degree in which the former element is introduced vitiates it for a scientific book; the condition of which, is, that an observer quite passionless & detached—a mere eye & pen—sees & records, without praise, without blame, without personal relation—like a god. But there runs throughout this book, as already intimated, a tone of scarcely less than prophetic pretension; which, however allowable in a gospel, is wholly out of place in philosophy, where truth, not duty, is the question. Or, in the second place, if such a tone is ever admissible, one thing only can justify it, to wit, the actual contributing a large amount of unknown truths, say, as Kepler, as Newton did. But this is not your object. The book neither abounds in new propositions nor writes out applications of old truth in systematic detail to existing abuses. This, you know, is my old song. I demand your propositions; your definitions; your thoughts (in the stricter use of that term, i. e. a new quality or relation abstracted); your facts observed in nature; as in solid blocks. But your method is the reverse of this. Your page is a series of touches. You play. You play with the thought: never strip off your coat, & dig, & strain, & drive into the root & heart of the matter. I wish you would, with this my complaint before you, open at a few pages of Psyche at random & see what a style this is to baulk & disappoint expectation. To use a coarse word—tis all stir & no go.—There is no progress. I become nervous at the patience with which my author husbands his thought—plays about it with a variety of fine phrases, each of which alone were elegant & welcome, but together, are a superfluity. Meantime, the present Ideas of Truth, of Love, of the Infinite, give, I allow, a

certain grandeur to the whole. I thought, as I read, of the Indian jungles, vast & flowering, where the sky & stars are visible alway, but no house, no mountain, no man, no definite objects whatever, & no change, or progress; & so, one acre in it is like another, & I can sleep in it for centuries. But mortal man must save his time, & see a new thing at every step. Moreover, I think it carries to an extreme the aphoristic style which is only good if dense with thought, but we must not multiply into many sentences. what could better be condensed into one. It is graceful when intermingled with a freer speech, but by itself is short & chopping like a cord of chips for a cord of wood.

If, therefore, the book is to be addressed to men of study, I think it demands;

1. The most resolute compression almost to a numbering of the sentences 1, 2,3,4, as they are *things*, & casting out the rest. Of course, enrich it by any additional pertinent matter, withholding nothing because it is a *pearl*, which seems to be intimated p. 289

2. The omission of all passages conveying this prophetic pretension, of which I have spoken; and shading or modifying all passages that are too obvious personal allusions, until they speak to the condition of all, or at least of a class. The author's Ego must be the human Ego, & not that of his name & town. (Some of these personal allusions seem to be in in pp. 198, 212, 259, 260, 289, &c)

3. The dropping of the Scriptural termination, as in do*eth*, work*eth;* of thou & thine; and the earnest adoption of the language you speak in your own house; and the more sparing use of several words which, through the MS., recur too frequently; such as, *Ideal*, image, ministry; genius; worthy, worthier, worthily; belie; mission; &c.

Thus far, my dear sir, go my axe & knife. You will see in the accompanying sheets a few verbal or local criticisms that occurred as I went along. I have also made an experiment or two at a condensation of one of your paragraphs to see if it would not gain thereby. I have indicated some passages that struck me more favorably. There are many such which I have not indicated. The book of Innocence, I esteem least valuable. I think the second & fourth books the best.

And now having said all these things in the relentless use of my critical bludgeon, I frankly tell you that I doubt entirely my jurisdiction in the matter; I may do great harm by inducing you to with hold the volume; & if you feel any promptings to print it as it stands, I will immediately &

cheerfully make my contract as I proposed with Messrs Metcalf & Co. In the circumstances, if you should feel undecided, I should think it best that some third person should be selected by you who should read it & decide.

Or if you would like to make trial of the public pulse, why would it not do to print one or two or three chapters successively & anonymously in one of the magazines, & if they drew such attention as you liked, then you would print the book with more confidence.

Your friend,
R. W. Emerson.

To Margaret Fuller, June 28, 1838

Concord 28 June 1838

My dear friend,

It is high time the Manuscript should go back & I am going to Boston tomorrow so although I am ashamed to have nothing to put in it in acknowledgment of your frank kindness I shall send it. I found no dulness in it but very sprightly sense & criticism & brave determination, & truth throughout. One thing struck me, the absence of abstract propositions. If I write too many aphorisms I think you write too few. Once, twice, or thrice at the most is a thought abstractly stated. Thus "One must live a great deal to think a very little." And yet perhaps that is formal merely, for on consideration I perceive that I owe several *things* to the book quite new to me & as a history of fine things, I prize it very highly. Can I see it again? & again as it grows? So shall I have presence in two places. It makes me very rich to think of your good will & bountiful construction of me & my flourishes, & certainly I will try never to do wrong any more. Friends on any high footing are surely very noble possessions and make the earth & the starred night, as you walk alone, more divine.

I have great pleasure in writing this letter for I have just closed a very irksome piece of work namely a faithful criticism of Psyche which I send home to Mr Alcott tomorrow with a letter of three sheets, & annotations beside. I had few smooth things to say but I hope he will feel the truth as better, as I should my brother's strictures. It seems very strange any should exist, be able to force their way out of nothing,—but perfect creatures. Of so many fine people it is true that being so much, they ought to be a little more, & missing that, are naught. The omnipresent tragedy of More & Less never moves us to such sadness as in these unperfect favorites, the missing window in Aladdins palace. Yet it is very impertinent in us to whine or to pity them. They never feel the want. In the compensations of nature they have some mysterious amends not to mention that they reward our condescension by reciprocal pity.

I had a very pleasant acquaintance say of two hours or less, with Caroline Sturgis whilst she stayed here, & that is a great deal too. I shall see her hereafter as an old acquaintance. She surprised me into very pleasant thoughts by her questions. For a hermit I begin to think I know several very fine people. I shall owe much to the picture sketches you showed me when here; that is, if I should come to see any pictures within a twelvemonth or so before the fine possibilities that floated before me are clear gone out of memory. But no, a genuine hint furnished out of a picture ought to serve us not in pictures only but also in seeing the lights of the landscape or the shadows on my study-wall. Yes and to an infinity of applications beside. I hope you are learning to live with moderation. I hate to think you should be the servant of a visiting-card-box. Ten people are a great deal better than a hundred. Put that down for one of the promised mottoes. I send you neither poem nor catalogue for Elizabeth Hoar has had hands too full with Sarah S.'s needs than that I could mention it to her to copy verses. When they come I will try to send the tardy book list. Send me I entreat you Mr Alcotts List of thoughts; and mine: Our *Thus far no farther.*

My mother, Lidian, & my talking boy are very well & send you—the two first—their love. I am working hard in the garden My tomatos rhubarb & potatoes do excellently but the bugs eat up my vines, if I do not watch the young entomologues.

Yours,

R. W. Emerson.

I design to send the Journal by the cars tomorrow (Friday) addressed to care of H. Fuller Esq, City Hotel. If it come not inquire with instant diligence at your side, & I will at mine. Has my kind friend Mr F. any subscribers to Carlyle. We finish printing this week.

TO HENRY WARE, JULY 28, 1838

Concord, July 28, 1838.

What you say about the discourse at Divinity College, is just what I might expect from your truth and charity, combined with your known opinions. I am not a stock or stone, as one said in the old time; and could not but feel pain in saying some things in that place and presence, which I supposed might meet dissent, and the dissent, I may say, of dear friends and benefactors of mine. Yet, as my conviction is perfect in the substantial truth of the doctrine of this discourse, and is not very new, you will see, at once, that it must appear to me very important that it be spoken; and I thought I would not pay the nobleness of my friends so mean a compliment, as to suppress my opposition of their supposed views out of fear of offence. I would rather say to them,—These things look thus to me; to you, otherwise. Let us say out our uttermost word, and be the all-pervading truth, as it surely will, judge between us. Either of us would, I doubt not, be equally glad to be apprized on his error. Meantime, I shall be admonished by this expression of your thought, to revise with greater care the "Address," before it is printed (for the use of the Class), and I heartily thank you for this renewed expression of your tried toleration and love.

Respectfully and affectionately yours,
R. W. E.

TO MARY MOODY EMERSON, SEPTEMBER 1, 1838

Concord, 1 September, 1838.

My dear Aunt,

We are all very glad to know by your letter to Elizabeth [Hoar] where you are, & by it & by Mr Farrar that you are pleasantly placed for the good Autumn that is coming. The months bring us few papers on their wings so much prized as your letters whose reading we owe to the charity of the two Elizabeths,—of Concord & Waltham. I have had Lockhart's seventh volume by me for some time & can send it if you wish it The sixth & seventh volumes have a deep manly interest, & show the best that Britain in these days can do for one who chooses actual Britain for his god. I have a different & very noble book which came to me lately Landor's Pericles & Aspasia that I know will interest you; for it is a Corinthian metal mixed of taste, wit, & heroism, in equal parts. I regret, I cannot send it immediately, even if I knew how to send,—as it is craved by several persons to whom it is successively promised.

I send you by mail a copy of my address lately to the Divinity School which if it offend you brings at least this mitigation that it offended good men at Cambridge also. We shall do the less harm? The Dartmouth Oration [on "Literary Ethics"] will be out in a day or two, & shall to Windham also. If you cared for Carlyle, his Miscellanies in two volumes are entirely at your service, to keep, or to give away, or to burn. But I will not send it, if you hate the sight. It is to most readers much less offensive than the History. I have had great satisfaction lately in Heeren who with great learning gathers up all the facts of oldest India, Egypt, Persia, Phœnicia; and, what is to me a recommendation, without philosophy. Such a book stimulates us to more thought than one where all is inferred & said for you. It is a rare book here,—5 large vols. and was loaned me.

We have had a short visit from E[lizabeth]. H[oar]. lately who spent a week in the house. We try to persuade her that she had better come & live with us the alternate months for at home with all their virtues, they do not understand her or leave her Peace. She bids me give you her love & say she shall write you in a few days. My little boy has passed out of the little heaven of his daily health into the Purgatory of teething & is miserable for a few days: Mother is very well. Lidian is well also. She was sadly checked by your calling her eager expressions of love & respect, "adulation," and knew not what to write; and indeed no creature in the universe is more incapable of that same: but she still reads with gladness all that comes from you to others. There is a young man at Cambridge named Jones Very who I think would interest you He studies Shakspear now & will presently finish & probably publish an Essay on S. and from a point of view quite novel & religious. He has been here twice yet be not uneasy on that account for he does not agree to my dogmatism. Henry Thoreau has just come, with whom I have promised to make a visit, a brave fine youth he is—Your affectionate nephew

To Margaret Fuller, September 28 and 29, 1838

Concord, 28 Sept. 1838—

My dear friend,

When you next are as munificent to me as you have now been (which I hope may happen next week) & the letter overruns the stingy single sheet, send it to the Concord Stage Office, Earl Tavern, & it will come to me forthwith. Only last night did I get your letter of the 17th, not having been in Boston this long time; &, until now, my good friends knew not how to send it. But it came in good hour to me as I got home—wife & I—from Elizabeth & Mary's *first party* at Waltham. Who could resist the seduction of cousinship on such an occasion & place, though he abhorred parties as Nature the vacuum? I heartily thank you for such a casket of brilliants as kept my eyes open a good hour of midnight. It was a golden week, & I delight from my corner to know that such society is no fable, can & does organize itself in this country, & so near—out of elements I have seen with eyes. Such rare pictures as you paint, make me suspect my own habitual skepticism in respect to the stimulus of society to be merely mine & springing from want of organs which others have. I contemplate with joy the meeting & relation of all the parties you name, without the least desire of nearer participation. Their very names daunt me, if the question be to go & seek them. Proportionally I prize in you & them the social faculty, & find my ample amends in the talent & good will that sketched for me the golden week. And I like very well that you should send me portraits of my friends & neighbors also, Mrs R[ipley]. & Dr. F[rancis]. I have thought this week that there is no cheaper way of giving great pleasure than when we simply describe from our centre the disk & direction of the ray of the surrounding orbs. How formidable it looks beforehand,—to estimate a fine genius, & write down his value in words— Gibbon, Rousseau, or whosoever. Yet the whole charm of the historical part of Goethe's Farbenlehre, and very charming it is, consists in the simplest statement of the relation betwixt the several grandees of European scientific history & John Wolfgang—the mere drawing of lines from John to Kepler, from John to Roger Bacon, from John to Newton. The drawing of this line is for the time & person a perfect solution of the formidable problem, & gives pleasure when Iphigenia & Faust do not, without any cost of labor comparable to Iphigenia & Faust. These of yours are excellent likenesses,—that of Mrs R. express & admirable; & Dr F's only wants a compensation, which exists, but which the occasion did not show.

Lately I have wished to be a scholar. Reading a little history & seeing how entirely the value of the facts is in the classification of the eye that sees them, I nourish the day dream of study, & what Bacon calls *longanimity.* I say, go to now, I will read, & watch, & know something. I verily believe that a philosophy of history is possible out of the materials that litter & stuff the world, that would raise the meaning of Book & Literature. Cause & effect, cause & effect forever! If we spend a little labor on a poor work of our own will, vamping & bolstering a silly theory we have resolved shall stand, we must not fret if we outlive it. If we bestow a great deal of labor, on God's facts, with the affection of a naturalist, our work shall have nature's colossal proportions.

29 Thus far wrote I yesterday afternoon but was too late for the mail, & so let my sheet lie. I have many things to say & little space left. Have you heard of the calamity of poor Very, the tutor at Cambridge? He is at the Charlestown Asylum & his case tho't a very unpromising one. A fortnight ago tomorrow—I received from him his Dissertation on Shakspeare. The letter accompanying it betrayed the state of his mind; but the Essay is a noble production: not consecutive, filled with one thought; but that so deep & true & illustrated so happily & even grandly, that I account it an addition to our really scanty stock of adequate criticism on Shakspear. Such a mind cannot be lost.

I have just had a naturalist here, John Lewis Russell, who showed me many things & suggested many an inestimable person in American society. Should you not like to live in a world where every pedlar was a philosopher a wit or a naturalist? Not I, & yet I wish Mr Russell would come to see me once every year. I thank you heartily again for your picture gallery of 17 September, but if nobody may see it I wish you would not paint so fine. I never showed any line of yours to Miss Peabody, nor, as I remember, to Mrs Brown: (who is however a person of uncommonly fine instincts—little cultivated.) I shall surely show this letter to one or two pair of eyes for whom it was meant though you knew it not. But I shall not print it in the Yeoman's Gazette. I am very happy in the happiness of your Muse in the Island in her poetry & wit. and shall be glad of all the scraps you will communicate. I heard you were sick & was the more refreshed by the letter which seems to say you are not. Waldo is very well. Lidian sends her love: & my mother.

R. W. Emerson.

To Henry Ware, Jr., October 8, 1838

Concord, October 8, 1838.

My dear Sir,

I ought sooner to have acknowledged your kind letter of last week, and the Sermon it accompanied. The letter was right manly and noble. The Sermon, too, I have read with attention. If it assails any doctrines of mine,—perhaps I am not so quick to see it as writers generally,—certainly I did not feel any disposition to depart from my habitual contentment, that you should say your thought, whilst I say mine.

I believe I must tell you what I think of my new position. It strikes my very oddly, that good and wise men at Cambridge and Boston should think of raising me into an object of criticism. I have always been,—from my very incapacity of methodical writing,—"a chartered libertine," free to worship and free to rail,—lucky when I could make myself understood, but never esteemed near enough to the institutions and mind of society to deserve the notice of the masters of literature and religion. I have appreciated fully the advantages of my position; for I well know, that there is no scholar less willing or less able to be a polemic. I could not give account of myself if challenged. I could not possibly give you one of the "arguments" you cruelly hint at, on which any doctrine of mine stands. For I do not know what arguments mean, in reference to any expression of a thought. I delight in telling what I think; but, if you ask me how I dare say so, or, why it is so, I am the most helpless of mortal men. I do not even see, that either of these questions admits of an answer. So that, in the present droll posture of my affairs, when I see myself suddenly raised into the importance of a heretic, I am very uneasy when I advert to the supposed duties of such a personage, who is to make good his thesis against all comers.

I certainly shall do no such thing. I shall read what you and other good men write, as I have always done,—glad when you speak my thoughts, and skipping the page that has nothing for me. I shall go on, just as before, seeing whatever I can, and telling what I see; and, I suppose, with the same fortune that has hitherto attended me; the joy of finding, that my abler and better brothers, who work with the sympathy of society, loving and beloved, do now and then unexpectedly confirm my perceptions, and find my nonsense is only their own thought in motley. And so I am

Your affectionate servant,
R. W. Emerson.

To Margaret Fuller, November 9, 1838

Concord, Nov. 9–1838

My dear friend,

I send Coleridge and greet you well in your fine studies. Except something in Johnson's Preface; and Lamb; Coleridge's seems to me the first English criticism on Shakspear that was at all adequate—and now it seems only introductory. Shakspeare has not done growing yet: and a great day it will be for any mind when it has come to put Shakspeare at a true focal distance. When you come here I will show you Very's two dissertations,—one on the general subject, & the other on Hamlet,—which are pretty great criticism. Very has been here himself lately & staid a few days confounding us all with the question—whether he was insane? At first sight & speech, you would certainly pronounce him so. Talk with him a few hours and you will think all insane but he. Monomania or mono *Sania* he is a very remarkable person & though his mind is not in a natural & probably not in a permanent state, he is a treasure of a companion, & I had with him most memorable conversations. I shall not fail to make diligent endeavors to secure you a residence here in our village, if you shall hold your good purpose of dwelling among us next spring. We are all very well; Lidian has broken out lately into wild hospitality & given two parties, or soirées, (if to avoid the equivoque we must go a-begging for a word which I hate,). We all desire you to rest & to get firm health

R. W. Emerson.

TO ELIZABETH HOAR, FEBRUARY 24, 1839

Concord, 24 February, 1839.

Dear Elizabeth,

I wish you will make the best haste you can, to come & see your little niece. A daughter was born to us this morning at eight o'clock. Lidian did not expect it quite yet: but the little soul was impatient for light & action, and came this morning, with all favorable circumstances. She seems to be a fair round perfect child, & very well contented with her new estate. Lidian is very well. Mrs Thoreau spent the night with her, & Miss Prescott is here today. And now we both claim the performance of your promise to come & take care of us all, whilst Lidian keeps her chamber.

I hope you will be able to come immediately, tomorrow afternoon. Do, if you can. Lidian sends her love & entreats you to love her babe; which, today, she calls Ellen.

Your affectionate brother,
Waldo E.

TO MARGARET FULLER, MAY 1 AND 2, 1839

Concord, 1 May, 1839.

My dear friend,

It is high time you should hear from me were it only to acknowledge the kind word I got through the Post Office—*weeks ago*—, I fear it is;—but I always postpone the letters that are easy & pleasant to write, for those letters that, like duns, do threaten & chide to be answered. But you was not very generous; you named topics & did not treat them; and have accustomed me to expect fine pictures so that I grieve when they are withheld. I want chiefly to know how the experiment Chapter goes forward. On our beginnings seems somehow our self possession to depend a good deal, as happens so often in music. A great undertaking we allow ourselves to magnify, until it daunts & chills us and the child kills its own father. So let us say; self possession is all; our author, our hero, shall follow as he may. I know that not possibly can you write a bad book a dull page, if you only indulge yourself and take up your work somewhat proudly, if the same friend bestows her thoughts on Goethe who plays now at the game of conversation & now writes a journal rich gay perceptive & never dull. But there are such & so many examples of fine wits overlaid by their subject, writing quite characterless & mechanical books,—so that the vivacious books are now only the exceptions,—that almost no wit seems to me sufficient guarantee against this mischance, & I dare hardly trust the very Muses. It seems too so very high a compliment to pay to any man, to make him our avowed subject, that the soul inclines to remunerate itself by a double self trust, by loftier & gayer sallies of joy & adventure, yes & I think by some wicked twitting & whipping the good hero himself, as often as occasion is, by way of certifying ourselves that he still keeps his place there & we ours here, and that we have not abated a jot of our supremacy over all the passengers through nature. *They* must all be passengers whosoever & howsoever they be, & *I* the inmate & landlord, though I were the youngest & least of the race. On these conditions, no subject is dangerous: all subjects are equivalent.

I began my letter on May day, but Mr Alcott is here and the usurping conversation breaks in on all writing so that it has become 2d May the while. His towering genius nobody has yet done justice unto, & he in his habits, in his whole day's conversation does not do justice to it. He is strangely attracted to the form, the circumstance of his life, expects events and external success, more a great deal than such a soul should, and whilst he talks about these I think it the old hum-drum I have met a hundred times. But the instant he seizes a general question he treats it so greatly & godlike, himself so self poised, eagle winged, & advancing, that he takes himself out of all competition or comparison & folds in his bosom far epochs & institutions. I must think very ill of my age & country, if they cannot discover his extraordinary soul.

Beautiful blows the south wind this P.M. Lidian is very well & sends her love to you The babies thrive every hour. Elizabeth, I saw yesterday. Neither she nor any of us have yet attained to see the Allston Gallery. I go next week. Henry Hedge is, I suppose, in Cambridge & Mrs Ripley promises to bring us all together at her house. I will add Alcott to the party if I can, unless you straitly forbid me.

Your friend
R. W. Emerson.

My brother William begs me to inform you that Mr Osborn was not in the house of Mr Jacob Barker or in his employ, he was a broker for Mr J. B.'s son

To Margaret Fuller, June 7, 1839

Concord, 7 June, 1839.

My dear friend,

I am so much in your debt by the Eckermann book that I must at least acknowledge the gift. The translating this book seems to me a beneficent action for which America will long thank you. The book might be called— Short way to Goethe's character—so effectually does it scatter all the popular nonsense about him, & show the breadth of common sense which he had in common with every majestic poet, & which enabled him to be the interpreter between the real & the apparent worlds. The Preface is a brilliant statement— with which I have no quarrel, but great contentment & thanks instead. I like it for itself, & for its promise. That you can write on Goethe, seems very certain in all this decision and intelligence; and moreover, you will give us the comfort of good English, as the whole book declares. So speed the pen, & do not let the 'dear five hundred' steal away all your summer. My own habits are much mended this summer. I rise at 6 o'clock, find my coffee in my study, & do not see the family until 12 or 1 o'clock. I like the result so well that I shall persevere. Though these precious & guarded mornings are not always better than others, yet if a day comes when you are fit for writing, this system secures its entire benefit; and it gives every day a better chance, as it defends you from being untuned. Unless the weather is so warm that I think you cannot write, I think I shall not come & see you before Commencement; so will you save one day. And if you properly use this edifying example among your friends, it may convert many. But truly I am sorry that you have sat down in a place so inaccessible to me, for there is a great deal to be said that will never be uttered if it must wait a semester,—and on gravest matters too. Well, you must be the more generous in writing to me.

We expect Caroline Sturgis tomorrow evening. Elizabeth Hoar is coming here presently to walk with Mary Russell & I am to show them my woods. Lidian & my babies two and my mother are well, & L. begs to be loved by you. I shall have a book full of Essays ready by autumn, and your Biography will not be half written. Mr Phillips came here the other day with Mrs Follen; talked very well for a good hour, & expressed the liveliest concern for your health. Does she take care of herself? Does she now take & follow advice?—Do you? I hope his anxiety is altogether groundless, & am your friend,

R. W. Emerson.

To Harrison Gray Otis Blake, August 1, 1839

Concord, Aug. 1, 1839.

My dear Sir,

I must seem very ungrateful for the confidence of your letter to have waited near a fortnight to answer it, but I have been for a few weeks back so miserably languid that I would not bestow my debility & indolence where I would rather express congratulation & courage. I am stronger again & take advantage of this reviving morning & west wind to say what it seems to say to you & to me.

You certainly apprehend the true position of the clergyman in relation to the community at this moment, & have described it with great precision. And the perception of the difficulties, in an honest man fast becomes the solution of them, and I infer from what you say at last of your present purposes that you see light already. That light, I am sure, is a greater selfreliance,—a thing to be spoken solemnly of & waited for as not one thing but all things, as the uprise & revelation of God. We talk of the Community & of the Church but what are these but what we let them be? When we are faithful we know them not—absorbed with our own thoughts sure of our duties we cumber ourselves never with the church, and in fact all that is alive in the church is with us. As soon as we step aside a little & consult history & facts straightway society grows a great matter & the soul a small circumstance. It seems to me that this holds not only in the whole, but in the particular. I have never known anyone fail as a preacher except by his own fault. Such is our happiness in the times & the country that the community will forgive any contradiction of their opinions so that they have a man to their preacher. But he must not be a half man or a third of a man addicted to dictionaries or pictures or sleep, & bringing them bad sermons half written, & doing ill the services he had rather forbear. His nerves must tingle first that their nerves shall tingle. If he gives them only the thoughts that have agitated his heart, they cannot choose but shake & fear. There is then no longer the "opinion of the community" to consider. One thought is now the community, of which you & I & all are members.

Man seems to me the one fact: the forms of the church & of society—the framework which he creates & casts aside day by day. The whole of duty seems to consist in purging off these accidents & obeying the aboriginal truth. I dare not say these things lightly—, I feel the shame of saying them at all.—The simplicity of Duty accuses our distracted & unholy lives. But I wish to say—at least, let our theory not be slavish; let us hope infinitely; & accustom ourselves to the reflection that the true Fall of man is the disesteem of man; the true Redemption self trust; the growth of character is only the enlargement of this, and year by year as we come to our stature we shall inherit not only forms & churches & communities but earth & heaven.

I really did not mean when you asked me for a letter to write a homily, but I have lived so much alone lately, that I find I acquire a sort of habit of generalizing or treating all things in the lump; and all my own compunctions & my resolutions take this turn of resisting the overweight of Society. I am sure I shall be able to show you better to what a range of topics this view extends, & perhaps make it look more amiable if you would come & spend a day with me when you are at leisure. I see that I have not said the obvious things that we are all now seeing—the changes that impend over the profession & the economical considerations that devolve on the individual. I think such changes promise a new culture & new powers to the man & so to the preacher but will not broach so large a subject at the end of a sheet. Your friend & servant,

R. W. Emerson.

To Margaret Fuller, August 14 and 16, 1839

Concord, 14 August, 1839.

My dear friend,

I write to beg you to roll up those several MSS, if they are detached,—or to write them out to the end, if they are in a book, that I may have them as viaticum in the mountains. I have written to Mr Bradford to decide between the 23d & the 26 Augt for the commencement of our journey. Now do not let me thus fail to see Recamier of whom I have heard somewhat that would make me grieve not to look upon her face though from afar. We shall not be absent much more than a week. Be a good countess now & weave such fast nets about your guest as to imprison her during your good pleasure.

16th Thus far had I written when a sudden wind blew me to Boston & kept my feet so busy there, that I had not a half hour to seek out Mr [Samuel Gray] Ward in, who had challenged me to go & see Day & Night. A young Southron whom I knew in college used to look in the glass on Saturdays, & say, "It is not one of Mr Coffin's good looking days" & so omitted his visits. Neither was it one of Boston's goodlooking days yesterday; I saw neither picture poem man angel or resurrection, not even the Botanic Garden; nothing but booksellers bankers & drays.

And pray who & what is the spectacle you so oracularly announce? Is it book or is it woman? I am very credulous on fine days & can still believe in the riches of nature And yet I have with my eyes transpierced so many goodly reputations & found them paper, that when the wind is east I make a covenant with my ears never to hearken to a new report. And yet to such a herald all faith is due, and at all events I will sit with meek expectation.—I am sorry you missed Mr Alcott who still gropes after & explores the irreconcileable light of your star. It is plain he cannot let you rest until he know whether this undeniable lustre be planetary or solar, kindred or alien. *I* surrender at discretion: he is sure of me: *You*, it seems, still pique his curiosity, and in riding to Concord perhaps he fancied that if worst came to worst, his party would be two to one when he got here. I understood him, when he was here, that he still intended to persuade you to ride so far. You must not baulk his astronomical intentions—I shall really look for you every day till next Friday. Undoubtedly too he wishes to see through your eyes his own present position & prospects. His position is to common sense perplexed & painful enough, but the power of the man is such that he can make (I will not say you, but) me suspend my common sense in his favor—for a time; And in talking with him I cease to urge my beggarly elements of justice & prudence against his justice & prudence of a loftier strain. Yet when all is said, I relapse into earnest wishes that he would work a small farm for his bread and dictate his gospel thence. And the last time we talked, he said, had things looked to him in the spring as now, he would have accepted such an offer, as was indeed made to him. If anything should prevent you from coming hither, as

I trust nothing will, will you not send to No 2 Winthrop Place that Olympian pacquet as soon as next Wednesday or Thursday morning—& I will send there for it on Thursday P.M. if, as is probable, I set out from Concord *via* Lowell, Friday Morng. In our house we are all well, & Lidian & my mother desire much to see your face. Elizabeth was here just now & required me to send her love to you.

R. W. Emerson.

Carlyle is gone to Scotland & will there he says consider intently the visit to America, & decide. He seems to halt between the impulse to commence a new book at home, or Lectures in America. He has seen Webster & written a masterly sketch of our Titan whom he prefers to all men. If Mr H. Fuller comes to Boston when I am here it would give me much pleasure to see him. I fear I have given him much trouble respecting Carlyles accounts.

To Margaret Fuller, September 6, 1839

Concord, 6 Sept. 1839

Gratitude for so generous a letter must even set my pen to the sheet though the Muse alone knows & not yet the mortal man what things can be said. I am glad to share this approximate ubiquity that comes of corresponding with two or three pairs of eyes, say, one pair in London, & one at Jamaica P. The account of the Davis Music, & especially the tender lines you have quoted accuse my indolence which has hitherto lost me the fairest opportunity of hearing the same strains. I remember I did lately see mountains & the snow on their summits, beheld the genesis of the cloud and the sources of great streams, but the New Hampshire landscape though savage & stern does not reach the surprising & overhelmimg grandeur that in some spots of this world draws a man as by the hair of his head into awe & poetry. Yet the Profile Mountain in the Franconia Notch is a pleasing wonder. Sternly that grave old Sphinx gazes eastward with an expression that may be called great & natural. The lofty Bust is a fine subject for verse, but I was not in the mood. Five miles further from Littleton, I went to see what is called "The Flume" as wild a piece of scenery as I ever chanced to see though the describable facts are nothing but a small stream pouring through a granite ravine over which at one point a natural bridge is made by a big stone which has fallen in to the top of the chasm. But we lowlanders so rarely see the aboriginal forest that here where it is in wildest wonder & strength it ennobles the strange spectacle & really healed me who had set out from Littleton that morning a sick man & doubtful whether I could crawl after my party, for we walked a mile in to the woods at this point. Mr Bradford moreover found this wild place the Gretna Green of Botany, for it was the den of all cryptogamous plants. These mountains what magnets they are to the eye! They are like men of genius too in society, the coachman the grocer do not ask their names, do not see them, but each ingenuous religious soul sees them & sees nothing else. You are accustomed to converse when you please. I suppose you hardly believe in the Tides of conversation, but I ride fifty miles & my tongue is dumb within my mouth, & then without visible cause it is loosed again. We had a good deal of various talk in this journey but I think it turned chiefly on this sad sore text of Reform that so wearies the eardrum of this country. We heard in one place blue sulphureous preaching, in another the most ominous shaking of Unitarian husks & pods out of which all corn & peas had long fallen, the men were base the newspapers base &, worse, the travellers did not find in themselves the means of redemption. I see movement, I hear aspirations, but I see not how the great God prepares to satisfy the heart in a new order of things. No church no state will form itself to the eye of desire & hope. Even when we have extricated ourselves from all the embarrassments of the social problem it does not please the oracle to emit any light on the *mode* of individual life. A thousand negatives it utters clear & strong on all sides, but the sacred affirmative it hides in the deepest abyss. We do not see that heroic resolutions will absolve men from those *tides* which a most fatal moon heaps & levels in the moral emotive & intellectual nature. It looks as if there was much doubt, much waiting, to be endured by the best,—the heavy hours.—Perhaps there must be austere elections & determinations before any clear vision of the way is given. Yet eternal joy & a light heart dwell with the Muse forever & ever and the austerity of her true lovers can never be harsh moping & low. Today is ours & today's action; why should I cumber myself with these morrows, these optical illusions, these cobwebs of time?—I hoped not to read lectures again, at least not in the old way but I am about determining to do that chore once more. Elizabeth Hoar & her friend have got away Bettine once more, or I would make up a pacquet. Now I will send this by mail & you shall expect the pacquet Monday or Tuesday—

I read somewhere that facts were the stuff of letters, but I lead the life of a blade of grass in mere wind & sun & have no other events than the weather. We are all very well in this house & all glad of the prospect of your visit here on a coming Sunday. I shall come to Roxbury as soon as you notify me, if not before; and so, farewell.

R. W. Emerson.

TO SAMUEL GRAY WARD, OCTOBER 3, 1839

Concord October 1839

My dear Sir

I received your letter & its enclosed verses immediately, though I acknowledge it so tardily. I write so slowly I believe because I liked the message so well & was willing to wait for a select hour to reply to what took my fancy with the most agreeable surprise. Certainly your friend [Ellery Channing] in these lines & in the very few others of his that I have seen, goes to the very end of the poetic license, & defies a little too disdainfully his dictionary & logic. Yet his lines betray a highly poetical temperament and a sunny sweetness of thought & feeling which are high gifts; and the voluminous eloquence of his Spenserian stanza is by itself an indication of great skill & cunning. Perhaps I judge the lines too partially for their subject & the affectionate playfulness with which he treats it, as indeed I was very happy to meet this kindness:— but I know the lines would have pleased me if addressed to a third person: & I think bad praise much more annoying than criticism. I entreat you not to despond of your friend's success because of any temporary inaction Wit & imagination, Milton said, are tender maidens,—and Margaret Fuller showed me not long ago a sentence of De Vigny—that the poet must lose a good many days in order to have a great one. Especially this sacrifice of good time seems almost universal among the contemplative class of persons in this country;—the very children are infected with skepticism & ennui. Even the active except in a very few happy instances seem to owe their health & efficiency to their foregoing the exercise of thought & the creative arts, and the more fortunate must wait for the less with a sure trust in the remedial force of nature. We outgrow our friendships and undoubtedly where there is inequality in the intellect must resign them but in a society as imperfect as ours I think no man can afford to spare from his circle a poet as long as he can offer so indisputable a token as a pure verse of his communion with what is highest in Being. It is possible that my love of these gifts might enable me to be useful to your friend if once I knew him. As lovers of English poetry we should certainly have common ground enough to meet upon though of course I should wish to meet him in the first instance only as scholars. I am not often in general society but if I should have an opportunity of making his acquaintance I will not fail to embrace it.

To Margaret Fuller, October 16, 1839

Concord, 16 Oct. 1839

My dear friend,

I have now your letter, the Portfolio, & the Commentary safely here. Bettina I sent to Mr Ward after peeping at the sortileges. I have also still glittering in new laid strokes of memory the fair image of your friend—so that I dare not defer writing to you any longer lest I incur new debts. These great ones I cannot acquit otherwise than by joyfully incurring them which to noble givers is a recompense. I would not on any account have failed to see Anna Barker that very human piece of divinity in whom grace goodness & wit have so constitutional a blending that she quite defies all taking to pieces. But my old slowness of sight which you deride still vexes me in this instance: I want more time & more opportunities to arrive at any steady vision of a person so excellent & so remote too from my usual experiences. But I shall see you next Sunday, & will tell you my dreams & guesses then. The Portfolio is very rich and I intended not to read any notes upon it until I had studied it over with unlearned eyes; my Mohawk eyes should see it without any tuition from Corinna; but when I had glanced at all, once, I seized the manuscript & read it through. I doubt not it will prove a good electuary,—at all events will make me more reverent. Certainly I read with great interest & respect. And yet these drawings need no praise. There is however such concentration of merits in every great work which though successive experiences in the mind of the master were primarily combined in his piece that we ought to come to the picture twenty times in the light of twenty new views of man & nature. How many times in the course of a year we entertain a thought that puts a new face on all things These are the strokes of our clock announcing that we have

The Letters

lived into another hour of True time But this the Master also had done, this divine realism rending the thin rinds of the Apparent he also had shared— could it be that his philosophy laid no color on the pallet, exalted no form? We are ready to allow the physical education to his eye new skill in costumes accessories & effects of light & shade but the difference between picture & picture is the age of thought in the painter's mind. Yet I had no idea when I begun, of writing notes on Painting & will stop here. I have a letter yesterday from Carlyle, but he has come to no decision about his American Visit. He talks pleasantly of Sterling who he says writes him that he has written a review of C. which will appear in the next Westminster. We shall have 500 copies of his new edition of Fr. Revn. here in Boston by next week I suppose. I should heartily greet any such Journal as would fitly print these Journals of yours, & will gladly contribute of my own ink to fill it up. But unless Mr. [George] Ripley would like to undertake it himself, or unless you would, I see not that we are nearer to such an issue than we have been these two years past. W[illiam]. [Henry] Channing would be a good conductor, if he were here. But next Sunday I hope you will not disappoint me but come; or Saturday night, will you not? And we will talk of these things or far better if any there be. Elizabeth Hoar is a great loss to me. She is gone to N. York. I miss her the more now this portfolio is come. We are all very well & little Ellen is worth a household.

R W Emerson

To William Emerson, November 8, 1839

Boston Nov 8 1839

Dear William,

C. C. Little & Co inform me that the 500 copies of Carlyles Fr. Revolution which we have expected for some time have now arrived per ship Ontario at New York. The duties & costs they compute at near $400. to be paid or promised at N.Y. Custom House before they can come here. In these circumstances will you go to Mr Charles Goff, Broker, Maiden Lane, who acts for Little & Brown & be with him bondsman for the payment of these duties, half of which amount is to be paid in 60 & half in 90 days. We depend on the sale of the book to pay this sum when it becomes due. If the book shall not sell fast enough, I must pay it otherwise. Anyhow, I will send you the amount when it is demanded. As no invoice has been sent us it becomes necessary to inclose to you a letter of Carlyle's which states the exact cost to him to be £95. This I understand C. C. L. & Co is a material fact, which will make the duties less than usual, as this cost is unusually small, in consequence of the largeness of the edition.

I see no personal risque to you in this affair & so boldly ask your attention to it. I understand that I & not Little & Co. am accountable to the Custom House for the whole amount. It may not exceed $300.

Your affectionate brother
R. W. Emerson

The knave teamster has gone to Boston again with my receipt in his pocket whereat R N Rice is heartily ashamed.

To Margaret Fuller, November 27, 1839

Concord, 27 Nov. 1839—

My dear friend,

You are as good—it may be better than ever—to your poor hermit. He will come yet to know the world through your eyes. The pacquet came safe & afforded me a rich hour last eve. on my return from a dubious society. I plunge with eagerness into this pleasant element of affection with its haps & harms. It seems to me swimming in an Iris where I am rudely knocked ever & anon by a ray of fiercer red, or even dazzled into momentary blindness by a casual beam of white light. The weal & wo is all Poetic—I float all the time—nor once grazed our old orb. How fine these letters are! I do not know whether they contented or discontented me most They make me a little impatient of my honourable prison—my quarantine of temperament where-from I deal courteously with all comers, but through cold water,—and while I get a true shrift of their wit, do now think I get never an earnest word from them. I should like once in my life to be pommelled black & blue with sincere words. That is the discontent—But all the while it seems to me that superlatives must be bought by many positives—for one eagle there go ten dollars—and that these raptures of fire & frost which so effectually cleanse pedantry out of conversation & make the speech salt & biting, would cost me the days of wellbeing which are now so cheap to me, yet so valued—I like no deep stakes—I am a coward at gambling—I will bask in the common sun a while longer; especially that this middle measure offers,—good friends who will recite their adventures in this field of fate. I will at least pay the price of frankness & you shall command such narratives in turn as a life so sequestered by temperament affords. I would send you Sterling's note today but that Mrs Ripley will be here Friday to whom I show all my playthings—and possibly you will come yourself.

I joy in your studies & success. Continue to befriend me. My blue eyed boy is ill today threatened with fever. I hope we shall have done with sickness some time.

R. W. E.

Ward has given me Endymion! I delight much in what I dreamed not of in my first acquaintance with you—my new relations to your friends.

To Mary Moody Emerson, December 22, 1839

Concord, 22 December, 1839—

My dear Aunt,

We have had no direct word from you for a long time until Ralph T. H. came to us the other day with a short note for Mother, and now we have learned through Uncle Samuel R. the death of Mrs [Phebe] Ripley. She loved all her blood so well, and had from nature so much dignity of manners & of form, that though I have never spent but a few hours in her company, I feel as if I had lost a great deal of *my family,* in her death. Mother who has recently lost her own sister Mrs Ladd, is greatly interested in this event, & has carefully gathered in the past months all the details that came from Waterford. Her departure will cut one of your own ties to your present abode, and as men say the apple never falls far from the stem, I shall hope that another year will draw your eyes & steps to this old dear odious haunt of the race

I am in these weeks busy at my old trade of lectures. I read them once a week in the Temple in Boston and my subject is, The Present Age. I hoped before I began this course to have got a volume of Essays ready for printing that I might send you a fair copy of some of the reveries of the past winters. But now you must wait for it until the summer. But you must come to Concord for we have a great deal that will interest you here. Elizabeth [Hoar], in the first place, who is more to us day by day, our court of appeal, our clear intelligence, the purest conscience and the constant heart. Now she is still at New London but in a few days will be here. Then we have Henry Thoreau here who writes genuine poetry that rarest product of New England wit. Thomas Carlyle we have not yet bodily but a good letter every two or three months from his eloquent & loving pen. and one day we look surely to see him. A few weeks since I had a letter from John Sterling his friend who wrote the Sexton's Daughter which I sent you in Blackwood. Then Margaret Fuller a most accomplished & growing woman sends us all manner of fine poetry & intelligence & in summer charms us by her varied & gay conversation. Lately I have one or two more valued additions to my little circle of friends—One whom I spent part of two days with in September last—Anna Barker—you should certainly have seen—a vision of grace & beauty—a natural queen— just returned from Europe, where as here she received incense every day, in all places, which she accepts with high glee & straightway forgets from her religious heart. She is the very heroine of your dreamed romance which you related to Charles & me at Elm Vale once. I would I could awaken your curiosity & old kindness in our fortunes & circumstance here. I could easily add to the little inventory of jewels that enchase our hearthstone. But for the hearthstone itself. Mother is not quite so well lately as usual, but firm & unchanged compared with any one else of her age. Lidian is not so well content with Waldo & Ellen but that she would be happier if she could show them to you. I assure you Ellen is a lovely child. Lidian has just been writing some pages out of my first lecture this winter to amuse you withal. The pages gravitate to you by the best right. We see S[arah]. A. R[ipley]. from Waltham every few weeks, and she certainly depends on living in Concord one day. I think you will not be able to resist us alway. We are talking of a certain wonderful Journal which is to be born next spring or summer of which Margaret Fuller is to be Editor & Geo Ripley Geo Bancroft & twenty more, whereof I am least, to be contributors.[23] I shall write to Thomas Stone, the moment the thing has certainty to crave the aid of his Platonic Muse.

---

23. *A reference to what would become the* Dial.

The good Grandfather at church this morning signified his own desire to be remembered in the prayer as a mourner for Mrs R. He is in usual health. Lidian says that she heartily wishes she had somewhat that would surely interest you & she would write but contents herself with joining her love to Mother's & that of your affectionate

R. Waldo E.

To William Ellery Channing the Younger, January 30, 1840

Concord Jan. 30, 1840.

My dear Sir,

Your friend Samuel G. Ward, whom though I have known but a little while I love much, has communicated to me a number of your poems which I have read & still read with great delight. I have seen no verses written in America that have such inward music, or that seem to me such authentic inspiration. Certainly I prize finished verses, which yours are not, and like best, poetry which satisfies eye, ear, heart, & mind. Yet I prize at such a dear rate the poetic soul, that where that is present, I can easily forgive the licence & negligence the absence of which makes the merit of mediocre verses; Nay, I do not know but I prefer the first draught and to be present at the secret of creation before the vamping & rhetoric are used which are but "the brushers of noblemen's clothes." I wish to thank you for the happiness I find in these little pieces which are wise, true & bold. Then, I wish that they should not be shut up any longer in the portfolios of a few friends but should be set free to fly abroad to the ear & heart of all to whom they rightfully belong.

Next Spring or Summer, probably in July, we are to have a new Journal of better promise than any we have had or have in America;—of which Margaret Fuller is to be the Editor. I have promised her my best assistance to write & to collect for her. And I have no plan so much at heart as to secure these poems for publication. I ask you to give me liberty to select some of these pieces & print them in her Journal. I think if you shall permit it, I could easily accompany them with a running commentary in prose that would shade the abruptness & fragmentary character of several pieces & give them due perspective. I feel my dear Sir, that the pleasure I take in this poetry fully authorizes me to make this request. My quarrel with our poets is that they are secondary & mimetic but you may thank the god for intuition & experience

I should regret that you have left Boston without my having seen your face if I did not feel a confidence that you will return hither with new stores of nature & life gathered for the language of your thought. Whenever you revisit your friends in these parts will you not count among them

Your affectionate servant
R. W. Emerson.

To Margaret Fuller, February 21, 1840

Concord, 21 February, 1840

I am sorry you should so hurry away from me, as this fragment of a visit seems only argument for a long conversation. With all my taste for letters, I have not the least disposition to write what I would say. So I will forget my yesterdays and hear only the sweet bells of today. And there is good reason; for the blue birds have come back this morning to their box on my barn; and the sun & air are so bland & good that I found a little summer in the edge of a woodlot an hour ago. Waldo watches the diminution of the snow banks & speculates on the probability of early grass for his Horse—that omnipresent Animation whereof & whereto his world is made.

These spring winds are magical in their operation on our attuned frames. These are the days of passion when the air is full of cupids & devils for eyes that are still young; and every pool of water & every dry leaf & refuse straw seems to flatter, provoke, mock, or pique us. I who am not young have not yet forgot the enchantment, & still occasionally see dead leaves & wizards that peep & mutter. Let us surrender ourselves for fifteen minutes to the slightest of these nameless influences—these nymphs or imps of wood & flood of pasture & roadside, and we shall quickly find out what an ignorant pretending old Dummy is Literature who has quite omitted all that we care to know—all that we have not said ourselves.

I value too the mnemonics of this season. I see plainly the old school-entry where at this time of year we spun tops and snapped marbles; and I see as plainly that life then was calendared by moments & not by days, threw itself into nervous knots or glittering hours, even as now, & not spread itself abroad an equable felicity. I am sure too that I see myself then more than now to have been a surprised spectator of the show,—less whole, less selfpossessed than now when I am not whole & not self commanding—But though the day be Syrian, I will not drivel any more, but subscribe myself your friend with good intention of writing speedily again.

R. W. E.

To Thomas Carlyle, March 18, 1840

New York
18 March 1840

My dear friend,

I have just seen the steamer "British Queen" enter this harbor from sea, and here lies the "Great Western" to sail tomorrow. I will not resist hints so broad upon my long procrastinations. You shall have at least a tardy acknowledgment that I received in January your letter of December, which I should have answered at once, had it not found me absorbed in writing foolish lectures which were then at high tide. I had written you a little earlier, tidings of the receipt of your "Fr. Revolution." Your letter was very welcome, as all your letters are. I have since seen tidings of the "Essay on Chartism," in an English Periodical, but have not yet got my proofsheets. They are probably still rolling somewhere outside of this port; for all our packet ships have had the longest passages; only one has come in for many a week. We will be as patient as we can.

I am here on a visit to my brother, who is a lawyer in this city, and lives at Staten Island, at a distance of half an hour's sail. The City has such immense natural advantages, & such capabilities of boundless growth, & such varied & ever increasing accommodations & appliances for eye & ear, for memory & wit, for locomotion & lavation, & all manner of delectation,—that I see that the poor fellows that live here, do get some compensation for the sale of their souls. And how they multiply! They estimate the population today at 350,000, and forty years ago, it is said, there were but 20,000. But I always seem to suffer from loss of faith on entering cities. They are great conspiracies; the parties are all masquers who have taken mutual oaths of silence, not to betray each others secret, & each to keep the others madness in countenance. You can scarce drive any craft here that does not seem a subornation of the treason. I believe in the spade and an acre of good ground. Whoso cuts a straight path to his own bread, by the help of God in the sun & rain & sprouting of the grain, seems to me an *universal* workman. He solves the problem of life not for one but for all men of sound body. I wish I may one day send you word, or better, show you the fact that I live by my hands without loss of memory or of hope. And yet I am of such a puny constitution, as far as concerns bodily labor, that perhaps I never shall. We will see.

Did I tell you that we hope shortly to send you some American verses & prose of good intent? My vivacious friend Margaret Fuller is to edit a journal, whose first number she promises for 1 July next, which I think will be written with a good will if written at all. I saw some poetical fragments which charmed me,—if only the writer consents to give them to the public.

I believe I have yet little to tell you of myself. I ended in the middle of February my ten lectures on the Present Age. They are attended by from 450 to 500 people, and the young people are so attentive & out of the hall ask me so many questions, that I assume all the airs of Age & sapience. I am very happy in the sympathy & society of from six to a dozen persons who teach me to hope & expect everything from my Countrymen. We shall have many Richmonds in the field, presently. I turn my face homeward tomorrow, & this summer I mean to resume my endeavor to make some presentable book of Essays out of my mountain of manuscript, were it only for the sake of clearance. I left my wife, & boy, & girl,—the softest & gracefullest little maiden alive, creeping like a turtle with head erect all about the house,—well at home a week ago. The boy has two deep blue wells for eyes, into which I gladly peer when I am tired. Ellen, they say, has no such depth of orb, but I believe I love her better than ever I did the boy. I brought my mother with me here to spend the summer with William E. and his wife & ruddy boy of four years. All these persons love & honor you in proportion to their knowledge & years. My letter will find you I suppose meditating new lectures for your London disciples. May love & truth inspire them. I can see easily that my predictions are coming to pass & that having waited until your Fame was in the flood tide we shall not now see you at all on western shores. Our saintly Dr Tuckerman, I am told, had a letter within a year from Lord Bryon's daughter *informing* the good man of the appearance of a certain wonderful genius in London named Thomas Carlyle, and all his astonishing workings on her own & her friends' brains—and him the very monster whom the Doctor had been honoring with his best dread & consternation these five years. But do come in one of Mr Cunard's ships as soon as the booksellers have made you rich. If they fail to do so come & read lectures which the Yankees will pay for. Give my love & hope & perpetual remembrance to your wife,—& my wife's also, who bears her in her kindest heart & who resolves every now & then, to write to her that she may thank her for the beautiful Guido.

You told me to send you no more accounts. But I certainly shall, as our financial relations are grown more complex & I wish at least to relieve myself of this unwonted burden of booksellers accts. & long delays, by sharing them. I have had one of their Estimates by me a year waiting to send. Farewell.

R. W. E.

To Waldo Emerson, March 19, 1840

New York. Thursday.

My dear Boy,

I cannot let Alexander go to Concord without sending you a little letter, for I do not think I shall see you until you have gone to bed thirteen or fourteen times, & waked up again just as many mornings. I hope you try to do a great many things to help Mamma, now that I am away & cannot help her. I think you can help little Ellen a good deal, by bringing her playthings, & playing with her. Though I cannot see you & little sister every day, yet I see you in my mind, every day, & every night. I believe you will be glad to know the boy who brings this letter. Willie is very fond of Alexander, who knows how to do a great many things, & Willie cried many times when he found that he was going away to Concord. Though you cannot write yourself an answer to me, I wish you would tell Mamma any thing that you think about, when you are playing, & she will put the words in her letter to me.

Your affectionate father.

Providence, March 30—
Monday Night

My dear friend,

I have just read your letter & its inclosure & your note, all which were given
me at my lecture room. If the outer wall gives way, we must retire into the
citadel. I do not wish any colleagues whom I do not love, and though the
Journal we have all regarded as something gay & not something solemn, yet
were I responsible, I would rather trust for its wit & its verses to the eight or
nine persons in whose affections I have a sure place, than to eighty or ninety
celebrated contributors. So on the matter of strength I cannot regret any loss
of numbers.—But I am very sorry for Henry Hedge.[23] It is a sad letter for
his biography: he will grieve his heart out by & by & perhaps very soon, that
he ever wrote it. As I have told you, we (H. & I) never quite meet; there is
always a fence betwixt us. But he has such a fine free wit such accomplishments & talents & then such an affectionate selfhealing nature that I always
revere him & subscribe gladly to all the warm eulogies that George Bradford & the Waltham people utter. Then I owe him gratitude for all his
manifest kindness to me, though he is wrong to say he loves me, for I am
sure he does not quite. All this makes me heartily sorry for him,—but I know
he will nigh kill himself with vexation at his own letter, after a few months
be past. So that I think you must only show it to such as it instantly
concerns, & to none others; for he will certainly beg it of you again, & beg
you to forget it. It is much for him, but it is not important to the book. The
book would be glad of his aid, but it will do as well without. I rely on Mr
Ripley, as far as he has promised his assistance, then on Dwight, then on
Parker,—as perfectly intelligent artists in this kind, then on Ward, who can &
will lend his eagle wings whilst the car is yours; then on Thoreau, whom I
shall now seriously ask to give his aid; then—if this letter is strictly private—

---

24. *In response to Margaret Fuller's request that he write for the Dial, Hedge replied that
he feared to be associated with the Transcendentalists and called "an atheist in disguise,"
and he clearly expressed his disagreement with the ideas of Emerson and Alcott (see Joel
Myerson, "Frederic Henry Hedge and the Failure of Transcendentalism,"* Harvard Library
Bulletin *23 [October 1975]: 402–404).*

(and if not, scratch out the line,) on Caroline S[turgis]. who will not refuse you anonymous verses whilst she writes such as you read me; Sarah Clarke is a noble person & wrote me a noble letter & she should write; Cranch; and Ellery Channing—where is his answer to my letter? Thomas Stone—probably Hedge has now neglected to write unto. I tell you if these persons added unto You, would promise me their assistance I should think I had the best club that ever made a journal.—And yet it is very far from being my wish to urge the Journal. I have not caused it & will not cause it to be. My own book is necessarily primary with me, and the Journal, if it exist, I only wish to aid. Yet I think I will write as many pages as you wish.

Hedge's view of the matter is to me quite worthless. The poor old public stand just where they always did,—garrulous orthodox conservative whilst you say nothing; silent the instant you speak; and perfectly & universally convertible the moment the right word comes. If three or four *friends* undertake the book, I will answer for the world.—But quite another consideration is your health. You say, you are ill—If you do not feel assured of being presently better, then drop all thoughts of this work, which will necessarily confine you a good deal. Indeed you must set yourself in earnest to get well.

I read my last lecture Wednesday eve. & do not go to Boston until Thursday. I will come & see you on that day, if you say the accn. train will leave me at your door. At least that is my expectation. Yet I have said in answer to many inquiries that perhaps I would stay to the end of the week, and I may yet be challenged to do so. Another letter from Carlyle yesterday. He is prospering in all ways, & promises in another letter an account of Landor & of Heraud.

There is so much that is yet to be seen & known & loved & done in this world of ours, that I pray you to make your health your first care. Yours,

R. W. E.

To Margaret Fuller, April 21? and 23? 1840

The Introductory Essay [to the *Dial*] is written with talent & strength I find very good things in it & on a second reading am better content with it. And yet I think I will give you my impressions from the first reading, & if they are unjust I am willing to drop them.

This paper addresses the public; and explains; it refers to the contemporary criticism; it forestals objection; it bows, though a little haughtily, to all the company; it is not quite confirmed in its own purpose.

But need we have a formal Introduction? If there be need of a new journal, that need is its introduction; it wants no preface. It speaks to persons who are waiting to hear, & on topics which they are already agitating

With the old drowsy Public which the magazines address, I think we have nothing to do;—as little with the journals & critics of the day. If we knew any other Journal, certainly we should not write this. This Journal has a public of its own; its own *Thou* as well as *I;* a new-born class long already standing waiting for this voice & wondering at its delay. They stand before their doors in the highway on tiptoe looking down the road for your coming.

Neither should I like to say before-hand with any particularity what this Journal would accomplish; rather considering that every good doctrine, sentence, verse, which we shall promulgate, is the best doing & the best trumpet.

Then in common prudence the less we promise, & the less we say about our relation to other journals, the less occasion we make for bickering. The world is wide enough for sense & nonsense too.

This form of our writing, this Journal, may not continue to please us, but our thought & endeavor we know will continue to please us, & to exist. I would not therefore insist much on this enterprize but solely on the Universal aims—

I do not like the early preparation for defence & anticipation of enemies in the sentence about—"this disclaimer may be forgotten" &c. &c. Simply say, 'We do not think alike' &c but leave out this canny bit of American caution. Don't cry before you are hurt.

Why not throw into a general form what upon criticism you have to say—perhaps by enlarging your Essay on Critics? These statements concerning the modern periodical literature &c are all just, and I think would be more graceful in another essay than the Preface. The Preface might say that we write for the love of writing & for the love of each other; might say in what form you please, who we are; might say what you have here written to your possible contributors.

But it is easy to criticise, hard to write. I will not urge an objection. Print what you write without asking me & I shall doubtless find it good. Ask me, & I can find a thousand reasons *why not.* If you wish me to solve any of my own problems I would even try to write now an essay on These Men & This Work. I say this as expiation for my petulance. But if you choose to print this & set me at work in another plot I shall be in less danger and quite content.

Dialling still.—

Ought there not to be in every number of the journal a Head of "Intelligence." for the communication of foreign & domestic tidings that interest us? Mr Ripley certainly from his foreign correspondence could always furnish something. You could from yours—Where is Calvert? where is Martineau? Carlyle is pretty sure to send me some fact once in a quarter; and any good reader of the London Journals will find extraordinary paragraphs from time to time.

Now appoint Miss Peabody your committee for this department: She will draw up the little chronicle with the utmost facility & perfectly well: & shall be supplied by such rills as I have named,—not to mention all our possibilities.

In connexion with the long discourse I have written on my first sheet-on a true philanthropical Dial why will you not authorize me to ask from Edward Palmer a short contribution? I send you his little tract.

I believe I shall roll up with this, Thoreau's paper. I read it through this morning & foresee that it may give you some hesitations. There is too much manner in it—as much as in Richter—& too little method, in any common sense of that word—Yet it has always a spiritual meaning even when the literal does not hold: & has so much brilliancy & life in it that in our bold bible for The Young America, I think it ought to find a place. I wish it were shorter. But the three divisions of the piece may be marked in the typography; & nobody need read it who cannot transpierce the imagery. Besides, when one article is too long, why not print a few pages more than the rubric, that so any thing material shd. not be excluded.

There is surely time for you to send this paper back to Thoreau for any corrections: a few words I noticed, but thought I would not keep it for them.

Thursday Eve—I have kept this letter & its company thus standing now two days on tiptoe, because I wished to send you my paper on the Ellery poetry which I suppose I have nearly ended, but I will not delay the rest any longer. I send you the old rhymes you asked for—You will see I have tacked them together so as to form a sort of whole—but it is so rude & unwieldy that it is not worth preserving if you prefer to print only one of them or two at two times. It was E. H[oar]. & not I who said they wd. pass muster. Farewell & forgive my dilatoriness.

> Can you not notice Miss Peabody's Bookstore in your "Intelligence" chapter. If I had not so overwritten, I would do that also like Peter Quince or his crone who wd. play all.

To Margaret Fuller, May 8, 1840

Concord, 8 May, 1840.

My dear friend,

Next Wednesday the club of clubs meet at my house. Will you not come & see me & inspire our reptile wits. Mr Ripley said he should like to bring you. I have asked Mrs S. Ripley & Sarah Clarke. Henry Hedge, Theodore Parker, Alcott, & Henry Thoreau will certainly be here. So that you see if the main senate should not be prosperous, we can sit in committees & settle all our affairs. You shall stay Wednesday Night & on Thursday shall transact business, for by this time things have arrived at that complexity as to demand an interview. Do not fail to come, & if you come bring with you T. T. Stone's letter & his paper that Hedge tells me of. I hope ere this you have digested your chagrin concerning the Introduction I sent you Nay have fairly got Mr Ripley at work to try his hand in drafting a Declaration of Independence. When he has tried, suppose we apply to Dr Channing—indeed I would send the requisition all round the Table to every member, & then print the Dial without any, & publish the Rejected Introductions in a volume.

One grave thing I have to say, this, namely, that you will not like Alcott's papers; that I do not like them; that Mr Ripley will not; & yet I think, on the whole, they ought to be printed pretty much as they stand, with his name in full. They will be differently read with his name or without. Give them his name & those who know him will have his voice in their ear whilst they read, & the sayings will have a majestical sound. Some things are very good: for the most part, they are open to the same fault as his former papers, of being cold vague generalities. Yet if people are properly acquainted with the prophet himself,—& his name is getting fast into the stellar regions,—these will have a certain fitting Zoroastrian style. I am glad to hear your portfolio grows so rich—you will need the less aid. I cannot find any fit topic for an exercitation, & wish you may not want me. Give me news of yourself, give me news of your friends: Your friend,

R. W. Emerson.

To John Sterling, May 29, 1840

Concord, Mass. 29 May, 1840.

My dear Sir,

I have trusted your magnanimity to a good extent in neglecting to acknowledge your letter received in the winter, which gave me great joy, & now lately your volume of poems, which I have had for some weeks. But I am a worshipper of Friendship, & cannot find any other good equal to it. As soon as any man pronounces the words which approve him fit for that great office, I make no haste; he is holy; let me be holy also; our relations are eternal; why should we count days & weeks. I had this feeling in reading your paper on Carlyle, in which I admired the rare behaviour, with far less heed to the things said,—these were opinions, but the tone was the man. But I owe to you also the ordinary debts we incur to art. I have read these poems & those still more recent in Blackwood with great pleasure. The ballad of Alfred delighted me when I first read it, but I read it so often to my friends that I discovered that the last verses were not equal to the rest. Shall I gossip on & tell you that the two lines "Still lives the song though Regnar dies

Fill high your cups again"

rung for a long time in my ear and had a kind of witchcraft for my fancy. I confess I am a little subject to these aberrations. The "Sexton's Daughter" is a gift to us all and I hear allusions to it & quotations from it passing into common speech which must needs gratify you. My wife insists that I shall tell you that she rejoices greatly that the man is in the world who wrote this poem. The "Aphrodite" is very agreeable to me, and I was sorry to miss the "Sappho," from the Onyx Ring. I believe I do not set an equal value on all the pieces, yet I must count him happy who has this delirious music in his brain, who can strike the chords of Rhyme with a brave & true stroke; for thus only do words mount to their right greatness, and airy syllables initiate us into the harmonies & secrets of universal nature. I am naturally keenly susceptible of the pleasures of rhythm, & cannot believe but that one day—I ask not where or when—I shall attain to the speech of this splendid dialect, so ardent is my wish; and these wishes, I suppose, are ever only the buds of power: but up to this hour, I have never had a true success in such attempts. My joy in any other man's success is unmixed. I wish you may proceed to bolder—to the best & grandest melodies whereof your heart has dreamed.— I hear with some anxiety of your ill health & repeated voyages. Yet Carlyle tells me that you are not in danger. We shall learn one day either how to prevent these perils of disease, or to look at them with the serenity of insight. It seems to me that so great a task is imposed on the young men of this generation that life & health have a new value. The problems of reform are losing their local & sectarian character & becoming generous profound & poetic.—If, as would seem, you are theoretically as well as actually somewhat a traveller, I wish America might attract you. The way is shorter every year & the object more worthy. There are three or four persons in this country whom I could heartily wish to show to three or four persons in yours, and when I shall arrange any such interviews under my own roof I shall be proud & happy. Your affectionate servant,

R. *Waldo Emerson.*

To Margaret Fuller, June 21, 1840

Concord 21 June

I am sorry that your fine holidays should be marred by editorial vexations—I am quite content to await on the hither side of Print, a ghost of three months probation, my investiture with flesh of types, & hope some seeds of sin may mortify & preexistently end in this interim. But I shall grieve if you are not content with what is printed. Can we not explode in this enterprize of ours all the established rules of Grub Street or Washington Street? leave out all the ballast or Balaam and omit to count pages? One hundred thirty six pages! Our readers, who, I take it, are the sincere & the sensible, will not ask, Are there 110 or 150 pages? but Is there one page? Every dull sentence vulgarizes the book and when we have inserted our gems from the papers of love & friendship we shall feel that we have wronged our angels by thrusting them into unfit company. But you do not mean that this number is not good. It is & shall be. Only with such friends as we have, and willing as three or four of us are to put the heart into what we write & sleep not, I think we ought not to be lax in our conditions of admittance for such a reason as to fill pages. Ellery Channing has granted the verses, which fills me with joy. They are what I wanted the Journal for.—He grants them on condition his name is not communicated to any. So we dear souls must seal our six or eight lips. They shall save the next number, shall they not? Then Ellen Hooper's *Poet, & Wayfarers,* and a few of Caroline's Spartan metres which I shall gladly elect & edit, as I was commissioned, shall enrich & ensoul the book.

Yesterday I went to Boston & found that Ward was ill with fever & ague You have told me nothing of it. He wrote me that he was not well, but I suspected nothing serious. His mother sent me a message, but I learned nothing exactly. He should be healed by a charm. Tell me all you know about him. I shall send to inquire, but I fear he may not write. I tried to see Channing, but he was not at home. You may be sure that Lidian & I will open our doors & hearts too to Anna & you, or to you & Anna, whensoever you shall make your joint Progress into the meadows. A woman in every part beautiful is a *practical poet,* is she not? awakening tenderness & hope & poetry in all whom she approaches. Write me all you can of Anna.

I am just finishing my chapter on Friendship and find a note in my old journal which points at a letter written to you a long time since which I shall beg again for the sake of a sentence as soon as I find the date. I am interrupted & have probably omitted some important matters—

Yours R. W. E.

To Margaret Fuller, August 4, 1840

Concord, Aug. 4, 1840

I fear you have accused me of great negligence in retaining the MSS so graciously sent me, beyond all limits of punctuality. I hasten now at last to restore them before the moon shall fill her horns. Thoreau was in my house this eve. & when I repeated to him some of your criticisms on his lines, he boggled at Nature "*relumes*," and prefers his own honest "doth have," which I told him should be restored. Othello's melodious verses "that can thy light relume," make that word sacred always in my ear. But our tough Yankee must have his tough verse, so I beg you will replace it. You need not print it, if you have anything better. He has left with me a piece of prose for you, which I will send now or presently. I am to read it first.

I begin to wish to see a different Dial from that which I first imagined. I would not have it too purely literary. I wish we might make a Journal so broad & great in its survey that it should lead the opinion of this generation on every great interest & read the law on property, government, education, as well as on art, letters, & religion. A great Journal people must read. And it does not seem worth our while to work with any other than sovereign aims. So I wish we might court some of the good fanatics and publish chapters on every head in the whole Art of Living. I am just now turning my pen to scribble & copy on the subjects of 'Labor,' 'Farm,' 'Reform,' 'Domestic Life,' etc. and I asked myself why should not the Dial present this homely & most grave subject to the men & women of the land. If it could be well & profoundly discussed, no youth in the country could sleep on it. And the best conceivable paper on such a topic would of course be a sort of fruitful Cybele, mother of a hundred gods and godlike papers. That papyrus reed should become a fatal arrow. I know the danger of such latitude of plan in any but the best conducted Journal. It becomes friendly to special modes of reform partisan bigoted. perhaps whimsical; not universal & poetic. But our round table is not, I fancy, in imminent peril of party & bigotry, & we shall bruise each the other's whims by the collision. Literature seems to me great when it is the ornament & entertainment of a soul which proposes to itself the most extensive the most kind the most solemn action whereof man is capable. Do not imagine that I am preparing to bestow my growing chapter on Reforms on your innocent readers Quite otherwise; as you know my present design is to compile a miscellany of my own. Elizabeth Hoar has just left us with the view of a visit to my Aunt Mary who is now at Portland. Do not fail to let me know when the fair Anna goes to Cambridge or to you.

To Caroline Sturgis, August 16? 1840

My dear friend, I should gladly make this fine style a fact, but a friend is not made in a day nor by our will. You & I should only be friends on imperial terms. We are both too proud to be fond & too true to feign But I dare not engage my peace so far as to make you necessary to me as I can easily see any establishment of habitual intercourse would do, when the first news I may hear is that you have found in some heaven foreign to me your mate, & my beautiful castle is exploded to shivers. Then I take the other part & say, Shall I not trust this chosen child that not possibly will she deceive a noble expectation or content herself with less than greatness When she gives herself away it will be only to an equal virtue, then will I gain a new friend without utter loss of that which now is. But that which set me on this writing was the talk with Margaret F[uller] last Friday who taxed me on both your parts with a certain inhospitality of soul inasmuch as you were both willing to be my friends in the full & sacred sense & I remained apart critical, & after many interviews still a stranger. I count & weigh, but do not love.—I heard the charge, I own, with great humility & sadness. I confess to the fact of cold & imperfect intercourse, but not to the impeachment of my will. and not to the deficiency of my affection. If I count & weigh, I love also. I cannot tell you how warm & glad the naming of your names makes my solitude. You give me more joy than I could trust my tongue to tell you. Perhaps it is ungrateful never to testify by word to those whom we love, how much they are our benefactors. But to my thought this is better to remain a secret from the lips to soften only the behaviour

But I do not get nearer to you. Whose fault is that? With all my heart I would live in your society I would gladly spend the remainder of my days in the holy society of the best the wisest & the most beautiful Come & live near me whenever it suits your pleasure & if you will confide in me so far I will engage to be as true a brother to you as ever blood made. But I thank you for saying that you were sure of me, in reply to M[argaret].s wish. The ejaculation & the reply were both delicious to me.

To Caroline Sturgis, August? *c.* 20? 1840?

I hate every thing frugal and cowardly in friendship. *That,* at least should be brave and generous. When we fear the withdrawal of love from ourselves by the new relations which our companions must form, it is mere infidelity. We believe in our eyes and not in the Creator We do not see any equal pretender in the field, and we conclude that Beauty and Virtue must vail their high top, and buy their Eden by the loss of that which makes them ours. But we are wiser with the next sun, and know that a true and *native* friend is only the extension of our own being and perceiving into other skies and societies, there learning wisdom, there discerning spirits, and attracting our own for us, as truly as we had done hitherto in our strait enclosure. I wish you to go out an adventurous missionary, into all the nations of happy souls, and by all whom you can greatly, and by any whom you can wholly love, I see that I too must be immeasurably enriched.

Not I, not thou, shall put on the God such an affront, as to fancy we know the best—have already seen the flower of his angels. This little coloured world, these few homely gossips we have chatted with, are not all of nature, nay not even the first scene of the first Act, but the poor prologue only. The rent and revenues of character, we have not yet computed: great spiritual lords walk among us hourly as benefactors, but how can we see them, we who look down and not up, who appropriate and not give? As we, dear sister, are *naturally* friends, we shall not need to have respect unto each other. We can carry life after its own great way, without lagging for the dull convoy, without bending to please or to explain, sure that we are then nearest when we are farthest on our own road. I feel how clearly the law of friendship requires the grandest interpretation, when I glance from the dearest lover to the vast spirit impatient of bounds, impatient of persons, foreseeing the fall of every fondness, of every specialty. Only that which *is* related, can weather His sky or grow with the growing world. It gives me joy to write over again to you the old creed of the heart, which is always new. So, dear child, I give you up to all your Gods—to your wildest love and pursuit of beauty, to the boldest effort of your Imagination to express it, to the most original choices of tasks and influences and the rashest exclusion of all you deem alien or malign;—and you shall not give me so great a joy as by the finding for yourself a love which shall make mine show cold and feeble—which certainly is not cold or feeble;

To Caroline Sturgis, August 28, 1840

Concord, 28 Aug. 1840 —

My dear friend,

How foolish to ask you if you would answer my letter as if I could not tell that as well as you. But I must not let the fresh memory of my three golden days fade without telling you how gladly I incur the debt of so much love to you all & severally, & how sensible I am of direct benefit to me in almost every kind,—personally, intellectually, morally,—from those few hours. And you have another claim on me which I hasten to own, for are you not my dear sister and am I not your brother? I cannot write to you *with others* any more than I can talk with you at a round table. From you I hear my own mother tongue, & not a patois of that, or a foreign language. And to you I can speak coldly and austerely as well as gently & poetically—and always truly. Will you not hear me; will you not so reply? Truly, my dear Caroline, it gives me great joy to claim this relation to you, and to insist on being that to you which it suggests. So you must put me to the proof on the first & on every occasion, & on your part must confide to me my sister's thoughts & purposes & history. I am greatly struck lately with the emphasis of this one fact in my history; the great event, as I think, in social life, the meeting namely of a strong mind by a strong mind. they understand each other so fast, so surely, & so dearly, yet so passionless withal, that not possibly henceforth can they ever be unrelated, but must occasionally beckon to each other across forests, seas, or ranks in society. And still the best value of this meeting of adequate & beautiful friends is what is prophetic in it. It is the broadest hint that God ever gave; it is the partial fulfilment of our earliest dream, & so the pledge that friends can be, friends shall be,—onward forever in the recesses of the future, and that the Best is the True. Against the host of chagrins & evils in the world, against the vulgarities, trifles, ennuis, and against the sins & temptations we must hasten to defend ourselves in time by this heavenly parapet of Friends, by true speakers & right doers & beauty-lovers. Let us exchange now & then a reasonable word: let us call one another now & then to a fair & honest act; and let us keep our youth by imbibing a spirit which is an Eternal Child. I read once that among wise men "rebuke was flattery." Can you not, my dear Caroline, sometimes sing me that sweet song. The web of our friendship is already old enough & firm enough if it were only an hour old, to bear that strain. But say what you will; only make haste to speak somewhat to me for I cannot hide from myself the probability that the friend may appear in any hour who by nearer ties shall draw you from all correspondence with your affectionate Brother

Waldo Emerson.

I wrote you another letter after a conversation with Margaret F[uller]. in the week before the last, which I need not send now, nor will I yet destroy. I only haste to write thus today admonished by the strange news I found at Cambridge.

To Margaret Fuller, August 29, 1840

Saturday 29 Aug. 1840, Concord.

Thanks, my dear Margaret, for the good letter of Wednesday, & thanks evermore to you & to our friends & to the Framer & inspirer of all beauty & love, for the joy I have drawn & do still draw from these flying days—I shall never go quite back to my old arctic habits—I shall believe that nobleness is loving, & delights in sharing itself. But what shall I say to you of this my sudden dejection from the sunlit heights of my felicity to which I had been as suddenly uplifted. Was I not raised out of the society of mere mortals by being chosen the friend of the holiest nun & began instantly to dream of pure confidences & "prayers of preserved maids in bodies delicate," when a flash of lightning shivers my castle in the air. The confessions the hope of being often & often shined on & rained on by these influences of being steeped in this light & so ripened to power whereof I yet dreamed not, are ended. the fragment of confidence that a wife can give to an old friend is not worth picking up after this invitation to Elysian tables. What of that? I have lived one day. "Tomorrow to fresh fields & pastures new." Ward I shall not lose. My joy for him is very great. I have never had occasion to congratulate any person so truly. What an event to him! its consequences to the history of his genius who can foresee? But ah! my friend, *you* must be generous beyond even the strain of heroism to bear your part in this scene & resign without a sigh two Friends; —you whose heart unceasingly demands all, & is a sea that hates an ebb. I know there will be an ardent will & endeavor on their parts to prevent if it were indeed possible & in all ways to relieve & conceal this bereavement but I doubt they must deal with too keen a seer and a heart too thoroughly alive in its affections to cover up the whole fact with roses & myrrh.

P.M.

Well & I too, it seems, have done you injustice and can never speak to you in the current day but always to the ghost of your yesterday. That must be snow in summer & a wound in the house of a friend. But how is it that you *can* leave me in this ignorance, with such a will on your part to teach & on my part to learn? I will not vex these vain questions but instead rejoice with you that from each other & from all these tormenting lovers we can retreat always upon the Invisible Heart upon the Celestial Love, and that not to be soothed merely but to be replenished,—not to be compensated but to receive power to make all things new. I am very happy & greatly your debtor in these days and yet I find my solitude necessary & more than ever welcome to me. Austerely kind, nature calms my pleasant fevers, flatters me never, tells me still what a truant pupil I have been, & how far I am behind my class. Nay my solitary river is not solitary enough; it interrupts, it puts me out, and I cannot be alone with the Alone. From these thoughts I would gladly write to these sons & daughters of time in this culminating hour of love & joy which I also have so gladly shared. Write to me from any mood: I would not lose any ray from this particular house of heaven in which we have lately abode.

R. W. E.

To Thomas Carlyle, August 30, 1840

Concord, 30 August, 1840.

My dear Carlyle,

I fear, nay, I know that when I wrote last to you about the 1 July, I promised to follow my sheet immediately with a bookseller's account. The bookseller did presently after render his account, but on its face appeared the fact,—which with many and by me unanswerable reasons they supported,—that the balance thereon credited to you, was not payable until the 1 October. The account is footed, "Nett sales of "Fr. Revolution" to 1 July 1840 due Oct. 1— $249.77" Let us hope then that we shall get not only a new page of statement but also some small payment in money a month hence. Having no better story to tell, I told nothing.

But I will not let the second of the Cunard Boats leave Boston without a word to you. Since I wrote by Calvert, came your letter describing your lectures & their success: very welcome news; for a good London newspaper, which I had consulted, promised reports, but gave none. I have heard so oft of your projected trip to America, that my ear would now be dull & my faith cold, but that I wish it so much. My friend, your audience still waits for you here willing & eager, & greatly larger no doubt than it would have been when the matter was first debated. Our community begin to stand in some terror of Transcendentalism, and the Dial, poor little thing, whose first number contains scarce anything considerable or even visible, is just now honoured by attacks from almost every newspaper & magazine; which at least betrays the irritability & the instincts of the good public. But they would hardly be able to fasten on so huge a man as you are, any party badge. We must all hear you for ourselves. But beside my own hunger to see & know you, and to hear you speak at ease & at large under my own roof, I have a growing desire to present you to three or four friends, & them to you. Almost all my life has been passed alone. Within three or four years I have been drawing nearer to a few men & women whose love gives me in these days more happiness than I can write of. How gladly I would bring your Jovial light upon this friendly constellation, & make you too know my distant riches! We have our own problems to solve also & a good deal of movement & tendency emerging into sight every day in church & state, in social modes, & in letters. I sometimes fancy our cipher is larger & easier to read than that of your English society. You will naturally ask me if I try my hand at the history of all this,—I who have leisure and write? No, not in the near & practical way which they seem to invite. I incline to write philosophy, poetry, possibility,—anything but history. And yet this phantom of the next age limns himself sometimes so large & plain that every feature is apprehensible, & challenges a painter. I can brag little of my diligence or achievement this summer. I dot evermore in my endless journal, a line on every unknowable in nature; but the arrangement loiters long, & I get a brick kiln instead of a house.— Consider, however, that all summer I see a good deal of company,—so near as my fields are to the city. But next winter I think to omit lectures, & write more faithfully. Hope for me that I shall get a book ready to send you by New Years Day.

Sumner came to see me the other day. I was glad to learn all the little that he knew of you & yours. I do not wonder you set so lightly by my talkative countryman. He has bro't nothing home but names, dates, & surfaces. At Cambridge last week I saw Brown, for the first time. I had little opportunity to learn what he knew. Mr. Hume has never yet shown his face here. He sent me his Poems from New York, & then went South, & I know no more of him.

My Mother & Wife send you kind regards & best wishes,—to you & to all your house. Tell your wife that I hate to hear that she cannot sail the seas. Perhaps now she is stronger she will be a better sailor. For the sake of America, will she not try the trip to Leith again? It is only twelve days from Liverpool to Boston. Love & truth & power abide with you always!

R. W. E.

TO ELIZABETH HOAR, SEPTEMBER 12, 1840

Concord, 12 Sept. 1840

Dear Elizabeth,

You stay a very long time and I trust you grow strong every day. We are very solitary—I am,—not only forsaken of companions but forsaken of thoughts—befriended only by the treacherous Sleep which hovers on all lids in these autumnal nights & *days.* Yet the sacred friends have not quite forgotten us. I have new letters from Raphael [i.e., Samuel Gray Ward] & Margaret & Caroline, and am myself sufficiently disposed to drink the last drop, if such there be, out of this horn of nectar which the new Hours offer me. Have I been always a hermit, and unable to approach my fellow men, & do the Social Divinities suddenly offer me a *roomfull* of friends? Please God, I will not be wanting to my fortune but will eat this pomegranate,—seed stem & leaves—with all thankfulness. So consider me as now quite friendsick & lovesick, a writer of letters & sonnets. Ask me again after a year or two how it sped with me. Sarah Clarke came hither Tuesday & spent a couple of days. We walked & talked: a very true person but with the right New England frost in her nature forbidding the streams to flow. Mrs Ripley came here also one evening—but nothing came of it. Will there not after so many *social* ages be now & here one *lonely* age? Tom Wyman at Walden Pond will be the saint & pattern of the time, and none of your Alcotts & Owens. Now for silence, scowls, Spanish Cloaks, & night walks! I think of occupying our Monument as a Stylite, and Zimmermann is your only book. Pray hasten home & hear my last words before I be perched.

Mamma & Lidian send you waves & tides of love. Waldo has lain in his bed ever since you went away, I believe,—with a sort of bilious fever which takes away his morals with his flesh, for a more difficult patient to please, lies not certainly anywhere on the banks of the Musketaquid. Dr Bartlett & his mother conclude that he is getting better. If you do not come quickly, Ellen will address you with sentences on your return.

I believe I have no news that you will care to know. All my conjectural emendations of our wonderful Manuscript Poet [Ellery Channing] came back to me dishonoured. Raphael & Margaret combined against me. I think the poet has given them philtres that they (and I believe thou also, O faithful sister mine,) do face me down with his bad grammar & his nonsense as all consecrated by his true *afflatus.* Is the poetic inspiration amber to embalm &

enhance flies & spiders? As it fell in the case of Jones Very, cannot the spirit parse & spell?[25] The wonders of the Bunker Hill Conventions & Fair Tables, you will hear as well as we. I did not go to town. My carnival had been too long already. My chapter on "Circles" begins to prosper and when it is October I shall write like a Latin Father. Do not complain that I have written you a letter & said no good word. What I think & feel, you think & feel also—Why should I sit down to write it out? Are you not the true sister of

Your affectionate brother
W.

To Margaret Fuller, September 25, 1840

Concord, 25 September, 1840.

My dear friend,

The day is so fine that I must try to draw out of its azure magazines some ray to celebrate our friendship, and yet nature does rarely say her best words to us out of serene and splendid weather. Twilight, night, winter, & storm, the muses love, & not the halcyon hours. You must always awaken my wonder: our understanding is never perfect: so was it in this last interview, so is it ever. And yet there is progress. Ever friendly your star beams now more friendly & benign on me. I once fancied your nature & aims so eccentric that I had a foreboding that certain crises must impend in your history that would be painful to me to witness in the conviction that I could not aid even by sympathy. I said, it is so long before we can quite meet that perhaps it is better to part now, & leave our return to the Power that orders the periods of the planets. But you have your own methods of equipoise & recovery, without event, without convulsion, and I understand now your language better, I hear my native tongue, though still I see not into you & have not arrived at your law. Absent from you I am very likely to deny you, and say that you lack this & that. The next time we meet you say with emphasis that very word. I pray you to astonish me still, & I will learn to make no rash

---

25. *Very, believing his writings to be those of the Holy Spirit as passed through him, had opposed Emerson's attempts at changing Very's verse in Emerson's edition of the younger man's* Essays and Poems *(1839).*

sentences upon you.—Now in your last letter, you, O divine mermaid or fisher of men, to whom all gods have given the witch-hazel-wand, or caduceus, or spirit-discerner which detects an Immortal under every disguise in every lurking place, (and with this you have already unearthed & associated to yourself a whole college of such,) do say, (for I am willing & resolute for the sake of an instance to fix one quarrel on you,) that I am yours & yours shall be, let me dally how long soever in this or that other temporary relation. I on the contrary do constantly aver that you & I are not inhabitants of one thought of the Divine Mind, but of two thoughts, that we meet & treat like foreign states, one maritime, one inland, whose trade & laws are essentially unlike. I find or fancy in your theory a certain wilfulness and not pure acquiescence which seems to me the only authentic mode. Our friend is part of our fate; those who dwell in the same truth are friends; those who are exercised on different thoughts are not, & must puzzle each other, for the time. For the time! But who dare say how quickly the old eternity shall swallow up the Time, or how ripe is already in either soul the augury of the dissolution of the barriers of difference in the glimpse of ultimate unity?—I am willing to see how unskilfully I make out a case of difference & will open all my doors to your sunshine & morning air. Nothing is to me more welcome nor to my recent speculation more familiar than the Protean energy by which the brute horns of Io become the crescent moon of Isis, and nature lifts itself through everlasting transition to the higher & the highest. Whoever lives must rise & grow. Life like the nimble Tartar still overleaps the Chinese wall of distinctions that had made an eternal boundary in our geography— and I who have taxed your exclusion in friendship, find you—last Wednesday, the meekest & most loving of the lovers of mankind. I thought you a great court lady with a Louis Quatorze taste for diamonds & splendor, and I find you with a "Bible in your hand," faithful to the new Ideas, beholding undaunted their tendency, & making ready your friend "to die a beggar." Honor & love to you ever from all gentle hearts,—a wreath of laurel, &, far better, the wreath of olive & of palm. My little boy for whom you promised good fortune was dressed & on his feet when I came home & is recovering his good health. All things go smoothly with me in these days but myself who am much of the time but a fat weed on the lazy wharf. Lidian sends her love to you & is overjoyed to hear of "the Bible."

Yours affectionately,
R. W. E.

To Samuel Gray Ward and Anna Barker, September, 1840

You treat me nobly & like yourselves to think & speak so and yet as I read again & again your letter I think perhaps you do not know me & in how remote antiquity I dwell. I was going to say to you, Dear Children! & you say to me Dear Brother! I suppose we may be each right in our turn. But Anna (which I only use as the short for Angelina) will remember Swedenborg's parable which may reconcile these differences.[26]

When I see you again I think I can talk with you. This is a great, perhaps, a rash hope. Certainly I have never yet got so far with *you*, my dear brother, (for so today at least I will joyfully call you;) we have halted hitherto on the precincts of speech with whatever confidence we have both augured our final relation—And Anna for the most of the time has quite overpowered all my talents And yet I must say in some moments your angel has appeared at all the doors melted my reserves & prepared me to say things never before spoken. But if you grow so fast on my love & reverence that I can dare believe that this dear style we are learning to use to each other is to become very fact then we can drop our words-of-course & can afford the luxury of sincerity. There are many degrees of sincerity, & persons like us three who know the elegance of truth may yet be far without their own highest mark of simple intercourse. Dear friends a divine beauty we are each conscious lies under all these weary wrappages constitutional or moral, & if once they drop, the Immortal will emerge in every word & deed. What benefactors then like those who by their celestial sincerity can speak to this high prisoner, can give me for the first time to hear my own voice & to feel the health of my own motion? Your frank love suggests to me the hope that I shall yet speak & yet hear. If we shall not be permitted to speak, I shall not trust you less:—we will pass on glad that more excellent communion is ripening for us than any we yet know.

But Anna, & thou my dear Raphael, one thing more I must say—that I cannot see the suddenness of our new meeting & new covenant & the joy it gives me without feeling a stern hint that other Hours & Powers may also be

---

26. *According to Swedenborg's elaborate system, the correspondence of "brother" is "charity, or the good of love," while the correspondence of "children" is "innocence and charity." Thus the differences are, as Emerson suggests, reconciled. [Rusk]*

at hand to balance for me so strange a condensation of prosperity. Perhaps our duties will lead us for the time wide apart, out of the sight of these radiant eyes, out of the hearing of these pleasant voices. When I dream by myself of my road, it sometimes shows itself lone rough & odious—possibly abhorred by the beautiful & happy & that I can only assure myself of your sympathy late late in the evening when we shall meet again far far from Here. And then I say, Do these lovers—(every hair of whose heads may the dear God keep from harm!) truly know me that they challenge me thus early by the thrilling name of Brother?—But perhaps I shall never deserve so high a call as the post of solitude & reproach. And I will not mistrust your fitness for every sweet & solemn emergency of your own blended fate. May the Infinite Goodness bind us all! Farewell, my brother, my sister!

To Sarah Ann Clarke, October 9, 1840

Concord, 9 October, 1840

We are so immersed in Nature, my dear friend, and our thinking so necessitated by our being, that we cannot diverge far from each other in our theories, phrase them how we will. I cannot see with my best heed any important difference between our two statements—I can only perceive that we are each overjoyed at the conviction that a great fact is, and have thrown ourselves into the attitude of vigilance to the end that no new light in this region of wonders shall escape us. Nature—what is it but the circumference of which I am the centre, the outside of my inside, object whereof I am subject? Always, to vary the expression, I behold this fact at the same angle, though sometimes it is near & trivial, a button or a fly, & sometimes it is far & vast as time space & systems; and always when my eye is sound & true, size makes no difference: kind or quality is so much, that degree is nothing. All parts of nature are equally low, external; servile; all parts of spirit central, regal, ordaining. The only question of *degree,* is, as to ourselves, as to the amount, that is, as to the purity of the spirit. Nature is the body which the spirit animates,—when impure faintly & to short reptile functions, but step by step with its purification, to greater energy & extent; as we familiarly see in so many incarnations baser & more beautiful which surround us; and at last the Soul pure dissolves all boundaries & resistance and sees the sap rise & the leaves fall, races coexist, and the whole connexion of beings live *at its will,* as truly as the bird is master of its own song or a man of the motion of his arm. For the only possible advance of the soul is in one line, namely, into itself, into that which is & causes, which is always one & invariable. It is by the soul that the world exists and planets revolve and as the soul enters into me I share & become the power will or science, call it what you please, by which the largest & all effects are wrought equally with the petty ones of my present experience.

This external unity & kindred of production and producer is the account of that feeling of self recognition we always find in the landscape. Strange if we were not domesticated in the house we have built, in the child we have begotten. The sea, the firmament, the forest are the work of pure soul; in them therefore we can so easily pray & aspire; whilst we are so easily checked in the presence of man & his works, or Impure Soul. In these beautiful days which are now passing, go into the forest & the leaves hang silent & sympathetic, unobtrusive & related, like the thoughts which they so hospitably enshrine. Could they tell their sense, they would become the thoughts we have; could our thoughts take form they would hang as sunny leaves. And yet it is not by direct study of these enchantments that their sense is to be extorted, but by manlier & total methods, by doing & being. Conscience is the key to botany by more life & not by microscopes must I learn the essence of a tree.—I hope the painting proceeds well in these sunny days. Whatever employments charm us & will not release us from their attraction must have a deep & friendly secret which we ought wholly to respect.

Your *affectionate servant,*
R. W. Emerson.

To Elizabeth Palmer Peabody, October 12, 1840

I have read the sheets on the Patriarchal Traditions. They certainly indicate great ingenuity & beauty of spiritual interpretation. In these days when no one cares for Moses or his Patriarchs, one might regret that so much labor & skill had been thrown away, for the public, if the habit of mind which these papers betray, were not itself an invaluable possession. Perhaps it is a critical fault of this essay that it looks at the Book of Genesis as if it had a cyclical integrity and did represent with some symmetry the primeval history, whilst a philosopher might rather esteem that book the fragment of fragments. It is moreover the obvious tendency of all our recent thinking to degrade history from its high place. Heretofore we have all travelled to it from far as to some old immovable collegiate city—now it waits on us as a travelling tutor. Instead of reverently exploring the annals of Egypt Asia & Greece as the cardinal points of the horizon by which we must take our departure, go where we will, it is too plain that the modern scholar begins with the fact of his own nature, and is only willing to hear any result you can bring him from these old dead men by way of illustration or ornament of his own biography. Instantly, therefore, our ancient & honorable acquaintances Abraham & Isaac & Jacob & Esau have a certain air of unreasonableness, like octogenarians at a young party, and one would willingly spare such valued friends the shadow of a disrespect. This, in regard to the condescension of their appearance in the Dial, if, as I understood your note, you contemplated that. The piece is too good to be lost and ought to appear in one of the theological journals, or in covers of its own. Nevertheless, the nine or ten first pages might easily if you fancied it, be separated into a short chapter, which I think Margaret Fuller might be glad to print in the Dial. And I will tell her of it, if you will. I shall probably be in town this week & will bring you the manuscript.

Elizabeth Hoar tells me you have new books, which I shall be happy to see. But you need keep no book for me from any purchaser. I seldom buy a book, alas! & yet will readily be a buyer in the last resort for books of a good name. I greet the arrival of the good periodicals E. H. tells of.

Yours with great regard,
R. W. Emerson.

Concord, 12 Oct. 1840.

To Caroline Sturgis, October 18, 1840

Concord, 18 October, 1840.

I am a slow scholar at magnetism, my dear sister, and always read the newspaper whilst that subject is discussed. I do not pretend to understand anything in your last letter but its lyric measures which are always beautiful to me. I went to school once to an archangel who taught me that the highest virtue was the most intelligible and that the road to power lay through the palm of the hand & the pupil of the eye, it was as straight as a ray of light, it lay in sight of all angels and every traveller on it was the more gloriously visible with every step he took. But there are new sects in heaven who teach an occult religion & describe the saints as men walking with dark lanterns in their hands which they turn the bright side on some passengers & the dark side on others and Virtue is a Will o' the wisp & not the sun in the firmament. I must even leave you & Margaret to your flights in the sky wishing you pleasant airs & a safe alighting.

See you not, Caroline, that we all (of whom is question here) are the pets & cossets of the gracious Heaven have never known a rough duty, never wrestled with a rude doubt, never once been called to anything that deserves the name of an action. Dare we name the great name or Virtue or pretend to translation & rapture. The scarred martyrs, the Seraphs of love & knowledge go silent by, yet every victory in their history, every coal of fire, every spark of light they have collected, augments their irresistible attraction for me & for all, & extends their being outward into all the kingdoms of nature. When we by acts of faith & courage yet unattempted shall have begun to develop character, be sure its language will be audible & musical to all ears It will not be a local & partial glow incommunicable & leaving old features of the individual unchanged. Understand me, then; I will not listen a moment to any narratives of heaven which come to my ears only; if they do not penetrate my heart & soul coming to me from an exalted nature & a transfigured form, I cannot tell what they say.

When I see how false our life is, how oppressive our politics, that there is no example of a noble household, no form of a Redeeming man appearing in the whole population, and myself & my friends so inactive & acquiescent in the main that our protest & the action of our character is quite insignificant, heroism seems our dream and our insight a delusion. I am daily getting ashamed of my life. If you have found a true energy—divine by the tests that it is humane, loving, universal,—comfort me by describing it & its workings in the sharpest terms your good sense can employ. I have written you down in my books & in my heart for my sister because you are a user of the positive degree. If you use the superlative you must explain it to

Your affectionate brother
W.

TO MARGARET FULLER, OCTOBER 20, 1840

Concord, October 20, 1840.

I should gladly have talked with you another day that we might have brought things to speech somewhat more reverently than in a cold room at abrupt & stolen moments. Yet what would another day have done to reconcile our wide sights? Much time much comparison habitual intercourse with an advancing private experience interposed, would do, will do the work of interpretation. A strong passion, or the opportunity of a great work accurately adapted to one's latent faculties,—these are the sudden schoolmasters who have short methods & teach the art of life in "six lessons." Nothing less than such as these could give me a look through your telescope or you one through mine;—an all explaining look. Let us float along through the great heavens a while longer and whenever we come to a point whence our observations agree, the time when they did not will seem but a moment. With you I do not quarrel when we do not understand; for, what degree of difference there is in any thought, there is the same in every faculty & act throughout our constitution. But I wrote Caroline a good scolding letter for presuming to differ from me & siding with you & pretending to see your lights which I know to her as to me must be stark naught.—A strong passion or a fit work, I said, were the abridged methods. The first will never come to such as I am; the second I do not absolutely despair of, especially in these days of Phalanx, though phalanx is not it. I delight to find that I have not quite done learning, nor have I absolutely cut off my hands, though my life for so many years might lead one to think so. But if new thoughts & new emerging facts should not renovate me as a better seer, let us not fail to practise still the sure old methods, for it is not divine to be in a hurry. I have today a letter from S[amuel]. & A[nna Ward]. at Brattleborough, as gay as health can write. They almost promise to come & see me on the 26th. I have yesterday a letter from Carlyle who is studying Cromwell again, and faintly praises The Dial Number I. Elizabeth Peabody sent me lately a MS of hers about the Patriarchal Religion with a view, as I understood her, to printing in the Dial. It has great merits, but the topics Abraham Isaac Jacob & Esau, I told her, were a little too venerable for our slight modern purpose. Yet the first ten pages would make a very good paper (there were 40 or 50 pp) if you want one. Eliza Clapp did not please me at first sight; better after talking; but I did not talk with her as I should now after seeing her poetry. I have written her a

letter to praise the verses. "Praise keeps good men good." Your friend yet,
Waldo E.

To Margaret Fuller, October? *c.* 22? 1840?

Dear Margaret,

None knows better than I—more's the pity—the gloomy inhospitality of the man, the want of power to meet and unite with even those whom he loves in his "flinty way." What amends can he make to his guests, he asked himself long since. Only to anticipate and thus if possible mitigate their disgust & suspicion at the discovery, by apprising them beforehand that this outside of wax covered an inside of stone. Ice has its uses when deception is not thought of and we are not looking for bread. Being made by chemistry & not by cooks its composition is unerring, and it has a universal value *as ice,* not as glass or gelatine. Would you know more of his history?—Diffident, shy, proud having settled it long ago in his mind that he & society must always be nothing to each other—he received with astonishment the kind regards of such as coming from the opposite quarter of the heavens he now calls his friends—with surprise and when he dared to believe them, with delight. Can one be glad of an affection which he knows not how to return? I am. Humbly grateful for every expression of tenderness—which makes the day sweet and inspires unlimited hopes. I say this not to you only, but to the four persons[27] who seemed to offer me love at the same time and draw to me & draw me to them. Yet I did not deceive myself with thinking that the old bars would suddenly fall. No, I knew that if I would cherish my dear romance, I must treat it gently, forbear it long,—worship, not use it,—and so at last by piety I might be tempered & annealed to bear contact & conversation as well mixed natures should. Therefore, my friend, treat me always as a mute, not ungrateful though now incommunicable. But the letter also says, that there is a change in him obvious to all observers. Of this I am not aware. I have no guess at what it points.

---

27. *Probably Margaret Fuller, Samuel Gray Ward, Anna Barker Ward, and Caroline Sturgis.*

To Margaret Fuller, October 24, 1840

Concord, 24 October, 1840.

My dear Margaret,

I have your frank & noble & affecting letter, and yet I think I could wish it unwritten. I ought never to have suffered you to lead me into any conversation or writing on our relation, a topic from which with all my persons my Genius ever sternly warns me away. I was content & happy to meet on a human footing a woman of sense & sentiment with whom one could exchange reasonable words & go away assured that wherever she went there was light & force & honour. That is to me a solid good; it gives value to thought & the day; it redeems society from that foggy & misty aspect it wears so often seen from our retirements; it is the foundation of everlasting friendship. Touch it not—speak not of it—and this most welcome natural alliance becomes from month to month,—& the slower & with the more intervals the better,—our air & diet. A robust & total understanding grows up resembling nothing so much as the relation of brothers who are intimate & perfect friends without having ever spoken of the fact. But tell me that I am cold or unkind, and in my most flowing state I become a cake of ice. I can feel the crystals shoot & the drops solidify. It may do for others but it is not for me to bring the relation to speech. Instantly I find myself a solitary unrelated person, destitute not only of all social faculty but of all private substance. I see precisely the double of my state in my little Waldo when in the midst of his dialogue with his hobby horse in the full tide of his eloquence I should ask him if he loves me?—he is mute & stupid. I too have never yet lived a moment, have never done a deed—am the youngest child of nature,—I take it for granted that everybody will show me kindness & wit, and am too happy in the observation of all the abundant particulars of the show to feel the slightest obligation resting on me to do any thing or say any thing for the company. I talk to my hobby & will join you in harnessing & driving him, & recite to you his virtues all day—but ask me what I think of you & me,—& I am put to confusion.

Up to this hour our relation has been progressive. I have never regarded you with so much kindness as now. Sometimes you appeal to sympathies I have not and sometimes you inquire into the state of this growth.—that for the moment puts me back, but you presently return to my daylight & we get on admirably.

There is a difference in our constitution. We use a different rhetoric It seems as if we had been born & bred in different nations. You say you understand me wholly. You cannot communicate yourself to me. I hear the words sometimes but remain a stranger to your state of mind

Yet are we all the time a little nearer. I honor you for a brave & beneficent woman and mark with gladness your steadfast good will to me. I see not how we can bear each other anything else than good will though we had sworn to the contrary.

And now what will you? Why should you interfere? See you not that I cannot spare you? that you cannot be spared? that a vast & beautiful Power to whose counsels our will was never party, has thrown us into strict neighborhood for best & happiest ends? The stars in Orion do not quarrel this night, but shine in peace in their old society. Are we not much better than they? Let us live as we have always done. only ever better, I hope, & richer. Speak to me of every thing but myself & I will endeavor to make an intelligible reply. Allow me to serve you & you will do me a kindness; come & see me & you will recommend my house to me; let me visit you and I shall be cheered as ever by the spectacle of so much genius & character as you have always the gift to draw around you.

I see very dimly in writing on this topic. It will not prosper with me. Perhaps all my words are wrong. Do not expect it of me again for a very long time.

I will go look for the letters you ask for & which should have been returned before; but I liked to keep them. And could you not send Alcott a remembrance that smacked not so much of Almacks?

You shall have whatever I can muster for the Dial—yet I do not now know what I can offer you.

Yours affectionately,
R. W. Emerson.

To Caroline Sturgis, November? 5? 1840?

I love the victories of the conscience, dear Caroline, everywhere, yet must think it almost prematurely or preternaturally irritable, if it will not suffer you to eat your bread or wear your robes in peace for the considering where these come from. A son may ask these questions, but I think a maiden lives as naturally in her father's house as the lily on its stalk, and as unquestioning.

The other question "What doest thou?", I suppose, has no sex, but is always emphatic in proportion to the force of the individual mind. "I tell no lie", is, I suppose, the negative answer, and it needs a brave woman to make it. "I love," is the great affirmative. The former seems to need Will, Talent, forethought. The last is the flowing of a divine Genius & taking no thought fulfils all the law. You are the angels that keep us You are the Sentiments— nearer to the heart of God—who glow & enkindle your else cold & opinion- ative brothers they without woman tending to be fantastic & insane. Woman seems to me essentially social—so much so that when weak she becomes merely relative. She is not to forecast & contrive, to invent like a man a new & solid life, but is the happy child of the Hour and the Day: wherever she is, she constitutes society, hallows & enchants it; and it is her greatness not to look beyond, but to bless the moment & the bystanders out of her oracular nature, her proximity to the Eternal Beauty. What has she to do with means & systems with commerce or the state? She carries Eden and its Seraphim into the camp of knights or the broker's shop and by ennobling the spirit of man regenerates institutions, & not by playing the Reformer in detail. *That* she may do or not do, but when she does it not, if a true woman, it is because of her greatness & preoccupation of mind.

I am glad if you found my boundaries & defied them. But you have not yet learned the whole history, if you fancied I was worse then & am better now. My dream is always divine, my interpretation always broken, hissing, almost epileptic. That week was probably like every other week, for I can detect no difference in my months & years as long as I can remember them. The present days & hours were always base & cheap to the point of remorse; the steadily accumulating result from month to month has been ever the perception ever more widely & variously illustrated of the circular & perfect Law which gazes at me from every point in nature from every thought in my heart. It goes ever to teach me calmness & self reliance,—but shall I say—I have learned both lessons better by heart than by rote. They are my faith & my habit, yet any person who saw me for a short time would probably say I had neither. Yet what am I? There is the Law new, alive, & yielding worlds for fruit from its branches, yes, making the same circumstance a new world every moment to its lover & adorer. I can well acquiesce to be nothing else than praise & wonder.

Concord, 9 November, 1840—

Dear William

For the sake of brotherly love & not that I have any thing to communicate I will send you a line by Mr Moore. I am but an indifferent Whig & do not care for Mr Harrison but since the election of J. Q. Adams I do not remember any national event that has given me so much content as this general uprising to unseat Mr Van Buren & his government. Would that his successors could carry into Washington one impulse of patriotism one aspiration for a pure legislation! But I think the hope is less & less daily, & the new administration will most likely begin with an ejectment of all existing officers as if they were rats & a universal scramble by our once holy Whigs, and then I shall be as glad to turn them out four years later. Beautiful Country! Honorable Nation! Well we are revenging ourselves on them by questioning the foundations of the state & preaching the advent of the Individual Man & utter confusion & rout to the law & the system which stand on force. It is a long time perhaps before this preaching will arrive at practice or this denouncing will turn out one post master. Certainly, it will not until it deserves to: it will not touch the state until it has built an individual.—But on all sides here in Massachusetts I can see the rise of the same spirit which I had known in a few, determining them to a simpler manlier more self-dependent life, & broaching every day multitudes of new questions in every part of life & practice. I hope it will not all end in pretensions.

We were all much relieved by your letter to mother. But I should be glad of more particular news of your health—precisely what you do or fear or hope in regard to the local complaints.—I am guilty of some negligence in the affair of the medallion, but of more want of opportunity, but I shall probably be in town this week & will ask Miss Peabody's attention to it. The Dial, Weeks, Jordan, & Co affirmed was at a store in N. Y., Wiley & Putnam's I believe, & should have been sent you at once, & they took order to have it go that day, & I hope it came. I am setting in order this week a Chapter on Art for that same learned Journal. Mother who sits beside me at her work is as well as usual & sends her love to you all. She went to Chelmsford last Friday & spent a day with Bulkeley who has not been so well. We hope he will escape a new attack on his nerves & he is better than he has been. Lidian is gone to Boston & the boy & girl are gone to bed.— We have little to brag of any of us, but when we get on into that divine State alluded to on my other page shall we not have wise & happy messages to send you every hour. I had a letter from Aunt Mary today from Waterford— in very good spirits. Elizabeth is well Love to Susan & Willie & John Haven from

Waldo E

Alexander is very well & very good I think a very rare boy. When he likes his work as he does all work in the garden or on the wood pile he makes it his own & toils with all his heart.

When you write again tell me what was the result of the trial of Sidney Masons case—

To Caroline Sturgis, November 11? 1840

You are such a prudent cautious Sister that I am not quite sure that you in what you say consult for the nature of Waldo Emerson or only for the *genus* of indolent poetical reflective discontented persons. But I will not be generalized. If you will not counsel *me,* I shall not hear what you say. Plainly then, do you think George & Sophia Ripley can by any arithmetic or combination give anything to me [at Brook Farm] which I can worthily accept? anything which with a little resolution & perserverance I cannot procure for myself. Would you have me like a green emigrant who jumps into the first wagon for Illinois throw myself into this gay brand new pretention because it uses words which I use, and is really well & generously intended by the projectors.

If the design meets my wants, shall I not feel it & love it afar off. My wants are very few & I need not surely encumber myself with a great apparatus to satisfy them. I much prefer a life of many privations to the annoyances of an economy which goes to remove them all. I fancy I have no taste for plans, for complex arrangements of any kind: I am willing & glad they should exist; but I comprehend them with so much difficulty that I think I ought not to meddle with them. Will any arrangements elude the good & evil which exist in all the persons. Whoever is deceived by the skill of the combination, I know that I must conquer my own sloth & cowardice, & devise & make my own instruments of action in that sort appointed to me, and I seem to play a ridiculous part in solemnly breaking up my house here & travelling to Newton & setting down my house there, to effect this. I greatly regret that an accidental importance should be given by Mr Ripley to my decision in this matter as it sorely wounds my good-nature to cast impediments in the way of a project so noble & pleasing—But do not you feel this complex character in the design? Does the eye fix on something True & Inevitable in it. (or do I not rather hope that amidst such a confusion of good things some may chance to fit me?) The company—the company!— are they United? Do I love them & will be poor & sick & slain for them?—I believe at last that my coldness to this enterprise arises from the fact that the eye of the planners rests on the circumstances & not on the men

I wish a grand thought or a Bleeding Heart or a fiery zeal to be at the bottom of it, shared thoroughly by all the members, melting them all into one. Then the circumstances will fall rightly, and a new line be surely written in history. But this movement is not yet commanding: has not yet enlisted either my Conscience or my Imagination.

Apart from these moral frigidities my confidence in the good economy of this project is by no means strong, & is shaken by every farmer & economist with whom I converse. Yet if I could fall in love with the plan it would be animating to make good these defects by sacrifices. We could throw ourselves into the breach. But it must first drive us nobly mad.

To William Emerson, December 2, 1840

Concord, 2 Dec 1840—

My dear brother,

We were surprised, the other day by the arrival of a double package containing the gayest & gorgeousest gifts for Waldo & Ellen which at their emerging into light from under the wrappages caused such explosions of joy and such happy silence from the young receivers as have not been witnessed here at home for many a day Their eyes were so glad that they could hardly see with them. The basket chariot bears away the bell for beauty but the rackets! & the ninepins! Waldo's vocabulary falls short, and Hobby horse has in the last fortnight grown decrepid & forgotten.

We were glad to hear of so much good health & now expect a good account of this surgery, if it must come. These touches of the dentist & the doctor—these interferences, seem very bold & profane at first; for our body is sacred as an angel's when we are young; but we find at last it is only a machine of the same stock & make as all matter & we learn to treat it like a truck or a wagon. 'Pero si muove,' as Galileo said;[28] I still believe, it is an angel's, & we shall learn to heal it by higher laws & without interference.

We are absorbed here at home in discussions of George Ripley's Community. I forget if I have mentioned it to you. He is very anxious to enrol me in his company, & that I should subscribe money to its funds. I am very discontented with many of my present ways & bent on mending them; but not as favorably disposed to his Community of 10 or 12 families as to a more private reform. G. R. wishes to raise $30,000.; to buy a farm of 200 acres in Spring St, Roxbury. for 12000—build $12000. worth of cottages thereon & remove himself with pioneers to the premises on 1 April next. The families who shall come are to do their own work which a studied cooperation is to make easier & simpler. The farm & such mechanical operations as are practised is to give subsistence to the company. A school or college in which the learneder clerks are to teach, it is presumed, will pay a profit—and out of many means the interest at 5 per cent of the capital is to be paid. If I should go there I get rid of menial labor: I learn to work on a farm under skilful direction: I am provided with many means & opportunities of such literary labor as I may wish. Can I not get the same advantages at home without pulling down my house? Ah my dear brother that is the very question we now consider. Lidian is gone today (as she goes every Wednesday) to Boston to attend Margaret Fuller's "Conversations." Elizabeth H. is very well. I suppose Mother has written you of Bulkeley's visit here & that he is gone to Charlestown—I hope for no long time. With thankful love to Susan & good greetings to my nephews

> *Your affectionate brother*
> *Waldo*

Bulkeley needs no new garments, says Mother.

---

28. *"But it is moving."*

Concord, 15 December, 1840.

My dear Sir,

It is quite time I made an answer to your proposition that I should join you in your new enterprise. The design appears to me so noble & humane,

---

29. *The manuscript of the letter Emerson sent to George Ripley in which he refused to join the Brook Farm community is unlocated. Two drafts exist in the Emerson collection at Harvard University: the text printed above is described by Tilton as "possibly closer to what was actually sent" than the other draft, which is printed in this note.*

My dear Sir

It is quite time I made answer to your proposition that I should enter into your new community. The design appears to me noble & generous proceeding as I plainly see from nothing covert or selfish or ambitious but from a manly & expanding heart and mind. So it makes all men its friends & debtors. It becomes a matter of conscience to entertain it friendly & examine what it has for its relation to us

I have decided not to join it and yet very slowly & I may almost say with penitence. I am greatly relieved by learning that you coadjutors are now so many that you will no longer attach that importance to the the defection of individuals which you hinted in your letter to me I or others might possess, the painful power I mean of preventing the execution of the plan.

My feeling is that the community is not good for me. that it has little to offer me which with resolution I cannot procure for myself that it would not be worth my while to make the difficult exchange of my property in Concord for a share in the new household. I am in many respects placed as I wish to be in an agreeable neighborhood in a town which I have some reason to love & which has respected my freedom so far that I have reason to hope it will indulge me further when I demand it. I cannot accuse my townsmen or my neighbors of my domestic grievances only my own sloth & conformity. It seems to me a circuitous & operose way of relieving myself to put upon your community this emancipation which I ought to take on myself I must assume my own vows.

The institution of domestic hired service is to me very disagreeable. I should like to come one step nearer to nature than this usage permits. But proceeding, as I plainly see, from a manly & expanding heart & mind that it makes me & all men its friends & debtors It becomes a matter of conscience to entertain it friendly & to examine what it has for us.

I have decided not to join it & yet very slowly & I may almost say penitentially. I am greatly relieved by learning that your coadjutors are now so many that you will no longer ascribe that importance to the defection of individuals which you hinted in your letter to me. it might attach to mine.

---

surely I need not sell my house & remove my family to Newton in order to make the experiment of labor & selfhelp. I wish am already in the act of trying some domestic & social experiments which would gain nothing

I ought to say that I do not much trust in any arrangements or combinations only in the spirit which dictates them. Is that benevolent & divine they will answer their end. Is there any alloy in that, it will certainly appear in the result

I have the same answer to make the proposition of the School. According to my ability & according to yours you & I do not now keep school for all comers and the energy of our thought & of our will measures our influence.

I do not think I should gain anything I who have little skill to converse with people by a plan of so many parts & which I comprehend so slowly & bluntly I think that where my opportunities are so great for doing as I will, that it especially becomes me not to throw them away but to show men how to keep house in those small private parties in which they are now set off throughout the world

I almost shudder to make any statement of my objections to our ways of living because I see how slowly I shall mend them. My own health & habits of living & those of my wife & my mother are not of that robustness that should give any pledge of enterprise & ability in reform. and I find Nor can I insist with any heat on new methods when I am at work in my study on any literary composition. Yet I think that all I shall solidly do I must do alone and I am so ignorant & uncertain in my improvements that I would fain hide my attempts & failures in solitude where they shall perplex none or very few beside myself. The result will of our secretest attempts certainly have as much renown as shall be due to it.

Neither am I good for it I do not look on myself as a valuable member to any community which is not either very large or very small & select. I fear that yours would not find me as profitable and pleasant an associate as I should wish to be & as so important a project seems imperatively to require in all its constituents.

The ground of my decision is almost purely personal to myself. I have some remains of skepticism in regard to the general practicability of the plan, but these have not much weighed with me. That which determines me is the conviction that the Community is not good for me. Whilst I see it may hold out many inducements for others it has little to offer me which with resolution I cannot procure for myself. It seems to me that it would not be worth my while to make the difficult exchange of my property in Concord for a share in the new Household. I am in many respects suitably placed. in an agreeable neighborhood, in a town which I have many reasons to love & which has respected my freedom so far that I may presume it will indulge me farther if I need it. Here I have friends & kindred. Here I have builded & planted: & here I have greater facilities to prosecute such practical enterprizes as I may cherish, than I could probably find by any removal. I cannot accuse my townsmen or my social position of my domestic grievances:—only my own sloth & conformity. It seems to me a circuitous & operose way of relieving myself of any irksome circumstances, to put on your community the task of my emancipation which I ought to take on myself.

The principal particulars in which I wish to mend my domestic life are in acquiring habits of regular manual labor, and in ameliorating or abolishing in my house the condition of hired menial service. I should like to come one step nearer to nature than this usage permits. I desire that my manner of living may be honest and agreeable to my imagination. But surely I need not sell my house & remove my family to Newton in order to make the experiment of labor & self help. I am already in the act of trying some domestic & social experiments which my present position favors. And I think that my present position has even greater advantages than yours would offer me for testing my improvements in those small private parties into which men are all set off already throughout the world.

But I own I almost shrink from making any statement of my objections to our ways of living because I see how slowly I shall mend them. My own health & habits & those of my wife & my mother are not of that robustness which should give any pledge of enterprize & ability in reform. And whenever I am engaged in literary composition I find myself not inclined to insist with heat on new methods. Yet I think that all I shall solidly do, I must do alone. I do not think I should gain anything—I who have little skill to converse with people—by a plan of so many parts and which I comprehend so slowly & imperfectly as the proposed Association.

If the community is not good for me neither am I good for it. I do not look on myself as a valuable member to any community which is not either very large or very small & select I fear that yours would not find me as profitable & pleasant an associate as I should wish to be and as so important a project seems imperatively to require in all its constituents Moreover I am so ignorant & uncertain in my improvements that I would fain hide my attempts & failures in solitude where they shall perplex none or very few beside myself The result of our secretest improvements will certainly have as much renown as shall be due to them.

In regard to the plan as far as it respects the formation of a School or College, I have more hesitation, inasmuch as a concentration of scholars in one place seems to me to have certain great advantages. Perhaps as the school emerges to more distinct consideration out of the Farm, I shall yet find it attractive And yet I am very apt to relapse into the same skepticism as to modes & arrangements the same magnifying of the men—the men alone. According to your ability & mine, you & I do now keep school for all comers, & the energy of our thought & will measures our influence. In the community we shall utter not a word more—not a word less.

Whilst I refuse to be an active member of your company I must yet declare that of all the philanthropic projects of which I have heard yours is the most pleasing to me and if it is prosecuted in the same spirit in which it is begun, I shall regard it with lively sympathy & with a sort of gratitude.

Yours affectionately
R W Emerson

To William Emerson, December 21, 1840

Concord 21 Dec. 1840

Dear William,

We had a good letter from you the other day which said nothing of your health, nothing of surgery, & so leaves us in doubt of what we wish to know. Otherwise we are glad of what you say. I shall not go to Mr Ripley's Community having sent him my final negative a week ago. Whatever inducements the design offers for others it is not good for *me*. I have or easily can have the same facilities where I am that his plan would laboriously procure me. But I am quite intent on trying the experiment of manual labor to some considerable extent & of abolishing or ameliorating the domestic service in my household. Then I am grown a little impatient of seeing the inequalities all around me, am a little of an agrarian at heart and wish sometimes that I had a smaller house or else that it sheltered more persons. So I think that next April we shall make an attempt to find house room for Mr Alcott & his family under our roof; for the wants of the man are extreme as his merits are extraordinary. But these last very few persons perceive, and it becomes the more imperative on those few—of whom I am in some respects nearest—to relieve them. He is a man who should be maintained at the public cost in the Prytaneum,—perhaps one of these days he will be—though of late it has rather seemed probable it would be in the county jail or poorhouse. At all events Lidian & I have given him an invitation to establish his household with us for one year, and explained to him & Mrs A. our views or dreams respecting labor & plain living; and they have our proposal under consideration

I really grudge to name all this to you tonight for it has been talked over & over for a fortnight past here at home to the point of ineffable weariness, only I thought you would like to know what way we look & how much & how little we are bitten by this madness of G. R's Socialism. Mother is very well & Lidian & both the young things. Ellen is a prodigious talker. She will make a town crier in a fortnights time. Dear love to you & Susan & the children from all & from particularly your affectionate brother Waldo—

No I don't lecture any where. No body asks me, Sir My book creeps along uncertain whether it shall be one volume or two. If one, it is ready now.

To Margaret Fuller, March 14, 1841

Concord, 14 March, 1841.

The young people wished to know what possessed me to tease you with so much prose, & becloud the fine conversation?[30] I could only answer that it was not an acute fit of Monday evening, but was chronic & constitutional

---

30. *On 8 March, Emerson had attended one of Fuller's conversations on Greek mythology in Boston, where, according to a participant, he "pursued his own train of thought" and "seemed to forget that we had come together to pursue Margaret's" (Caroline W. Healey [Dall], Margaret and Her Friends [Boston: Roberts Brothers, 1895], p. 46).*

with me, & I asked them in my turn when they had heard me talk anything else? So I silenced them. But how to reply to your fine eastern pearls with chuckstones of granite & slate. There is nothing for it but to pay you the grand compliment which you deserve, if we can pay it, of speaking the truth. Even Prose I honor in myself & others very often as an awkward worship of truth—it is the plashing & struggling in the water of one who would learn to swim & though not half so graceful as to stand erect on the shore, yet more brave, & leads to something. He who swum by nature, that is, the poet, and he who has learned to swim, that is, the cultivated, will see that this floundering results from genuine admiration & is the straight road to the Fortunate Isles.—I know but one solution to my nature & relations, which I find in the remembering the joy with which in my boyhood I caught the first hint of the Berkleian philosophy, and which I certainly never lost sight of afterwards. There is a foolish man who goes up & down the country giving lectures on Electricity;—this one secret he has, to draw a spark out of every object, from desk, & lamp, & wooden log, & the farmer's blue frock, & by this he gets his living: for paupers & negroes will pay to see this celestial emanation from their own basket & their own body. Well, I was not an electrician, but an Idealist. I could see that there was a cause behind every stump & clod, & by the help of some fine words could make every old wagon & woodpile & stone wall oscillate a little & threaten to dance; nay, give me fair field,—& the Selectmen of Concord & the Reverend Doctor Poundmedown himself began to look unstable & vaporous. You saw me do my feat—it fell in with your own studies—and you would give me gold & pearls. Now there is this difference between the Electrician,—Mr Quimby— is his name?—(I never saw him)—and the Idealist, namely, that the spark is to that philosopher a toy, but the dance is to the Idealist terror & beauty, life & light. It is & it ought to be; & yet sometimes there will be a sinful empiric who loves exhibition too much. This Insight is so precious to society that where the least glimmer of it appears all men should befriend & protect it for its own sake. You, instead of wondering at my cloistered & unfriendly manners should defend me if possible from friendship from ambition, from my own weakness which would lead me to variety, which is the dissipation of thought. You & those others who are dear to me should be so rightly my friends as never to suffer me for a moment to attempt the game of wits & fashionists, no nor even that of those you call Friends; no, but by expecting of me a song of laws & causes, only, should make me noble and the encourager of your nobility. Our friendship should be one incompatible

with the vicious order of existing society, and should adjourn its fulness of
communion into pure eternity. And so, my dear Margaret, in spite of my
deep humiliation for all the years of dereliction, I write myself with joy &
hope Your friend,

Waldo E.

To Caroline Sturgis, March 15, 1841

Concord, 15 March, 1841

Sometimes the air is so full of poetry that the very streets look magnificent, &
sometimes we must remember all our walls. The hour is always coming when
we shall flow in a full stream without drought, without night, & always to an
ocean, that is, to an end commensurate with our force. How pitiful that the
circumstance of a city, that is, a thousand houses laid along the ground
instead of two or three, should check our thought or feeling, should tend to
depress or freeze us. Yet I must bring a stock of health & spirits to town—I
shall not find it there. It is always a pleasure to see you & though there were
no intercourse it would be a pleasure, for I associate you with all the fine arts
and all the high truths. But who is fit for friendship? Not one. Who assumes
it with mastery & grandeur so that his demeanour speaks for him to all
passengers, saying, 'I am that finished & holy person who is called a Friend;
hinder me not, but cherish my purpose, all men! & all women! for I seek the
furtherance of one soul by means that must advance the whole commonwealth of souls.' I think it plain that there is no friend, until the heart is
grown so great as to pour an unquestionable majesty into the eye, that shall
take place everywhere. What hypocrites are we to make free with these great
words, and be all the time the fools of the weather & of events,—to slide, &
sidle, & fear, & hope, as profane persons do!—What we now call friendship,
like what we call religion & poetry, is but rudiments & gymnastics.

But our highest presentiment unceasingly affirms that it shall yet be.—
This selection that we make in friendship, so odious to the excluded, is more
odious to the godlike souls. Certainly the good feel most keenly the livelong
tragedy of conversing with or avoiding (for here to converse & to avoid are
the same thing,) the incapable & wicked. Multitude in our philosophy is a
sort of name & title for the devil, yet one would dream away soul in extasy
at the faintest prophecy of dwelling in a universe of angels. And yet the

profound Voice whispers forever that this will be whenever *One* is clean. the plumage will follow the bird, the radiance the Star, and when this soul is cloudless love, the populous universe will be perfect beauty.

Ever your brother,
Waldo E.

To William Emerson, March 30, 1841

Concord 30 March 1841
Tuesday Eve—

Dear William

I ought to have said a few hours earlier that I received this day your letter with its enclosed order for one hundred seventy two dollars $^{21}/_{100}$—and find you as always not only the surest but promptest of paymasters.

Thanks for all the information you give us of your house. We grieve to hear that Susan should suffer from that tenacious complaint. The most that I know of it is from Mrs Abel Adams who seems sometimes to lose it entirely but she refers its obstinacy to some fall, in childhood, if I remember; Susan has two boys to comfort her which Mrs A has not. Thanks for the account of Alexander, which we all have waited for. He is very kindly remembered here by all the household. Louisa & Lydia say, he was very good company, & they miss him very much. Let me tell you a word touching the progress of our projects. You know Lidian & I had dreamed that we would adopt the country practice of having but one table in the house. Well, Lidian went out the other evening & had an explanation on the subject with the two girls. Louisa accepted the plan with great kindness & readiness, but Lydia, the cook, firmly refused—A cook was never fit to come to table, &c. The next morning Waldo was sent to announce to Louisa that breakfast was ready but she had eaten already with Lydia & refuses to leave her alone. With our other project we are like to have the same fortune as Mrs Alcott is as much decided not to come as her husband is willing to come.

I was very glad to hear of Mr Calvert's execution of our commission. Will Ralph Emerson send the prints to you or to me? I have made no inquiries.

We have nothing of special note to tell you. F. H. Hedge is to deliver the Φ B K Oration. You must some time have him read a course of lectures in

your city He has read six this winter in Boston which were excellent whereof
I heard two; one here in Concord. I have an invitation a few days ago to
deliver an oration in August before a literary society in Waterville College in
Maine—a Baptist seminary. The force of candor could no farther go I am
strongly tempted to say, Yea. such an appetite I have to these things. I have
received from Carlyle some sheets of his Six Lectures spoken last spring in
London on Heroes & Hero Worship & which he is now printing & we will
reprint. He has written Lidian a most courteous letter. We shall grieve if the
addition of that little stout boy is to put an end to your annual migrations
from Ecbatana to Susanopolis or Portsmouth *via Concord,* for you can go by
no better way. We dare not say when any of us will come to see you for no
necessity of health or business or filial duty draws us yet in your direction
But we shall gladly obey any such leading when it appears. Send us good
news of Susan of Willie & the babe who is ceasing to be such.

Waldo.

To Lidian Emerson, June 14, 1841

Concord 14 June, 1841.
Monday Noon.

Dear Lidian,

The blue sky, health & labor have not forsaken us though you have quitted
your fold—We all remain as busy as idle & as languidly happy as the last
week knew us. The children have both been very well and have lived out of
doors all the daylight hours at home yet Waldo wishes you would come
home, when he wakes in the morning & Ellen affirms that you will return
quickly. Mother is well, & presides with great serenity, although sometimes
at thinly attended tables, for in these fine afternoons she finds some difficulty
in clucking her chickens home to tea from the river & the pond. Caroline
prepared to go home today, but we have persuaded her to stay until tomorrow; she is a good child, & I have had a good visit from her, yet I am willing
she should go now,—else I shall not have Margaret Fuller's matters ready,
which she is impatiently demanding for the Dial. Yesterday Mr Saml Ripley
preached the farewell sermon to the old church, which goes down, the spire
at least, this week. But your sinful household were for the most part worship-

ping each in his or her separate oratory in the woodlands—What is droll, Henry Thoreau was the one at church. This P.M. he carries Caroline to Fairhaven in his boat. Margaret Forbes's letter is not yet written, but then my corn & melons are hoed. We all congratulate you on the fine weather of your riding & sailing, & believe this morning in your safe arrival at the City & the Island. Peace & love dwell with all the inmates of my brother's house, & O be sure, dear Lidian, to have no care from home upon your brow: but if you will, you shall select a spot on William's plantation whither we may transport ourselves & build up our Community, when we get quite tired of Concord, or Concord of us. If the United States will sell me Fort Tompkins perhaps I will come. Give my hearty love to William & Susan,—& to Elizabeth my blessing for her labor of love. I am sure the angels will make her journey fair & prosperous to herself also.—Here are verses that I find scribbled in a latest page. You shall give them to her. Yours affectionately

Waldo

I am neither faint nor weary,
Fill thy will, O faultless Heart!
Here from youth to age I tarry,
Count it flight of bird or dart.
My heart at the heart of things
Heeds no longer lapse of time,
Rushing ages moult their wings
Bathing in thy Day sublime.

Write as quick as you can. You need not write but a few lines, if you dread writing: but tell me how you speed: & then again write soon. Love from Mamma

To ———, JULY 3, 1841

Concord, July 3, 1841.

I am very much moved by the earnestness of your appeal, but very much humbled by it; for in attributing to me that attainment & that rest wh. I well know are not mine, it accuses my shortcomings. I am, like you, a seeker of the perfect & admirable Good. My creed is very simple; that Goodness is the only Reality; that to Goodness alone can we trust: to that we may trust all &

always: beautiful & blessed & blessing is it, even though it should seem to slay me. Beyond this, I have no knowledge, no intelligence of methods; I know no steps, no degrees, no favorite means, no detached rules. Itself is gate & road & leader & march. Only trust it; be of it, be it,—& it shall be well with us forever. It will be & govern in its own transcendent way, & not in ways that Arithmatic & mortal experience can measure. I can surely give no account of the origin & growth of my trust, but this only: that the trust accompanies the incoming of that which is trusted. Blessed be that! Happy am I when I am a trust; unhappy & so far dead if it should ebb from me. If I, if all should deny it, then not the less would it be & prevail & create. We are poor, but it is rich: as every wave crests itself with foam, so this can incarnate itself everywhere into armies of ministers, inorganic, organic, plant, brute, man, angel, to execute its will. What have we to do but to cry unto it All Hail, Good Spirit!—it is enough for us that we take form for thy needs: thou art in us; thou art us. Shall we not learn to look at our bodies with a religious joy, & empty every object of its meanness by seeing how it came to be?

But the same Goodness in which we believe, or rather, which always believes in itself, as soon as we cease to consider duties & consider persons, becomes Love, imperious love, that great Prophet & Poet, that Comforter, that Omnipotency in the heart. Its eye falls on some mortal form, but it rests not a moment there, but, as every leaf represents to us all vegetable nature, so love looks through that spotted, blighted form to the vast spiritual element of which it was created & which it represents. We demand of those we love that they shall be excellent in countenance, in speech, in behavior, in power, in will. They are not so: we are grieved, but we were in the right to ask it. If they do not share the Deity that dictated to our thoughts this immense wish, they will quickly pass away; but the demand will not die, but will go on accumulating as the supply accumulates; & the virtues of the soul in the remotest ages will only begin to fulfil the first craving of our poor heart.—

I count you happy that your heart suggests to you such affectionate & noble errands to other spirits as the wish to give them your happiness & your freedom. That the Good Heart, which is the heart of us all, may still enrich you with new & larger impulses of joy & power, is the wish of your affectionate servant—

R Waldo Emerson.

TO A. D. WOODBRIDGE, JULY 6, 1841

Concord, 6 July, 1841.

Miss A. D. Woodbridge—

I owe you an apology for neglecting to acknowledge the receipt of your note enclosing a copy of verses for the Dial—I will not count how many weeks ago. I am not quite so guilty as the date of your note would seem to make me, for it was addressed *Boston* and forwarded to me thence by your friend unknown sometime later. In reply to the inquiry respecting our little journal, the *Dial,* I have to say that all the contributions to that paper are gratuitous. It was set on foot by a party of friends and is furnished with matter by them. A very few persons in whose pen a constant dependence is placed, receive each a copy of the work & no other reward. The occasional contributors have not received even this reccompense, so entirely is this journal an experiment, hitherto uncertain whether its subscription list would pay its printing and publication. Miss Fuller, the Editor, who is to have some contingent allowance from the publishers, has thus far, I believe, received none.

Will Miss Woodbridge now allow me to show her a stroke of the petty tyranny of my office as poetic critic or "Fadladeen" to the Dial and to tell her why I did not press my friend Miss Fuller to insert these harmonious lines you have sent me in the Dial for this month?

I believe I am very hard to please in the matter of poetry, but my quarrel with most of the verses I read, is this, namely, that it is conventional; that it is a certain manner of writing agreed on in society,—(in a very select society if you will) and caught by the ear; but is not that new, constitutional, unimitated and inimitable voice of the individual which poetry ought always to be. I think I ought always to be apprised by any person's poetry, of that individual's private experience. The imagery ought to reveal to me where or with whom he or she has spent the hours, & ought to show me what objects (never before so distinguished) his constitution & temperament have made affecting to him. In short, all poetry should be original & necessary. The verses you sent me are uncommonly smooth & elegant, and happily express a pleasing sentiment; but I suppose I should prize more highly much ruder specimens from your portfolio, which you, perhaps would as much underrate, which recorded in a way you could not repeat, some profound experience of happiness or pain. I have written a long letter, yet have given but a hint of what I should say. You must not, however, judge me so ill, as to think me quite contented with such verses as we have published in our magazine; yet I please myself much with the marked taste for poetry which is showing itself everywhere in the country, & I congratulate you in the possession of an ear & talent which promise so much.

> *With great respect, Your obedient servant,*
> *R. W. Emerson.*

To Lidian Emerson, July 15, 1841

Thursday—

Dear Lidian,

I misinformed you in my last letter about the days of the Hingham & Plymouth Stage line. It meets the one' o'clock Boat at Hingham on Tuesdays Thursdays & Saturdays.—going to P. from H. on the arrival of the boat from B[oston].

But what is the reason that my wife never writes to me. I have written her three letters already since I have been here [Nantasket Beach] & not had so much as a message requesting me not to jump overboard. Well I have no such intention but am always glad to hear from you, being neither an oak nor a rock. But I can never persuade you to make my distinctions, and if I postpone persons & things in my high times you are resolved I shall never know about persons & things, are you not, O Asia, friendly mourner for human calamities! I too who read the Transcript & listen to all the gossip of bar rooms: Surely I am no philosopher: send me word of the very peas & beans: I have got into a pretty good way of reading & writing at last, and so rather grudge to write letters; yet I mean to write one to Elizabeth H. before I go hence. I always fancy that when I once have got myself up to the writing temperature, I have made sure of myself and may then go home with security that the 'barm' will still work. And here I have accomplished some reading that has been lying in wait for me a year or two & so I have not lost the whole time, & I see at least how such materials as I have will work into an oration although I have not had any of those visitations of the high Muse which make a few moments of every life memorable, & one of which would have given me the golden seed of a new Discourse that should have defied all my old readings & writings & been a new plant a new flower in me as in the world. Yet sometimes it is piety, is it not, to accept thankfully the daily moss & manna & not ask that a bird should bring bread & meat or angels should bring us wine? But I hope I have not made my letter too long for the chance of going today. Farewell, with love to all.

W.

To Thomas Carlyle, July 31, 1841

Concord,
31 July, 1841.

My dear Carlyle,—Eight days ago—when I had gone to Nantasket Beach, to sit by the sea and inhale its air and refresh this puny body of mine—came to me your letter, all bounteous as all your letters are, generous to a fault, generous to the shaming of me, cold, fastidious, ebbing person that I am. Already in a former letter you had said too much good of my poor little arid book,—which is as sand to my eyes,—and now in this you tell me it shall be printed in London, and graced with a preface from the man of men [31] I can only say that I heartily wish the book were better, and I must try and deserve so much favor from the kind gods by a bolder and truer living in the months to come; such as may perchance one day relax and invigorate this cramp hand of mine, and teach it to draw some grand and adequate strokes, which other men may find their own account and not their good-nature in re-peating. Yet I think I shall never be killed by my ambition. I behold my failures and shortcomings there in writing, wherein it would give me much joy to thrive, with an equanimity which my worst enemy might be glad to see. And yet it is not that I am occupied with better things. One could well leave to others the record, who was absorbed in the life. But I have done nothing. I think the branch of the "tree of life" which headed to a bud in me, curtailed me somehow of a drop or two of sap, and so dwarfed all my florets and drupes. Yet as I tell you I am very easy in my mind, and never dream of suicide. My whole philosophy—which is very real—teaches acquiescence and optimism. Only when I see how much work is to be done, what room for a poet—for any spiritualist—in this great, intelligent, sensual, and avaricious

---

31. *Emerson's* Essays [First Series] *was published in Britain with a preface by Carlyle.*

America, I lament my fumbling fingers and stammering tongue. I have sometimes fancied I was to catch sympathetic activity from contact with noble persons; that you would come and see me; that I should form stricter habits of love and conversation with some men and women here who are already dear to me,—and at some rate get off the numb palsy, and feel the new blood sting and tingle in my fingers' ends. Well, sure I am that the right word will be spoken though I cut out my tongue. Thanks, too, to your munificent Fraser for his liberal intention to divide the profits of the *Essays*. I wish, for the encouragement of such a bookseller, there were to be profits to divide. But I have no faith in your public for their heed to a *mere* book like mine. There are things I should like to say to them, in a lecture-room or in a "steeple house," if I were there. Seven hundred and fifty copies! Ah no!

And so my dear brother has quitted the roaring city, and gone back in peace to his own land,— not the man he left it, but richer every way, chiefly in the sense of having done something valiantly and well, which the land, and the lands, and all that wide elastic English race in all their dispersion, will know and thank him for. The holy gifts of nature and solitude be showered upon you! Do you not believe that the fields and woods have their proper virtue, and that there are good and great things which will not be spoken in the city? I give you joy in your new and rightful home, and the same greetings to Jane Carlyle! with thanks and hopes and loves to you both.

R. W. Emerson.

As usual at this season of the year, I, incorrigible spouting Yankee, am writing an oration to deliver to the boys in one of our little country colleges, nine days hence. You will say I do not deserve the aid of any Muse. O but if you knew how natural it is to me to run to these places! Besides, I always am lured on by the hope of saying something which shall stick by the good boys. I hope Brown did not fail to find you, with thirty-eight sovereigns (I believe) which he should carry you.

To Margaret Fuller, July 31 and August 2, 1841

Concord, 31 July, 1841.

Dear Margaret, ever to me a friendly angel with a cornucopia of gifts. Tonight came your pacquet whose contents I instantly divined, although the superscription and the seal were foreign. All the parts of this pacquet are of one stuff: they are filled with names & allusions now so near & domestic to me, that I read it as a piece of my life, and love my brothers and sisters. I have had no dealings with you fine Samaritans, for I know not how long past, and have been groping in quite another region, between which & you a Lethe River flows; and now superterraneously you break in on me in a flood and carry me (for this night) all too willingly away. They say in heaven that I am a very awkward lover of my friends. Granted, O Raphael, Urania, Margarita, & Carolina,[32]—but a sincere one. My love reacts on me like the recoiling gun: it is pain:—I was going to add something concerning the capacity to love of this reputed icicle, but the words would tell nothing, and we shall certainly pass at last with each other for what we are.—I give you joy of your two friends—for W. C. will be there—Give me tidings as much as you can of these relations Say to them You have a deaf & dumb brother,—by nature & condition the equal friend of all three,—but who, being hindered by this slight mishap to the organ, from joining the Conversation, claims a full report—to the finest particulars. I am sure they would be Feejee Islanders to grudge me any whisper or glance.—To my especial sister Caroline, I beg you to say, that I cease not to wonder every morning at mail hours that I have no letter from her, and am convinced that she has sent me a letter or letters which have never reached me. I have had but one, since she went to Newbury & I think I have written her *four,* since the date of that.

Yet is it not strange that our love & our labor should ever be so disunited streams. I can plunge me at will in either, but how little they help each other's fulness, and yet each seems spectral and Acherontian, until that confluence takes place. "How little ye bestead!"—But I beseech you to know that for a day or two I have been growing very wise. My wit is lynx-eyed: I detect twenty contradictions which hedge me round where I saw nothing but white walls in all my previous good easy days. Among other things I have discovered that the cause of that barrier some time talked of between us two, is that I have no barrier, but am all boundless conceding & willowy: and many other such like wisdoms have I, too numerous to be sounded by any trumpet. Friends are luxuries, are they not? things that honest poor people can do without but indispensable as serenades & ice to all fanciful persons. Thus the other night I found myself wishing to die because I had friends,—which sounds very like nonsense but was a veritable reverie very pleasant to enter-

---

32. *Samuel Gray Ward, Anna Barker Ward, Margaret Fuller, and Caroline Sturgis. [Rusk]*

tain. Do not fail to write me as often as you can find it in your heart &
charge that cold sister Charity sometimes called Caroline to do the same.

Waldo E.

Monday. I have a letter from C. this morning forwarded from Cohasset of
an old date but it rings like a seashell. Still, still she is in my debt. I will write
directly to Dr Francis, who is neither an oak nor a stone.

To Margaret Fuller, August 16, 1841

Concord, 16 August, 1841

Dear Margaret,

I should gladly have written to you on my journey if I had alighted anywhere
on an inkstand and a quiet half hour; but these are not the gifts of stage
roads & small ocean-steamboats; so with many friendly thoughts cast southward to Newport by way of ventilation & perfume to our dull carting &
boating, I finished my transits in silence. But here at home last night I found
one letter, & this morning, by mail, another, of good remembrance, to be
thankful for; and so I greet you well,—you & Caroline, that the sea is full,
the sunshine & moonshine not yet dim, and the good heart as capacious of
love and as glad of any straw or fibre of virtue or even the hope of such to
cling unto, as ever. I dream I dream that we shall yet meet—all of us and
more than we three—on a far higher ground than ever hitherto with less to
explain with nothing to explain with less to depress or retard or benumb
Strange that there is almost no attempt to realize a fine & poetic intercourse
but that always there should be such vast allowance made for friction until
the best of society gets to be a mere diminution of the friction. I think if you
should read the letters & diaries of people you would infer a better conversation than we ever find. Yet I must preach a little & say that nothing excellent
can ever come of our partial & irregular merits: the delicacy & lustre of our
Corinthian capitals, the carving, inlaying, & painting of our tablets must rest
on the hidden but perfect, foundations of the just & laborious life. I suppose
what is finest in life comes neither out of poverty or riches but out of heights
of character which make themselves so conspicuous that they will not suffer
us to attribute anything to condition, scarcely to know what the condition

was. So jealous is the Godhead of his own praise so unwilling to share it with persons, that we know no great career that is continuous, (—a man goes by steps;—it is the worm that leaves a trail;—) but dots its way along by interrupted points of light so that we do not think the man the master of his work, but ascribe the authorship to a higher will. Well, Courage! courage! the way to God is always as near as it was to our brightest & happiest hour. Do we not feel that we were never younger than we are now? My poverty, my importunate need shall be, O all enriching Soul! itself a childhood and the nakedness of infancy. Teach us whom thou permittest to love thee simply to meet and truly & godlike to converse each standing so fast against the sun as to seem & to be wholly illuminated to the other

I had a good journey & reached Boston Saturday night; saw one or two agreeable & sensible persons—Henry C. Whitaker of N. Y. whose connections live at Providence & Mr Peabody of Portsmouth, & a Mrs Fuller of Augusta. Write me exactly how long you will stay at N. and whither next. When do you wish to confer with the "Committee on the Dial"?

Give my love to Caroline. On the way to Portsmouth I gazed out of the cars at the hills & woods of Newbury, if peradventure I might see any track of light or hint of a spirit. Farewell.

Waldo E.

To Mary Moody Emerson, September 21, 1841

Concord, Sept 21, 1841
Tuesday P.M.

My dear Aunt

Dr [Ezra] Ripley died this morning soon after four o'clock. He suffered nothing and lay quite insensible since Friday morning when he sustained a paralytic shock. The evening before, he received his brother with great gladness and conversed with his usual sympathy & spirit, &, as they testify who heard, made a wonderful prayer before retiring.

The fall of this oak makes some sensation in the forest, old & doomed as it was, and on many accounts I could wish you had come home with me to the old wigwam & burial mounds of the tribe. He has identified himself with the forms at least of the old church of the New England Puritans: his nature was eminently loyal, not in the least adventurous or democratical, and his whole being leaned backward on the departed, so that he seemed one of the rear guard of this great camp & army which have filled the world with fame, and with him passes out of sight almost the last banner & guide's flag of a mighty epoch; for these men, however in our last days they have declined into ritualists, solemnized the heyday of their strength by the planting and the liberating of America. Great, grim, earnest men! I belong by natural affinity to other thoughts & schools than yours but my affection hovers respectfully about your retiring footprints, your unpainted churches, strict platforms & sad offices, the iron gray deacon and the wearisome prayer rich with the diction of ages. Well the new is only the seed of the old. What is this abolition and Nonresistance & Temperance but the continuation of Puritanism. though it operate inevitably the destruction of the Church in which it grew, as the new is always making the old superfluous. I admire the letter of your friend T. T. Stone. Nothing can be better in the way of general statement on the subject of Transcendentalism than his third page. I should not say the same things or all of the same, but he should: and I have copied that page to show to others. Write as much as you please of him & from him, whenever you do not write of yourself.

I am sorry to have bro't home, as I ignorantly did, the Dial which I carried you. Examiners Jouffroys or the like come never into my study, however they may at Waltham. No paper, no review—Nothing but old Plotinus, Iamblichus, Mores, Cudworths, & Browns. Bettina I offered you, but you quite excluded it with contempt. Do you want Carlyle's "Six Lectures.," his last book? I will have it bound immediately—tis in sheets—& *lend* it to you: and Lidian will send her "Beggar Girl," and in a few days you shall have a new Dial with brand new poetry & prose of Antony White's! I will also attend to the paper & sealing wax with great joy & much penitence for my constitutional short comings. I have no time to say anything today which you wish to hear except that I am your affectionate

Waldo E.

Mamma's love & heartily wishes you could see the corpse of the old man, which she says is "the beauty of the dead," a rare expression you will say from my mother. It was indeed a soldier's or a sachem's corpse. & lies on the old couch we all know.

To William and Susan Haven Emerson, November 22, 1841

Concord, 22 November, 1841

Dear William & Susan, Be it known unto you that a little maiden child is born unto this house this day at 5 o clock this afternoon; it is a meek little girl which I have just seen, & in this short dark winter afternoon I cannot tell what color her eyes are, and the less, because she keeps them pretty closely shut: But there is nothing in her aspect to contradict the hope we feel that she has come for a blessing to our little company. Lidian is very well and finds herself suddenly recovered from a host of ails which she suffered from this morning. Waldo is quite deeply happy with this fair unexpected apparition & cannot peep & see it enough. Ellen has retired to bed unconscious of the fact & of all her rich gain in this companion. Shall I be discontented who had dreamed of a young poet that should come? I am quite too much affected with wonder & peace at what I have & behold and understand nothing of, to quarrel with it that it is not different. So love remain with you and all your house!

R. Waldo E

Mother who has not been quite as well as usual for some two or three weeks past by reason of a cold & cough, sends you her love; She must perforce get well at once at sight of this rosebud.

To Mary Moody Emerson, January 28, 1842

Concord, 28 January, 1842

My dear Aunt,

My boy, my boy is gone. He was taken ill of Scarlatina on Monday evening, and died last night. I can say nothing to you. My darling & the world's wonderful child, for never in my own or another family have I seen any thing comparable, has fled out of my arms like a dream. He adorned the world for me like a morning star, and every particular of my daily life. I slept in his neighborhood & woke to remember him. Elizabeth was his foster mother filled his heart always with love & beauty which he well knew how to entertain [blank space] and he distinguished her arrival always with the gravest joy.

This thought pleases me now, that he has never been degraded by us or by any, no soil has stained him he has been treated with respect & religion almost, as really innocence is always great & inspires respect. But I can only tell you now that my angel has vanished. You too will grieve for the little traveller, though you scarce have seen his features.

Farewell, dear Aunt.

Waldo F.

To Margaret Fuller, January 28, 1842

Concord, 28 Jan. 1842.

Dear Margaret,

My little boy must die also. All his wonderful beauty could not save him. He gave up his innocent breath last night and my world this morning is poor enough. He had *Scarlatina* on Monday night. Shall I ever dare to love any thing again. Farewell and Farewell, O my Boy!

W.

To Elizabeth Palmer Peabody, January 28, 1842

Thanks for your kind invitation, my friend, but the most severe of all afflictions has befallen me, in the death of my boy. He has been ill since Monday of what is called Scarlet Fever & died last night & with him has departed all that is glad & festal & almost all that is social even, for me, from this world. My second child is also sick, but I cannot in a lifetime incur another such loss. Farewell.

R. W. Emerson.

Concord, Jan 28, 1842.

TO ANNA AND SAMUEL GRAY WARD, JANUARY 28, 1842

Concord, 28 Jan. 1842.

My dear friends,

You have made yourselves a right to be informed of my extreme sorrow, though, I thank Heaven, you have no experience that can give you any sympathy for me. My little Boy died last night, after an illness of three days. Seems to me never was such a hope blasted, so many hopes dragged to the ground. All is best, but I cannot see now beyond the fatal fact. I had much in my heart to say to you at the beginning of this week, but nothing nothing today. Yet my little Angel shall, I hope, shed a blessing on yours.

Waldo E.

TO CAROLINE STURGIS, FEBRUARY 4, 1842

Concord, 4 February 1842

Dear Caroline,

The days of our mourning ought, no doubt, to be accomplished ere this, & the innocent & beautful should not be sourly & gloomily lamented, but with music & fragrant thoughts & sportive recollections. Alas! I chiefly grieve that I cannot grieve; that this fact takes no more deep hold than other facts, is as dreamlike as they; a lambent flame that will not burn playing on the surface of my river. Must every experience—those that promised to be dearest & most penetrative,—only kiss my cheek like the wind & pass away? I think of Ixion & Tantalus & Kehama. Dear Boy too precious & unique a creation to be huddled aside into the waste & prodigality of things! Yet his Image so gentle, yet so rich in hopes, blends easily with every happy moment, every fair remembrance, every cherished friendship of my life. I delight in the regularity & symmetry of his nature. Calm & wise calmly & wisely happy the beautiful Creative Power looked out from him & spoke of anything but Chaos & interruption, signified strength & unity & gladdening, all-uniting life What was the moral of sun & moon of roses & acorns,—that was the moral of the sweet boy's life softened only & humanized by blue eyes &

infant eloquence. It gladdens me that you loved him & signalized him as you did, and a thousand thanks for your letter. Write to me as soon as you can find it in your heart. Your loving brother

W.

To Lidian Emerson, February 10, 1842

Thursday Night Feb 10
1842
Providence

Dear Lidian I am very sorry to find that I cannot come home on Saturday night but must stay here to lecture on that evening, as my audience are all engaged elsewhere tomorrow Evening; and my nights are to be Saturday, Monday, Tuesday, & Thursday; so that I shall end my engagement a week from tonight & go home the next day. Tonight I read two lectures into one, the Introductory, & the Conservative: But my audience was not large. If it do not grow larger, I shall have to go to New York, I think, to make another adventure to retrieve my losses.—At all events I am sorry not to go home on Saturday, on your account, & on mine, on your friend's who is within your gates, on Mamma's, & on the children's, & lastly on Mr Alcott's, to whom on Sat. Eve. I was to make report of my success. I think to write to him in the course of tomorrow a letter which he shall receive on Monday.

And now how art thou, Sad wifey? Have the clouds yet broken, & let in the sunlight? Alas! alas! that one of your sorrows, that our one sorrow can never in this world depart from us! Well perhaps we shall never be frivolous again, eating of this everlasting wormwood. Meantime Ellen & Edith shall love you well, & fill all your time, and the remembrances of the Angel shall draw you to sublime thoughts. I look out from the window of the cars for him as Ellen does from the chamber window.

I am here at the City Hotel, well enough provided for. As I have brought books with me, I can live easily, but am not permitted to stay in my chamber for the goodness of twenty or thirty friendly people who wish you to drink tea sociably. Shall I not tell them that I live in Concord, and in Concord we never drink tea sociably?—I hope Mary Russell has known how to recall your spirits. I am sorry to lose thus much of her visit. Write to me quickly that you are all well, and give my love to Mamma & to the babies. Farewell! fare best!

Waldo.

To Caroline Sturgis, February 23? 1842

Very grateful & dear to me are your remembrances of the Boy, almost the only ones out of my house which give me any pleasure, for the eye that could see him must extol and enshrine him, and if it could not see him so truly, let there be peace & silence between us. I am stripped of all generosity of nature: He was my ornament, I had need of no other, and from the greatest patrician I am become plebeian at a blow. He as much as any, perhaps he more than any of my little company of friends (all of whom you know) gave a license to my habitual fancy of magnifying each particular in my modest round of experiences to stand for a general & mundane fact, for I cannot tell you what pleasing depths of gentleness & courtesy & friendship I found for myself in little private passages between that boy & me, in giving & taking, in his coming to draw or to play at my study-table, or, last summer, in his first walks with me at some distance from the house. And now that he is gone, every thing looks contemptible: I fancied one day that the boys insulted me in the street: And well they might, for Time & Nature had done so too. Charles Newcomb read me at Providence his two pieces, of Dolon, & in the distinction he drew between genius in children & the intellect in adults, brought the Boy to my mind. His pieces seemed to me full of genius, and I am glad you made for him those beautiful pictures.

O yes, if you have pictures of this Child also in your memory, in your head, do not fail, I entreat you, to draw them all for me on paper. But you will not have,—I sadly believe;—the Real refuses to be represented when it is taken to heart, and a copy is heartily wanted. I who have words & descriptions for everything which moderately interests me, have no line, no memorandum, in these dark weeks to set down, wherewith I might keep my little strong Beauty freshly before me. And because I should be overglad that you could draw for me now, I may know you will not be able? Nevertheless draw or write what you will & I will find in it remembrances & affection for the Boy & for me.

New York, 25 Feb. 1842

Dear Sir,

In Boston yesterday on my way hither from Concord, I learned that you are about editing an American Edition of Sterling's Poems. I hope it is not quite too late to entreat you & the publishers to withhold your hands. Mr Sterling is a valued friend & correspondent of mine now for some years, & I transmitted to him, more than a year ago, the offer volunteered by an admirer of his writings, Andrew L. Russell, an iron-master at Plymouth, Mass., who proposed to get all Sterling's writings republished in this country with the intent to secure the profits of the sale to the Author, provided that Sterling should send us a correct list of the same. Mr Sterling accepted the proposition thankfully & promised the list on his return to London, from which he was then absent for some time. He has since written to beg a little farther delay on account of a Tragedy, "Strafford," which he means shortly to send us, to add to our collection; and which I am constantly expecting. Had I known of your intention I should have earlier informed you of ours; & can now only hope you have not gone too far to stop.

If so, will you not enforce the claim of forbearance on the publisher by informing him that Mr Sterling has been a great pecuniary loser by the unfortunate circumstance that a friend of his invested a considerable sum of money for him in American stock—the Morris Canal Company,—which, I believe, is bankrupt; & we pleased ourselves with thinking that by means of our Edition, America would make him some small amends. If you should have any communication to make to me, I shall probably remain here a fortnight, and a letter addressed to the care of William Emerson, Esq. 64 Wall Street, would reach me.

Yours respectfully,
R. W. Emerson.

R. W. Griswold.

TO MARGARET FULLER, MARCH 1, 1842

Castleton,
Staten Island, 1 March, 1842

Dear Margaret, I was born to stay at home, not to ramble. As soon as I get thus far from my hearthstone, I feel, as two years ago, when I sat in this same apartment, new reason for writing to you, namely, that I may feel myself again, may expand these northern lungs for northern air, somewhat too contracted in this realm of the Knickerbockers—realm strange to me. Through some misunderstanding my first lecture in the city is appointed not until Thursday, so I came down here to stay a little at my brother's. Tomorrow I go to N. Y. & establish myself probably at the Globe Hotel, for a week or two: Yesterday I dined with Horace Greeley and with [Albert] Brisbane the socialist at their Graham boarding house. Greeley is a young man with white soft hair from New Hampshire, mother of men, of sanguine temper & liberal mind, no scholar but such a one as journals & newspapers make, who listens after all new thoughts & things but with the indispensable New York condition that they can be made available; likes the thought but must keep the power; What can I do with such an abettor? He declares himself a Transcendentalist, is a unitarian, a defender of miracles, &c I saw my fate in a moment & that I should never content him. Brisbane wished to know how the "Trans." &c established the immortality of the soul. He had never believed it until he learned it of Fourier, who completely established it! Alas, how shall I content Mr Brisbane? For me was nothing but disclaimers & still disclaimers. Mr B. wished to know if I was master of Fourier? No. Then he must come directly on my arrival at the Globe Hotel & possess me of it by full illimitable personal explanation. So I am to come home an understanding man, if a sad one. These kindly but too determinate persons, the air of Wall Street, the expression of the faces of the male & female crowd in Broadway, the endless rustle of newspapers all make me feel not the value of their classes but of my own class—the supreme need of the few worshippers of the Muse—wild & sacred—as counteraction to this world of material & ephemeral interest. Lidian sometimes taxes me at home with an egotism more virulent than any against which I rail. Perhaps she is right. Greeley, like Hedge, talks of Eclecticism. I mistake,—not like Hedge, but like Cousin & Geo. Ripley. I was driven at once to say, as, I believe I have heard Hedge say, "there was no hope for an Eclectic"; I must unfold my own thought. Each must build up his own world, though he unbuilt all other men's, for his materials. So rabid does egotism, when contradicted, run;

Pity me & comfort me, O my friend, in this city of magnificence & of steam. For a national, for an imperial prosperity, everything here seems irrevocably destined. What a Bay! what a River! what climate! what men! What ample ample interior domain, lake mountain & forest! What manners, what histories & poetry shall rapidly arise & for how long, and, it seems, endless date! Me my cabin fits better, yet very likely from a certain poorness of spirit; but in my next transmigration, I think I should choose New York. Said you that you should not believe me if I subscribed myself your friend?

Waldo

Mr Greeley is greatly interested in Ripley's community. His wife an amiable pleasing woman wishes to board there. I told her what I knew of it. He said he should write to G. R. very soon.

To Margaret Fuller, March 18, 1842

Friday Evening

Dear Margaret

I have tonight your sad & sudden conclusion.[33] That you should be such a lavish spender of time labor & health for our poor Dial, with such a bankrupt's return, makes me very sorry. We are all your debtors & must always be. What to do, now? Miss Peabody has omitted to enclose in the pacquet the Address to the Public, you speak of. But there ought to be time—the press waiting or working,—for the needful questions to be asked— Whether Parker will undertake it? alone? if not so, with me? I think I could

---

33. *In this letter Margaret Fuller announced that she could no longer afford to sacrifice the health and labor which the editorial duties demanded and suggested that Theodore Parker or Emerson might take over the Dial. She had hoped to get the facts before Emerson had returned from New York, but he had come back sooner than she expected. She asked a prompt reply, as she had already written a notice about possible suspension and the press was waiting. [Rusk; and see (17? March 1842) in* The Letters of Margaret Fuller, *ed. Robert N. Hudspeth (Ithaca: Cornell University Press, 1983–1994), 3:53–54]*

easily edit & fill *per alios vel per se* one Number. Two look formidable, & Four incredible. We must have so much time to consult upon & determine this matter as until the last days of this month when our determination may be printed on the covers or on a slip of paper accompanying the title page.

I would even promise for the July Number, but I am not ready tonight to say I will take it for a year. So tell your printers that we must have time to consult. I insert the page written this morning in quite other thoughts of our Future. But I hate to hear of your weakness & needs. Nobody is brave & faithful & self sufficing but you, so I think tonight, and "Rectitude God has taken to heart" forever & ever. And so you who cheer such & so many friends shall be of good cheer undoubtedly, & come to an issue of pure prosperity.

Yours
Waldo—

To Margaret Fuller, March 21, 1842

Monday Morng 21 March 1842

Dear Margaret,

After thinking a little concerning this matter of the Dial, I incline to undertake it for a time, rather than have it stop or go into hands that know not Joseph. I had rather it should not be suspended. Your friends are my friends & will give me such aid as they would have given you and my main resource is to adopt the expedient of Selection from old or from foreign books almost with the liberality to which Alcott would carry it—certainly to make Synesius or Lucian or Chaucer speak whenever a dull article is offered and rejected. Perhaps I shall rue this day of accepting such an intruder on my peace such a consumer of my time as a Dial Perhaps then I shall find some friendly Hercules who will lend a shoulder to uphold the little world. At all events you have played martyr a little too long alone: let there be rotation in martyrdom! Yet shall you not forget to help to help. I think also I had rather undertake it alone than with any partnership of oversight such as Mr Parker or Mr Ripley for example—So little skill have I in partnership that I am sure we should make each other mutually uneasy. Now I will ask of them their whole aid & furtherance. So I think you shall withhold your Notice to subscribers & I will immediately consult Fabricius *on Authors* for solid continent to fill up July withal. You will see at once what folios of information on details & good advice for my first adventure I need Send me word that your head aches less with such prospect of present relief & we will hope that our Dial will one day grow so great & rich as to pay its old debts.

Yours Waldo.

To Frederic Henry Hedge, March 23, 1842

Concord, 23 March, 1842.

My dear Hedge,

Be it known to you that our poor Dial after staggering through two years of external weakness, friendlessness, *public*lessness, and *publisher*lessness, (forgive the words, they are too true) threatened last Saturday on an inspection that was made of its accounts—to die of atrophy. The publishers, Weeks & Jordan, were not only extremely negligent but when they became bankrupt, were much in debt, I am told, to the little Journal. Margaret Fuller has never had a penny for all her time & toil; & now J F Clarke & E P Peabody discovered that they could rely only on 300 subscribers to yield, after deductions for agency but 750. dollars a year, and that the expenses of publishing amounted to 700. There was no chance, therefore, that Margaret should receive anything this year of fit remuneration. She decided to go on no farther. She has been too generous already, and is now far from well in bodily health. She sent me word of all this & put it to me whether the Dial should stop. Very unwillingly I assume the load for a time until a better person appears, more fit for this service & more fond of it. Meantime thus suddenly a new Number, the Number for July, is to be provided for. I recall the friends & favorers of the book, & you among the first. Frederic Henry Hedge, What say you? Have you any word to print on these Times? fact or thought; history, poem, or exhortation? I heartily wish you would send me some fragment of verse or prose that interests you, if you have not leisure or readiness to settle yourself to any labor for our thankless Magazine. Poor Dial! It has not pleased any mortal. No man cried, God save it! And yet though it contains a deal of matter I could gladly spare, I yet value it as a portfolio which preserves & conveys to distant persons precisely what I should borrow & transcribe to send them if I could. Then with all its demerits, it is regarded by several youths & maidens whom I have chanced to see, far-sundered about the country, with such religion, tenderness, & hope, that I dare not let it perish without an effort. It wants mainly & only, some devotion on the part of its conductor to it, that it may not be the herbarium that it is of dried flowers, but the vehicle of some living & advancing mind. But nobody has yet conceived himself born for this end only.

There is public enough, I am sure, for a spiritual writer. I was at New York lately & conversed with many persons who would gladly read him. The old things rattle louder & louder & will soon blow away. Yet this is not a question of *time* All obstructions are already blown away from him who has a thought a purpose in his mind. We cheat ourselves with hunting for phantoms of Church & State. When we awake they are fled dreams. But I wish to say of the Dial that I rely on one expedient to make it valuable namely a liberal selection of good matter from old or from foreign books when dull papers are offered & rejected. Every number can easily be so enriched that they shall certainly have a permanent value for the library. If now, my dear friend, you have any hints for its better conduct or any matter in possession or in prospect or contingency for its pages will you not for the love of America & of your friends & of me, send me it, or promise of it. Yours affectionately

R. W. Emerson.

A young genius whom I found in Providence the other day read a beautiful tale which he promises to give. Excellent verses have I called "Autumn Leaves" from another correspondent. Alcott is just setting out for England & promises chapters of Intelligence. Stearns Wheeler goes to Europe in August & shall do the same. If you see Stone or Prest Wood engage them to befriend us. What is Intelligence from England to real spiritual intelligence from Maine or from Wisconsin?

To Theodore Parker, April 6, 1842

Concord 6 April 1842

My dear Sir,

I ought to have written you many days ago to say, that since Margaret Fuller has put it on me to decide whether the Dial should live or die, saying that if it lived it must be by my nursing; and since I have decided that it shall be reprieved for another year; in this state of things, I must crave your countenance & aid as an element of its life. I am very well aware of the importance of your past contributions to the fame and to the existence of the Journal; & I have always heard from Miss Fuller testimonies to the uniform accuracy & generosity which she could rely on finding in yourself in reference to these matters. By these merits I adjure you to renew & multiply the same for the time to come in favor of our little Journal. I hope it will one of these days be stronger & better. Its days of infancy are somewhat prolonged already. Can you not give me a paper for the July Number? Can you not give me such as early as the 1st May?

Perhaps you have Foreign Literary or Theological Intelligence that would be valuable to us. Perhaps you have some good suggestions for the better conduct of the paper. I shall receive thankfully any communication from you on the subject. And if you should come into Middlesex I beg you will give me the pleasure of seeing you at my house.

Yours respectfully,
R. W. Emerson

Theodore Parker.

To Margaret Fuller, April 10, 1842

Concord, 10 April, 1842.

My dear Margaret, You write as if there was something unexpected to you in my Editorship? I have not seen it announced in the newspaper, but supposed it all settled in my first reply to you weeks ago. Mr Presbury's poem is not in the collection you gave me: I have therefore made no reply to his letter, I ought to have told you this earlier. I have written to Hedge & to Parker for aid, & have good letters from both.

I shall rejoice in such a paper as you propose on the Boston Entertainments; or in any other paper you shall have spirit & leisure to prepare; but I had rather you should send me none than have one headache: and if you will take care to have no headaches, I shall have more papers from you in time to come.

I am reading & writing a little lately with interest, & putting far from me all thoughts of the Dial until 1 May. I have had some guests, now & then a passage of conversation, and a glance at the bright wonder of life but when I read geology I observe that sandstone is a more frequent formation than coal, & coal more frequent than the fossil of beast or bird with fossil eye that records the existence of light & the sun glowing as today on the fens of billions of ages behind. I read a little lately in the "Scientific Surveys" of Massachusetts by Messrs Harris Dewey Storer Gould Emmons By what chance or lucid interval or kindly overruling, came our good Legislature to give itself this bright vacation from Whig & Tory voting lists, from New Valuations, & Revised Statutes, and lend itself to be led for a time by the Boston Society of Natural History? I went, when I was in Boston last time, to the Secretary's office at the state house & begged of him this series of Reports. All of them but Hitchcock's, which is a swollen quarto, I got; and this day I have, as I hope, set Henry Thoreau on the good track of giving an account of them in the Dial, explaining to him the felicity of the subject for him as it admits of the narrative of all his woodcraft boatcraft & fishcraft. Henry is quite unable to labor lately since his sickness, & so must resign the garden into other hands, but as private secretary to the President of the Dial, his works & fame may go out into all lands, and, as happens to great Premiers, quite extinguish the titular Master. My reading lately is to the subject of Poetry, which has at least this advantage over many others, that it pays the student well day by day, even if it should fail to reward his inquisition with one adequate perception after many days & nights. The custom of that enchanted hall I have often heard of, I have often experienced. The Muse receives you at the door with Godlike hospitality gives bread & wine & blandishment will turn the world for you into a ballad drives you mad with a ballad with a verse with a syllable, leaves you with that, & Behold! afar off shines the Muse & her mountain, shines Homer & Shakspeare, shines the world unexplained; and I torturing my syllable. So it will be until we deserve a better fate. Farewell my dear friend, let not me be visited by all courteous & all tedious persons & never compensated by a visit from wise & endeared spirits.

Waldo

To Margaret Fuller, June 9, 1842

Concord, 9 June, 1842—

Dear Margaret,

Wonderful sleepless working loving child, with such aspiration! and with all this doubt & selfreproach! Whether to admire or chide or soothe you? I can no less than do all at once, if there existed any word of such a wondrous mixture of meaning. Failing the word or the skill to find it I must enumerate my emotions in detail. First I thankfully acknowledge the wise & ample chapter you have sent me for the Journal, which operates for me first a great relief by giving me a breathing space, time to consider & prepare things, whilst they are printing this; then calms me with the sense of so much possession, for it is a fine *manly* (that is the word that fits the thing) deliberate criticism on the men & the things before us, so flowing too & so readable, that I am glad & proud of my friend. Then you say you will send me 50 or 60 pages on Romaic poems for October! I am afraid for your health & life. I will not be the axe to cut down the sandaltree which sheds so profusely its perfume on the woodcutter. I hoped you were going to sleep—to sleep a solid month or trimester, and then wake newborn; but now you shall be harried, like the mesmerised, with more work in your night than in your day. Well, I want the article. but I had rather continue to want it, than that you should thus overstrain yourself always.—In respect to the new piece I have sent it to the printer with instruction to get the first proof to you at Dr Randalls on Saturday, if possible, & that you will give directions when you return it, where the remainder shall go.—I beseech you not to think me so irritable & shallow as to fall out with my rich versatile friend at every word or note that is not written in *my* mood. Interpret my largeness by your own, my long suffering & generous friend. Yet that is a compliment too costly to be paid. I believe that we do not believe in any body's heart but our own. Well I am yet glad of the doubts & tenderness which gave occasion to the two letters. I often suppose myself quite incompetent to do you any justice in these years & think I shall in some hour of power roll up all your letters in cloth of asbestos & shooting across this lunar & solar sphere alight on the star of Lyra or the shoulder of Orion and there in some grotto of light meditate your genius until I have computed its orbit & parallax, its influence, its friend & its enemy. In the meantime I wish you to know that I have Dolon in black & white, & that I account Charles K [Newcomb] a true genius: his writing fills me with joy, so simple so subtle & so strong is it. There are sentences in Dolon worth the printing the Dial that they may go forth. Caroline came & staid four days & was tormented with ennui—We exerted ourselves honestly for her amusement, but nothing was of any use but the legs of horses. a remedy never to be applied but in extreme cases.

I shall have more to say presently as indeed I thought I needed a quire of paper when I begun my letter but the presence of very unexpected company in my very writing apartment conceals from me everything else but that I am the dear valuer of your genius & virtues, & wish to know when you shall be in Cambridge, for you must come hither & I will fetch you if I can.

Waldo

To Thomas Carlyle, July 1, 1842

Concord,
1 July, 1842—

My dear Carlyle,

I have lately received from our slow friends James Munroe & Co $246. on account of their sales of the Miscellanies—and I enclose a bill of Exchange for £51. which cost 246.50/100 dollars. It is a long time since I sent you any sketch of the Account itself, & indeed a long time since it was *posted,* as the booksellers say; but I will find a time & a clerk also for this.

I have had no word from you for a long space—You wrote me a letter from Scotland after the death of your wifes mother, and full of pity for me also; and since, I have heard nothing. I confide that all has gone well & prosperously with you; that the iron Puritan is emerging from the Past, in shape & stature as he lived; and you are recruited by sympathy & content with your picture; and that the sure repairs of time & love & active duty have brought peace to the orphan daughter's heart. My friend Alcott must also have visited you before this and you have seen whether any relation could subsist between men so differently excellent. His wife here has heard of his arrival on your coast—no more. I submitted to what seemed a necessity of petty literary patriotism—I know not what else to call it,—& took charge of our thankless little Dial, here, without subscribers enough to pay even a publisher, much less any laborer; it has no penny for editor or contributor, nothing but abuse in the newspapers, or, at best, silence; but it serves as a sort of portfolio, to carry about a few poems or sentences which would otherwise be transcribed and circulated; and always we are waiting when somebody shall come & make it good—But I took it, as I said, & it took me, and a great deal of good time, to a small purpose. I am ashamed to compute how many hours & days these chores consume for me. I had it fully in my heart to write at large leisure in noble mornings opened by prayer or by readings of Plato or whomsoever else is dearest to the Morning Muse, a chapter on Poetry,—for which all readings all studies are but preparation: but now it is July, & my chapter is in rudest beginnings. Yet when I go out of doors in the summer night, & see how high the stars are, I am persuaded that there is time enough, here or somewhere, for all that I must do; and the good world manifests very little impatience. Stearns Wheeler the Cambridge tutor, a good Grecian, and the editor, you will remember, of your American Editions, is going to London in August, probably, & on to Heidelberg, &c. He means, I believe, to spend two years in Germany, and will come to see you on his way; a man whose too facile & good-natured manners do some injustice to his virtues, to his great industry & real knowledge. He has been corresponding with your Tennyson & editing his poems here. My mother, my wife, my two little girls are well: the youngest, Edith, is the comfort of my days; Peace & Love be with you, with you both, & all that is yours!

R. W. Emerson

In our present ignorance of Mr Alcotts address I advised his wife to write *to your Care,* as he was also charged to keep you informed of his place. You may therefore receive letters for him with this.

TO JOHN F. HEATH, AUGUST 4, 1842

Concord, 4 August, 1842.

My dear Sir,

I cannot let Wheeler go from me to you without carrying an acknowledgment of the letter you wrote me from London almost a year ago. I was glad of the good defence of travelling it made. & have been interested since to hear once & again from your friends of the good use to which you have put your journeys & your residences. To hear Schelling might well tempt the firmest rooted philosopher from his home, and I confess to more curiosity in respect to his opinions than to those of any living psychologist. Oken, of whose speculations I have read something, I take to be a scholar first, & then a continuator of Schelling's thought. There is a grandeur in the attempt to unite natural & moral philosophy which makes him a sort of hero. Well you will bring home all his best thoughts, or perhaps, better yet—a result at which he cannot arrive namely the action & reaction which his doctrines awaken in your own mind,—and the general impression which a doctrine makes on us, I think is the test of its truth. If it frees & enlarges,—if it helps me, then it is true; and not otherwise. But you have many more resources & occupations than Schelling & the lecture room; and at Berlin amidst all the brilliant society have doubtless seen the Frau von Arnim, our wonderful Bettine. I have seen two or three travellers who have seen her and who did not much distinguish her in their memories, but we are indebted to her for the most remarkable book ever written by a woman. She is a finer genius than George Sand or Mme de Stael, more real than either, more witty, as profound, & greatly more readable. And where shall we find another woman to compare her with. Then you have the grand Humboldt the Napoleon of travellers an encyclopaedia of science, a man who knows more of nature than any other one in it—What can you tell me of him? It seems to me you are very rich in men to have in one city so large a proportion of the most conspicuous persons in Europe. I heartily congratulate you on your happy position, which must have a rich & happy sequel. You will bring the best home to your countrymen. I shall count it a great kindness if you will make me acquainted with any particulars of your academic life and the course & tendency of your studies, and of the men and the ideas which now attract you. Does the high Platonic Beauty still hover for you in that eastern heaven?

Or is it left behind for realities less fair but nearer, and, as it is pretended, more fit for man? I hope & will believe, it still holds its place and will hold it evermore, changing its names, & becoming more distinctly visible, but by drawing man up to itself, not by any descent on its part. We have little American literary news, and the less to write, that Wheeler will tell you more than any letters. I think it an important fact in our literary history that Cambridge should have both of you in the neighborhood of Berlin at so capital a conjuncture as the present, and I entreat you to send us a loaded journal from that great feast of the Muses.

In return, I will gladly send you any good news I can collect for you from the towns of men or the world of thought. With auspicious hopes for your present & advancing welfare, I am your affectionate servant

R. W. Emerson.

To Margaret Fuller, August 12, 1842

Concord, 12 August, 1842.

Dear Margaret,

I am glad to get your long expected letter as I was grieved to learn on my return last eve that our plenipotentiary sister failed to see you at Cambridge. Well, now please to come, for this I have always desired that you will make my house in some way useful to your occasions & not a mere hotel for a sleighing or summering party. I admire the conditions of the treaty, that you shall put on sulkiness as a morning gown, & I shall put on sulkiness as a surtout, and speech shall be contraband & the exception not the rule. I say nothing, I think nothing in these days, & shall be glad of so fair a diplomatic veil for dulness. Besides, the immense responsibilities of 1 October already are mounting into my horizon, & will shortly overcloud the sky: and I must work like a beaver, or with sharp scissors, for the strong men fail. me. As to the coming hither, if you will consent this time to the Queensberry Diligence or Concord Fly, why, I, in return, will promise my gig for commencement, or for the road to Concord another day; I have grown slight, dissipated, & disturbable in my habit of study by slight things, so that I am very apt to lose more than the day I give to the ride. I have consulted with the Queen & she can muster no objection to the plot more than this that if a visiter or two who may be expected should come to spend a night you will be disturbed for such night in your possession of the bedroom below & driven upstairs into the prophet's chamber or Hole in the Wall, a contingency I suppose to which all mortals in this circumnavigable are occasionally exposed by their fellow circumnavigators. Ellery came up with me yesterday P.M. & I comfort myself with the hope that he will find Concord habitable, and we shall have poets & the friends of poets & see the golden bees of Pindus swarming on our plain cottages & apple trees. Mrs Ripley holds a soirée on Phi Beta night which it will behove us all to attend & we will descend in solid column on Waltham plain. Lest my letter should miss this day's mail, I will not delay longer to send Lidian's message of love and expectation of your coming on Wednesday. Yours,

Waldo.—

To Samuel Gray Ward, September 30, 1842

30 September

My dear Sam,

I received your note on the moment of departing from home on a two days stroll into the country with Mr Hawthorn. At the same time came to me the last proof of the Dial, which I confided to Henry Thoreau for correction—& pursued my walk. You had been so much better to me than my request that I had no right to ask more. So I had absolved you for not writing, & now my book was done. It is curiously composed too. Four articles have been sent me from London, no, five, of which I have printed two & a fraction. Margaret has made a fine selection & translation of Rhine & Romaic Ballads. Ellery has written verses Yourself has written Art; and yet I fear we need all to balance the grim parish politics which the brave Parker has sent & which I printed without reading, pro honoris causa to the writer.

Hawthorn & I visited the Shakers at Harvard, made ourselves very much at home with them, conferred with them on their faith & practice, took all reasonable liberties with the brethren found them less stupid, more honest than we looked for, found even some humour, and had our fill of walking & sunshine.

R. W. E.

To Mary Moody Emerson, October 18? 1842

Nothing has occurred to interest us so much as Dr [William Ellery] Channing's departure, & perhaps it is saddest that this should interest us no more. Our broad country has few men; none that one would die for; worse, none that one could live for. If the great God shined so near in the breast that we could not look aside to other manifestations, such defamation of our Channings & Websters, would be joy & praise, but if we are neither pious, nor admirers of men,—. I wish you would write me what you think after so long a perspective as his good days have afforded, of your old preacher. For a sick man, he has managed to shame many sound ones, and seems to have made the most of his time, & was bright to the last month & week. A most respectable life; and deserves the more praise that there is so much merely external, and a sort of creature of society, in it;   that sort of merit of which praise is the legitimate fee. He seems sometimes as the sublime of calculation, as the nearest that mechanism could get to the flowing of genius. His later years,—perhaps his earlier,—have been adorned by a series of sacrifices which unhappily he rated high, & knew every pennyworth of their cost. His intellect dispensed its stores with the same economy; & he did not omit to intimate to the humble hearer that this truth was only seen by himself. Yet although thus stopping short in both respects of the generosity of genius, he has been, whilst he lived, the Star of the American Church, & has left no successor in the pulpit. He can never be reported, for his eye & his voice cannot be printed, & his discourses lose what was best in wanting them. He was made for the Public; he was the most unprofitable private companion, but all America would have been impoverished had it wanted him. I think we cannot spare a single word he uttered in public,—not so much as the reading a lesson in Scripture, or a hymn. The sternest Judges of the Dead, who shall consider our wants & his austere self application to them, & his fidelity to his lights, will absolve this Soul as it passes, and say, This man has done well. Perhaps I think much better things of him too. His Milton & Napoleon were excellent for the time (the want of drill & thorough breeding as a writer, from which he suffered, being considered) & will be great ornaments of his biography.

Washington, 13 January, 1843

Dear Margaret,

You shall have a word from your friend escaped from his village to the Capitol, if only that he may s'orienter in the fine place. I came hither day before yesterday from Baltimore, & fell instantly & softly on the kind offices of two or three young men who have shown me the best things. The Capitol deserves its name & singularly pleases by its mass,—in this country where we never have the satisfaction of seeing large buildings; satisfies too, by its commanding position, & fine entrances. The interior passages are inconveniently small from the doors to the Rotunda & from thence to the legislative chambers, but the Rotunda I admire. Night before last I went thither to see the Washington, which Greenough was endeavouring to show by torch light. It was his private experiment merely to see if it were practicable to show it so, for now in the daylight it is a statue in a cave. The experiment did not turn out well: a sufficiently powerful light could not be shed on the whole of so great a figure but it must be shown part by part by removing the light,— which is not easy, as there are no fixtures to which the sconce could be attached excepting a standing pole which had been erected & rigged for the purpose. The statue is simple & grand, nobly draped below & nobler nude above, the right Washington head in its plain strength pretty well adhered to, the left arm resigning his sheathed sword, the right arm uplifted. Ill lighted as it is, I suppose this uplifted arm will not please, will not seem sufficiently motived. Greenough wishes to light the face that we may see the reason of the action. It happened that night that our sconce did not succeed very well for it soon set on fire the wooden case which held the lamps & was let down rapidly lamps melting & exploding & brilliant balls of light falling on the floor By the time it was fairly down it was a brilliant bonfire & it was necessary in order not to fill the rotunda (picture hung) with smoke to drag it out of the doors on to the piazza where it drew together a rabble from all parts.—Afterwards with a humbler contrivance the details of the figure which are of great beauty were successively brought out.—But the two hours I spent here were very pleasant. I sat on the stone floor in all parts of this grand area & watched the statue with its great limbs & the colossal shadows of the five or six persons who were moving about; the great height above, & the

moonlight looking in at the sky light and the resonance of every word &
footstep and the electric air of this place, the political centre of the continent
made it a very fanciful & exhilarating spot—John C. Calhoun was one of the
company. Greenough talks very well about his work. He is not confident he
says that he has translated the public sentiment of this country for Washington into marble, but he is very sure of his own diligence & that what has
been in his mind must sooner or later appear. I told him I had rather have it
in this Rotunda, in the worst light, than any where else in the best: The
genius of the place is omnipotent here; but he wishes a separate structure.
But I have not written you what I would; I have been driven to the wall here
with many sights & much company, & shall, I hope, have the more to tell
you hereafter. I go to Baltimore Saturday P.M. Yours Waldo

Give my sure love to Ellery.

To Rufus Wilmot Griswold, April 7, 1843

Concord, 7 April, 1843

Dear Sir,

When Mr Greeley told me he thought Graham's Magazine would be a
desireable medium for the publication of my lecture, I entertained the
proposition for a time, but made no decisive reply. He afterwards wrote me
that Mr Graham would pay me $50.00 for the Introductory Lecture on New
England. It is not easy to set a money value on these things: two persons
would never set the same price. I fancied my work worth twice so much as
the sum named; and immediately wrote him, that I would keep it, as it might
prove to me of great convenience if I should decide to prepare a course of
lectures on New England, to read in Boston next fall. I hope no inconvenience will arise to you from expecting my contribution for a given time.

Yours respectfully,
R. W. Emerson.

Rufus W. Griswold.

TO MARGARET FULLER, APRIL 20, 1843

Concord, April 20, 1843.

Dear Margaret,

I now think to make the effort of continuing the Dial for a new year: unwilling that a book of so good intent & which can avail itself of such costly veins as volunteer to bleed for it, should die; and whilst it has such sincere wishes from a few good people that its life should be prolonged, which wellwishers we will gladly believe represent a larger unknown company hovering in distance, or even in the Future. A great part of the reason why it should continue comes from you. You like that it should go on, & you offer so liberally after your liberal nature. You shall then do for it what you see fit, only I am always tempted in writing to you on this subject to bespeak your continence & not give too precious hours to writing articles even for Liverpool poets & critics or Cambridge acolytes to study. I will not have those divine bees who sting the brutish or you may read British world, *animasque in vulnere ponunt,*[34] lay their deaths at my door. So be as dull as a muse can who is also a friend, & very much wanted under the moon.

I have the subscription list this morning, in which I do not count but 220 subscribers: but Miss Peabody, affirms what I willingly hear that there is a change operating in the business of magazines—viz. that people incline rather to buy single numbers than to subscribe: and of all our journals, the Dial ought best to stand this test,—of merit in single numbers.

I will make the amendment of securing its publication on the first day of each quarter, which seems so important to booksellers. & I will try what can be done for more efficient publishing: but my main reliance of course must be in the goodness of the book; we are not magazine makers, but wish to represent &, by representing, further the best culture of New England. If possibly, if possibly, the Dial could look beautiful to you, my friend, & to me, I could well forgive its slender popularity.

I have a letter from Carlyle today announcing the arrival by the new come Brittania of his new book half in print half in MS—called "Past & Present," for us to print here. It is in four parts the Proem; the Monk; the Worker; the Horoscope;—Something like this is the division; but I have not seen the

---

34. *"They put their souls in pain."*

book. It comes an inconvenient moment for it requires hurry, & I was getting
meditative on a chapter which I greatly wish to write. But the great brilliant
friend must be served on the instant when he is 3000 miles off. Yours,
Waldo.—

> Lidian greatly desires to hear of her St Johns' friends, the twins. Let the first
> news that come, come to her,—prithee.

TO THOMAS CARLYLE, APRIL 29, 1843

Concord,
29 April, 1843

My dear Carlyle,

It is a pleasure to set your name once more at the head of a sheet. It signifies
how much gladness, how much wealth of being, that the good, wise, man-
cheering, man-helping friend, though unseen, lives there yonder, just out of
sight. Your star burns there just below our eastern horizon, & fills the
lower & upper air with splendid & splendescent auroras. By some refraction
which new lenses or else steamships shall operate, shall I not yet one day see
again the disc of benign Phosphorus? It is a solid joy to me that whilst you
work for all, you work for me & with me, even if I have little to write, &
seldom write your name.

Since I last wrote to you, I found it needful, if only for the household's
sake, to set some new lectures in order, & go to new congregations of men. I
live so much alone, shrinking almost cowardly from the contact of worldly
and public men, that I need more than others to quit home sometimes, &
roll with the river of travellers, & live in hotels. I went to Baltimore, where I
had an invitation, & read two lectures on New England. On my return, I
stopped at Philadelphia, & my Course being now grown to four lectures,
read them there. At New York, my snowball was larger, and I read five
lectures on New England. 1, Religion; 2, Trade; 3 Genius, Manners, &
customs. 4, Recent literary & spiritual influences from abroad. 5 spiritual
history.—Perhaps I have not quite done with them yet, but may make them
the block of a new & somewhat larger structure for Boston, next winter. The
newspaper reports of them in N.Y., were such offensive misstatements, that I
could not send you, as I wished, a sketch. Between my two speeches at

Baltimore, I went to Washington, 37 miles, and spent four days. The two poles of an enormous political battery, galvanic coil on coil, self-increased by series on series of plates from Mexico to Canada, & from the sea westward to the Rocky Mountains, here meet & play, and make the air electric & violent. Yet one feels how little, more than how much, man is represented there. I think, in the higher societies of the Universe, it will turn out, that the angels are molecules, as the devils were always Titans, since the dulness of the world needs such mountainous demonstration, & the virtue is so modest & concentrating.

But I must not delay to acknowledge the arrival of your Book [*Past and Present*]. It came ten or eleven days ago, in the Britannia, *with* the *three* letters of different dates announcing it.—I have read the superfluous hundred pp. of Ms. and find it only too popular. Besides its abundance of brilliant points & proverbs, there is a deep steady tide taking in, either by hope or by fear, all the great classes of society,—and the philosophic minority also, by the powerful lights which are shed on the phenomenon. It is true contemporary history, which other books are not, and you have fairly set solid London city aloft afloat in bright mirage in the air. I quarrel only with the popular assumption, which is perhaps a condition of the Humour itself, that the state of society is a new state, and was not the same thing in the days of Rabelais, & of Aristophanes, as of Carlyle. Orators always allow something to masses, out of love to their own art, whilst austere philosophy will only know the particle. This were of no importance, if the historian did not so come to mix himself in some manner with his erring & grieving nations, and so saddens the picture: for health is always private & original, & its essence is in its unmixableness.—But this Book, with all its affluence of wit, of insight, & of daring hints, is born for a longevity which I will not now compute.—In one respect, as I hinted above, it is only too good, so sure of success, I mean, that you are no longer secure of any respect to your property in our freebooting America.

You must know that the cheap press has, within a few months, made a total change in our book markets. Every English book of any name or credit is instantly converted into a newspaper or coarse pamphlet, & hawked by a hundred boys in the streets of all our cities for 25, 18, or 12 cents. Dickens's "Notes" for 12 cents, Blackwood's Magazine for 18 cts., & so on. Three or four great New York & Philadelphia printing houses do this work, with hot competition. One prints Bulwer's novel yesterday, for 25 cents; and already in twenty four hours, another has a coarser edition of it for 18 cents, in all thoroughfares.—What to do with my sealed parcel of Mss & proofs? No bookseller would in these perilous circumstances offer a dollar for my precious parcel. I inquired of the lawyers whether I could not by a copyright protect my edition from piracy until an English copy arrived, & so secure a sale of a few weeks. They said, no; yet advised the taking a certificate of copyright, that we might try the case if we wished. After much consulting & balancing for a few hours, I decided to print, as heretofore, on our own account, an edition, but cheap, to make the temptation less, to retail at 75 cents. I print 1500 copies, & announce to the public that it is your edition, & all good men must buy this. I have written to the great Reprinters, namely to Park Benjamin, & to the Harpers, of New York, to request their forbearance; & have engaged Little & Brown to publish, because, I think, they have something more of weight with Booksellers, & are a little less likely to be invaded than Munroe. If we sell a thousand copies at 75 cents, it will only yield you about 200 dollars: if we should be invaded, we can then afford to sell the other 500 copies, at 25 cents, without loss. In thus doing, I involve you in some risk; but it was the best course that occurred.—Hitherto, the "Miscellanies" have not been reprinted in the cheap forms; and in the last year, J[ames]. M[unroe]. & Co have sold few copies; all books but the cheapest being unsold in the hard times; something has however accrued to your credit there. J. M. & Co. fear that if the new book is pirated at N. Y. & the pirate prospers, instantly the "Miscellanies" will be plundered. We will hope better or at least exult in that which remains to Wit & Worth unplunderable, yet infinitely communicable.

I have hardly space left to say what I would concerning the Dial. I heartily hoped I had done with it when lately our poor good careless publishing Miss Peabody, who sent your number so wisely through the English post office, wrote me that its subscription would not pay its expenses (we all writing for love.) But certain friends are very unwilling it should die & I a little unwilling, though very unwilling to be the life of it, as editor. And now that you are safely through your book, & before the greater Sequel rushes to its conclusion, send me, I pray you, that short chapter which hovers yet in the limbo of contingency, in solid letters & points. Let it be, if that is readiest, a criticism on the Dial, and this too Elysian race, not blood, & yet not ichor.— Let Jane Carlyle be on my part, &, watchful of his hours, urge the Poet in the golden one. I think to send you a duplicate of the last Number of the D. By Mr [Horace] Mann who with his bride [Mary Peabody Mann] (sister of the above-mentioned Miss Peabody) is going to London & so to Prussia. He is little known to me, but greatly valued as a philanthropist in this State. I must go to work a little more methodically this summer, and let some thing grow to a tree in my wide straggling shrubbery. With your letters came a letter from Sterling, who was too noble to allude to his books & mss. sent hither, & which Russell all this time has delayed to print; I know not why, but discouraged, I suppose, in these times by booksellers. I must know precisely, & write presently to J.S. Farewell!

R. W. Emerson.

To Henry James, Sr., May 6, 1843

Concord, 6 May, 1843

My dear Sir,

It is hardly true to the relation between us that no intercourse should occur until I shall sometime go to your city or you shall pass through my village; and yet a friendly silence is more grateful than inadequate communion, as most Communions are. I recall with lively pleasure our free conversations, cheered to me by the equal love, courage, & intelligence I met, and if I were a day younger or had a few grains more of reliance on circumstances, I should have already more than once obeyed my inclination to ask how your dice were falling and furthermore whether there were no hope that they might fall within the Massachusetts line. For I could not help feeling in talking with you how much you would enjoy the society of a few persons whom I most value, & with the assurance of being valued in return. But this & the like of this, I leave with the silent Disposer who loveth not meddlers, & often allows them to punish themselves. I live in Concord, & value my nest, yet I will not promise to myself or another that I shall not in a year or two flee to Berkshire from so public & metropolitan a place as this quietest of country towns.

But the reason of my writing now is to inform you that a friend of mine who has been an inmate of my house for the last two years, Henry D. Thoreau is now going, tomorrow, to N. Y. to live with my brother William at Staten Island, to take charge of the education of his son. I should like both for Mr Thoreau's & for your own sake that you would meet and see what you have for each other. Thoreau is a profound mind and a person of true magnanimity, and if it should happen that there is some village pedantry &

tediousness of facts, it will easily be forgotten when you come at what is better. One can never be sure that these delicatest of all experiments, experiments of men & intercourse, will prosper, but if you remain in the city this summer, which seemed uncertain, I wish you would send your card to him through my brother at 64 Wall Street. I want that he should tell you about our Dial, which has just escaped the fate of being extinguished. Can you not send me some brief record of your faith or hope to enliven our little journal with a new element?—I have never learned from [William] Tappan whether he carried home your Montaigne & found you, That also I had much at heart and now the 'other friend' G[iles]. Waldo, has come to N. Y. & as I understand it, the two are in the same office. Gladly I would learn how you prosper with [William Henry] Channing also.—I had nearly forgotten to say that if you meet Mr [Parke] Godwin, as I believe you know him, you would mention Thoreau to him, as one of our main contributors to the Dial, and as one who would be very glad of literary employment and would make on many subjects very valuable papers. He hopes to make his pen useful to him through the Journals or Booksellers. Here is a longer letter than I dreamed of when I began, yet I wish to be remembered to Mrs James.

Your affectionate servant,
R. W. Emerson.

To Henry David Thoreau, June 10 and 15, 1843

Concord, 10 June 1843

Dear Henry,

It is high time that you had some token from us in acknowledgment of the parcel of kind & tuneful things you sent us, as well as of your permanent rights in us all. The cold weather saddened our gardens & our landscape here almost until now but todays sunshine is obliterating the memory of such things. I have just been visiting my petty plantation and find that all your grafts live excepting a single scion, and all my new trees, including twenty pines to fill up interstices in my "Curtain," are well alive. The town is full of Irish & the woods of engineers with theodolite & red flag singing out their feet & inches to each other from station to station. Near Mr Alcott's the road is already begun.—From Mr A. & Mr [Charles] Lane at Harvard we have yet heard nothing. They went away in good spirits having sent "Wood Abram" & Larned & Wm Lane before them with horse & plough a few days in advance of them to begin the Spring work. Mr Lane paid me a long visit in which he was more than I had ever known him gentle & open, and it was impossible not to sympathize with & honour projects that so often seem without feet or hands. They have near a hundred acres of land, which they do not want, & no house, which they want first of all. But they account this an advantage, as it gives them the occasion they so much desire of building after their own idea. In the event of their attracting to their company a carpenter or two, which is not impossible, it would be a great pleasure to see their building which could hardly fail to be new & beautiful. They have 15 acres of woodland with good timber. Ellery Channing is excellent company and we walk in all directions He remembers you with great faith & hope thinks you ought not to see Concord again these ten years, that you ought to grind up fifty Concords in your mill & much other opinion & counsel he holds in store on this topic. Hawthorne walked with me yesterday P.m. and not until after our return did I read his "Celestial Railroad" which has a serene strength which one cannot afford not to praise,—in this low life.

Our Dial thrives well enough in these weeks. I print W.E.C.'s "Letters" or the first ones, but he does not care to have them named as his for a while. They are very agreeable reading, & their wisdom lightened by a vivacity very rare in the D.—Ward too has sent me some sheets on architecture, whose good sense is eminent. I have a valuable manuscript—a sea voyage, from a new hand, which is all clear good sense, and I may make some of Mr Lane's graver sheets give way for this honest story; otherwise I shall print it in October. I have transferred the publishing of the Dial to Jas. Munroe & Co.—Do not, I entreat you, let me be in ignorance of any thing good which you know of my fine friends Waldo & Tappan Tappan writes me never a word. I had a letter from H. James, promising to see you, & you must not fail to visit him. I must soon write to him, though my debts of this nature are perhaps too many. To him I much prefer to talk than to write. Let me know well how you prosper & what you meditate. And all good abide with you!

R. W.E.

15 June—Whilst my letter has lain on the table waiting for a traveler, your letter & parcel has safely arrived. I may not have place now for the Winter's Walk in the July Dial which is just making up its last sheets & somehow I

must end it tomorrow—when I go to Boston. I shall then keep it for October, subject however to your order if you find a better disposition for it.—I will carry the order to the faithless booksellers. Thanks for all these tidings of my friends at N. Y. & at the Island. & love to the last. I have letters from Lane at "Fruitlands"[35] & from Miss Fuller at Niagara. Miss F. found it sadly cold & rainy at the Falls.

TO BENJAMIN PETER HUNT, AUGUST 8, 1843

Concord, 8 August, 1843.

My dear Sir,

It is much more than time that I should acknowledge directly to you the joy with which I found the prize which you had put at my disposal in the Journal which Mr Dennis sent me. As I read it the first time it seemed to me the best of all sea voyages, and I made no delay in assuring myself that Mr D. had printed no part of it; for a year's experience of editorship has not a little whetted my natural appetite to a good Manuscript by the insatiate Secondary or Editorial hunger. It delights me by its directness & veracity, by its plain strength and its insight, and by its capital art of compression & of omission which in all writing seems so much. To me too it has another quite additional to all its rhetorical values inasmuch as it realizes so fully for me the promise of the large wise boy who made my school days in Chelmsford so glad by his lively interest in books, & his native delight in ethical thought; and life looks more solid & rich to me when I see these many years keep their faith, and when I rejoin a principal figure in my group so accomplished & perfected after so long a separation One thing seems plain to me that your distrust of your talents for a success in literature is quite unfounded and that you need never shudder at the danger of being confounded with the very small practitioners whom I have heard you name. I am quite sure that there are none of the Messieurs nor Mistresses of the New York magazine press who could dare to handle your steel pen, or write one line of this Journal. My friend & neighbour Mr Hawthorne who is a better critic than he is a writer

---

35. *Bronson Alcott, his family, Charles Lane, and a few others had begun "Fruitlands," their attempt at communal living, at nearby Harvard, Massachusetts, earlier in June.*

quotes this piece in the Dial as a solitary example of facts which had not lost their vigour by passing through the mind of a thinker. He set a very high value on the whole piece. I have many other distinct testimonies to its rare merit, so that if any other voice were to be heeded than the inward summons of the Muse herself, I think you would have ample reason for making a fair experiment of your powers of instructing & entertaining the public. Why will you not with these repeated visits to the W[est]. I[ndies]., add to this journal what is most striking in your unreported experience and make a narrative which if not a picture of the Islands will be what is much better a daguerrotype of the observer's mind & character. The printing in the Dial, such is the happy obscurity of that Journal, will be a very harmless rehearsal to a very small private audience, whom yet I cannot refrain from gratifying with another portion of the Manuscript I hold. Mr Dennis has been recently in Concord & though quite ill for a time seemed to enjoy talking of you, & gave me many particulars which greatly contented me. I heartily wish to see you, & when you come to this region again, I beg you to come directly to my house; so shall I be surest of seeing you. Meantime I wish you would write me some account of your present position & plans, & specially what you think of this design of writing: & tell me if I cannot aid you in such an enterprise with our booksellers.

> *Your affectionate servant*
> *R. W. Emerson.*

To Elizabeth Hoar, August 31, 1843

Concord, 31 August, 1843—

Dear Elizabeth,

If Windsor is pleasant to you you shall stay there with the good leave of all & of me also. but if it is not better than Concord, I wish heartily you would come home in the first stage. Caroline S. is here since last Monday until next Monday, & rejoices me by her love & reverence of you, and a long conversation yesterday made me wish for your participation & counsel. I could not help wishing as I heard the description of social disadvantages that some effort might be made for the relief of sensible people Their sufferings seem too so susceptible of remedy. They fancy that by living within reach of each other's society they could work & suffer better, & very reasonably anticipate from the instructions of sympathy an unlimited benefit: The experiment of Brook Farm is just so far valuable that it has shown the possibility & eminent convenience of living in good neighborhood, and that part of the institution may be borrowed & the rest left. I can think of nothing so certain to stop the perpetual leakage of the continent—letting all the best people flow off continually in the direction of Europe—than to make them fond of home by concentrating good neighborhoods. Is not the universal rule for the prevention of rovers & bad husbands, to make their own house pleasant to them. Every week I hear of some conspicuous American who is embarking for France or Germany, and every such departure is a virtual postponement of the traveller's own work & endeavour. I do not know how much my sensibility to this mischief is sharpened by hearing yesterday that William Tappan proposes to sail for Italy by the first vessel: Simmons sails next week I believe, & [Theodore] Parker next week & Henry James prepares to go, & Charles Newcomb may go at any time, & I suppose in a fortnight I shall have a farewell letter from Henry Thoreau. I have not yet learned that Rockwood has engaged his berth, but Tom Appleton who is a sort of fine genius, I am told, has gone again. Now if these very persons or such of them as could bring their books & works, & Ellen Hooper & Margaret F. & Caroline & others as readily named, would by the slightest concert whenever & as far as it is in their power choose one place as Concord or Cohasset or Berkshire, the whole world would not be the poorer and all of us would be incomparably richer. Perhaps we should be ashamed to be idle or to be mean. Perhaps we should find a common end in the diffusing something good—Let us hope it!—I can easily suggest good sequences that might come, but the strength of the argument of Concord Socialism lies herein that half a dozen rare persons are at this moment available as recruits or conscripts for a Sacred Phalanx who would forever esteem him as their benefactor who should embody them in the name of the most holy Trinity Truth, Goodness, & Beauty. Let me not be crowded out of my message by want of room, that William Prichard also grieves over your absence & begged me to pray you to return. Write that you will come immediately & I will ask Caroline to prolong her visit. I think I must write to Henry James and inquire why he should go to Europe when America has such claims & invitations. There is a strong way of putting this as well as weak cries of dilettantism. What do you think. Shall there be a reasonable neighborhood or only foolish ones. Your loving brother

Waldo.

To Charles Anderson Dana, October 18, 1843

Concord, October 18, 1843

My dear Sir,

I am sorry I have suffered weeks to pass without a direct answer to your note, & yet there is a kind of fitness in waiting so long. Be it known to you, then, on the part of the total Senate of the Dial, that you shall not have that Journal. It does not seem to be known to you that the moral character of that paper from the beginning through three tedious years & two quarters, has been uniformly masked by a black ingratitude. It has coaxed & wheedled all men & women for contributions: it has sucked & pumped their brains, pilfered their portfolios, peeked into their journals, published their letters, and what it got, it has mutilated, interpolated, & misprinted, and never so much as said, Thank you, or Pardon me; on the contrary, a favourite method has been to extract by importunity a month's labor from its victim, & when it was done, send it back or suppress it as not fit for our purpose. The Dial Senate may possibly know that you have contributed some poems to its numbers. The more excellent they are, the more in character will it be to say, you shall not have the Dial for them, but the Dial must have some more of the poems, & for the next number. If this reasoning from character is not satisfactory, our beggar is almost too proud to whine that the Book is in debt to its gratuitous editor seventy or eighty dollars, & that the edition of the last number it was thought prudent to reduce from 500 to 350 copies, so that it is necessary to sell all the numbers copies to make an honest Dial of it, except the few which are given to large Contributors.

Very respectfully & unthankfully—on the part of the Dial,

C. A. Dana, Esq.

To Margaret Fuller, October 18 and 19, 1843

Concord, 18 October, 1843

Dear Margaret,

It is good to hear from you again, and though I have begun to blot, I will not turn back. Thanks for your beneficent proposals in behalf of Lidian, who, I doubt not, will be glad to do as you say, as she certainly entertains it happily today. Health is a pregnant name, and Hygeia shall prove a metonomy for every muse in turn. Your conversation-room, I judge, *is* that which Bettine projected, and in the long winter into which our times have fallen is the search of the best after the sun. Strange strange absence of the soul of our souls. I have gone trifling the other day, the finest day, to the top of a hill with Ellery, & was surprised on turning, with the beauty in which I found myself like some profane person. 'How camest thou hither unprepared, O child!' said the gracious presence. I wondered this morning at the hard shallow fruitless worldliness in which I spend my days, & felt, as often before, that I should fly to profoundest solitude & the quittance of care—I, who in comparison with others am a hermit & an exempt. They say the railroad has made Massachusetts Boston, and I fear my habits & affections will make every cave Massachusetts. Yet would it not be best to accept the first omen of this kind & be driven into the wilderness humbly & gladly. Nature would wear a new face to the pilgrim who sought her thus holily & with so awful a guide. It is to such that she confides laws on tables of stone for half mankind, or opens the ever sealed senses & embodies for them all current tendencies in panoramas of Heaven & Hell. Yet one would ask no reward but the high sense of newness & true communiion with the Power which was obeyed. Every epoch in a private spirit is a new kingdom for mankind, opens new leaves in the intellectual & moral world. Our antiquities & poetries are commonplaces, & have become stale. We are but a step from the Temple wherein all things shall become new. I am glad you have recovered Charles N[ewcomb], for yourself he should be the truest votary. A high & plain speech should be used among all faithful men & women, and the hidden worthiness would answer unexpectedly.—Charles shall be silent with my goodwill ten years, if his silence is commanded,—but if he have any doubts, I find his silence already too long. Let him come & spend a couple of days with me, now: he shall be greatly welcome. Thanks evermore for your goodwill to the Dial. Yes if you will write of Strafford, it will be very grateful to me. I have written to Sterling to acknowledge the kindly pleasing book, and shall most gladly give him that gratification you offer.

19 My letter waited too long & will not find you at B[rook]. F[arm]. I had a good letter the same day as yours from C[aroline]. S[turgis]. and one from S[amuel]. G[ray]. W[ard]. & one from my Aunt. Forgive & love if you can or as you can your incommunicable yet affectionate W. There must be somewhat analogous in the factories of heaven to those of earth and as we

make all of cast iron now & not of wrought, so are the men now made run in moulds, but do not yield or expand.

To Margaret Fuller, December 17, 1843

Concord, 17 December, 1843.

Dear Margaret

My life is made up of excuses, I have thought lately, and I will not add new ones to you—Meantime the deed the affirmation which burns up all apologies delays to be born. The felon Dial, the felon lectures, friend, wife, child, house, woodpile, each in turn is the guilty cause why life is postponed If life were a hoax, what an admirable devil must he be who puts it on us, delay breeding delay & obstruction obstruction until the seventy years are fully told, & we are bowed out before we have even begun. Truly the founders of Oxford fellowships & of celibate orders & the administrators of oaths of silence & of solitude were wise endeavourers & many failures should not discredit their prudence. Deception endless deception,—tis wonderful how rich the world is in this opium. The inexorable demand of every hour, of every eye that is fixed on us, of every friendly tongue, is that we lead the impossible right life; and every step in that direction has a ridiculous & an insane appearance. It requires an enormous perspective, some centuries perhaps, to correct these obliquities & wild refractions of our vision, but we cannot wait for the aesthetic gratification, but must keep the road to Heaven though it lead through Bedlam. It is lucky for the peace of Boston & all honest cities that the scholars & the religious generally are such puny bodies; if they had any vigour answerable to their perception, they would start aside every day from expectation & their own prescription, and destroy the peace of all burgesses. For me, I have only impulse enough to brood now & then on the conditions favorable to thought & life, but not enough yet to make me either pirate or poet. And this "Not Yet" is the arch deceiver of all the ages, and when we sleep will deceive our children.—Will it be any consolation to you in these clouded days—which you describe—of your muse, to hear the confessions of weakness? No no we have very quickly enough of the litanies of "miserable sinners."—I am, as always, so now newly bound to you, for this good deed of yours to Sterling, which you so depreciate. I make up my mind that it will be good. Yes, do write of Mrs [Lydia Maria] Child's book, a thankful sentence. Your copy, it is said, has disappeared, then I will send you mine. Mr Lane was here lately again for two or three days having been arrested for his taxes as he stopped with the Harvard Stage at the tavern. He declined bringing any friend to answer for him & was put into jail. Rockwood Hoar heard of it & paid the debt, & when I came home from seeing you in Boston I found him at my house. He was sad & indisposed. Now he & Mr Alcott think they have been wrong in all these years with Pestalozzi in lauding the Maternal instinct, & the Family, &c. These they now think are the very mischief. These are selfish & oppose the establishment of the community which stands on universal love: You shall see.

Ellery is actually chopping now for more than a week past oak trees in Lincoln Woods. He puts all poets & especially all prophets far far in the background. Your friend

Waldo—

To Sarah Margaret Fuller, January 6, 1844

It is the least like writing & the most like vital affluent communication that can be. It is an infinite refreshment to me to see it in the dry stone "Dial." The hardened sinners will be saved for your sake, O living friend! I think, that, when, (if you should do such a thing, & many many years hence may it be!) you shall lay your body in the ground, the dust will beat & palpitate above, & the flowers that grow there thrill & tremble to the eye.

To Margaret Fuller, January 30, 1844

Concord, January 30, 1844.

Thou steadfast loving wise & dear friend, I am always astonished at thy faith & truth—I cannot tell whether they be more divine or human. How have you adopted the life of your poor friend and the lives that are dear to him, so easily, & with a love at once connate & prophetic, which delights & admonishes me at the same time. I am glad of guardian angels, but life is a treasure of soberer worth under the fanning of their wings.

When last Saturday night Lidian said, "It is two years today—" I only heard the bellstroke again.[36] I have had no experiences no progress to put me into better intelligence with my calamity than when it was new. I once had occasion to transfer before the Probate Judge the guardianship of an Irish child who had been the ward of my brother Charles, to a new guardian, a gentleman in Boston. A poor Irishman who was her Uncle wished himself to have the charge of her little estate & opposed the new appointment but his counsel—seeing the persons interested, forsook him,—the judge slighted his objections, & appointed the gentleman, & the poor Roger could only say to all of us strangers, as he did very distinctly, "I am not satisfied." I am often in his condition; I feel all his impotence; and have only to say after my fashion, 'I am not satisfied.' I read lately in Drummond of Hawthornden, of Ben Johnson's narrative to him of the death of his son who died of the plague in London: Ben Johnson was at the time in the country, & saw the Boy in a vision, "of a manly shape, & of that growth he thinks he shall be at the resurrection." That same preternatural maturity did my beautiful statue assume the day after death, & so it often comes to me to tax the world with frivolity.—But the inarticulateness of the Supreme Power how can we insatiate hearers perceivers & thinkers ever reconcile ourselves unto? It deals all too highly with us low-levelled & -weaponed men. Does the Power labour, as men do, with the impossibility of perfect explication, that always the hurt is of one kind & the compensation of another. My divine temple which all angels seemed to love to build & which was shattered in a night, I can never rebuild,—and is the facility of entertainment from thought or friendship or affairs, an amends? Rather it seems like a cup of Somnus or of Momus. Yet flames forever the holy light for all eyes, & the nature of things against all appearances & specialties whatever assures us of eternal benefit. But these affirmations are tacit & secular. if spoken, they have a hollow & canting sound; and thus all our being, dear friend, is evermore adjourned. Patience & Patience & Patience! I will try, since you ask it, to copy my rude dirges to my Darling & send them to you. And warm thanks for Richard's, which I had neither seen nor heard & which are original with love & thought. Lidian also desires me to thank you in her behalf for your love of the Child & of her husband & she rejoices in your existence & powers. Your affectionate Waldo—

---

36. *Young Waldo had died on 27 January 1842.*

I enclose one of the M[ercantile] Library [lecture] tickets for Wednesday 7 Feb which is my evening. I was mortified to find that the "Ethnical Scripture" which I gave you at Cambridge was printed on, which I did not find till I came home. I have since been to the printer & am to have more that are not.—

To Christopher Pearse Cranch, June 7, 1844

Concord, June 7, 1844.

My dear Sir,

I received a few days ago, in Boston, the beautiful little volume of poems which you had sent me, and on opening them & your letter, I found the deeper obligation you had put me under, by the inscription. Had you asked me beforehand, I should have said, Be it far from thee, Lord! for I dare not sit for a moment in the chair, and all the skill I have is to study in the youngest class. As you have thrust me into place I must only hope that your fair & friendly book shall not suffer by the choice, and then thank you for the noble gift. I am glad to find my old friends in the book, as well as new ones, &, throughout, the same sweetness & elegance of versification which I admired in the pieces which adorned our first Dials. But I should like to talk over with you very frankly this whole mystery & craft of poesy. I shall soon, I hope, send you my chapter on "the Poet," the longest piece, perhaps, in the volume I am trying to bring to an end, if I do not become disgusted with the shortcomings of any critical essay, on a topic so subtle & defying. Many, many repentances he must suffer who turns his thoughts to the riddle of the world, & hopes to chant it fitly. each new vision supersedes & discredits all the former ones, and with every day the problem wears a grander aspect, and will not let the poet off so lightly as he meant; it reacts, & threatens to absorb him. He must be the best mixed man in the Universe, or the universe will drive him crazy when he comes too near its secret. Of course, I am a rigorous, cruel critic, & demand in the poet a devotion that seems hardly possible in our hasty, facile America. But you must wait a little, & see my chapter that I promise, to know the ground of my exorbitancy; & yet it will doubtless have nothing new for you. Meantime I am too old a lover of actual literature, not to prize all real skill & success in numbers, not only as a pledge of a more excellent life in the poet, but for the new culture & happiness it promises to the great community around us. So I am 'again your debtor, and your grateful & affectionate servant.

R. W. Emerson.

To William Emerson, October 4, 1844

Concord, 4 October, 1844.

Dear William

I received on my return from Boston three days ago your letter with its enclosure of $174. and was very glad to hear that your long recusant partner Mr F. was willing to render reason. We are all disconcerted by Elizabeth's illness which may be tedious and may hinder Mother's long projected visit, for the season. I have been confined at home this rainy day by a cold, & yesterday & cannot go out to know how Elizabeth prospers I suppose she may suffer many weeks with a slow bilious fever Let us hope not. Aunt Mary is at Waltham from Waterford. I detected her in Roxbury the other day when I was in & about the city, & laid two successive trains of arrest & conveyance to get her to Concord, but, as usual, she slipped from them both, &, in a sort of spite, planted herself at Waltham, where it is house-crowded term-time. I have lately added an absurdity or two to my usual ones, which I am impatient to tell you of. In one of my solitary wood-walks by Walden Pond, I met two or three men who told me they had come thither to sell & to buy a field, on which they wished me to to bid as purchaser. As it was on the shore of the pond, & now for years I had a sort of daily occupancy in it, I bid on it, & bought it, eleven acres for $8.10 per acre. The next day I carried some of my well beloved gossips to the same place & they deciding that the field was not good for anything, if Heartwell Bigelow should cut down his pine-grove, I bought, for 125 dollars more, his pretty wood lot of 3 or 4 acres. and so am landlord & waterlord of 14 acres, more or less, on the shore of Walden, & can raise my own blackberries. I am now, like other men who have hazarded a small stake, mad for more. Since Mrs Brown wishes me to build her a cottage on some land near my house; & the dreaming Alcott is here with Indian dreams that I helped him to some house & farm in the Spirit Land! These are the light headed frolics of a hack of a scribe when released at last from months of weary tending on the printers devil! I expect to grow fat & plump now for weeks to come. My book [*Essays: Second Series*], I prayed the publisher to secure me some copies of in time to send you tomorrow but he did not seem willing to promise any before Monday or Tuesday.

Yours with love to Susan & boys!
Waldo.

To John Chapman, December 30, 1844

Concord, Dec 30 1844

Mr John Chapman
Dear Sir,

I am in your debt for two or three unanswered letters, & for important good deeds, besides. I received your reprint of my First of August Address, & was very well contented with the handsome pamphlet[37] I have also the reprint of the Essays[38] which Mrs Lee bro't me & your letter & accompanying newspapers; for all which you will accept my particular thanks. The style of the reprint is unexceptionable, &, wherever I have looked into it, appears carefully correct. There is an unlucky for (keeps) for (keep) on the second page, in the second poetical motto to "the Poet." And though I have no motto to substitute, I should be glad if you print any more copies, to suppress the motto on the title-page. If your plan requires a motto for each member of your series, I will keep an eye open for any sentence I may meet which will serve. Also I should willingly drop the motto on the "Address": but it is a trifle. I shall be sorry, & on your account also, if your public do not, as you intimate, like this book as well as its forerunner but I shall by no means accept their opinion in the first month as final. What I have not made, but only recorded, I am sure the experience of other men will confirm. I could easily give you a list such as you ask for of the few writings I have published in our literary journals, but I should not like to have them reprinted without

---

37. *The London publisher John Chapman had published Emerson's* The Emancipation of the Negroes in the British West Indies *in early October.*
38. *Chapman's edition of* Essays: Second Series *had been published on 9 November.*

a careful revision & correction by myself: which, if you think it desirable, I may undertake. But I doubt—Old pieces are not sufficiently attractive to me to seem worth the labor. Our booksellers have repeatedly asked me to collect my verses into a volume, which perhaps I shall adventure.

> *Respectfully, your obliged servant,*
> *R. W. Emerson.*

To Thomas Carlyle, December 31, 1844

Concord, 31 December, 1844

My dear friend,

I have long owed you a letter & have much to acknowledge. Your two letters containing tidings the first of the mortal illness, & the second of the death of Sterling, I had no heart to answer. I had nothing to say. Alas, as in so many instances heretofore, I knew not what to think. Life is somewhat customary & usual; and death is the unusual & astonishing: it kills in so far the survivor also, when it ravishes from him friendship & the most notable & admirable qualities. That which we call faith seems somewhat stoical & selfish, if we use it as a retreat from the pangs this ravishment inflicts. I had never seen him, but I held him fast: now I see him not, but I can no longer hold him. Who can say what he yet is & will be to me? The most just & generous can best divine that. I have written in vain to James to visit me, or to send me tidings. He sent me, without any note, the parcel you confided to him, & has gone to Albany, or I know not whither.

I have your notes of the progress of my London printing, &, at last, the book itself. It was thoughtless in me to ask your attention to the book at all in the proof state: the printer might have been fully trusted with corrected printed pages before him. Nor should Chapman have taxed you for an advertisement: only, I doubt not he was glad of a chance to have business with you; and, of course, was too thankful for any *Preface*.[39] Thanks to you for the kind thought of a "Notice," & for its friendly wit. You shall not do this thing again, if I should send you any more books. A preface from you is

---

39. *Carlyle's two-page "Notice" appeared in Chapman's edition of* Essays: Second Series.

a sort of banner or oriflamme, a little too splendid for my occasion, & misleads. I fancy my readers to be a very quiet, plain, even obscure class,— men & women of some religious culture & aspirations, young, or else mystical, & by no means including the great literary & fashionable army which no man can count, who now read your books. If you introduce me, your readers & the literary papers try to read me, & with false expectations. I had rather have fewer readers & only such as belong to me.

I doubt not your stricture on the book as sometimes unconnected & inconsecutive is just. Your words are very gentle. I should describe it much more harshly. My knowledge of the defects of these things I write is all but sufficient to hinder me from writing at all. I am only a sort of lieutenant here in the deplorable absence of captains, & write the laws ill as thinking it a better homage than universal silence. You Londoners know little of the dignities & duties of country Lyceums But of what you say now & heretofore respecting the remoteness of my writing & thinking from real life, though I hear substantially the same criticism made by my countrymen, I do not know what it means. If I can at any time express the law & the ideal right, that should satisfy me without measuring the divergence from it of the last act of Congress. And though I sometimes accept a popular call, & preach on Temperance or the Abolition of slavery, as lately on the First of August, I am sure to feel before I have done with it, what an intrusion it is into another sphere & so much loss of virtue in my own. Since I am not to see you from year to year is there never an Englishman who knows you well, who comes to America, & whom you can send to me to answer all my questions. Health & love & joy to you & yours!

R. W. Emerson

To John Sullivan Dwight, April 20, 1845

Concord, April 20, 1845

My dear Sir,

Your letter was very kind & friendly, and one is always glad that anything is adventured in the midst of so much excusing & impediments; and yet, though I should heartily rejoice to aid in an uncommitted journal, not limited by the name of any man, I will not promise a line to any which has chosen a patron.[40] We shall never do anything, if we begin with being somebody else. Then, though I admire the genius of Fourier, since I have looked a little into his books,—yet it is only for his marvellous tactics; he is another French soldier or rather mathematician, such as France is always turning out, and they apply their wonderful ciphering indifferently to astronomy, chemistry, war, or politics. But they are a sub-type, as modern science would say, deficient in the first faculty, and therefore should never be allowed the lead in great enterprises, but may very well serve as subordinate coadjutors, where their power as economists will stand in good stead. It seems sadly true that the scholars & philosophers, & I might say also, the honest & well disposed part of society, have no literary organ or voice which is not desperately sectarian, and we are always impelled toward organization by the fear that our little power will become less. But if things come to a still worse pass, indignation will perhaps summon a deeper voiced & wiser muse than our cool New England has ever listened to. I am sure she will be native, and no immigrant, least of all will she speak French. But she will, I doubt not, have many wreaths of honor to bestow on you & your friends at Brook-Farm; for courage & hope & real performance, God & man & muses love. You see how little & how much faith I have. As far as your journal is sectarian, I shall respect it at a distance: if it should become catholic, I shall be found suing for a place in it.

Respectfully & affectionately yours,
R. W. Emerson

To Evert Augustus Duyckinck, August 25, 1845

Concord, 25 August, 1845.

Evert A. Duyckinck, Esq
Dear Sir,

I have delayed my reply to your letter for several days because I did not wish to send a refusal, when you had kindly opened so many doors for my

---

40. *Dwight had hoped to enlist Emerson as a contributor to the new Brook Farm paper* The Harbinger. *[Tilton]*

compliance. But I believe it is not in my power to undertake either to furnish Messrs Wiley & Putnam with a new book, or with a compilation of my scattered papers. The principal objection to the second, lies in this, that I have a sort of friendly understanding with Mr John Chapman of London, bookseller, who some time ago proposed to publish my things in London, on a system of half profits, and has not ceased to solicit me from time to time to collect these very 'scattered pieces,' correct, & reprint them there. If I should compile the book, I should be disposed at present to send it to Mr Chapman (for an English sale,) in acknowledgment of his friendly & prior proposals,— whilst your friends W. & P. have, I am aware, an English house. For your third proposition, that respects an edition of Mr Landor's works, I think I might make the selection, if I knew how many numbers you wished it to consist of. Would you reprint Pericles & Aspasia (the best fitted on many accounts for a cabinet book)? The whole Pentameron ought to be printed; the whole Pentalogia omitted. I should omit the whole "Examination of Shakspere": And the whole question will be what proportion will you publish of the 5 English octavos of "Imaginary Conversations." *For* of his volume of poems, I suppose there are & can be no readers here. I could easily select one volume, and, if I should look at the work, I suppose I should say, two volumes, of your size, from the "Imag. Conversations."—And I suppose I might adapt & enlarge a little that critique in the Dial to which you refer. If you will give me your opinion on this matter, I will decide at once whether I will undertake it.

Yours respectfully,
R. W. Emerson

TO CAROLINE STURGIS, OCTOBER 1, 1845

I do not know whether the fine sentence in your letter concerning the Children of the Mist, points at any sentence of mine it is of no importance, it is certainly elegant & I admired it. But all things with me are of a sad earnest, and I am very negligent of professing love, since whatever really draws me, draws me as daylight & gravitation do, & many years do not release me from my friends. I do not know whether I have ever dared to expect in recent years any concurrence of the circumstance to my affection & scarcely more any concurrence of affection to my affection. The guiding Genius has required a covenant of the heart that it shall adjourn to a quite infinite future its rightful satisfactions. If at any time I rebel, the Genius knows very well how to whip me with my defects & send me to my cell again; so that I had long ago in one plane of life almost ceased to believe that any peer of mine, my quantitative & qualitative peer, if you will forgive the expression, could see through so many & many surfaces, and nobly love me, nor can I now perhaps for any long time together maintain the belief. Against this skepticism I have, dearest friend, our singular friendship, every passage of which I religiously regard. But the Genius is sometimes sinister then when he should be best, and fine as are your influences, & noble as is your appreciation, I am not quite contended. We do not wish to feel the weight of ourselves in the presence of our friend, but only power to unite, to rise & to raise. If we have powers which our friend never saw exerted, we long to summon them also from their subtle cells to elevate the hour. With you therefore it must happen that I should say, well there is a better friendship yet for both of us to dwell in together. How then can you tolerate this? and I anticipate your discontent, and fortify myself again in my solitude.—This whiff of sentiment has expanded itself, you see, into a very long dull smoke— to end in my old saw, that I dearly love my friend, but never expect a return in the world that now is. Great & generous wonderfully is my friend's nature, and great demands are made on her by her brother's infirmities, but, though I have not ended my shrift, I will break it off.—The lost letter came, & this day came the new letter, with tidings that you were ill, & do remain. Last night I looked for you in the down train. May the fever be gone. As for Concord, Sophia Hawthorne goes out of town on Thursday, they quit us then.[41] The house is to be vacant all winter, except during the repairs of some rooms by carpenters. I asked Mr Ripley if he would not have you for a tenant until spring? "Yes, if she will endure the hammering." So you had better bring Margaret Curson & a manservant & live there. I think I may escape out of Concord for a day or two on one of my pen & ink excursions presently but it will not last longer. If you come & make the promised visit, call Lidian to council as to houses & places. Margaret has not come but is I believe daily expected. Come here by all means and to this house and if I should not be at home stay till I come, and then, only stay long enough to tell me all you

---

41. *Nathaniel and Sophia Peabody Hawthorne, who had lived in Concord since their marriage in July 1842, left for their new home in Salem on 2 October.*

have learned in Brattleboro, unless you decide to sit down & board with Lidian; for I am a spacious reader for these six or eight weeks to come have I answered any of your questions? Ellen Hooper and Anna H. and Susan Sturgis came hither the other day & called at this & other houses—. I was very sorry that I was in Boston all the while.

1 October

To Evert Augustus Duyckinck, October 14, 1845

Concord, 14 October, 1845

My dear Sir,

I fear you find me a very dilatory correspondent: I wish you may not think me also a very impracticable one. It seems to me you make me a very liberal offer on the part of Messrs Wiley & Putnam for my book of Poems; and yet it does not in fact promise me the advantage I had expected from the book, nor an equal advantage to that I do derive from my prose books, which may be presumed to be less popular. I do not well carry figures in my head, but I believe I have received or am to receive between 5 & 600 dollars for each edition of my "Essays," the first series, counting 1500 (all sold), the second 2000 copies. I print them at my own risk, & Munroe & Co have 30 per cent as their commission. This, by means of a little better style of book, and its higher price. If I print my Poems in Boston, I suppose the book will cost 75 cents; and if we sell 2000 copies, I should receive more money than by the sale of 2500 on the scale you propose.

Our people too say that a large proportion of purchasers prefer in works of this kind a costlier style of book. Perhaps then it would be better for author & readers to print a costlier edition first, & a cheaper afterwards. I think Munroe told me this. But to say what I ought to have said in the beginning of the sheet, it has been for a few days growing almost certain that I must postpone my printing a little, & lose the advantage of the New Year. My engagements to the Lyceum will not now permit the attention to the Poems which they seem to require. I shall not take any new step in regard to their publication without communicating further with you. J. M. & Co have announced them as *in press* without any authority. As for the "Lectures" which made the subject of a note also from you, I will see what they grow to, and can better answer you after some weeks.

> *Yours respectfully,*
> *R. W. Emerson.*

To William J. Rotch, November 17, 1845

Concord, Nov. 17th, 1845.

W. J. Rotch, Esq., Secretary

Dear Sir:—If I come to New Bedford, I should be ready to fix, say the first Tuesday of March, and the second. But I have to say, that I have indirectly received a report of some proceedings in your Lyceum, lately, which, by excluding others, I think ought to exclude me. My informant said, that the application of a colored person for membership by purchase of a ticket in the usual manner, had been rejected by a vote of the Lyceum; and this, for the first time. Now, as I think the Lyceum exists for popular education, as I work in it for that, and think that it should bribe and importune the humblest and most ignorant to come in, and exclude nobody, or, if any body, certainly the most cultivated,—this vote quite embarrasses me, and I should not know how to speak to the company. Besides, in its direct counteraction to the obvious duty and sentiment of New England, and of all freemen in regard to the colored people, the vote appears so unkind, and so unlooked for, that I could not come with any pleasure before the Society.

If I am misinformed, will you—if they are printed—have the goodness to send me the proceedings; or, if not printed, their purport; and oblige,

> *Yours respectfully,*
> *R. W. Emerson.*

To Samuel Gray Ward, February 16, 1846

Concord, 16 Feby 1846

My dear Ward,

Ellery Channing has suddenly found out that he must see Europe, that he must see it now,—nay, that it is a matter of life & death that he should set out for Havre & Italy on the first of March. I played with the project when he first broached it, thinking that after a week I might never hear of it again, but hearing from his wife as well as from himself that he was as serious as he is capable of being in this design I challenged him to a dinner & an evening yesterday, & talked it through with him. He thinks it indispensable that he should see buildings, & pictures, & mountains, & peasantries, part of his poetic education—never was poet who did not see them—that he has seen this country through—there is no hope for him but in the excitement of that. Art, Art alone is his object. &c, &c. He talks well enough about it and I can see well enough that it is all in his system, truly enough.

Well, how to do it? He says in reply to my suggestions about this & that method, that he knows perfectly well that no newspaper whatever will give him a penny for his "Correspondence," and that therefore he will not apply to them, that's flat. What next? He has calculated, Heaven knows how, that he can go for a year to Italy (England is not in his plan; nor Paris even, except on the way) for 250 or at most 300 dollars, including the passage money. He can go, he says, & will, in the steerage, to Havre, for 25 dollars. Well, he has written letters to various persons, to Mr Ticknor Mr Cushing & others (I know not what secrets I am blabbing but you can burn the sheet) asking aid in this design of a poet for the Muse's sake. Ticknor refused; all refused; except Mr Cushing, who will cheerfully give the hundred dollars he asked for. Caroline Sturgis is to give $75. . I am to give as much more: We want fifty dollars of you, if you can spare them, and behold his three hundred complete. It is not desireable (secret still) that he should have any more than a poor artists provision, for (his wife said this to me) for said she, if he has money, he only spends it in idlest indulgences. Write me what you think & can advise. With love & joy to you & yours, your friend

Waldo Emerson.

To John Chapman, Concord, May 15, 1846

Concord 15 May 1846

Mr John Chapman,
Dear Sir,

I was sorry to have let slip the occasion of the writing by the last steamer to acknowledge your letter. I am sorry again that I have so little good account to give of my forwardness to take advantage of the good opportunities you continue to offer me. This volume of poems though now pretty certain I hope to be ready for the next Christmas still remains in imperfectness. The Seven Lectures which I read in the winter in Boston, I shall, no doubt, print some day; but they are quite too incomplete for print now. I am, in these very days, revising & enlarging them, but I dare not fix a time when they will be ready to send to you. Munroe & Co have pressed me to reprint the first & second series of Essays in two uniform volumes. But I do not find even that easy, for I wish, if I can, to keep the first series in one volume; & the second needs a considerable addition to go as its companion. In one or another way we must soon execute this last plan.

Though I have so little satisfaction to give you on these points I believe you must take my word for it that I am not quite idle & after a few months I shall hope to give you something to print.

With great regard,
Yours,
R. W. Emerson.

To William Henry Furness, May 22, 1846

Concord, 22 May, 1846.

My dear Friend,

I have nothing to send to the new Diadem. I am sorry for it. But I have promised to do what I can to make a volume of poems, and those which I can suffer to pass for publication are so few, that I dare not diminish the number by a single quatrain or couplet. Then for prose, I am like some bookdealers who will never sell me the thing I want, for it will break a set.

With the most vigorous recollections, I cannot remember that I ever wrote anything detached & of reasonable dimensions. You see my desperate imbecility, & will leave me to time & my tub for recovery.

I am trying to put into printable condition my seven Lectures on Representative Men; but the topics were so large, & seem to require such spacious & solid reading, that what might pass to be spoken, does not promise to be fit to print in a hurry.

Your abominable
R. W. Emerson

To The Corporation of Harvard University, June 25, 1846

To the Corporation of Harvard
University.
Gentlemen,

I request the privilege of borrowing books from the College Library, subject to the usual rules for their safety & return.

I do not find myself included in any class of persons entitled by law to this privilege. I ask it as an alumnus of the College engaged in literary pursuits, & constantly in want of books which only the University can supply, & which it has provided for precisely such needs as mine; and as, in my residence, conveniently situated for easy access to Cambridge

I have formerly endeavoured to borrow books by special orders signed, in each case, by the President. But this mode is very troublesome to the President, & very inconvenient to the borrower. It may easily happen, as it has happened to me, that after I have selected my books at the Library, the President is not at home, or not at liberty; then I must return to my house, fourteen miles distant, without them.

Presuming the willingness of the Corporation to extend the usefulness of their valuable Library to the utmost limits compatible with safety, I pray them to grant me the right of taking books thence, from time to time, in my own name.

R. Waldo Emerson.

Concord, 25 June 1846.

To William Emerson, September 21, 1846

Concord 21 Sept 1846

Dear William,

I am absurd in not answering earlier your letter concerning Mr Appleton's proposition the days are so fast diminishing in which it can be entertained— But I am settling into the belief that the best offers of the booksellers are not good and that it is best for me to keep the property of my own book as I have usually done and only employ them as publishers. I have usually found that in that way, I received at last only a little less than 33 per cent on the retail price of the book or if I cheapen the book to the trade say 30 or 25 per cent. There is no risk in so doing, for my books uniformly pay for themselves, and this book of poems is much more sure of an easy sale than its foregoers. The objection to this course is, that the bookseller will not press the sale of the book at a distance which he prefers to sell at his own counter and monopolize the retail commission, which is larger. But if the book is good, the distant trader will have to send for it, & then it will go to him at trade prices. If I publish it myself, as I incline to, I shall have to employ, I suppose, my old agents here; as I can more easily work with them, & can know if they do me any wrong; but at a distance I cannot work so well, nor know if I am fairly treated.

Our people in Boston like a costly book So I think to get a good edition of the poems first; and if it seems advisable I will presently after print on coarser paper.

Mr Appleton's offer is about as good or nearly as good as Wiley & Putnam's last fall. Munroe would readily rise on either of them. I believe, a bookseller who had capital, & knew what Munroe & I know, could make me a much better offer, which I might accept.

I ought to have apprised Mr Appleton when it was in his consideration,— that I mean to offer only the American sale of the poems, as I have promised Chapman in London to send him a copy that he can copyright. The book itself is about done: I mean it shall end with this month. And it is never separable from my person long enough to go to N.Y. & Staten Island, as I meant it should, in its callow state.

Lidian has not yet returned from Plymouth The children have come home well Mother went on Saturday to Littleton in cars without escort; & found Bulkeley well & happy; & returned safely at night. Mr Hall charges board for the 3 months last, at $1. per week, & credits 6.00 for his work. I think he might have rendered a still more favorable account by mother's statement, and am sorry I cannot go there a day. Mother's eyes are improved & she thinks shortly to write you a letter with her own hand. With love to Susan, & to the boys, Yours,

Waldo—

To John Abraham Heraud, January 31, 1847

Concord, 31 January, 1847.

Mr John A. Heraud,
Dear Sir,

I received your letter & the accompanying programmes of the "Half Yearly Review." I have spread them abroad among such persons here, as I thought would like to know the design. Very direct aid in any way I think it would be sanguine to promise you. There is no reason to expect in Boston any other pecuniary support to the work, than simply a number of subscribers for single copies: and as for aid in the composition of the book itself, it will not be very easy to draw our few writers into any engagement with what may seem to them a distant enterprize. And yet, perhaps I ought to say, this will be in the power of the Journal to effect. One or two numbers of a paper of a truly superior tone, belonging equally to all countries, may easily persuade men of genius that it alone speaks their native language. But we have very few writers, as yet, to add to the few already known to you. Elizur Wright, now the editor of a very successful daily paper in Boston, called "the Chrono-type," has a great deal of talent with courage & catholicity. Mr H. D. Thoreau is a man of profound & symmetrical nature, who, if he lives, will certainly be heard from in this country, & I think in yours also. Mr Alcott may never succeed, as he has not hitherto succeeded, in giving a written expression to his original & religious thinking; but he may be reckoned on as a sure ally of everything great & good. You must not fail to talk with Margaret Fuller, on the subject, who is well acquainted with the best people in New York, as well as Boston,—& is the most eloquent & independent of women. I am also acquainted with a few young men of whom I entertain high hopes. For myself, I do not like to promise any very efficient aid; for, though I may easily contribute a paper or two, as the work goes on, yet my papers, when good for anything, have no timeliness, and I am the worst periodical writer.

Meantime, I shall not fail to keep the programme before such friends as I shall meet from time to time, &, if your purpose is really to go into effect, next spring, I shall be glad to be informed of it, & will send you the names of such subscribers as I can, & more aid by word & deed, if more arrives.

> *Respectfully, Your friend &*
> *servant,*
> *R. W. Emerson.*

I requested Mr Chapman of Newgate Street to send you a volume of my Poems,—which I hope he did not neglect.

To William Emerson, February 13, 1847

Concord, 13 February, 1847

Dear William,

I have been driven lately into a scrutiny of my accounts to make myself ready for some approaching payments and as usually happens on such investigations do not find my results perfectly gratifying. The immediate occasion of my counting is the necessity of paying on 1 April next $500. for the field east of my house which, after some years talking about, I agreed with Warren last year that I would buy during this, and, a month ago, I received the deed & gave my note payable on the 1 April. But I have other debts; $450. to the Concord Bank, for one; & the discovery, too, not quite unexpected, that our present system of boarding costs me more than did our own housekeeping.[42] Another circumstance occurred last year, which makes a part of my affair, and which I do not know that I have communicated. Aunt Mary, in some of her fancy-practice in real estate, sold a valuable part of her farm for a trifle to

---

42. *"The feeble health of my wife having made it necessary that she should be relieved of the care of housekeeping, I engaged Mrs [Marston] Goodwin [in April 1846] to take my family to board in my house. She removed with her family to Concord & remained with us sixteen months and we had the opportunity of knowing very intimately her manner of conducting the affairs of a household comprising much of the time 16 or 18 persons"* (L, 4:117).

a Mr Matthewson, a jeweller in Providence. Mr Robert Haskins who, you know, always fancied the farm was his, & acted on the fancy, found himself embarrassed by this new owner. He came to me for help—and in reply to all his unintelligible histories, I told him I had no cent to give him, but, that a good farm need not be lost for want of a hundred dollars, I would borrow for him a hundred dollars on his bringing to me Gore Ripley's assurance that there was security from the farm for that money.

Gore looked into it, & immediately came out here to tell me that he found Aunt Mary was owner, & had "got herself into a scrape" by the Matthewson dealing, & that he Mathewson must be bought off by all means. I told him that I would try to raise the money necessary for the purpose, but must borrow it, & he must secure it on the land. He negotiated with Matthewson, who demanded 400. for what I believe cost him 25 dollars at first, and I, at last, paid, in all, $325.00, for which I hold Aunt Mary's note & a mortgage. Again, in the course of the last year, Aunt Mary wrote me, that she had borrowed of somebody 25.00, a year or two ago, & given a deed of one acre, (a deed not acknowledged or recorded, I believe, but meant as a memorandum to the parties) as payment. She wished me to pay this debt, & have the amount added to my claim on her estate. This also I have done; paid $29.00, & have or am to have some sort of security. But these dealings with Aunt Mary, you are aware, withdraw just so much money as they involve, entirely from present use; as she pays no interest in these years. Of course it appears in that balance of 450. against me at the Concord Bank.

Well I carried my results to Abel Adams & told him I should want money in April & must sell stock though unwillingly. Abel talked the matter over & inquired about my account with W. E. & G. F. and, on my saying, that you had proposed to make a transfer & a partial settlement (?) within a year or some short time,—he advised that I should write you the facts & inquire whether you could not without inconvenience reduce 5800 (is it not?) to 5000 by the 1 April.

I have the expectation of some advantage from the sale of my new book, but not to any solid purpose before next January. So you shall send me your counsel in this matter, and if what I suggest can not be done without straits & hurts, do not attempt it, as I can certainly get the money through Mr Adams.

Your affectionate brother
Waldo

To Alexander Ireland, February 28, 1847

Concord, 28 February, 1847

My dear Sir,

I owe you new thanks for your friendly & faithful attention to the affair of Lectures which you have put me on. But I had not anticipated so prompt an execution of the project. as you now suggest. Certainly, I cannot think of it for April. For September—I will think of it, but cannot at present fix any thing.

I really have not the means of forming an opinion of the expediency of such an undertaking It would be very displeasing to me to make a visit of literary propagandism in England All my impulses to work of that kind would rather employ me at home. It would be still more painful to me to put upon a few friends the office of collecting, an audience for me by puffing & coaxing. At the same time, it would be very agreeable to me to accept any invitation to read lectures from societies or a number of friendly individuals who sympathized with my studies, But although I possess many decisive tokens of interest in my pursuits & way of thinking from sundry British men & women they are widely sundered persons, & my belief is that in no one city unless it were London could I find any numerous company to whom my name was favorably known. So that you see my project requires great frankness on your part. You must not suffer your own friendly feelings to give the smallest encouragement to the design.

In regard to the remuneration of Lectures here, we have all rates as we have all merits. I have formerly read courses of Lectures on my own account to classes collected by advertisement in the newspapers: and for a course of ten lectures I once received, after the payment of all expenses, 576 dollars; or, 57 dollars for each lecture. That is the highest payment I ever received. From the Boston Lyceum, last winter, I received 50 dollars for each lecture of a course of seven; by a previous agreement. And the Lyceum was no loser, as I was told. These are city prices. I often read lectures to our country Lyceums, which usually pay their Lecturer $10.00, & his travelling expenses.

If I were younger, it would give me great pleasure to come to England & collect my own audience as I have done at home here, & I have that confidence in my favorite topics that I should undertake the affair without the least distrust. But perhaps my ambition does not give to a success of this

kind that importance it has had for me. At all events in England I incline
rather to take than give the challenge.

To Evert Augustus Duyckinck, March 12, 1847

Concord, 12 March, 1847.

E. A Duyckinck, Esq.
Dear Sir,

Mr Henry D. Thoreau of this town has just completed a book of extraordinary merit, which he wishes to publish. It purports to be the account of "An Excursion on the Concord & Merrimack Rivers," which he made some time ago in company with his brother, in a boat built by themselves. The book contains about the same quantity of matter for printing as Dickens's Pictures of Italy. I have represented to Mr Thoreau, that his best course would undoubtedly be, to send the book to you, to be printed by Wiley & Putnam, that it may have a good edition & wide publishing.

This book has many merits. It will be as attractive to *lovers of nature,* in every sense, that is, to naturalists, and to poets, as Isaak Walton. It will be attractive to scholars for its excellent literature, & to all thoughtful persons for its originality & profoundness. The narrative of the little voyage, though faithful, is a very slender thread for such big beads & ingots as are strung on it. It is really a book of the results of the studies of years.

Would you like to print this book into your American Library? It is quite ready, & the whole can be sent you at once. It has never yet been offered to any publisher. If you wish to see the MS. I suppose Mr Thoreau would readily send it to you. I am only desirous that you should propose to him good terms, & give his book the great advantages of being known which your circulation ensures.

Mr Thoreau is the author of an Article on Carlyle, now printed & printing in Graham's last & coming Magazine, & of some papers in the Dial; but he has done nothing half so good as his new book. He is well known to Mr Hawthorn also.

Yours respectfully,
R. W. Emerson.

To Mary Rotch, March 28, 1847

Concord, 28 March, 1847.

My dear friend,

It was a great pleasure to hear from you, if only by a question in philosophy. And the terrors of treading that difficult & quaking ground shall not hinder me from writing to you. I am quite sure however that I never said any of those fine things which you seem to have learned about me from Mr Griswold, and I think it would be but fair, as he deduces them, that he should explain them, &, if he can, show that they hold. No, I never say any of these scholastic things, and when I hear them, I can never tell on which side I belong. I never willingly say anything concerning "God" in cold blood, though I think we all have very just insights when we are "in the mount," as our fathers used to say. In conversation sometimes, or to humility & temperance the cloud will break away to show at least the direction of the rays of absolute Being, and we see the truth that lies in every affirmation men have made concerning it, & at the same time the cramping partiality of their speech. For the science of God our language is unexpressive, & merely prattle: we need simpler & universal signs, as algebra compared with arithmetic. Thus I should affirm easily *both* those propositions, which our Mr Griswold balances against one another, that, I mean,—of "Pantheism" & the other *ism*. Personality, too, & impersonality, might each be affirmed of Absolute Being; and what may not be affirmed of it, in our own mind? And we when we have heaped a mountain of speeches, we have still to begin again, having nowise expressed the simple unalterable fact. So I will not turn schoolman today, but prefer to wait a thousand years before I undertake that definition which literature has waited for so long already. Do not imagine that the old venerable thought has lost any of its awful attraction for me. I should very heartily,—shall I say, *tremulously* think & speak with you on our experiences or gleams of what is so grand & absorbing: and I never forget the statements so interesting to me you gave me many years ago of your faith & that of your friends. Are we not wonderful creatures to whom such entertainments & passions & hopes are afforded?

Yours with respect & affection,
R W Emerson

Concord,
30 April, 1847.

My dear Carlyle,

I have two good letters from you, & until now you have had no acknowledgment. Especially I ought to have told you how much pleasure your noble
invitation in March gave me. This pleasing dream of going to England dances
before me sometimes. It would be, I then fancy, that stimulation which my
capricious, languid, & languescent study needs. At home, no man makes any
proper demand on me, and the audience I address is a handful of men &
women too widely scattered than that they can dictate to me that which they
are justly entitled to say. Whether supercilious or respectful, they do not say
anything that can be heard. Of course, I have only myself to please, and my
work is slighted as soon as it has lost its first attraction. It is to be hoped, if
one should cross the sea, that the terror of your English culture would scare
the most desultory of Yankees into precision & fidelity: and perhaps I am not
yet too old to be animated by what would have seemed to my youth a proud
privilege. If you shall fright me into labour & concentration, I shall win my
game; for I can well afford to pay any price to get my work well done. For
the rest, I hesitate, of course, to rush rudely on persons that have been so
long invisible angels to me. No reasonable man but must hold these bounds
in awe:—I—much more,—who am of a solitary habit, from my childhood
until now—I hear nothing again from Mr Ireland. So I will let the English
Voyage hang as an afternoon rainbow in the East, and mind my apples &
pears for the present.

You are to know that in these days I lay out a patch of orchard near
my house, very much to the improvement as all the household affirms,
of our homestead. Though I have little skill in these things, and must
borrow that of my neighbors, yet the works of the garden & orchard
at this season are fascinating, & will eat up days & weeks, and a brave
scholar should shun it like gambling, & take refuge in cities & hotels from
these pernicious enchantments. For the present, I stay in the new orchard.

I gave Clark his letter sealed, and I doubt not you will hear from him.

Duyckinck, a literary man in New York, who advises Wiley & Putnam in their publishing enterprises, wrote me lately, that they had $600. for you, from Cromwell. So may it be.

Yours,
R. W. E.

To Ellen Emerson, May 10, 1847

Nantucket, 10 May, 1847.

Dear Ellen,

I was very glad of your journals This island is like a ship sixty miles out at sea: anything that comes from the mainland is highly valued. And papas that leave their homes, and wander here, you may be very sure are glad to hear from their daughters. This is a strange place, the island is fifteen miles long, but there are no woods and no trees upon it, and hardly any fence. As soon as you have walked out of the town or village of Nantucket (in which there are a few little gardens and a few trees) you come on a wide bare common stretching as far as you can see on every side, with nothing upon it but here & there a few nibbling sheep. And if you walk on till you have lost sight of the town, and a fog rises, which is very common here, you will have no guide to show you the way, no houses, no trees, no hills, no stones, so that it has many times happened here that people have been lost, & when they did not come back, the whole town came out & hunted for them. All the people here live by killing whales, which in old times used to swim about the island & the men went out in boats & killed them with harpoons; but now they go to the Pacific Ocean for them in great ships. But one day when the ship Essex was sailing there, a great sperm whale was seen coming with full speed towards the vessel: in a moment he struck the ship with terrible force, staving in some planks, and causing a leak: then he went off a little way, & came back swiftly, the water all white with his violent motion, & struck the ship a second frightful blow; the crew were obliged instantly to escape in boats, and the ship sunk in a few minutes. The Captain is now here.—Tell Mamma that I have received Mrs Goodwins letter today & her own enclosed

note and am uneasy at hearing of Eddy's cold. You must all take care of
him & make him well.

With a kiss for Edie, too,
Your affectionate father.
R. W. E.

To Harrison Gray Otis Blake, July 4, 1847

Concord, 4 July, 1847

My dear Sir,

I cannot afford in my hermit state which sometimes closes round me more like a sheath than a cell, to let your friendliest voice go unanswered. Of course, I have nothing to do with your fine exaggerations which are only astonishing in this that they have stayed by you so long. Like the fleetingest mists these persistent ones will blow off presently, and leave the looming figures dwarfed to the size of life, but real fixed & related to you. But I have to thank you for this fine generous criticism which furnishes a new portrait such as none of my critics have drawn, & which has certainly this certificate of its goodness, that it touches & admonishes me. I accept the omen, at least. I believe that more comes to a head in every sound well developed man than he or any body wots of. Men are the pores of Nature, and Nature cannot do without the perspirations. But in this grand body, each pore has a special function—not to be supplied or superseded by any of the other innumerable pores, which have their own organism, as reliable & indispensable. We must have not cotton only, but cotton, hemp, flax & mulberry; & every other weed in our flora will, no doubt, have its turn to be as famed a staple as the cotton pod is now. So that life teaches at every point the bifold lesson of assurance & humility. We cannot do without you—you cannot do without us. You may easily have too much salt, & be tired of it; but salt need not kill itself for that, knowing that it occupies a point in nature's economy which nothing else can fill, & you will come back to it. So does potash, sulphur, brandy, & milk,—so does each of them keep a good heart, since it is not here for nothing, & will presently be the one thing wanted. Only let each wear his own manners, and milk not try to be brandy, nor sulphur to be soap.— We may well go to sleep, for our Friend wakes. We may put off our clothes, we may put off our bodies, but it is not possible for the mind to divest itself of the faith that a beneficent tendency rounds in all these varieties, impresses itself on every atom, persuades every intelligence,—and carries its point. It beguiles the freest of his freedom—on the Fourth of July, and on all other days & centuries, and brings back the wildest democrat,—the practical as well as the theoretical *mauvais sujet* Barnburner, Antirenter, Burglar, Man-stealer &-Killer as gently & surely as the Mother the Babe, to his own & the common weal. These two facts—that our selves are somebodies, & may be relied on as good for some performance, and then that our private roots run down into the great Perfection;—if trite & truistical—are still the two articles of my creed, and they both certainly furnish the just basis for the doctrine of inspiration, and for every other piece of courage and forwardness. But if I write you such long sermons you will not try me again, so I will quit the generalities.—I hear with interest what you tell me of your private history. I cannot criticise at a distance, and will believe that you do not use the microscope too much in your affairs. What was it that the sad Samuel Johnson said, that things were always happening where little was to be said & much was to be done.—Well I also believe that in affairs we must not anatomize, that the spade is better than the trowel, & the plow better than the spade. And so in general the wholesale gross style in farming & in garden and in our economies is often a great prudence

Write to me, certainly, when you have anything for me. I have a little leaning now towards a project that has been pressed on me lately from England to go out thither next autumn and read some lectures before some Institutes that have been growing up there. But perhaps I shall not go. But I find I must stop, so will bid you goodbye affectionately,

To William Henry Furness, August 6, 1847

Concord, 6 August, 1847.

Dear Furness,

It was very wrong in you not to come & see me in any of these your northern flights. The last of your Boston visits, for example, I set down as a clear case of contumacy, that you would neither come to me nor be at home where I went to see you. I hope you had my card, which I left at Dr Gannett's. But now I write because Henry D. Thoreau has a book to print. Henry D. Thoreau is a great man in Concord, a man of original genius & character who knows Greek & knows Indian also,—not the language quite as well as John Eliot—but but the history monuments & genius of the Sachems, being a pretty good Sachem himself, master of all woodcraft, & an intimate associate of the birds, beasts, & fishes, of this region. I could tell you many a good story of his forest life.—He has written what he calls, "A Week on the Concord & Merrimack Rivers," which is an account of an excursion made by himself & his brother (in a boat which he built) some time ago, from Concord, Mass., down the Concord river & up the Merrimack, to Concord N.H.—I think it a book of wonderful merit, which is to go far & last long. It will remind you of Isaak Walton, and, if it have not all his sweetness, it is rich, as he is not, in profound thought.—Thoreau sent the manuscript lately to Duyckinck,—Wiley & Putnam's literary Editor, who examined it, & "gave a favorable opinion of it to W. & P." They have however declined publishing it. And I have promised Thoreau that I would inquire publishing it. And I have before we begin to set our own types. Would Mr Hart, or Mr Kay like to see such a manuscript? It will make a book as big as my First Series of Essays. They shall have it on half profits, or on any reasonable terms. Thoreau is mainly bent on having it printed in a cheap form for a large circulation.

You wrote me once & asked about Hedge. I esteem & respect him always more & more. He is best seen at Bangor. I saw him there last October & heard him preach all day. He is a solid person who cannot be spared in a whole population of levities. I think he is like one of those slow growing pear trees whose fruit is finer every year & at last becomes a *Beurré Incomparable*. I bade him goodbye seven or eight weeks ago, on board the "Washington Irving," & expect to see him in England next spring. Do you know that I am going thither in October? Will not Henry Thoreau serve as well as another apology for writing to you. Yours ever,

R. W. Emerson.

It may easily happen that you have too many affairs even to ask the question of the booksellers. Then simply say that you do not; for my party is Anacharsis the Scythian, and as imperturbable as Osceola.

TO MARGARET FULLER, AUGUST 29, 1847

Concord, 29 August, 1847.

Dear Margaret,

I believe there is a French steamer to go that can as well carry a word to you from us as from others. And I have to thank you for the good letter from Florence, which brought one to E. H[oar]. also. I am very busy in these days in setting my hous*es* in order, before my English excursion, for it is determined that I should go to Liverpool in October, and houses carnal & intellectual must surely be arranged. For I am to read lectures according to "*numerous*" engagements, it seems; there should then be much to say. And when odd men, indulged men are to go away from home, it is with them a sort of day of quittance, when all their debts, pecuniary, social, ceremonial, the arrears of years must be paid. Garden, orchard, woodlot, peat meadow, all must be remembered, and the exigences of the next Spring provided for. As at a funeral or a wedding, one makes a census of his cousins. It is for our sin that these things are remembered, which should be disposed of as by a wave of the hand, if our errand were a little nearer the heart. What said the stout Luther,—that if he came to count his puddings like Pomeranus, he should die quickly. You have always been magnificent & have not moped in corners, and so have, as you deserve, some good Italian sunshine & beauty & nobility to bask in. That you find the roads so smooth & welcome, & the climate so cordial, is a great happiness to us all. I fear I shall not see you till you have seen all, & come richly laden with all your conquests, & acquests home. I shall spend my winter in England, probably may go to Paris in the spring, or not till May or June, & I think it very doubtful if I take another step *from* home. America the great listless dumb lifeless America has urgent claims on her children, which, as yet are all unanswered. If by staying at home, or returning home,—they could be any nearer to a satisfaction! Do not think, as you will not, that there is any thing to tell of, not a blush on her cheek, not a morning hymn, not a dream of a nobler future—nothing has chanced to make the social state less sordid or to open man's eye to the prodigalities of Nature.

I can tell you nothing of Ellery. He & his family have disappeared for 5 or 6 weeks past & when he is gone no tidings of him ever transpire. I believe his wife is in Cambridge. His little book on Rome is a pretty good success, is more readable than any thing he has published, and finds some readers & praisers. This perseverance of his in writing & printing, read they or read they not, is an unexpected indemnity which Nature seems to have added to our poet for some small discontinuity which she suffered to occur somewhere in these fine wires. Lidian has just come home from Waterford, whither she went with Elizabeth H. whom she has left there. E plays through life the part of good angel. Our other parts are still sustained by the stock performers. Thoreaus book is not yet published. though now on the point of concluding the contract. Alcott (in whom do you know a Palladio was lost?) is building me (with Thoreau) a summerhouse of growing—alarming dimensions— peristyle gables, dormer windows, &c in the midst of my cornfield—for I have pulled down my eastern fence, alas! & added 2 1/2 acres to my lot in an evil hour. In my absence Mamma will go to Staten Island for the winter, & Lidian probably continue to board with Mrs Goodwin till my return. The Mass. Quarterly Review is resolutely pushed to light by Parker & Cabot & is to appear in December As they have used my name, I am sorry I cannot much help them at first. Charles Newcomb spent a day with me here lately good & calm & superior & so quietly putting behind him into oblivion all defects. Every one else is a little penitent. Edward Bangs I like very much. A letter from Sam Ward who has been strolling in the Adirondack Mts. Mrs [Sarah] Ripley remains a glowing domestic & scholastic centre. Longfellow is writing a poem. Wilkinson has written a piece preliminary to Swedenborgs "Outlines on the Infinite" which you ought to see Tis much the best piece of criticism on Modern Opinions, especially Transcendentalism, which has been written. If an equal painter could exhibit the other side of the shield, it would be the "sufficient reason" for the new Journal. Live well & long & happy, and let me know of all. Dear love from all your friends dear Mother, Lidian, & Waldo E.

To Lidian Emerson, October 21 And 22, 1847

October 21, 1847.

Dear Lidian.

Here is the finest of mornings after the best of nights and it has shown us poor sailors the coast of Ireland as we enter St Georges Channel. We have had the most prosperous & rapid voyage from Cape Sable to this point. The first four days of the voyage were quite lost with calm weather in the near neighborhood of Cape Cod But on Saturday night we took a good wind & from that moment have made a speed across the ocean which the Captain thinks so unusual that he has just now been drawing the line in red ink on his chart for the encouragement or for the envy of all future navigators. Every thing has been pleasant & prosperous aboard. We have had a very kindly & well ordered company, three ladies with nine children, four gentlemen and the Captain in our cabin; three gentlemen & a child in the second cabin; (which twenty one souls, you are to understand are entitled to walk or to be carried on the spacious quarter-deck.) sixty five in the steerage sixteen sailors and one little boy who had stowed himself away in the provision room for concealment, & did not appear until we were out at sea the second day. The prattle & play of the children who never seem to have been sick or suspicious of danger or even impatient of confinement one moment during the passage has been as pleasant as the song of birds, and the good fellowship of the cabin has been complete. The Captain is an excellent master, full of exact information about his ship & all that relates to Boston & Liverpool trade and so good a sailor as to make us all sleep securely, and the rather that since this ship was built, he has never taken off his clothes at night, at sea. For our company, one of the gentlemen is Mr Kennedy a partner formerly of Mr Hemmenway (whom we knew in the summer) at Valparaiso. Another was Mr Pollock of Boston a young merchant; and Mr Watson of Exeter, a machinist. Of the ladies, one is Mrs White of Demerara, a sister of the last wife of Mr Russell Sturgis of Boston. The others are, I believe, Salem ladies. In the second cabin is a Mr Bartlett, who is a young colleague of Burritt the philanthropist, whom he is seeking in England. And an Englishman of some connexion who is a graduate of Oxford. By night & by day we have exchanged experiences, and have all learned something. I find the voyage with all these alleviations quite tedious It is forlorn to have the room in which you stand or sit always sloped at an angle of from 20 to 40 degrees, and besides what seems some one at every moment actually tipping it up. At night in my berth home pictures come very palpably before me. The children I see plainly, & Ellen actually called me the other night to come to her & them. Eddie tells no bad news May none arrive of them or you. I cannot send you my rough & blotted scrap journal, it is pity for Ellen at least that I cannot give her my experiences here, while they are fresh. Tell her that I have seen whales spouting, schools of porpoises or sea-pigs swimming by the bowsprit & throwing themselves out of the water, great shoals or beds of mackerel jumping out of water by thousands Little land birds, sparrows & one pigeon woodpecker alighted on the masts & bulwarks of the ship & even took temporary refuge in the cabin. I fear they never came to land again. One of them I saw drowning in the sea.

On Friday, we came every now & then into floating drift of boards, logs, & chips, which the rivers of Maine & New Brunswick pour out into the sea after any freshet. The next day, I saw what seemed a tub with two ears, floating, but, on nearer inspection, it was judged a valise of who knows what traveller. When nature was exhausted, we retreated upon novels and Dumas, Dickens, & Marryatt are our sea-gods. I read Mrs Butler's "Year," which Mrs Alcott gave me, with great pleasure & the Captain & passengers have read it. Then the book of Modern Painters,—which if any one wishes to know was written by a young man named Ruskin.

But the reading & writing are soon tedious & we come back to the deck every half hour whilst the weather is clear. Tell Ellen that the poor boy who hid himself in the bread closet that he might go to England, though he had no money to pay his passage & not even a coat over his shirtsleeves, is working about very contentedly after the sailors, who have equipped him already in a Guernsey frock, with a knife in a belt buckled round his body. His name is Walters, and, it seems he is English, & came out to America, in *the same way*, in the "Ocean Monarch"; &, not finding republics to his mind, smuggles himself back. He says, he likes the work of the ship "firstrate," &, if the captain will take him, means to go back again. The mate tells me, that this is the history of all sailors. Ask them all their history, & nine out of ten are runaway boys: and, as he farther says, all of them disgusted with the employment, but stay in it out of pride.

Today, at noon, we have yet 234 miles to reach Liverpool. But instead of the bubbles along the ships side by which the passenger always measures his progress at sea we have Kinsale, Cork, Ardmore, & Waterford. Ireland looks like a country as well cultivated & plentiful as Brookline & Brighton I see towers, towns, & grain & turnip fields, & fishermen, but no curse.

22 Oct. This morning finds us off Holyhead & the mountainous coast of Wales in full view. At 10 o clock we took in a pilot under the mountains of Penmanmaur, but the weather is too thick to show us Snowdon.

And, after dark, we dropped anchor in the port of Liverpool, and in a little dangerous-looking dangerously dancing boat, first by oars & then by sail, four of us passengers with the Captain have touched the land. With all good thoughts & holy love to that which loveth us, and with all kindest & thankfullest thoughts to you, dear Lidian, & to Mamma and to the three blessed children, & to Elizabeth Hoar, and to Henry Thoreau & to every kind friend, may love & peace abound!

Waldo E.

To Lidian Emerson, October 27 and 30, and November 1, 1847

Chelsea London 27 October 1847

Dear Lidian,

I found at Liverpool after a couple of days a letter which had once been there seeking me (& once returned to Manchester before it reached my hands) from Carlyle addressed "to R W E. on the instant when he lands in England," conveying so hearty a welcome & so urgent an invitation to house & hearth, that I could no more resist than I could gravitation; and, finding that I should not be wanted for a week in the Lecture rooms, I came down hither on Monday, and, at 10 at night, the door was opened to me by Jane Carlyle, and the man himself was behind her with a lamp in the entry. They were very little changed from their old selves of fourteen years ago (in August) when I left them at Craigenputtock and the floodgates of Carlyle's discourse are very quickly opened, & the river is a great & constant stream. We had a large communication that night until nearly one o clock and at breakfast next morning it begun again. At noon or later we went together, C. & I—to Hyde Park and the palaces (about two miles from here) to the National Gallery and into the "Strand" to Chapman's shop Carlyle melting all Westminster & London down into his talk & laughter as he walked. We came back to dinner at 5 or later, then Dr Carlyle came in & spent the evening, which, again was long by the clock but had no other measures—But I can hardly write to you at all: London days are very short, London distances are so long, and, as the day & night are hardly distinguishable in colour, there is every excuse for late hours & all & any hours to suit your own convenience. Here in this house we breakfast about 9, and Carlyle is very apt, his wife says, to sleep till 10 or 11, if he has no company. An immense talker he is, & altogether as extraordinary in his conversation as in his writing. I think even more so. You will never discover his real vigor & range, or how much more he might do than he has ever done, without seeing him. I find my few hours discourse with him in Scotland, long since, gave me not enough knowledge of him; and I have now at last been taken by surprise by him. He is not mainly a scholar, like the most of my acquaintances, but a very practical Scotchman, such as you would find in any sadler's or iron dealer's shop, and then only accidentally and by a surprising addition the admirable scholar & writer he is. If you wish to know precisely how he talks, just suppose that Hugh Whelan had had leisure enough, in addition to all his daily work, to read Plato, & Shakspeare, & Calvin, and, remaining Hugh Whelan all the time, should talk scornfully of all this nonsense of books that he had been bothered with,— and you shall have just the tone & talk & laughter of Carlyle. He has too the strong religious tinge, in the way that you find it in people of that temperament. That, & all his qualities have a certain virulence, coupled though it be, in his case, with the utmost impatience of Christendom & Jewdom, and all existing presentments of the good old story. He talks like a very unhappy man, profoundly solitary, displeased & hindered by all men & things about him, & plainly biding his time, & meditating how to undermine & explode the whole world of nonsense which torments him. He is obviously greatly respected here, by all sorts of people, understands his own value, quite as well as Webster, (of whom too his behaviour sometimes reminds me—especially when he is with fine people—) and can see *"Society"* on his own terms. Carlyle and his wife live on beautiful terms: Nothing can be more engaging than their ways, and in her book case all his books are inscribed to her, as they came from year to year, each with some significant lines. His brother has ended his travels as a physician, and lives near them in his own house, a bachelor, & is a good scholar on his own account. He is getting out a translation of Dante into English prose.

Liverpool 30th But you will wish to hear more of my adventures, which I must hasten to record. On Wednesday, Mr [Charles] Lane came to see me whom I had summoned from Ham by letter: with him I went up to the counting house of the Barings, presented my letter from Mr Ward to Mr Bates, who had much to say of my father, whom he remembered, & something also of myself, he gave me money on my account, & I paid Lane £92.17s.9 pence—(of which payment let this record be kept until I get it into my Journal at home) then, after looking into the Bank, I went to the National Gallery, and was there accosted by Alexander Bliss, whom I did not at first know, but he brought his mother, Mrs [George] Bancroft, to me, who greeted me with the greatest kindness, and insisted on presenting me to Mr Rogers, who chanced to come into the Gallery with ladies. Mr Rogers invited me to breakfast, with Mrs B, at his house, on Friday. The smoke of London, through which the sun rarely penetrates, gives a dusky magnificence to these immense piles of building in the West part of the City, which makes my walking rather dreamlike. Martin's pictures of Babylon, &c. are faithful copies of the West part of London, light, darkness, architecture & all.

Friday morning at 9 1/2 I presented myself at Mr Bancrofts door, 90 Eaton Square, which was opened by Mr Bancroft himself! in the midst of servants whom that man of eager manners thrust aside, saying that he would open his own door for me. He was full of goodness & of talk with news from America by the steamer, & his own theories to explain the English calamities in trade. Mrs Bancroft appeared and with young Butler of New York & young Bliss we rode in her carriage to Mr Roger's house. You know how famous this old man is for his collection of works of art, and for his good company. I suppose, no distinguished person has been in England during the last fifty years, who has not been at this house, so that it appears to you like some modern pantheon. Mr Rogers received us with cold quiet indiscriminate politeness, and entertained us with abundance of anecdote, which Mrs Bancroft very skilfully drew out of him about people more or less interesting to me. Scott Wordsworth Byron Wellington Talleyrand, Madame de Stael, Lafayette, Fox, Burke, & crowds of high men & women had talked & feasted in these rooms in which we sat, and which are decorated with every precious work. The mantle piece was carved by Flaxman. An antique marble head Canova had brought in his own arms & set down in the place it now occupies. Sir F. Chantrey, dining one day here, asked Mr R. if he remembered the workman who made a cabinet for him? (which I saw) "I was that man," continued the Sculptor. Here are vases from old Rome, & some of the best pictures in England. And casts of the Elgin Marbles are in an excellent way let into the wall above the staircase, so as to be everyway examinable. Mr R. showed me Milton's autograph, and Pope's original bust, and autograph letters of Washington, & Franklin, & Mozart, & Fox, & Burke, & Dr Johnson, &c He read letters of Byron to himself & I saw original manuscript of pages of Waverley. And so on to any extent. I think it must be the chief private show of London, this man's collection. But I will not bore you with any more particulars. From this house Mrs Bancroft carried me to the Cloister of Westminster Abbey, to the Abbey itself, & then insisted on completing her bounties by carrying me in her coach to Carlyle's door at Chelsea—a very long way. I surrendered at discretion to so much real & friendly & graceful information as she gave me concerning persons & modes here. At last she set me down with injunctions to give you her love & to send her affectionate remembrances to Elizabeth Hoar also. At Carlyle's, I presently saw Mrs Rich, a daughter of Sir James Mackintosh. Yesterday, I was presented to Milman the sometime poet & historian of the Jews, & I am promised any number of introductions, when I return. At 5. P.M. yesterday after spending four complete days with my friends, I took the fast train for Liverpool, & came hither 212 miles in 6 hours, which is nearly twice our railway speed. In Liverpool, I drank tea last Saturday night with James Martineau, & heard him preach on Sunday last. He is a sincere sensible good man & though greatly valued as a preacher (I found pictures & busts of him in the houses of his friends here as if he were some great man) yet I thought him superior to his books & his preaching. I have seen Mr Ireland also at Manchester, on my way to London, and his friends. It seems I am to read six lectures in this town in three weeks, and, at the same time, three lectures in each week in Manchester, on other evenings. When this service is ended, I may have as many new engagements as I like, they tell me. I am to begin at Manchester next Tuesday Evening.

Nov. 1, Monday Evening. I am heartily tired of Liverpool. I am oppressed by the seeing of such multitudes: there is a fierce strength here in all the streets, the men are bigger & solider far than our people, more stocky, both men & women, and with a certain fixedness & determination in each person's air, that discriminates them from the sauntering gait & roving eyes of Americans. In America you catch the eye of every one you meet: here you catch no eye almost. The axes of an Englishman's eyes are united to his backbone. So their speech & all their manners have a certain concentration & solemnity. If they bow in the street, it is no trifle, but a duty performed. They rarely introduce persons to each other, & mean something when they do, and they are slow to offer the hand. But I assure you the mechanics porters carters smiths & even shopkeepers have such a Patagonian size, that I can remember few Americans who would not be slight & insignificant figures. I do not think there is so slender a person as I in the 2, or 300,000.

Dear Lidian, Perhaps I shall not get time to write more before the steamer sails, (in which Mr Geo. H. Pollock, who came out with me, returns, & will carry this letter;) so I hasten to say, that never was wardrobe or outfitting so carefully & affectionately complete as mine. Every inch of my trunk & valise is a praiser of your love & forethought. Only I have too many things, &, if I understood it well enough, would send some of them back. Yesterday morning, I got your welcome letter (by Mr Ireland) & today called on Barings here, to ask them to send immediately to London for the other letter wh. I shall not have until day after tomorrow. But I am greatly contented to know that all is so well with you. I shall write now to Abel Adams, whom you should know I have left with a power of attorney to act for me in all cases, so you must refer any question on business to him. Ever affectionately yours

Waldo E

To Henry David Thoreau, December 2, 1847

Manchester, 2 Dec. 1847.

Dear Henry,

Very welcome in the parcel was your letter, very precious your thoughts & tidings. It is one of the best things connected with my coming hither that you could & would keep the homestead, that fireplace shines all the brighter,—and has a certain permanent glimmer therefor. Thanks, evermore thanks for the kindness which I well discern to the *youth* of the house, to my darling little horseman of pewter, leather, wooden, rocking & what other breeds, destined, I hope, to ride Pegasus yet, and I hope not destined to be thrown, to Edith who long ago drew from you verses which I carefully preserve, & to Ellen who by speech & now by letter I find old enough to be companionable, & to choose & reward her own friends in her own fashions. She sends me a poem today, which I have read three times!—I believe, I must keep back all my communication on English topics until I get to London which is England. Everything centralizes, in this magnificent machine which England is. Manufacturer for the world she is become or becoming one complete tool or engine in herself—Yesterday the *time* all over the kingdom was reduced to Greenwich time. At Liverpool, where I was, the clocks were put forward 12 minutes. This had become quite necessary on account of the railroads which bind the whole country into swiftest connexion, and require so much accurate interlocking, intersection, & simultaneous arrival, that the difference of time produced confusion. Every man in England carries a little book in his pocket called "Bradshaws Guide", which contains time tables of every arrival & departure at every station on all the railroads of the kingdom. It is published anew on the first day of every month & costs sixpence. The proceeding effects of Electric telegraph will give a new importance to such arrangements.—But lest I should not say what is needful, I will postpone England once for all,—and say that I am not of opinion that your book should be delayed a month. I should print it at once, nor do I think that you would incur any risk in doing so that you cannot well afford. It is very certain to have readers & debtors here as well as there. The Dial is absurdly well known here. We at home, I think, are always a little ashamed of it,—*I* am,—and yet here it is spoken of with the utmost gravity, & I do not laugh. Carlyle writes me that he is reading Domesday Book.—You tell me in your letter one odious circumstance, which we will dismiss from remembrance henceforward. Charles Lane entreated me, in London, to ask you to forward his Dials to him, which must be done, if you consent, thus. Three bound vols are among his books in my library The 4th Vol is in unbound numbers at J Munroe & Co's shop received there in a parcel to my address a day or two before I sailed & which I forgot to carry to Concord It must be claimed without delay It is certainly there, was opened by me, & left. And they can enclose all 4 vols. to Chapman for me.—Well I am glad the Pleasaunce at Walden suffered no more but it is a great loss as it is which years will not repair.—I see that I have baulked you by the promise of a letter which ends in as good as none But I write with counted minutes & a miscellany of things before me. Yours affectionately,

R. W. E.

To Edith Emerson, December 9, 1847

Derby, 9 December, 1847

My dear Edie,

I have been walking this afternoon up & down the street which you see in this little picture, because the tower of the church called All Saints Church is so rich & handsome that I could not look at it enough. It is a great deal handsomer than you can think it from this print, and has been standing here three hundred years. In the high belfry, there is a chime of bells, & they played today a pleasant tune. I have a larger & better picture of it, but I am afraid the Postmaster will not let me send it in his bags. But the tune of the bells did not please me so much as it would to hear the voices of Edie & Ellen & Eddie again, and you was a dear little girl to write me a letter, which is a kind of picture of a voice. Here in England the grass is green everywhere, and I have had roses in my buttonhole, this morning, which were taken from bushes growing in the open garden. In Concord it is cold & snowy. As soon as the snow & cold are gone, I hope to come home again, and to tell you all about the English boys & girls. And you must give a kiss to Eddy from Papa, and tell him so.

Good night!
Papa.

To Elizabeth Hoar, February 28 and 29? 1848

Dear E—

I have been here [Ambleside] with Miss [Harriet] Martineau a couple of days, & ere I pack my bags again for Manchester, & London, you shall have a token of the fine pleasures of this country & its tenants. Miss Martineau lives here in great advantage & comfort, in a good stone house which she has built in a beautiful position, where, to be sure, all possible sites are excellent, and with Windermere before her windows, the rude hill Loughrigg on one side, Wansfell a higher hill on the other & Fairfield which rises 2900 feet & more, not far off, behind her. Her two maids make all her family; & her days, as you will believe, are spent with perfect method. She is in perfect health, as I can bear witness, after this day's riding & running. I came here yesterday morning, from the North, &, about 3. oclk. we set forth for Mr Wordsworth's house which is a mile & a half from her gate. Wordsworth waked up a little heavily from his after dinner nap on the sofa, but soon began to talk on the great French news. He had, of course, all the strongest English prejudice against the French. He had lived in France a year & a half, & they were an idle people; the women did the work in the manufactories, in the shops, even in the counting houses; the men carried out a fowling piece, or only liked to play at billiards, or faire le cour aux dames. Even the disasters of poor old Louis Philippe, a vagabond at this day, did not seem much to touch the Tory poet. His opinions, however, about many important things are capricious, & rest on anecdotes & narrow experiences. We talked of Jeffrey—No Scotchman could write English. Robertson has only two or three set forms of sentences. (Gibbon, no Scot, could not because he first learned French. Carlyle could not, he was a high offender. Tennyson we came upon, & he expressed great regard & respect for him, whom he personally knew, thinks him to have most genius of all the poets, but some affectation; in short Wordsworth had just such opinions good & bad, as you in your chamber could write out for him. Why should I tediously remember them? And yet it is good to see his great rough weather-beaten face, the dome of his brow, & sometimes a fine smile. His nose is so large & corrugated as no picture would dare to represent it. But he is very temperate, and is all his life long, of a very frugal habit. Mrs Wordsworth was present, & took part in the conversation, Miss Martineau leaving me there, after a little while, to finish my visit. I stayed an hour & a half, & we ran over many topics, & he set out to walk towards Miss M's with me, but it rained, & I would not suffer it. He is 77 years old, but assured me he does not feel his age in walking or journeying. That night, in a tempest of rain, the Arnolds came & spent the evening—very beloved people here, & very well deserving.—The next day Mr Greg provided three ponies, & with him & Miss M. I rode seven or eight miles, & saw, I think, the best of their mountains & lakes; then walked to Fox How, (of the Arnolds); then to Stock Gill Force, a waterfall; then dined with the Arnolds again at Mr Greg's. And so ended the day—Can my letter choose but end? Your brother Waldo.

To Lidian Emerson, April 20 and 21, 1848

London, 20 April, 1848

Dear Lidian,

The steamer is in, every body has letters, & I have none. none from you, nor the dear little Ellen who writes me short pert good notes—all blessings fall on the child—It must be that you too have decided that boats run a little too often for mere human pens moved by hands that have many more things to drive. Another boat is to arrive next week & I shall have your letter then. I will believe all goes well with you all. You wrote me the kindest & best account of your reading in the precious file of letters. Your feeling was just & noble. And they deserved all you have said. For they came out of a heart which nature & destiny conspired to keep as inviolate, as are still those three children of whom you send me such happy accounts. But I am deeply gratified by your pleasure & sympathy in them. Ah how we wander from goal to goal of our life, and often it seems as if one thread of consciousness did not tie the far parts together. Who am I that roam these desarts, & knew this & that in old years? But you should have seen Ellen. When she left this world, I valued every body who had seen her, and disliked to meet those who had not.—Another time.—I have a letter from William, with a truly kind proposition. I have a letter from George P. B[radford]. who speaks of you & the children, so I have no mistrust. I have been busy during the last fortnight, but have added no very noticeable persons to my list of acquaintance. A good deal of time is lost here in their politics, as I read the newspaper daily; & the Revolution, fixed for the tenth instant, occupied all men's thought until the Chartist petition was actually carried to the Commons: and the rain, too, which falls at any time almost every day,—these things & the many miles of street you must afoot or by bus or cab achieve to make any visit, put me, who am, as you know, always faint-hearted at the name of visiting, much out of the humour of prosecuting my social advantages. I have dined with Mr & Mrs Lyell, one day, & one with a good Dr Forbes who carried me to the Royal Institution to hear Faraday who is reckoned the best lecturer in London. I dined too with Mr Morgan (Hampden in XIX Century), and have visited Wilkinson at Hampstead, & dined with Mrs Wedgewood, who is daughter of Sir J. Mackintosh & with several other people, who, like these, must be but names to you. I breakfasted with John Forster, Editor of the Examiner, and am to dine with him & meet Dickens & Carlyle next Tuesday. It seems very doubtful whether I shall read lectures here even now. Chapman makes himself very busy about it, & a few people, and I shall, no doubt, have a good opportunity, but I am not ready, and it is a lottery business, and I do much incline to decline it, on grounds that I can only tell you of at home, & go to Paris for a few weeks, get my long promised French lesson, & come home to be poor & pay for my learning. I have really been at work every day here with my old tools of book & pen. and shall at last have something to show for it all. The best sights I have seen lately are; the British Museum; whose chambers of Antiquities I visited with the Bancrofts on a private day, under the guidance of Sir Charles Fellows who brought home the Xanthian marbles, & really gave us the most instructive chapter on the subject of Greek remains that I have ever heard or read of. On this, I hope to bear catechism when I come home. Then, the Kings Library, which I saw under the guidance of Panizzi, the Librarian, and afterwards of Coventry Patmore, a poet, who is a sub-librarian. Then I heard Grisi, the other night, sing at Covent Garden Grisi & Alboni, the rivals of the Opera. Being admitted an honorary member of the Reform Club (that is having one month's free admission to its privileges) I went over all that magnificent house with Mr Field;—through its kitchen—reckoned the best in Europe—which was shown me by Soyer, renowned in the literature of saucepan & soup—. Another day, through, over, & under the new Houses of Parliament begun 13 years ago, and of which as yet no chamber but the House of Lords is complete; but it is a vast pile covering eight acres, and among the chiefest samples of the delight which Englishmen find in spending a great deal of money. Carlyle has been quite ill, lately, with inflamed sore throat, and as he is a very intractable patient, his wife & brother have no small trouble to keep him in bed, or even in the house. I certainly obtained a fairer share of the conversation when I visited him. He is very grim lately on these ominous times, which have been & are deeply alarming to all England.

I find Chapman very anxious to establish a journal common to Old & New England, as was long ago proposed—Froude & Clough & other Oxonians & others would gladly conspire. Let the Mass. Q. give place to this, & we should have two legs, & bestride the sea. Here I know so many young goodminded people, that I am sure would well combine; but what do I, or what does any friend of mine in America care for a journal? Not enough, I fear, to secure any energetic work, on that side. I have a letter from Cabot lately, and do write to him today. Tis certain that the M. Q. J. will fail unless Henry Thoreau & Alcott & Channing and Charles Newcomb,—the fourfoldvisaged four,—fly to the rescue. I am sorry that Alcott's editor, the Dumont of our Bentham, Baruch of our Jeremiah, is so slow to be born.—I am very glad to know that Ellery Channing & Mrs Ripley have become neighbors at last.

Thanks for the very satisfactory piece of good sense & good feeling that you send me in W. E. C's article on the Ether business.[43] It was a cordial after the sad story of the letter. I send it in a letter to Mrs Howitt; but she will hardly publish it. I have mentioned the matter from time to time to people here but nobody takes the smallest interest in the thing. Edward Forbes &

---

43. *Emerson's brother-in-law Charles Thomas Jackson and W. T. G. Morton argued for many years about who should properly receive credit for first using ether as an anesthetic.*

others knew Dr Jackson as the inventor, but the chloroform has superseded ether, & they care nothing for what an Englishman did not invent. The pertinacity of the opposition to Dr J's claims with us does indeed astonish me & I can easily understand should dishearten him. But he who discovered so much, can discover a great deal more, which his swindlers & enviers can not. He ought to leave defending his rights—(*ab iniquo certamine indignabundus recessit,*[44]—as I used to read of old Bentley,) & forget it in his laboratory. Tell him the story I used to tell you of Wordsworth making his election on the death of his father whether to prosecute his lawsuit with a Sir Giles Overreach of a man (Sir J. Lowther) for his fathers property, or to throw it up & retire to poverty & poetry. He decided on the last. Time went on, Sir J. L., (afterwards Lord Lonsdale), died; the new lord Lonsdale owned the debt, & paid £10 000 to the Wordsworths, & W. W. had now not only his share of the money, but his poetry also.

Dear love to all the children,—. and to the severalties whom I dare not name.

Miss Martineau has sent me her new book which I must try to send home to you. It will interest you much. Margaret F. has written me another letter from Rome indicating sad health & spirits.

I have not ventured at this long space to say anything of garden or orchard. Henry & Mr Hosmer must advise & act or rather Henry by & with the counsel & practice of Hosmer The main object is the trees; and there is a good heap of manure, & more to be made by bringing peat to the sewer in the garden. But we ought, I suppose, to have good corn & potatoes also. I hope Henry will not decline to arrange it. He says I do not write to him, or you say it, but I have, almost sheet for sheet, as I believe.—A Mrs Gaskell, a lady of much consideration, has just died. I received a few days ago a note from her inviting me to dine on a certain day. That night she was struck with palsy, and she lingered but a few days—. Wilkinson my Swedenborgian sage is to my surprise a Fourierist, & I think rapidly losing his interest in the great Mystagogue. There are in England the usual sprinkling of enthusiastic young ladies. I wish to anticipate Elizabeth H's remark on some of my acquaintances when she comes to know them. Love to Mother & William & Susan, when you write—as I write not to them.

---

44. *"Enraged, he departed from that disadvantageous fight."*

London, 21 April, 1848.

My dear Sir,

I was very glad to get your letter touching the Massachusetts Quarterly. I am verily useless to you, but I gag my conscience by remembering that when I found I was to leave home, I entreated that the Journal might wait a semester. I have not found myself here in England in any position to help you. I am a very bad traveller, not social, not adroit, and all I get comes by the grace of God. The distraction of travelling puts all writing of my sort out of the question Yet I have been compelled here to write some new lectures, nor has any literary information come to me which seemed fit for both you & me.

The Journal certainly discloses character & talent but in the present competition it should have a great deal of both. I am sure it would gain for the best English readers, and for ours, by dropping this Review form, & obtaining short miscellanies also; prose & verse. Then I am only confirmed in my first feeling that Thoreau should be immediately set to write—animas in vulnere.[45] Alcott still wants his editor, but that which he stands for would be presently & permanently valuable. George P. Bradford could write something valuable on Dante, perhaps an abstract of the Ozanams & historians of the mystical theology. Sam G. Ward cannot be spared, though I think he has done himself no justice in his contributions to Number I. But here is another scheme opening. John Chapman the bookseller here is eager to have a journal for New & Old England published simultaneously in London & Boston, and as he constantly affirms, substantially on the plan of the Dial. I found some young men lately at Oxford, Fellows of Colleges, who entered willingly enough into his thought. Froude & Clough, particularly, good men of Oriel & Exeter Coll. It deserves consideration,, whether our book would not be better, & certainly, easilier supplied from two countries. At the end of the year, we can change it.—For me, I think to go to Paris in a few days, & shall probably turn my steps homeward about 1 June, though tis not certain, & could not come into bonds for work before the September Number.

With kind remembrances to Mr Parker.

---

45. *"A soul in pain."*

I shall see what can be done by way of exchanges for the Journal; but am told that the great Reviews hold their heads high. & at any rate that we must pay the difference of our several costs. In Chapman's plan of a common Journal, we should really secure a phœnix of a publisher a man of integrity & of talent in his trade with the liveliest interest in the project itself.

I have not thanked you for the very kind expressions in your letter, which I very heartily appreciate. I am fully sensible how much your generosity has been & is taxed in this adventure.—In the hope of soon seeing you, Yours,

R. W. Emerson.

To Lidian Emerson, May 24 and 25, 1848

Paris, 24 May, 1848

Dear Lidian, I have this night received your letter of 7 May, describing the several & general joy of you all in the most beautiful of spring days. And beside Ellen's joys, she or Edie has sent me an honest violet which I heartily accept as a kind of "dry light." This time you send me none but good news and Elizabeth Hoar sends pure wine too. I wish Ellery, & Henry Thoreau had written a benediction also. From what you say & from what they do not say, I infer, that I write very bad letters all the time. Tis very likely, for in every letter you say that you show them to all your friends, and at the same time entreat me if I have any confessions to make not to omit them by the next post. I find Paris a place of the largest liberty that is I suppose in the civilized world & I am thankful for it just as I am for Etherization as a resource when the accident of any hideous surgery threatens me; so Paris in the contingency of my ever needing a place of diversion & independence; this shall be my best bower anchor. All winter I have been admiring the English and disparaging the French. Now in these weeks I have been correcting my prejudice & the French rise many entire degrees Their universal good breeding is a great convenience, and the English & American superstition in regard to broadcloth seems really diminished if not abolished here. Knots of people converse everywhere in the street, and the blouse or shirtsleeves-without-blouse becomes as readily the centre of discourse as any other, & Superfine and Shirt,—who never saw each other before,—converse in the most earnest yet deferential way. Nothing like it could happen in England. They are the most joyous race and put the best face on every thing. Paris, to be sure, is their main performance, but one can excuse their vanity & pride, it is so admirable a city. Nothing can be finer than the arrangements for splendor & gaiety of living. The Seine adorns Paris the Thames is out of sight in London the Seine is quayed all the way so that broad streets on both sides the river as well as gay bridges have all the good of it, & the sun & moon & stars look into it & are reflected—At London I can not remember seeing the river Here are magnificent gardens neither too large nor too small for the convenience of the whole people who spend every evening in them Here are palaces truly royal. If they have cost a great deal of treasure at some time, they have at least got a palace to show for it; and a church too in Notre Dame: whilst in England there is no palace, with all their floods of millions of guineas that have been spent. I witnessed the great national Fete on Sunday last when 1200000 people stood in the Champs de Mars and it was like an immense family the perfect good humour & fellowship is so habitual to them all. At night the illumination in the Champs Elysées was delicious they understand all the capabilities of the place & of the whole city as well as you do your parlour and make a carcanet of jewels of it all. The skill with festal chandeliers were hung all up & down a mile of avenue gave it all the appearance of an immense ballroom in which the countless crowds of men & women walked with ease & pleasure. It was easy to see that France is far nearer to Socialism than England & it would be a short step to convert Paris into a phalanstery. You will like to know that I heard Lamartine speak yesterday in the Chamber, his *great* speech, the journals say, on Poland. Mr Rush lent me his own ticket for the day. He did not speak however with much energy, but is a manly handsome greyhaired gentleman with nothing of the rust of the man of letters, and delivers himself with great ease & superiority. Instead of water the huissier put wine beside him, and he also refreshed himself occasionally with snuff. The whole chamber listened to him gladly, for he has mystified people a good deal lately, & all were eager for any distinct expressions from him. The chamber appeared like an honest country representation. [Arthur Hugh] Clough is still here, & is my chief dependence at the dining hour & afterwards

Love to all dear children & to dear sisters too who write best letters & get nothing but ingratitude. And to Mother & Aunt Mary & W. & S

Mr Tom Appleton also I like better than any other. I go to London in a few days & am bound there three weeks from 6 June. Then I mean to come home. Farewell, dear wife

Waldo.

25 May. I hoped last night that I might win a little time today for a letter to Elizabeth but I find it impossible, and Aunt Mary must forgive me in her great heart a little longer, though I fear she no longer expects anything from me,—and the dear children who sent tidings of the Day & violet, sweet-briar & sweet [blank] , must wait also,—more's the pity; and you must send word to Mrs Goodwin, who has sent me the kindest report of yourself, that I have grieved to make no answer, and I must bear the impossibility of any one of you comprehending why a writer cannot write who has nothing else to do.—I have seen Rachel once more, since I wrote you before, and now in Mithridate. France is vexed because her slight form has never acquired any roundness or height, nor her voice any resonance, since she came to the stage. But you feel her genius at first sight, and trust her resources. The Marseillaise is the finest chant,—but should not be heard but once.—But you do not care for any of these things. Well, I am glad if the kind spring winds have given you new health & courage, & will make you forget the dismal winter. The children will cheer you with new games, new hymns. The garden will hide all memories under a million leaves & petals: and, I doubt not, I shall have my own share of news out of this poor Old World to add to the solace of your celandine & chocolate. But you must not be uneasy if, in the expectation of telling you all this gossip so quickly, I shall not write letters—perhaps not one in the next fortnight or three weeks, when I shall certainly be very little master of my time. Hedge I have not seen, he must have suddenly taken to the sea. Dr Parsons I saw in the Louvre & Hillard in the street. Geo. Summer has called on me, but I have not seen him. I am to go to a soirée at [Alexis] De Tocqueville's tonight. My French is far from being as good as Madame De Stael's

To Edith Emerson, June 23, 1848

London 23 June 1848

My dear Edie,

Your little letter & flower & some drawings your mother sent me made me very glad about you, & I am making ready as fast as I can to finish my visit and come home and find you again.

I shall have a great many stories to tell you about little boys & girls in England and in France; and you will have a hundred things to tell me, now that you have learned to read, & can choose books & stories for yourself. I am delighted to hear that you take such good care of Eddy, & tell him what is in your books, & teach him verses to say. I long to hear him say them; & you must not let him forget them. A few days ago there were fifty hundred children, all in the uniforms of their different schools, met in the great church of St Paul's, and they sung hymns together, & people say, they sung well. I was very sorry I could not go to hear them. But I should not have liked it better than I like *"Now condescend,"* and so forth, when sung by three little people whom I know. I hope they will sing it for me & Mother together again in five or six weeks.

So goodbye for today!

Papa.

To Samuel Gray Ward, July 22, 1848

At sea
Steamship Europa
22 July 1848.

My dear friend,

The daily presence & cheerful smiles of your brother make it almost imperative, if I had not besides a just debt, to write you a page, and it will be some sunshine in these headwinds & long disgust of the sea, to remember all the gallery of agreeable images that are wont to appear with your name. What games we men so dumb & lunatic play with one another! What is it or can it be to you that through the long mottled trivial years a dreaming brother cherishes in a corner some picture of you as a type or nucleus of happier visions & a freer life. I am so safe in my iron limits from intrusion or extravagance, that I can well afford to indulge my humour with the figures that pass my dungeon window, without incurring any risk of a ridiculous shock from coming hand to hand with my Ariels & Gabriels. Besides, If you & other deceivers should really not have the attributes of which you hang out the sign, you were meant to have them, they are in the world and it's is with good reason that I rejoice in the tokens. Strange that what is most real & cordial in existence should lie under what is most fantastic & vanishing. I have long ago found that we belong to our life not that it belongs to us, & that we must be content to play a sort of admiring & secondary part to our genius. But here to relieve you of these fine cobwebs, comes an odd challenge from a fellow passenger to play chess with him; me too, who have not played chess, I suppose, for 20 years. Tis of a piece with the oddity of my letter, & I shall accept that, as I write this. Shadows & Shadows. Never say, I did it. Your loving fellow film.

Sea weeds. Two very good men with whom I spent a Sunday in the country near Winchester lately, asked me if there were any Americans, if there were any who had an American idea? or what is it that thoughtful & superior men with us would have? Certainly I did not retort, after our country fashion, by defying them to show me one mortal Englishman who did not live from hand to mouth but who saw his way. No, I assured them there were such monsters hard by the setting sun, who believed in a future such as was never a past, but if I should show it to them, they would think French Communism solid & practicable in the the comparison. So I sketched the Boston fanaticism of right & might without bayonets or bishops, every man his own king, & all cooperation necessary & extemporaneous. Of course, my men went wild at the denying to society the beautiful right to kill & imprison. But we stood fast for milk & acorns, told them that musket-worship was perfectly well known to us, that it was an old bankrupt, but that we had never seen a man of sufficient valour & substance quite to carry out the other, which was nevertheless as sure as copernican astronomy, and all heroism & invention must of course lie on this side. Tis wonderful how odiously thin & pale this republic dances before blue bloodshot English eyes, but I had some anecdotes to bring some of its traits within their vision, & at last obtained a kind of allowance; but I doubt my tender converts are backsliders before this.—But their question which began the conversation was so dangerous, that I thought of no escape but to this extreme & sacred asylum, & having got off for once through the precinct of the temple, I shall not venture into such company again, without consulting those same thoughtful Americans, whom their inquiry concerned. And you first, you who never wanted for a reason of your faith, choose now your colours & styles, & draw in verse, or prose, or painted outline, the portrait of your American. Yours, at least, will have verisimilitude marrow & mountain life. Forgive these ricketty faltering lines of mine; they do not come of infirm faith or love, but of the quivering ship. Ever your friend,

R. W. E.

At Sea, on board the Europa,
27 July, 1848.

Dear William,

In the near prospect of reaching Boston, you shall have a line, if only to assure you, & Mother, if she is with you, that I have had a good run home, thus far, having met with no mischance, excepting the loss of six hours yesterday in entering the harbour of Halifax, where we waited for the fog to disperse. We have an admirable steamer, excellently provided, good captain, good company, Tom Appleton, Dr Loring, Tom G. Bradford, Jonathan Amory, and young Tom Ward (T. W. Wards youngest son) being of the party The steamship table was full of books & we have made the Atlantic spaces as little dreary as we could. I cannot tell you how heartily glad I am to approach home, & to resolve never to travel more—until my children force me to. I fear I have been a bad correspondent, & you certainly have a good right to complain. But really I did what I could, & there is hardly in your acquaintance a person of narrower possibilities & stricter limits than I. I take to myself great praise for hiding my intellectual poverties by my diligence, to such a creditable extent, & not being cashiered long ago. Weak eyes, that will only serve a few hours daily; *no animal spirits,* an immense & fatal negative with our Anglican race. No Greek, no mathematics, no politics,—How the deuce man do you contrive to live & talk with this nervous exigent race? Alas, I know not how they have borne with me so long—, and the oddity & ridicule of it all, is,—given me a literary reputation too, which I make dangerous drafts upon, every day I live. The will o' the wisp, the light invisible except in certain angles, & in all but impossible circumstances, seems to me how often the type & symbol of us all. We cannot overestimate or underestimate these strange goodfornothing immortal men that we are. When shall I see you? You must come to Concord: I have had enough of riding & sailing for my share and I have I suppose a great many long stories to tell. So bring Susan & Mother to see us, & be a good brother to your affectionate

Waldo.

TO THEODORE PARKER, AUGUST 17? 1848

Concord 18 August 1848

My dear Sir,

Tis bad that we cannot talk of the Quarterly,[46] but must write. Is it certain that it should go on? Who is it for? *Not for you*—who sell 20,000 copies of your article with its own proper name; you surely need no partnership: *not for Cabot,* who works for good nature, and, among other reasons as he is pleased to say, for me: *not for the unwilling martyr-contributors, who write* because you are resolved they shall: not for me, lastly, who also have my own little platoon who will read my chapter as readily out of as in the Journal. I fear that we are taking a world of pains we might save We began the journal in the belief that the time was critical & a good political journal might do essential service. But we have found no new political writer. All that part you have done, & would have done it at the least as effectually in your usual ways. None of those whom I am wont to depend on as my section in our company, have volunteered any aid, as I hoped they would. I fear it will cost me much toil to wake them to exertion. For myself, I am so puny in my constitution that it is only by the strictest parsimony in husbanding my resources that I ever bring anything to pass & I have not any willingness to waste an ounce. I fear we are to work blindly for these poor publishers to the certain wasting of our wits. Consider twice, my dear profuse friend, before you put forth any new prospectus.—If it is to be done, if I could see any good in it, I would write my article, & coax others to write theirs. But I have a great deal of work quite other than this, which I wish to do.

It is a long story & can better be spoken: but you have sickness in your house, & I in mine. My mother is very ill today If there were time, & health, I should come at once to see you. Write your sense of it [manuscript mutilated]

Horrible certainly is my position, I who have done nothing, to you who have done all.—But the question is for a new year—a year!

---

46. *Parker was trying to get Emerson involved as an editor and contributor with his new* Massachusetts Quarterly Review.

To Theodore Parker, September 15, 1848

Concord, 15 September, 1848.

My dear Sir,

Your letter announcing your resolution respecting the Journal reached me duly, but I waited to see Cabot who delayed his coming until yesterday. As Cabot has been so prompt in throwing down his arms, I who was plotting to throw down mine, must persist in my mutiny, even though I should repent it one of these days with tears. I could heartily wish that communication with you were a little easier, as I should like well to exculpate myself from what may easily seem to you very little performance, after much implied promise. But I wanted what perhaps is here & now an impossibility, a journal of pure literature & ethics, which must be very jealous of its philanthropic & political contributors, every man writing on oath, and the journal much preferring to go without its complement of pages than to have less than the best. But I understand very well—though I did not until I saw you last week—your own interest in the enterprise, and you have every right to make it good, & I shall gladly aid you, if I can, by some contribution; though it becomes me henceforward to be very discreet in promising aid, after this experience. And now I shall promise myself great public results from your courage & energy in dealing with the great questions of the day; which, if I, warned by vision or by no vision, do not touch, I do not the less but the more honour & thank those who can & do.

Yours ever gratefully,
R. W. Emerson.

To William Buell Sprague, October 25, 1848

Concord, October 25, 1848.

My dear Sir: It will be easy, as it is grateful, to me to answer your inquiries in regard to Dr. [Ezra] Ripley, as I still have by me some sketches which I attempted of his character very soon after his decease. Indeed, he is still freshly remembered in all this neighbourhood. He was a man so kind and sympathetic, his character was so transparent, and his merits so intelligible to all observers, that he was very justly appreciated in this community. He was a natural gentleman; no dandy, but courtly, hospitable, manly, and public spirited; his nature social, his house open to all men. I remember the remark made by an old farmer, who used to travel hither from Maine, that "no horse from the Eastern country would go by the Doctor's gate." Travellers from the West and North and South could bear the like testimony. His brow was serene and open to his visitor, for he loved men, and he had no studies, no occupation, which company could interrupt. His friends were his study, and to see them loosened his talents and his tongue. In his house dwelt order, and prudence, and plenty; there was no waste and no stint; he was open-handed and just and generous. Ingratitude and meanness in his beneficiaries did not wear out his compassion; he bore the insult, and the next day his basket for the beggar, his horse and chaise for the cripple, were at their door. Though he knew the value of a dollar as well as another man, yet he loved to buy dearer and sell cheaper than others. He subscribed to all charities, and it is no reflection on others to say that he was the most public spirited man in the town. The late Dr. Gardiner, in a Funeral Sermon on some parishioner, whose virtues did not readily come to mind, honestly said,—"He was good at fires." Dr. Ripley had many virtues, and yet all will remember that, even in his old age, if the fire bell was rung, he was instantly on horseback with his buckets and bag.

He was never distinguished in the pulpit as a writer of sermons, but in his house his speech was form and pertinence itself. You felt, in his presence, that he belonged by nature to the clerical class. He had a foresight, when he opened his mouth, of all that he would say, and he marched straight to the conclusion. In private discourse or in debate, in the vestry or the lyceum, the structure of his sentences was admirable,—so neat, so natural, so terse, his words fell like stones, and often, though quite unconscious of it, his speech was a satire on the loose, voluminous, patch-work periods of other speakers. He sat down when he had done. A man of anecdote, his talk in the parlour was chiefly narrative. I remember the remark of a gentleman, who listened with much delight to his conversation, at the time when the Doctor was preparing to go to Baltimore and Washington, that "a man who could tell a story so well was company for kings and John Quincy Adams." With a very limited acquaintance with books, his knowledge was an external experience, an Indian wisdom, the observation of such facts as country life, for nearly a century, could supply. He watched with interest the garden, the field, the orchard, the house and the barn, horse, cow, sheep and dog, and all the common objects that engage the thought of the farmer. He kept his eye on the horizon, and knew the weather like a sea-captain. The usual experiences of men,—birth, marriage, sickness, death, burial, the common temptations, the common ambitions, he studied them all, and sympathized so well in these that he was excellent company and counsel to all, even the most humble and ignorant. With extraordinary states of mind, with states of enthusiasm, or enlarged speculation, he had no sympathy and pretended to none. He was very sincere, and kept to his point, and his mark was never remote. His conversation was strictly personal, and apt to the person and the occasion. An eminent skill he had in saying difficult and unspeakable things; in delivering to a man or a woman that which all their other friends had abstained from saying; in uncovering the bandage from a sore place, and applying the surgeon's knife with a truly surgical spirit. Was a man a sot, or a spendthrift, or too long time a batchelor, or suspected of some hidden crime, or had he quarrelled with his wife, or collared his father, or was there any cloud or suspicious circumstance in his behaviour, the good pastor knew his way straight to that point, believing himself entitled to a full explanation; and whatever relief to the conscience of both parties plain speech could effect, was sure to be procured. In all such passages he justified himself to the conscience, and commonly to the love, of the persons concerned. Many instances, in which he played a right manly part, and acquitted himself as a brave and wise man, will be long remembered. He was the more competent to those searching discourses, from his knowledge of family history. He knew everybody's grandfather, and seemed to talk with each person, rather as the representative of his house and name than as an individual. In him has perished more local and personal anecdote of this village and vicinity than is possessed by any survivor. This intimate knowledge of families, and this skill of speech, and still more his sympathy, made him incomparable in his parochial visits, and in his exhortations and prayers with sick and suffering persons. He gave himself up to his feeling, and said on the instant the best things in the world. Many and many a felicity he had in his prayer, now forever lost, which defied all the rules of all the rhetoricians. He did not know when he was good in prayer or sermon, for he had no literature and no art; but he believed, and therefore spoke.

He was eminently loyal in his nature, and not fond of adventure or innovation. By education, and still more by temperament, he was engaged to the old forms of the New England Church. Not speculative, but affectionate; devout, but with an extreme love of order, he adopted heartily, though in its mildest forms, the creed and catechism of the fathers, and appeared a modern Israelite in his attachment to the Hebrew history and faith. Thus he seemed, in his constitutional leaning to their religion, one of the rearguard of the great camp and army of the Puritans; and now, when all the old platforms and customs of the Church were losing their hold in the affections of men, it was fit that he should depart, fit that, in the fall of laws, a loyal man should die.

> *Yours, with great respect,*
> *R. W. Emerson.*

To Arthur Hugh Clough, January 11, 17? 1849

Concord, 17, January 1849

My dear Clough,

I cannot tell you how great a joy to me is your poem. It came to me on the very day when a frightful calamity had come into the house of a dear friend here, whom I was on the way to visit,—and I had that night a strange balance to adjust, of grief & joy. For this poem is a high gift from angels that are very rare in our mortal state. It delights & surprises me from beginning to end. I can hardly forgive you for keeping your secret from me so well. I knew you was good & wise, stout of heart & truly kind, learned in Greek, & of excellent sense,—but how could I know or guess that you had all this wealth of expression, this wealth of imagery, this joyful heart of youth, this temperate continuity, that belongs only to high masters. It is a noble poem. Tennyson must look to his laurels. It makes me & all of us richer, and I am recalling every passage of speech & action of my staid & reticent friend, to find the hints & parallels of what I read. I have no time now to write at all, much less to tell you what I think. But I sent the poem to many friends, each for one night, & have the best report from all. Three of them have ordered copies immediately, & you shall have a sale here quickly. Longfellow I sent it to, & he writes moderately enough, yet I will transcribe his note, as Longfellow is prized on your side the water. "Altogether fascinating, & in part very admirable is the poem of Mr. Clough. Tom Appleton read it aloud to us the other evening, the audience consisting of my wife; my brother, an engineer; Lowell, the poet; a German friend, a man of letters, well versed in our vernacular; &

myself. All were much delighted with the genial wit, the truth to nature, & the extreme beauty of various passages & figures; all agreed that it was a poem of a very high order of merit; no one criticized.—In the morning, I found Appleton reading it again to himself; in the afternoon, my wife doing the same thing, &c"—then he praises "the fine delineation of the passion of love," & congratulates himself on the hexameters, &c &c

Well, Carlyle has written me, & never mentioned this. I looked into your journals, & find no notice yet. It is named somewhere, but they have not found out that they have got a new book! Well, keep your secret if you can, & as long as you can. Alas for you! Your silent days, I believe, are now nearly ended. Thanks & joy & love to you!

R. W. Emerson.

To Thomas Wentworth Higginson, May 16, 1849

Concord, 16 May 1849

My dear Sir,

I was in town yesterday & Mr Alcott showed me the list of subscribers to the Town & Country Club and I read at or near the end of the list the names of two ladies, written down, as he told me, by your own hand. On the instant, I took a pen & scratched or blotted out the names. Such is the naked fact. Whether the suggestion I obeyed was supernal or infernal, I say not But I have to say that I looked upon the circumstance of the names of two ladies standing there upon our roll as quite fatal to the existence of our cherished Club. I had stated to the Club the other day that "men" was used design-edly & distinctively in the first draft, & the Club by vote decided that it should stand so. I had moreover yesterday just come from a conference with some gentlemen representing the views of an important section of the mem bers, who, alarmed by the pugnacious attitudes into which the Club was betrayed the other day, were preparing to withdraw, & whom I had assured that all those who had long been projecting their literary Club, would not be deprived of their object, & something else thrust on them,—when to my surprise I found this inscription of names of ladies. I erased them at once, that no man might mistake our design. I really wish that you would join with us in securing what we really want,—a legitimate Club Room; & very many of us will, I doubt not, heartily join with you in obtaining what is also legitimate, but not what we now seek, a social union of literature, science, &c for the sexes. But we claim a priority of time in our project, & do not wish to be hindered of it, when it is now ripened & being realized. I am quite sure it is the wish of the great majority of persons who have acted in it hitherto, to establish a club house; & you must let us do it, & you must heartily join & help us do it.

Yours with great regard,
R. W. Emerson.

To Ellen Rendall, May 22, 1849

Concord, Massachusetts,
22 May. 1849

My dear Miss Rendall,

Your beautiful gift of Psyche arrived safely at my door, many months ago, & the very kind letter which accompanied it. Then came a note from Mrs Fisher, saying, that your friend Mrs Adams, (wife, too, of another of my benefactors) had died:—And neither you, nor Mrs F., nor Mr A., have had any syllable from me. I cannot think of detailing to you the weary reasons that have kept me silent. Indeed, I seldom write, & must risk with generous people the imputation of ingratitude. My wife is a victim of ill-health, my housekeeping unskilful, &, besides my own studies which are exacting, I fancy that I have either some bad facility of assuming, or else a bad luck in being engaged in other people's affairs. I think this an unpardonable infirmity in others; but I find always some exceptional feature in each new case, which pleads for that one. I have seen a fortnight ago, Mr & Mrs Flower, who spent a part of a day with me on their way to the West, who claimed kindred with your friend. I have no studies to tell you of: Only one study that I hope to make proficience in, Ethical Science. I should like well to write, or, at least, to read, a better statement of its Results than any I know. But perhaps this needs a life lease of some centuries; for the experiences that make Bibles, form like stalactites in caverns, particle by particle, in slow ages.

I wish you would say thus much to my friends Mr & Mrs Fisher at

Sheffield, whom I remember with lively affection, & whom I am not without hope of greeting in America. There is nothing very good to tell you of the people here, no books, no poets, no artists; nothing but their incessant activity as pioneers & geographers. The material problem is great & engrossing, the opening of new countries every year. In so great a population as ours,—all readers & writers,—we must now & then be entitled to a good & happy soul. The probability of a great one increases every hour. I ought to say, however, that my friend Thoreau is shortly to print a book called "A Week on the Concord & Merrimack Rivers," which, I think, will win the best readers abroad & at home. I have owed much pleasure & instruction to Mr Adam's papers in the Repository, & Westminster Review and my friends have borrowed them Their originality, their cheerfulness & variety makes them favourites with us all. Psyche is planted on the mantel piece in my library, & will keep me in mind to send you better & the best news of us, when my neighbours & countrymen shall afford me any thing that ought to interest you. With the kindest wishes & assurances of your welfare,

Your obliged friend,
R Waldo Emerson

To Henry Wadsworth Longfellow, May 24, 1849

Concord ⎱
24 May ⎰ *1849*

My dear Longfellow,

I am heartily obliged to you for Kavangh, which I read on Sunday afternoon with great contentment,—though hindered by "the Steamer" & other accidents, from acknowledging it. It had, with all its gifts & graces, the property of persuasion, & of inducing the serene mood it required. I was deceived by the fine name into a belief that there was some family legend, & must own (like palates spoiled by spices) to some disappointment at the temperate conclusion. But it is good painting, & I think it the best sketch we have seen in the direction of the American Novel: for here is our native speech & manners treated with sympathy, taste, & judgment. One thing struck me as I read,—that you win our gratitude too easily; for, after our much experience of the squalor of New Hampshire & the pallor of Unitarianism, we are so charmed with elegance in an American book, that we could forgive more vices than are possible to you. Is it not almost June, & did you not agree to trust yourself for one day to my guidance?

Yours,
R. W. Emerson

To Ellen Emerson, July 4, 1849

Concord, July 4, 1849

Dear Ellen,

Do not write to Mr Thoreau or any one else without good reason, and then you will have no doubt what to say, or what address to give. We are glad to get your accounts of your new home [at school] You must tell us how the music prospers, & how the daily lessons. Ask Uncle William to please show you how to fold your letter, before you seal it. And sometimes you must sit alone in your chamber.

Papa.

To Elizabeth Dodge Kinney, April 8, 1850

United States Hotel
Philadelphia 8 April 1850

My dear Mrs Kinney,

You will have thought it has taken me a great while to read your two poems, & no doubt have looked for their return many days ago. But you are quite mistaken. If I did not fear that you were packing your portfolios & preparing for Italy, I should not think of sending home the verses for many days to come: and then should perhaps accompany them with notes longer than the poems. So you must congratulate yourself on your escape from an elaborate critique. But, seriously, though I am hard to please in poetry, yet I am very sensible of the variety of power that appears in it, & I find in these verses a fine literary talent, though it seems to me somewhat accidentally thrown into the poetic form. Yet the metre is sweet & flowing, and there is a continuity & fulness of expression, which is rare & valuable. My quarrel with it, if I have any, is what is almost a national quality, the inwardness or "subjectiveness" as they call it of our lyrics, & which somewhat marks these poems. If I were a professor, I should make all young people with a poetic talent, read Chaucer, Herrick, & Shakspeare, for their objectiveness. But you, on your way to Italy, and in Florence itself, will read Dante, at once the most outward & inward of bards. With many thanks for this kind trust you have committed to me, & with congratulations on the bright year that now opens before you, of planting a home in Italy, and with a lively interest to know its effect on your genius,—I shall watch for news of your goings. Make my kind regards & congratulations also to Mr Kinney, who must enjoy the general pleasure which, I observe, his appointment gives.

R. W. Emerson.

To Margaret Fuller, April 11, 1850

United States Hotel
Philadelphia 11 April 1850

Dear Margaret,

I know you have not much more faith than I have in my skill as a factor for you or myself with booksellers; but I have more experience than formerly, & more acquaintances in that craft; and, if you will send me the statement of your intentions & wishes respecting your proposed book, I will do all that I can, (&, I doubt not, more than you could if you were here,) to make the best terms for you with a publisher. If it shall prove adviseable to publish in Boston, my new friends, Phillips & Sampson, are excellent men, & will do better than any house there. If, as I can easily believe, it is better to print in New York, I can certainly procure the assistance of the same friends there to whom you, if there, would apply, as advisers & mediators with the Parnassian brokers of Cliff Street or Broadway. If, on general grounds, as I gathered in talking with Mr Spring & other friends, you prefer to remain in Florence for the present, I am sure it is needless that you should cross the Ocean only to make a bargain for your book, whilst I am here, even if I were a far clumsier agent than I am. I can see plainly, too, the very important advantages which continued residence in Italy will give to your factors at home, not only as adding solidity to your testimony, but new rays of reputation & wonder to you as a star,—advantages which no bookseller can overlook for a moment. It is certainly an unexpected side for me to support,—the advantages of your absenteeism,—I, who had vainly imagined that one of these days, when tired of cities, our little Concord would draw you to itself, by the united claims of four families of your friends,—but surprise is the woof you love to weave into all your web. Well, we shall only postpone our claim a little more patiently. I go home tomorrow & the next day, being here only to read lectures, for the past week. I shall find, I trust, Ellery full of thoughts, if fitful & moody as ever. I could only wish he were born as much for his own happiness, & for yours, as he is for mine. To me, he is, from month to month, from year to year, an incomparable companion, inexhaustible even if it be, & more's the pity, the finest luxury, rather than a necessity of life. Elizabeth is always sacred & dear, and never ceases to love you. You may stay in Italy, for now, but all the more we shall want you & must have you at last. Lidian is never well, but perhaps not much more invalid than you knew her Mamma is well both are ever your friends, & Ellen, Edith, & Edward, I hope will be yet.

Yours affectionately,
Waldo Emerson.

TO LIDIAN EMERSON, MAY 20, 1850

Burnet House
Cincinnati, 20 May 1850

Dear Lidian,

I arrived here safely on Saturday night. I left Cleveland (whence I wrote you) on Friday evening, about 7 o clock, in the steamer Saratoga, had a rough pleasant ride over the lake to Sandusky, about 5 hours, slept there until nearly 5 o'clock, A.M., then took the cars for the South, and travelled 218 miles to this city. Beautiful road, grand old forest, beeches, immense black walnuts, oaks, rock maples, buckeyes (horse chestnuts) in bloom, cornels in white flower, & red buds—a forest tree whose bloom is precisely the colour of the peach-blossom,—made all the miles rich with beauty; enormous grapevines I saw too: Most of the houses were log-huts, with log-barns. Cities are everywhere much the same thing, but this forest is very unlike ours. The land was all heavy with wood, and, of course, the poor Germans buy it with confidence that it will bear wheat & corn. I saw the land that is never manured, and they say that when the manure heap has grown too big, they move the barn to another place. As we drew nigh Cincinnati, the wheat was from a foot to 18 inches high, & the corn 5 & six inches. Yet the season here, they tell me, is very backward. Yesterday morning, I found several friendly people, Mr William Greene, Mr Vaughan, Mr Urner, and today I have seen Judge Walker Mr Cranch, & many others. Young Stackpole is here, & I particularly like him, tell Mrs Ripley. Mr Storer, tell Elizabeth H. left his card for me, but I have not seen him. I live in a magnificent hotel, the best & largest building of that kind I have ever seen. And the growth of the city, which is incessant, warrants it. Here are, it is said, 120 000 souls, and in 1840 only 36,000. I have seen, tell Mother, Mrs Inman Haskins & her family, & Joseph B. Ladd. Inman Haskins himself is gone to California. I went yesterday across the river in a ferry, & walked along the Kentucky shore to see Cincinnati from the hills on that side. I have seen a young man here who is worth all the rest, named Goddard, and am to see him again tomorrow, fine scholar, clear-sighted, ardent, with a poetic taste, & a deal of strength. He keeps a school here, but is going into the law. In short, I think I shall be able to weather the nine days I am to stay here. And yet I am already asking my best way home. For when I hear how many fine ways I have to choose among, by the great lakes, by Harper's Ferry, by the Juniata, &c I am like a boy with a cent who is puzzled to know which of all Mr Potter's things he shall buy. Of course you are all well. May it be so & continue so! Love to Mother, and love to all the children. I will write you again quickly when I have any news as to my return to send. W.

Mrs Vaughan, whom I find here, was Sarah Clarke, an old pupil of mine in Boston in 1824. She presented me to her daughter who is as old as she was then, yet the mother to my eyes still looks young. Pray send any letters promptly to me at the Burnet House, Cincinnati, Ohio I shall be here eight or nine days yet.

To Marcus Spring, July 23, 1850

Concord, 23d July, 1850.

My dear Sir

The morning papers add no syllable to the fatal paragraphs of last night concerning Margaret Fuller,[47] no contradiction and no explanation. At first I thought I would go myself and see if I could help in the inquiries at the wrecking ground, and act for the friends. But I have prevailed on my friend, Mr Henry D. Thoreau, to go for me and all the friends. Mr Thoreau is the most competent person that could be selected; and in the dispersion of the Fuller family, and our uncertainty how to communicate with them, he is authorized by Mr Ellery Channing to act for them all.[48]

I fear the chances of recovering manuscript and other property, after five or six days, are small, and diminishing every hour. Yet Margaret would have every record of her history for the last three or four years; and whatever is found by anyone would easily be yielded up to a diligent seeker. Mr Thoreau is prepared to spend a number of days in this object, if necessary, and you must give him any guidance or help you can. If his money does not hold out, I shall gladly pay any drafts he may make on you in my name. And I shall cordially unite with you in any expense that this painful calamity shall make necessary.

Yours faithfully,
R. W. Emerson.

Marcus Spring, Esq.

---

47. *Margaret Fuller, her husband, and their son had all perished in a shipwreck off Fire Island, N.Y., on 19 July.*
48. *Ellery Channing was married to Margaret Fuller's sister, Ellen.*

To Samuel Gray Ward, August 2, 1850

My dear friend,

William Henry Channing asked me to write some Life of Margaret, defining his thought by calling it "Margaret & her Friends."[49] On his invitation, I spent an hour or two with him yesterday, to talk of it. Many questions rise;— whether the materials will be surrendered, on all hands? Whether it can be done by one? Whether it is publishable, if done? I think it could really be done, if one would heroically devote himself, and a most vivacious book written, but it must be done tête exaltée, & in the tone of Spiridion, or even of Bettine, with the coolest ignoring of Mr Willis Mr Carlyle and Boston & London. But no step of this kind could be taken without the concurrence of yourself & Anna, & Caroline S. & of Margaret's own family. Nay, if for the glory & honour of Margaret such a hecatomb were prepared, and all scruples magnificently renounced, I think, when the first experiments came to be made, it might turn out to be a work above our courage. If you had leisure, you & Channing & I would sit as committee? What is your opinion?

R. W. E.

Concord, 2 August, 1850.

To Paulina W. Davis, September 18, 1850

Concord, 18 September, 1850.

Mrs. P. W. Davis
Dear Madam,

I have waited a very long time since I had your letter, because I had no clear answer to give, and now I write rather that I may not neglect your letter, than because I have anything very material to say. The fact of the political & civil wrongs of woman I deny not. If women feel wronged, then they are wronged. But the mode of obtaining a redress, namely, a public convention

---

49. *William Henry Channing, James Freeman Clarke, and Emerson edited and wrote sections of* Memoirs of Margaret Fuller Ossoli *(1852).*

called by women is not very agreeable to me, and the things to be agitated for do not seem to me the best. Perhaps I am superstitious & traditional, but whilst I should vote for every franchise for women,—vote that they should hold property, and vote, yes & be eligible to all offices as men—whilst I should vote thus, if women asked, or if men denied it these things, I should not wish women to wish political functions, nor, if granted assume them. I imagine that a woman whom all men would feel to be the best, would decline such privileges if offered, & feel them to be obstacles to her legitimate influence. Yet I confess lay no great stress on my opinion, since we are all liable to be deceived by the false position into which our bad politics throw elections & electors. If our politics were a little more rational we might not feel any unfitness in accompanying women to the polls. At all events, that I may not stand in the way of any right you are at liberty if you wish it to use my name as one of the inviters of the convention, though I shall not attend it, & shall regret that it is not rather a private meeting of thoughtful persons sincerely interested, instead of what a public meeting is pretty sure to be a heartless noise which we are all ashamed of when it is over. Yours respectfully

R. W. Emerson.

To Samuel Gray Ward, September 23, 1850

Concord 23 September.

My dear friend,

On Saturday P.M. I tried to find you at your office—to tell you at large what I find & what I think of Margaret's MSS. Perhaps one person should undertake the whole work, & everything should be put unreservedly in his hands. If you could, & would, you should be that person. I think I am the next best candidate—if I can be induced to undertake it. But it is the last imprudence in me to hold out any flag. My own tasks press on me, & require indefinite time, & my eyes can be used only for a few hours daily. Perhaps William Channing was too much her friend to leave him quite free enough. But whoever is editor, it will not be quite plain what he is to take & what he is to leave of these manifold threads, some pale coloured, & some glowing.

The personalities are essential;—leave them out, & you leave out Margaret. It would be prudentest for all parties to abdicate any part in the matter,—all but the editor,—& make up their hearts to take their fate from his discretion.

But when he has finished his task, I think, he must bring it to our jury to decide whether it shall go to the press, or to the flames. *You,* of course, have nothing to fear. In one of her books I read a pleasing narrative of a journey to Niagara, on which you were one of the party, & you will be gratified with all the characteristic if slight notes of her growing regard for the new acquaintance. And all her pictures, afterwards, are faithful & appreciating, even when written in sad moments. And, universally, constancy is one of her shining traits.

R. W. E.

To Caroline Sturgis Tappan, November 17 and 18, 1850

Concord
Sunday noon 17 Novr.

Dear Caroline,

The parcel came safely & on Friday morning. I read much & I believe the largest part of it. I find it perfectly like all I had read before of Margaret's, & thoroughly creditable to her. So much wit, ready & rapid learning, appreciation, so much probity constancy & aspiration, when shall we see again? Then what capacity for friendship! Her discriminating & proud election of her friends from afar, her brave & flowing intercourse with them, her quarrels, patience, pardons with & of them, are all good. But if I could have had any doubt earlier, I can have none now that those elevations & new experiences of which she sometimes wrote & spoke, & which she well knew how to adorn with a whole literature of mystical symbols, were quite constitutional, & had no universal sense whatever—The best effect of these fervid pages is the fine praise they give to every thing liberal, and the admonition to self reliance & courage. I grieve to find in them so much grief, belief in a bitter destiny, &c., which her clear mind & great heart should not have admitted, though the head ached & the knees shook. But she used her gifts so well, & against so much resistance, that almost none has a right to blame her.—Yes, it is too obvious that all her estimates of men, books, pictures, were distorted a little or much by her highly-refracting atmosphere, & therefore her statement is never catholic & true. But as an impulse & inspiration to whole files & companies of young men & women, & these the best, the memory of her decisive choices & of the marvellous eloquence in which she conveyed them will remain one of the best things our time has afforded us.—I had large & vague expectation of what amount of manuscript you would send, & perhaps had some disappointment in the actual reading.—I had hoped from what Ellery said, there were two or three Journals, & that you would not burn them; and I hoped there would be more recent letters, from New York, & from Europe. But a seal seems to be set when she leaves Boston. Nothing of any importance comes to me, after that time. I saw William Story & his wife, last week; they give the friendliest pictures of Margaret; that was pleasant,— and describe her agreeable relations with her Italian ladies & with the Brownings. and repeated the story I had heard from the Springs of the first acquaintance with Ossoli. But no *mots* & no action. William Channing will use his own materials so that I have nothing more to look for. Charles K. N[ewcomb]. has written again to say that he has been ill & is not quite yet able to come.—The whole reading has been an Egyptian chamber to me, filling me with strange regrets that my first dealing with the facts themselves was hardly more substantial than with these shadows of them. But I shall have more to say. Ever Yours,

R. W. E.

18 Nov

You ask of Jenny Lind. I heard her but once in Boston, and, as it chanced for me it was much more satisfactory than my seeing her in the Opera in Lon-don; I know no more than to be entirely contented, though, as you know, my musical suffrage is worth nothing. Your allusion to Eastern Sages almost tempts me to send you the Megha Duta, which I believe you have not seen. But it is not, at least in metrical translation, up versions from Von Hammer, which are always attractive to me till they in plain English.

Body & Soul   Enweri

In China, once painted a painter a hall,
O hearken! no better did ever befall!
One half from his brush with rich colors did run,

The other he touched with a beam of the sun,
So that all which attracted the eye in one side.
The same, point for point, in the other replied.
In thee, friend, the well-painted chamber is found,
Thine the high vaulted roof, & the base on the ground;
Is one half depicted with colors less bright?
Beware that the counterpart blazes with light.

To Mary Merrick Brooks? March 18, 1851

New York, 18th March, 1851.

Dear Friend:

I had more reasons than one to regret leaving home at this time, and, if my present engagements were not of two seasons' standing, I should have made every effort to relieve myself. For your Liberty meeting,[50] I think it has a certain importance just now; and, really, at this moment, it seems imperative that every lover of human rights should, in every manner, singly or socially, in private and in public, by voice and by pen,—and, first of all, by substantial help and hospitality to the slave, and defending him against his hunters,— enter his protest for humanity against the detestable statute of the last Congress. I find it a subject of conversation in all cars and steamboats, and everywhere distributing society into two classes, according to the moral feasibility of individuals on one part, and their habitual docility to party leading on the other. I do not know how the majority of to-day will be found to decide.

Sometimes people of natural probity and affection are so warped by the habit of party, and show themselves so unexpectedly callous and inhuman, that it seems we must wait for the Almighty to create a new generation, a little more keenly alive to moral impressions, before any improvement in institutions can be looked for. But, as far as I have observed, there is, on all great questions, a tide or undulation in the public mind—a series of actions

---

50. *The Liberty Meeting, held 3 April in the orthodox church to protest the Fugitive Slave Law, had the compelling event of the arrest of Thomas Sims to make the meeting of more than usual importance. [Tilton]*

and reactions. The momentary interest carries it to day; but, presently, the advocates of the liberal principle are victorious,—and the more entirely, because they had persisted unshaken under evil report. And, as justice alone satisfies every body, they are sure to prevail at last.

If the World has any reason in it, it is forever safe and successful to urge the cause of love and right. I know it is very needless to say this to you, and others like you, who cannot, if they would, help serving the truth, though all the world be gone to worship Mammon. But it is the only answer I know how to make to our mathematical compatriots. So, wishing you a day of happy thoughts and sympathies on Thursday, I remain,

Yours respectfully and gratefully,
R. W. Emerson.

TO WILLIAM EMERSON, JUNE 28, 1851

American House
Boston, 28 June, 1851

Dear William,

I had not time to write you yesterday of Mother's unhappy accident. In the night before last she had bad dreams, & rolled out of her bed on to the floor. She lay there unable to help herself for a long time, neither calling out, nor able to reach her bell-rope or so much as a shoe to make a noise with, & wake us in the next room It was between 1 & 2 o'clock, & she thinks it was nearly an hour before she succeeded in getting into her bed again, with difficulty & pain. In the morning, she waited till the girl came to her room, then sent to me, & I called Dr Bartlett The Doctor found no dislocation, but believes that the capsule of the hip bone is fractured, and that she can never walk again: that, at 83 or 84, nothing can be hoped from the power of nature under a treatment of splints, & so does not try that treatment. But the Doctor is always an alarmist, & has given mother up already two or three times, on account of attacks, which she presently rallied from; and I have much confidence that she will walk again. Still it is a grievous calamity to her. The day before, she had walked with Charlotte Haskins to Mrs Ripley's, & home again. You must write to her immediately. She is very happy in having Charlotte H., as we all are. I am here, last night & this morn. on my way to Lenox for a day.

> *With love to you all,*
> *Waldo E.*

TO MONCURE DANIEL CONWAY, NOVEMBER 13, 1851

> *Concord*⎱ *13 November 1851*
> *Mass* ⎰

Dear Sir,

I fear you will not be able except at some chance auction to obtain any set of the Dial. In fact, smaller editions were printed of the later & latest numbers; which increases the difficulty.

I am interested by your kind interest in my writings, but you have not let me sufficiently into your own habit of thought, to enable me to speak to it with much precision. But, I believe, what interests both you & me, most of all things, & whether we know it or not,—is, the morals of intellect: in other words, that no man is worth his room in the world, who is not commanded by a legitimate object of thought. The earth is full of frivolous people who are bending their whole force and the force of nations on trifles; & these are baptized with every grand & holy name, remaining of course totally inadequate to occupy any mind; & so skeptics are made. A true soul will disdain to be moved except by what natively commands it, though it should go sad & solitary in search of its Master a thousand years. The few superior persons in each community are so by their steadiness to reality, & their neglect of appearances. This is the euphrasy & rue that purge the intellect & ensure insight. Its full rewards are slow but sure; & yet I think it has its reward on the instant, inasmuch as simplicity & grandeur are always better than dapperness. But I will not spin out these saws farther, but hasten to thank you for your frank & friendly letter, & to wish you the best deliverance in that contest, to which every soul must go alone.

> *Yours, in all good hope,*
> *R. W. Emerson*

M. Conway.

TO ELIZUR WRIGHT, JANUARY 7, 1852

Concord, 7 January, 1852

To the Editor of the Commonwealth.
Dear Sir,

I am exceedingly vexed by finding in your paper, this morning, precisely such a report of one of my lectures, as I wrote to you a fortnight since to entreat you to defend me from. I wrote, at the same time, to the other newspapers, & they have all kindly respected my request, & abstained. My lectures are written to be read as lectures in different places, & then to be reported by myself. Tomorrow, I was to have read this very lecture in Salem, & your reporter does all he can to kill the thing to every hearer, by putting him in possession beforehand of the words of each statement that struck him, as nearly as he could copy them. Abuse me, & welcome, but do not transcribe me. Now that your reporter has broken the line, I cannot expect the Traveller, & other journals to respect it, for it is a thing of concert. Defend me, another time.

Respectfully,
R. W. Emerson

Elizur Wright, Esq.
    I have been very sensible of repeated kind notices of my things, I have found in the Commonwealth.

TO FRANCIS R. GOURGAS, APRIL 8, 1852

Concord, 8 April, 1852

To the Town Clerk,

Dear Sir,
    I give you notice that I am no longer a member of the First Parish in this town.

Respectfully,
R. W. Emerson

To John Albee, 1852?

To a brave soul it really seems indifferent whether its tuition is in or out of college. And yet I confess to a strong bias in favor of college. I think we cannot give ourselves too many advantages; and he who goes to Cambridge has free the best of that kind. When he has seen their little all he will rate it very moderately beside that which he brought thither. There are many things much better than a college; an exploring expedition if one could join it; or the living with any great master in one's proper art; but in the common run of opportunities and with no more than the common proportion of energy in ourselves, a college is safest, from its literary tone and from the access to books it gives—mainly that it introduces you to the best of your contemporaries. But if you can easily come to Concord and spend an afternoon with me we could talk over the whole case by the river bank.

To Horatio Greenough, September 6, 1852

Concord ⎱ *6 September*
Mass. ⎰ *1852*

My dear Sir,

I have read your little book twice through, to say the least.[51] I have gone back, & up & down, & criss cross, & now am in a course of reading passages to my neighbors: and I assure you, it is, a very dangerous book, full of all manner of reality & mischievous application, fatal pertinence, & hip- & thigh-smiting personality, and instructing us against our will. I am not sure of its success as a popular book. The air of haste & of the newspaper, the negligence of some indispensable trifles in literary etiquette will hide its value from some readers,—and its own kindred & lovers whom it goes out to seek will imperatively ask a more elaborate redaction,—a sinking of the ephemeral, & some bridging to the eminent parts: but it contains more useful truth than any thing in America I can readily remember; & I should think the

---

51. The Travels, Observations, and Experience of a Yankee Stonecutter *(1852), published under the pseudonym "Horace Bender."*

entire population well employed if they would suspend other work for one day & read it. As long as they do not, you may be very sure a few of us will profit by the secret & deal it out to them little by little. Meantime, you have been unpardonably careless in your proofreading, and the book now needs a long table of Errata;

The book does not take me by surprise, as it would if I had not seen the man three weeks before; but it was all the more interesting & luminous. So right & high minded as it is, I am only the more sorry that it should confound things on the negro question, & put reason, from a most unexpected quarter into the hands of the base & greedy partisan. That the negro was a pre Adamite, I early discovered, but now that he too reads books, the courtesy to present company seems to require that it be a little parliamentarily stated. Then, though some fond Las Casas or two might fetch negroes to save Indians, tis very certain that the first planter who turned them or their work into doubloons, if he used Las Casas's words lied & knew he lied. Early Grey "would stand by his order." I hold it to be a paramount law of every aristocracy, that its members do so. I require of every reasonable Saxon man not to hold slaves or praise the holding,—because he belongs by blood & bond to the other party, & nature has not a Saxon ounce to spare. There is plenty of Celtic or Roman blood that can hold slaves as innocently as sharks bite, & the grand harmonies of nature round them all admirably in: yet we are all pained when either quits *his order,* when a Turk unturks himself to be a democrat, or a Saxon unsaxonises himself for some accidental sympathy When I begun this leaf I did not mean to be betrayed into preaching.

But man & book are a great possession to me. I wish to get the power of them. I am driven once more to revolve the old question, why not a Journal in this country that will combine the sanity & talent of really liberal men? There is plenty of power in New England wasted for want of concentration—& of which the population has need. I am tempted to go out into the highways & drum the Rappel, now that I see this new strength, But lest I should make no end of this letter, I subscribe myself

Yours faithfully,
R. W. Emerson

Horatio Greenough.

My brother William, a lawyer in New York, has lately sold his house on Staten Island & is proceeding to build another on his adjacent land. I have written to him to say that if I were about to build, I should apply to you for professional counsel, though I suppose a working plan for a house is not a thing to go to Phidias for. Yet I should not the less wish to know what Phidias would say on the subject. I mean to inclose to my brother a note to you, & if you chance to have any leisure, I bespeak your attention It is an easy trip to the Island & the site of his dwelling is noble. William E is no artist but is docile and is an honest & worthy man.

I find I have omitted to say what struck me not less than the broad good sense of the book, that is the splendor of statement, which is better than Canning.

To Wendell Phillips, February 19, 1853

Concord
19 February 1853

My dear Sir,

I read the Petition [for women's suffrage] with attention, & with the hope that I should find myself so happy as to do what you bade me. But this is my feeling in regard to the whole matter: I wish that done for their rights which women wish done. If they wish to vote, I shall vote that they vote. If they wish to be lawyers & judges, I shall vote that those careers be opened to them But I do not think that wise & wary women wish to be electors or judges; and I will not ask that they be made such against their will If we obtain for them the ballot, I suppose the best women would not vote. By all means let their rights of property be put on the same basis as those of men, or, I should say, on a more favorable ground. And let women go to women, & bring us certain tidings what they want, & it will be imperative on me & on us all to help them get it.

I am sorry that you should have had to write twice. Though I am a slow correspondent, I should have written today, without a second urgency. Do not despair of me. I am still open to reason.

Yours gratefully,
R. W. Emerson

TO THEODORE PARKER, MARCH 19, 1853

Concord, 19 March 1853

My dear Parker,

Be sure that book came to me, though not until several weeks after it was sent, & I read the inscription,[52] if with more pride than was becoming, yet not without some terror. Lately, I took the book in hand, & read the largest part of it, with good heed. I find in it all the traits which are making your discourses material to the history of Massachusetts,—the realism, the power of local & homely illustration, the courage & vigor of treatment, & the masterly sarcasm—now naked, now veiled,—and, I think, with a marked growth in power, & *coacervation*—shall I say?—of statement. To be sure, I am, in this moment, thinking also of speeches out of this book as well as those in it. Well; you will give the time to come the means of knowing how the lamp was fed, which they are to thank you that they find burning. And though I see you are too good natured by half in your praise of your contemporaries, you will neither deceive us, nor posterity, nor,—forgive me,—yourself, any more, in this graceful air of laying on others your own untransferable laurels. We shall all thank the right soldier whom God gave strength & will to fight for Him the battle of this day. I have not yet seen the new "Webster." It has not come with your letter. Ever new strength & victory be to you!

R. W. Emerson

Theodore Parker.

TO ABEL ADAMS, APRIL 8, 1853

Concord, 8 April, 1853

My dear Sir,

Mr Hosmer has two cows in his view, and is eager that I should tell you that one of them is black. He does not like to buy a black cow for you, until he

---

52. Parker's Ten Sermons of Religion *(1853)* was dedicated to Emerson.

knows that you have not an invincible objection to the colour. This cow is represented to him as yielding 14 quarts of good milk a day, and is five years old. The other is six years, of a chestnut color, & described as a very good milker. Cows & oxen are high-priced, at this moment; the first cow costs $75—the second $55.

I told Mr H., that, if he would buy at all, he must buy at his best discretion, without consulting you at all, & you would be content But, to ease his mind, at last, I promised, last night, to report his progress thus far. He will go on to buy one, & perhaps, the first, unless you send him word that you detest a black cow.

Ever yours,
R. W. Emerson

Mr. Abel Adams.

To Abel Adams, April 30, 1853

Concord, 30 April, 1853

My dear friend,

Mr Hosmer came home last night well pleased with having seen you, & very proud of the praises his cow had obtained from Mr Hagar, & other farmers on the way. I gave him your cheque for cheque for $55. and asked him what his own charges were. He said he had paid nearly or quite $2. for the cow; and when I proposed to pay him this, & 5.00 for himself,—he said, that would not pay him more than a dollar a day for his time. He thought he ought to have ten dollars. So I paid him ten dollars. I have no doubt that he has taken a good deal of time & pains about it; and I never dispute his charges, to myself, as I always find him fair.

He was offered, on the way, $80. for the cow in Lincoln.

I hope you are well & strong, or will be so when you are righted & rested.

Ever yours,
R. W. Emerson

Abel Adams.

To Ellen Emerson, July 8, 1853

Concord—
8 July 1853

Dear Ellen,

Do not omit to find or make an occasion to tell Miss Grace that it is a principal point with you to learn to speak French; &, at all events, that papa, who knows that no French man or woman ever set foot in Concord, was on the verge of sending you to a convent in Montreal, for no other purpose. I was glad that when the bell called you downstairs, & your friend called you upstairs, you obeyed your friend, & disobeyed the bell. Earl Grey said, when the nobles were threatened, "I shall stand by my order,"—and that is the rule of good sense. I am glad to see by your letters that your time is well filled, & the days are not long enough at Lenox to allow you to be homesick. Mrs Tappan[53] wrote me that she was, one day, on her way to call upon you, & met you. Since, she has lost her sister, whom you might have seen at Mrs Hoopers, apparently in brilliant health. I enclose $21.00 for your debt to Mrs Farley.

Papa.

To Caroline Sturris Tappan, July 22, 1853

Concord,
22 July 1853

Dear Caroline,

You say truly & wisely, we must learn from our losses not to let our friends go; yes; one would not willingly omit one good office: and yet when we do not speak or write, it is out of a confidence that we know our party, & are known for our own quality, once for all. I believe, my slowness to write letters has grown from the experience, that some of my friends have been very

---

53. *Caroline Sturgis had married William Aspinwall Tappan on 12 December 1847.*

impatient of my generalizings, as we weary of any trick, whilst theirs are still sweet to me. So I hesitate to write, except to the assessors, or to the man that is to slate my house. And my friends are an ever narrowing troop. Yet I am incurable, &, to this day, only rightly feel myself when I meet somebody whose habit of *thought*, at least, holds the world in solution, if I cannot find one whose will does. Friends are few, thoughts are few, facts few—only one: one only fact, now tragically, now tenderly, now exultingly illustrated in sky, in earth, in men & women, Fate, Fate. The universe is all chemistry, with a certain hint of a magnificent *Whence* or *Whereto* gliding or opalizing every angle of the old salt-&-acid acid-&-salt, endlessly reiterated & masqueraded through all time & space & form. The addition of that hint everywhere, saves things. Heavy & loathsome is the bounded world, bounded everywhere. An immense Boston or Hanover street with mountains of ordinary women, trains & trains of mean leathern men all immoveably bounded, no liquidity of hope or genius. But they are made chemically good, like oxen. In the absence of religion, they are polarized to decorum, which is its blockhead;— thrown mechanically into parallelism with this high *Whence* & *Whither*, which thus makes mountains of rubbish reflect the morning sun & the evening star. And we are all privy-counsellors to that Hint, which homeopath- ically doses the System, & can cooperate with the slow & secular escape of these oxen & semioxen from their quadruped estate, & invite them to be men, & hail them such. I do not know—now that stoicism & Christianity have for two millenniums preached liberty, somewhat fulsomely,—but it is the turn of Fatalism. And it has great conveniences for a public creed. Fatalism, foolish & flippant, is as bad as Unitarianism or Mormonism. But Fatalism held by an intelligent soul who knows how to humor & obey the infinitesimal pulses of spontaneity, is by much the truest theory in use. All the great would call their thought fatalism, or concede that ninety nine parts are nature, & one part power, though that hundredth is elastic, miraculous, and, whenever it is in energy, dissolving all the rest.

Forgive this heavy cobweb, which I did not think of spinning, & which will put you too out of all patience with my prose. But I see sun-colours over all the geometry, & am armed by thinking that our wretched interference is precluded.

Thanks for the new invitation. I very much wish to come & see you, & will use the occasion of Ellen's wants to come. Did you read Van Artevelde Taylor's "Notes on Life" I think he calls it? The first look of the book was sinister, but I found some things I would not have missed Alexander Smith I have not read, my attempts were not successful. "History & tradition" which you so characteristically disdain, are good in the interim, when no clarion of the muse is heard from the steeps, and are as good as bibles, when we ourselves are full of light, to read the three meanings from. And so may all high & happy thoughts dwell with you!

Your friend,
W. E.

To Charles F. Smith, August 31, 1853[54]

Concord, 31 August.
1853.

Dear Sir,

I have not received any communication from your society prior to your own.

It will give me pleasure to read a lecture before your association during their course.

If I come, your association shall pay me twenty five dollars.

Respectfully,
R. W. Emerson

Charles F. Smith. Committee

To William Emerson, November 19, 1853

Concord, 19 November, 1853.

Dear William,

I have been heartily sorry not only for your painful accident, but also that it should occur at this moment. Mother's death, at the last, surprised me by its suddenness She was so well on Saturday, & was so perfectly intelligent, whenever spoken to, in the midst of her lethargic state on Monday &

---

54. *This is typical of the letters Emerson wrote accepting lecture engagements.*

Tuesday, that I had no hesitation in leaving her on Tuesday afternoon till the next morning to fulfil an engagement at Charlestown. Happily, most happily, Elizabeth Ripley, who had promised to watch with her that night, & Elizabeth Hoar, who had promised herself to watch with her as long as she existed, were present; & not the good Nova Scotian Annie, her latest attendant, who with Irish Catherine had watched & slept alternately on Monday night. I told you she had asked on Monday that you should come to her, & said that she had been long expecting to hear from you. Something I believe was in her mind of some particular provisions or notices that you two had left unsettled in conversation which were to be added or altered in her will. She never said what,—and, as I never had confidence that she perfectly understood herself in these matters, since she ever had hanging before her vague notions of a great deal of "business" to be done, I never inquired; but usually adjourned over such things to the day which could not be distant, when you would come. Had you been in travelling condition I should have pressed your instant coming on Monday, but even that would not have availed. Yet it is a great loss that you & Susan should not have been here as she seemed so entitled to go to her rest with the fulness of her family & friends around her. And it was an end so graduated & tranquil, all pain so deadened, & the months & days of it so adorned by her own happy temper & by so many attentions of so many friends whom it drew to her, (as Martha Bartlett, Mr Mackay, Miss Joy, & others) that even in these last days almost all gloom was removed from death. Only as we find there is one less room to go to for sure society in the house, one less sure home in the house. Every thing yesterday was well & properly done. I could gladly have asked, had it been anywise practicable, that the English liturgy should have been read at her burial; for she was born a subject of King George, had been, in her childhood, so versed in that service, that, in her old age, it seemed still most natural to her, & the Common Prayer Book was on her bureau. She had lived through the whole history of this country. But all the proprieties & her own acts held her to the modern church here, & so it must be. Mr Frost very considerately & cordially performed his part yesterday as he has uniformly held Mother in veneration. I had informed all our few Boston relatives as well as I could & written to Dr Frothingham. But the Shepards were gone I believe & the Ladds & Haskinses perhaps did not receive my notes in time None appeared except Greene Haskins. George B Emerson & Abel Adams came also. Dr Frothingham wrote a kindest letter, in which he "still thought he might be there" but the weather was stormy, though not quite rain.

Messieurs Hoar, Reuben Brown, Deacon Wood, Deacon Ball, Mr John Thoreau, Edmund Hosmer, Mr Stow [blank space] were the bearers. Henry Thoreau saw beforehand to all necessary points & went to Littleton & brought home Bulkeley. Geo M. Brooks, Esq took charge of arranging the funeral from the house.

There was no change but for the better in Mother's face for two days It seemed perfect sleep Yesterday morning it was changed & became less natural. Her body was beautifully dressed & laid in a black walnut *casket,* I have never seen more pleasing arrangements.

You know it was her wish to be buried in her fathers tomb unless I should own a tomb. I have for these last three years been prevented from buying & dressing a "lot," by the uncertainties of our proposed "Cemetery" here. It has been the wish of the citizens to buy Sleepy Hollow for a cemetery & Mr Keyes mainly who has the charge of Public Grounds has discouraged me from selecting a lot repeatedly (in the existing ground) by his confidence that as soon as the Bedford Road should be finally laid out the difficulties in the way of establishing the Cemetery would end. The Road is now laid out & it will presently appear what can be done. Some lot I shall very soon possess. I therefore thought it best to keep these remains here to be therein placed hereafter, and with those of my little Waldo. So I asked of Mrs Ripley again hospitality for our dead, in her tomb, for a time. And so she was buried.—I believe I have told you all you will have to ask. Now it remains that you shall get well as soon as you can, & that you shall come here as soon as you can. I shall take no step in regard to the settlement of Mothers few affairs until you advise me. Her drawers have not been locked: there has been no necessity. But some early attentions will, I suppose, be necessary. What useful & what few ornamental articles she had, Lidian would like to consult with you about bestowing the last especially on such friends as ought to be remembered. Her expenses there is no need at present for you to consider, as, I doubt not, in my account, I hold a considerable balance in her favor. What must I do in reference to the Probate? In regard to Bulkeley, whom I shall keep here till Thanksgiving, I wish to advise with you. But this letter is grown so long, I will add no word. Tell Susan, we have her letter this morning, but deplored her absence yesterday. Persuade her to come with you when you come; & give all love to Wm & the boys twain.

Lidian sends her love, & Elizabeth who leaves us today.

Waldo E.

To Theodore Parker, November 22? 1853

Concord
22 Novr. 1853

My dear Parker,

Our Village Lyceum is ambitious of distinguished lecturers in direct proportion to its poverty & humble claims. So I am instructed to invite you to come & read us a lecture one evening, nay, on a named evening, Wednesday February 8. Meantime, we can only pay $15. for a lecture. Now if you wish to help & comfort mightily the hearts of many & all good-willing persons in this town & in particular of me & my wife who are to be your hosts on the occasion, say grandly yes, & come on the above-named, or some other Wednesday (or Thursday) Evening of the winter. Or we will deviate to a Tuesday or a Friday, I suppose, to give you place.

Ever yours,
R. W Emerson.

for
　　Rev B. Frost
　　A. G. Fay　　} Curators
　　R W E
Rev. T. Parker.

To Nathaniel Langdon Frothingham, December 3, 1853

To Rev. Dr Frothingham.

Concord, 3 December, 1853

My dear Sir,

My mother was born in Boston, 9 November 1768, & had therefore completed 85 years, a week before her death. Her father Captain John Haskins whose distillery on Harrison Avenue was pulled down not many years ago was an industrious thriving man with a family of thirteen living children He was an Episcopalian & up to the time of the Revolution a tory. My mother was bred in the English church, & always retained an affection for the Book of Common Prayer. She married in 1796 and all her subsequent family connexions were in the Congregational Church At the time of her marriage her husband was settled in Harvard, Masstts. In [blank space] they removed to Boston on his installation at First Church. He died in 1812 and left her with six children & without property. She kept her family together & at once adopted the only means open to her by receiving boarders into her house & by the assistance of some excellent friends, she carried four of her five sons through Harvard College The family was never broken up until 1826, when on the death of Dr Ripleys daughter (my fathers half-sister) she accepted the Doctor's earnest invitation to make her home at his house. She remained there until my marriage in 1830, when she came to live with me After my housekeeping was broken up in 1832, and on my return from Europe in 1833, she went with me to Concord, & we became boarders in Doctor Ripley's family, until I bought a house & took her home with me in 1835. This was her permanent home until her death. I hardly know what to add to these few dates. I have been in the habit of esteeming her manners & character the fruit of a past age. She was born a subject of King George, had lived through the whole existence of the Republic, remembered & described with interesting details the appearance of Washington at the Assemblies in Boston after the war, when every lady wore his name on her scarf; & had derived from that period her punctilious courtesy extended to every person, and continued to the last hour of her life. Her children as they grew up had abundant reason to thank her prudence which secured to them an education which in the circumstances was the most judicious provision that could be made for them. I remember being struck with the comment of a lady who said in my family when some debate arose about my Mother's thrift in her time, the lady said, "Ah, but she secured the essentials. She got the children educated."

To Richard Bentley, Concord, March 20, 1854

Concord ⎱ *20 March*
Masstts. ⎰ *1854*

Dear Sir,

I regretted extremely the interruption which has delayed the completion of my Book, and I have feared that you might think yourself ill used in this long delay of a work in which you had acquired some interest. But the hindrances have been unavoidable. (I ought to say, meantime, that I never authorized the advertising the book here or in England.) Nor am I yet ready to fix a day when the book shall be done, though I am now seriously at work, again, on it with a good hope of bringing it to some end.

I write today to bring another matter to your attention.

A friend of mine, Mr Henry D. Thoreau, is about to publish, by Ticknor, Fields, & Co. Boston, a book he calls "Walden, a life in the woods." It will make a volume about the size of Carlyle's "Past and Present." Mr Thoreau is a man of rare ability: he is a good scholar, & a good naturalist, and he is a man of genius, & writes always with force, & sometimes with wonderful depth & beauty. This book records his solitary life in the woods by Walden (a lake in this State,) for a couple of years. and his observations of life & nature. He has mother wit. I have great confidence in the merit & in the success of the work.

This book Ticknor & Co begin to print this week, & will stereotype 2000 copies. I should be glad if you inclined to publish it, in London. Will you do so? Ticknor & Co. mean to have the book ready about 1 May, and they can send you the revises as fast as they are printed, &, at the end, might wait for you the needful time. If you incline to print it, have the goodness to write immediately what terms you will offer Mr Thoreau for copyright.

Respectfully, your obedt servt.
R. W. Emerson

Mr Richard Bentley

I forgot to say that Mr Thoreau is known here by a remarkable book called "A week on the Concord & Merrimac Rivers."

To Charles Sumner, June 9, 1854

Concord⎱ 9 June
Masstts ⎰ 1854

My dear Sumner,

I thank you heartily for your brave temperate & sound Speeches,—all rooted in principles, and, what is less to my purpose, but grateful also to me,— rooted in history. It is an immense advantage to an honest man,—what seems none, at the moment,—that all the argument & all the elevation of tone should be on his side. For I hold it certain that water & intelligence *work down,* & that each man takes counsel of him whom he feels to be a little higher than he; and this one of the next higher; & so on, & up, in an ascending gradation; so that, however slowly, the best opinion is always becoming known as such. I can easily believe you have a rude winter of it, on your "north wall of opposition";—but not comfortless,—when you see the vast importance which the times & circumstance have added to the good fortune of Massachusetts in having you in the Senate in these eventful years. Well done! But no release yet to be so much as thought of! Stand fast to the end! making all of us your honorers & debtors; and none more than Yours faithfully,

R. W. Emerson

Hon. Charles Sumner.

To Charles Sumner, April 4, 1855

Concord 4 April 1855

My dear Sumner,

Can you not, will you not come & read your lecture on Slavery, in this place? It is very warmly desired, & you shall be affectionately heard. We will pay twenty five dollars: and my wife will with pride of heart make her best cake

for you on the occasion. Choose your own earliest time, & come to my
house.

Yours faithfully,
R. W. Emerson.

Hon. Charles Sumner.

TO FREDERICK BECK, JUNE 29, 1855

Concord, 29 June
1855

My dear Sir,

I am in these days looking round in all directions, or, perhaps I should say, to all degrees of spiritual affinity, in search of aid to Mr Alcott. I am by no means sure that you come within the allowed degrees. If not, you shall say so, & pardon me as having been led into error by what I have observed of your large & catholic tendencies. At all events you shall have the facts.

Mr Alcott has lately been proposing a visit to England. He has found some friends in Providence R I., who have promised him money in aid of his plan. When he came to me, I set my face against it, & told him I would not only not help it, but I would try to persuade his friends at P. to withhold their money from this, & give it a new direction, namely, to make it the basis of a permanent, if small, fund for his support at home. And I would add a hundred dollars within a year to theirs. Professor Longfellow subscribes $50. in the form of a poem, for which Putnam will pay that sum; & urges that poets shall subscribe a poem; lecturers, a lecture; journalists, an article; & so on; & believes that twenty subscribers, at the rate of $50 each, can be found. Whipple, Parker, & Starr King, have each promised a lecture. Horatio Woodman, J. G. Fisher, R. E. Apthorp have promised a contribution. Lowell will give, & others, whom I have not yet heard from, or have not yet seen. There is a sum already invested, long since, of $500., to which these present collections being added, will, I hope, enable us to buy for him a small annuity that may at least secure him a philosophic loaf every day. Mr Sam G. Ward is willing to take care of it, & will probably add to it. I ought to have said just now, that the Providence men consent gladly to give this direction to their $150. and I believe that Mr A. has many friends who can & will add small sums. Will it be in your power, and will it be in your system & wishes, to aid in this benefit? I think his case extraordinary & exceptional; &, though it is a very bad precedent to release a man from the duty of taking care of himself, yet Alcott has unique claims as a natural Capuchin, or abbot of all religious mendicant orders. I have just received a noble letter from King, on the subject. Your often obliged,

R. W. Emerson.

Frederic Beck, Esq.

To Charles King Newcomb, July 9, 1855

Concord ⎱ *9 July*
Mass ⎰ *1855*

My dear Charles,

This is the second letter I have written or begun to write to you since I so gladly saw your autograph once more in my box at the Post Office. That the first sheet did not go forth, may show what mixture of terror, even in the old, your love inspires. You are surely a strange perverse son of the light fighting against light, and it requires all the resignation which days & the corrections of largest nature teach, to acquisce in the waste of your genius on I know not what theory of your dear mad master Swedenborg, that genius is pernicious. As if the world were not full already of sad blockheads, & perception had not enemies enough, & they had not managed to draw the agreed mundane line of Duty on this side of the vital culture & offices of the intellect, & leave that outside: so that halfness & dwarfishness result, love itself becomes drivel, & for the voice of man is the squeal of cats & swine. To be sure, it seems verbiage to praise light & defend thought. We must leave the "glad primal creatures," as Dante calls them, to vindicate themselves. But what extreme caprice made you their accuser! I must admire with pain. Of course it comes, at last, of the hatred every good soul has to be fractional, & of some accidental cloy or disgust at cold magpie talent, which has given you this regretted bias. Years ago, when I first knew it I lamented this overcasting of my brightest star, but, as it was frankly avowed the creed, I mean, of suppression of all thought,—there was of course no choice for me; I must submit to the silence of the wise lips I coveted to listen. But, I trusted, a new moon or at most a new year would bring a righter feeling. It seems more sad than droll—a quixotism that hovers on the tragicomic twilights, and yet to me as a patriot of the Muses' country, purely regretable. An arrested mind, a bud that is principled against flowering, a resistance of the eternal flowing & transition of nature. Well, I must still confide. There is no great error but has its great return; only shows larger periodicity, and each of us has his own sure laws. Tis very fine to be sure for you & me to be dictating to each other.

You have not been to see Caroline Tappan, since her postponed voyage. I am told, she is still less sanguine than before to go; but I suppose she will. I remember your mother with great kindness. You shall offer her my respects. I used to think, & still must think, what new varied happy element for me, if your house had stood near mine, across the street, or over the hill, an easy walk! But of course the dear Power knew best. Well, that which lived in the genius of your youth abideth forever.

Yours affectionately,
R W Emerson

Charles K. Newcomb.

To Walter Whitman, July 21, 1855

Concord ⎱ *21 July*
Masstts. ⎰ *1855*

Dear Sir,

I am not blind to the worth of the wonderful gift of "Leaves of Grass." I find it the most extraordinary piece of wit & wisdom that America has yet contributed. I am very happy in reading it, as great power makes us happy. It meets the demand I am always making of what seemed the sterile & stingy Nature, as if too much handiwork or too much lymph in the temperament were making our western wits fat & mean. I give you joy of your free & brave thought. I have great joy in it. I find incomparable things said incomparably well, as they must be. I find the courage of *treatment,* which so delights us, & which large perception only can inspire.

I greet you at the beginning of a great career, which yet must have had a long foreground somewhere for such a start. I rubbed my eyes a little to see if this sunbeam were no illusion; but the solid sense of the book is a sober certainty. It has the best merits, namely, of fortifying & encouraging.

I did not know until I, last night, saw the book advertised in a newspaper, that I could trust the name as real & available for a post-office. I wish to see my benefactor, & have felt much like striking my tasks, & visiting New York to pay you my respects.

R. W. Emerson.

Mr. Walter Whitman.

To Theodore Parker, October 11, 1855

Concord
Masstts 11 Oct. 1855

My dear Parker,

I am extremely sorry that I cannot accept the invitation you send. I should like the courage it would cost & bestow to stand in your pulpit, which looks to me like the military pulpits of Cromwell & of the Covenanters. I am too closely promised, day by day, now for many weeks or months, to my few but exclusive tasks, to leave me the leisure for proper preparation at any one time: for there is neither strength nor flow nor sudden counsel vouchsafed to me,— nothing but petty husbandry & tortoise continuance, as a poor offset to your lion leaps. I am just now printing and writing, but with a slavish & linear poverty; and, in December, am forced to go westward once more, sorely against my will. Give me, on my return, a like opportunity to relieve you on some day, with any few days of leisure before me, & I shall gladly make the venture. I looked first into my portfolio before I would write, & found nothing fit for you.

Yours ever,
R W Emerson

TO THEODORE PARKER, NOVEMBER 11, 1855

Concord, 11 Nov. 1855.

My dear Parker,

I have read into your book,[55] but have not yet read it:—it is in great demand here at home, &, if my hands are not on it, the ladies carry it away: indeed, I understand, it is to be read to the Anti Slavery Society of ladies at their meeting tomorrow or the next day. I shall not wonder at its popularity. People love war too well, now, as aforetime, not to love the best soldier of these days. I see well the book has all the dangerous merits of that mystery; and I, not understanding the mystery, am yet glad & grateful that the best soldier fights on our side. The historical researches of the book are right welcome, & will make it a permanent reference. And as a piece of American history, the courage & the conduct of this onset are above praise, when I think how huge majorities you assail, and with what few & feeble allies. I shall take up the book again with my earliest leisure, and, very likely, may have criticisms to send you, if your commanding position in the front fight & the consecration of danger did not make all criticism unseasonable, & only prayers for your success, & blessings right & fit. Your friend,

R. W. Emerson

Theodore Parker.

---

55. *Parker's* The Trial of Theodore Parker, for the "Misdemeanor" of a Speech in Faneuil Hall against Kidnapping, before the Circuit Court of the United States, at Boston, April 3, 1855. With the Defence, by Theodore Parker *(1855)*.

To Henry Wadsworth Longfellow, November 25, 1855

Concord
25 November
1855

My dear Longfellow,

Sanborn brought me your good gift of Hiawatha, but I have not read it without many interruptions nor finished it till yesterday. I have always one foremost satisfaction in reading your books that I am safe—I am in variously skilful hands but first of all they are safe hands. However, I find this Indian poem very wholesome, sweet & wholesome as maize very proper & pertinent to us to read, & showing a kind of manly sense of duty in the poet to write. The dangers of the Indians are, that they are really savage, have poor small sterile heads,—no thoughts, & you must deal very roundly with them, & find them in brains; and I blamed your tenderness now & then, as I read, in accepting a legend or a song, when they had so little to give.) I should hold you to your creative function on such occasions. But the costume & machinery, on the whole, is sweet & melancholy, & agrees with the American landscape. And you have the distinction of opening your own road. You may well call it an Indian Edda. My boy Edward finds it "like the story of Thor," meaning the "Hammersheimt," which he admires. I found in the last cantos a pure gleam or two of blue sky, and learned thence to tax the rest of the poem as too abstemious. So with thanks & greeting

Yours affectionately,
R. W. Emerson.

To Henry David Thoreau, December 26, 1855

American House
Boston
26 Dec 1855

Dear Henry,

It is so easy at distance, or when going to a distance, to ask a great favor, which one would boggle at near by. I have been ridiculously hindered, & my

book [*English Traits*] is not out, & I must go westward. There is one chapter
yet to go to the printer, perhaps two, if I decide to send the second. I must
ask you to correct the proofs of this or these chapters I hope you can & will,
if you are not going away. The printer will send you the copy with the proof,
and yet tis very likely you will see good cause to correct copy as well as proof.
The chapter is "Stonehenge"; & I may not send it to the printer for a week
yet; for I am very tender about the personalities in it, and of course you need
not think of it till it comes. As we have been so unlucky as to overstay the
market day, that is, New Years, it is not important a week or a fortnight now.
If any thing puts it out of your power to help me at this pinch you must dig
up [Ellery] Channing out of his earths, & hold him steady to this benefi-
cence. Send the proof, if they come, to Phillips, Sampson, & Co. Winter St
  We may well go away, if one of these days we shall really come home.

Yours,
R. W. Emerson

  Mr. Thoreau.

To Lidian Emerson, January 3, 1856

Dixon, Ill.
3 January—56

Dear Lidian,

A cold raw country this, & plenty of night travelling and arriving at 4 in the
morning, to take the last & worst bed in the tavern. Advancing day brings
mercy & favor to me, but not the sleep. But I suppose this rough riding will
not last long. I was yesterday at Lasalle and at 12:10 P.M. took the train for
Dixon, the mercury at 15 below zero. The pinch of all this is the impossibility
of sending out of such circumstance the last sheets which the printers are
waiting for. But I pick up some materials as I go for my chapter of the Anglo
American, if I should wish to finish that. I hope you are not so cold and not
so hard riders at home. I find well disposed kindly people among these
sinewy farmers of the north; but in all that is called cultivation they are only
ten years old, so that there is plenty of non-adaptation & yawning gulfs never
bridged in this ambitious lyceum system they are trying to import. Their real
interest is in prices, & sections & quarter sections of swamp lands. I go

tomorrow to Freeport, and, if you have sent me any letters, shall find them there. Mr H H. Taylor there is my general committee for ten or eleven towns. You must send the children to Aunt Mary, as they go by, with a pear, & go to see her yourself, & invite her to dine. I will send you a hundred dollars the first time I come to a town with a broker's office in it. Dear love to my girls & boy. W.

To Oliver Wendell Holmes, March 1856 [56]

Concord
March 1856

My dear Sir,

I am very sensible of the kindness which dictates your note. I have not seen a true report of your speech,[57] & confess to have drawn my sad thoughts about it from the comments of the journals I am relieved to know that they misreported you and the more they misreported or the wider you are from their notion of you, the better I divide men as aspirants & desperants. A scholar needs not be cynical to feel that the vast multitude are almost on all fours; that the rich always vote after their fears, that cities churches colleges all go for the quadruped interest, and it is against this coalition that the pathetically small minority of disengaged or thinking men stand for the ideal right, for man as he should be, &, (what is essential to any sane maintenance of his own right) for the right of every other as for his own. When masses then as cities or churches go for things as they are, we take no note of it, we expected as much. We leave them to the laws of repression, to the checks nature puts on beasts of prey, as mutual destruction, blind staggers, delirium tremens, or whatever else, but when a scholar, (or disengaged man,) seems to throw himself on the dark a cry of grief is heard from the aspirants side

---

56. *Rusk prints this "rough draft" with cancellations and interlineations. It is printed here in a clear text.*
57. The Boston Daily Advertiser *of 22 December 1855 had reported the celebration by the New England Society of New York on 21 December. Holmes, as the orator of the occasion, created a sensation when, according to the newspaper, he "denounced the abolitionists of New England in good round terms, as 'traitors to the Union.'" [Rusk]*

exactly proportioned in its intensity to his believed spiritual rank. Of course, this must be so, and you might well complain if, on their misapprehension of your meaning, they had not exclaimed. It would have been a poor compliment to your fame, if every humblest aspirant had not showed sorrow & anger at the first rumor that such a leader were lost.

The cant of Union like the cant of extending the area of liberty by annexing Texas & Mexico is too transparent for its most impudent repeater to hope to deceive you. And for the Union with Slavery no manly person will suffer a day to go by without discrediting disintegrating & finally exploding it. The "union" they talk of, is dead & rotten, the real union, that is, the will to keep & renew union, is like the will to keep & renew life, & this alone gives any tension to the dead letter & if when we have broken every several inch of the old wooden hoop will still hold us staunch

You see I am not giving weight to your disgust at the narrowness & ferocity of their virtue for they know that the side is right & it is leading them out of low estate into manhood & culture

With constant regards
of R. W. E.

To Thomas Carlyle, May 6, 1856

Concord
6 May, 1856.

Dear Carlyle,

There is no escape from the forces of time & life, & we do not write letters to the gods or to our friends, but only to attorneys landlords & tenants. But the planes or platforms on which all stand remain the same, & we are ever expecting the descent of the heavens, which is to put us into familiarity with the first named. When I ceased to write to you for a long time, I said to myself,—If any thing really good should happen here,—any stroke of good sense or virtue in our politics, or of great sense in a book,—I will send it on the instant to the formidable man; but I will not repeat to him every month, that there are no news. Thank me for my resolution, & for keeping it through the long night. One book, last summer, came out in New York, a nondescript monster which yet has terrible eyes & buffalo strength, & was indisputably American,—which I thought to send you; but the book throve so badly with the few to whom I showed it, & wanted good morals so much, that I never did. Yet I believe now again, I shall. It is called "Leaves of Grass,"—was written & printed by a journeyman printer in Brooklyn, N. Y. named Walter Whitman; and after you have looked into it, if you think, as you may, that it is only an auctioneer's inventory of a warehouse, you can light your pipe with it.

By tomorrow's steamer goes Mrs Anna Ward to Liverpool & to Switzerland & Germany by the advice of physicians, and I cannot let her go without praying you to drop your pen, & shut up German history for an hour, & extend your walk to her chambers, wherever they may be. *There's* a piece of republicanism for you to see & hear! That person was, ten or fifteen years ago, the loveliest of women, & her speech & manners may still give you some report of the same. She has always lived with good people, and in her position is a centre of what is called good society, wherein her large heart makes a certain glory & refinement. She is one of nature's ladies, & when I hear her tell I know not what stories of her friends, or her children, or her pensioners, I find a pathetic eloquence which I know not where to match. But I suppose you shall never hear it. Every American is a little displaced in London, & no doubt, her company has grown to her. Her husband is a banker connected in business with your Barings, and is a man of elegant genius & tastes, and his house is a resort for fine people. Thorwaldsen distinguished Anna Ward in Rome, formerly, by his attentions. Powers the Sculptor made an admirable bust of her; Clough & Thackeray will tell you of her. Jenny Lind like the rest was captivated by her, & was married at her house. Is not Henry James in London? he knows her well. If Tennyson comes to London, whilst she is there, he should see her for his "Lays of Good Women." Now please to read these things to the wise & kind ears of Jane Carlyle, and ask her if I have done wrong in giving my friend a letter to her? I could not ask more than that each of those ladies might appear to the other what each has appeared to me.

I saw Thackeray, in the winter, & he said he would come to see me here, in April or May; but he is still, I believe, in the South & West. Do not believe me for my reticency less hungry for letters. I grieve at the want & loss, and am about writing again, that I may hear from you.

Ever affectionately yours,
R. W. Emerson

To Samuel Longfellow? October 14, 1856

Concord, Oct. 14, 1856.

My Dear Sir,

Could I give a series of five lectures on five successive days, say, beginning on Monday, 24 November? or is that inadmissible, & must the evenings alternate? At least it would be practicable to put four into a week & so to read 5 or 6 lectures in 8 or 10 days. I had left the space between 21 Novr & 10 Decr open, with another view, &, if you still think it desirable, I can attempt this. Perhaps *Five* Lectures is the safer announcement. I ought to receive not less than $50. for each lecture. You see therefore your dangers. Be dissuaded in time from any rash undertakings. If you ask for my subjects, I have a new lecture not quite ready, which I call "Conduct of Life." Of those which I read in Boston, last winter, two with bad names turned out to be successful enough 1. "Poetry," &, 2. "The Scholar." Perhaps we can mend the names. Then I have a chapter on France, or French traits, with which I like to reward the young people for good behaviour at the foregoing metaphysical lessons and one called the Anglo American, which is a pendant to that. But if I prosper in my present writings for a week or two, I hope to bring you something different & better,—if I come. With kindest regards to Col M'Kay, whom I wish to see, I must go to my brother. Yours constantly,

R. W. Emerson

To Moncure Daniel Conway, January 16, 1857

Syracuse, 16 Jany. 1857

My dear Sir,

I have your note, which causes me no little uneasiness, when I see you working so earnestly & efficiently in my behalf, whilst I am hardly prepared to meet the claims you are creating for me. I fear I was inconsiderate in not reckoning my means more exactly in the hasty conversation in Concord about lectures, & that I counted eggs hatched & not quite hatched, for what seemed to me so improbable a contingency as a *course* in Cincinnati. My chapter on "Memory," the most matured in my studies of "Intellect," is not yet presentable. An essay which I call "Days," which may yet deserve the Hesiodic title of "Works & Days," is not yet presentable. At this moment, after I shall have read my lecture on "Life" to the Mercantile Library, I shall only have two more with me. which I care to read at C., one "on Beauty," & one "on Poetry." A third, "the Scholar," which was an address at Amherst, did very well at Boston, last spring, & might pass at C. and "France."; but I think, that, unless the project can be postponed until April, so that I can go home & prepare for it, it had better be dropped. I am sorry to meet your kind zeal for me so very ill; but though one or two additional lectures were spoken of, I did not look beyond that, and I believed before this, that the scheme was out of your mind, for indeed you have enough to do, & as I learn & read, are doing it well. Shall we not say, then, that Mr E. who does not mean to read in many places another winter, may yet come, *then,* to Cincinnati as he will to Philadelphia & to Boston? Or, if you think the late spring of this year will serve, I will come.

Yours gratefully,
R. W. Emerson

Rev Mr Conway.

To Evert Augustus Duyckinck, March 5, 1857

Concord
5 March 1857

My dear Sir,

I can have no objection to your use of the verses you wish to republish; only I wish they were better.

Respectfully,
R. W. Emerson

Mr Duyckinck.

Concord, 9 March, 1857.

My dear Sir,

You will think me very ungrateful in my slow acknowledgment of your letter, which breathes such enthusiastic good will: but I am slow to write letters, and, at the time when I had your sheet, dwelling in such a cold aphelion of trifles & tasks, that I had no right to entertain any spark of generosity & heroism, but must wait until I were worthier & happier. Besides, do you know that you run huge risks in venturing that great warm heart of yours against my congelations of nearly fifty four years? I dare not be responsible for the hurts you would suffer in my churlish solitude. I must defend you from myself I am happy in the heroic tone in which you speak of your duty to the Country. We, & that third & that fourth person, though he were a son of God, must keep & show our loyalty to each other & to ideas, by our truth to the poor betrayed imbruted America, infested by rogues & hypocrites. In our corners, in days of routine & unfit society, we will speak plain truth & affirm the old laws, heard or not heard, secure that thus we acquit ourselves, & that our voices will reach unto & cheer our distant friends, who will find them on the same key with their own. This is all I dare say, on this cold day of obstruction with me; for I will not have your gifts of youth & genius profaned. And when the Muses are nearer, & the Virtues which are their Mothers, I may be prompted to write you again.

> *Meantime, Yours gratefully,*
> *R. W. Emerson*

Mr Kaufmann.

TO JAMES ELLIOT CABOT, *c.* APRIL? 1857

Concord, Saturday

My dear Cabot,

I give you all joy of the welcome news your note brought me, last evening. Nothing can be more seriously or deeply gratifying that we mortals know, than these new days of a connection which all good omens attend. I must think him happy who seeks & finds in wise daylight the mate whom the most of mankind grope for in the dark, & fatally mis-find. In your instance, I read a well-founded joy, which the following years shall raise & enlarge. Beautiful are the gates to a road on which all that is most real & grave in human lot lies. Woman brings us so much good, that I think the right condition of the union is, when the man is conscious that it is very much which he offers;—too happy almost, when fate allows that the counterpart is as variously, more sweetly gifted. It is so little that I know of your friend,—& yet how much we know of each other at the first glance,—& on this ground of divination I send you most assured greetings. I shall use the privilege you give me to make that brief acquaintance better with every opportunity. I shall be in town on the first days of the week, and hope to see Miss Dwight, to whom I beg you to offer my sincere congratulations.

Yours faithfully,
R. W. Emerson

To Caroline Sturgis Tappan, October 13, 1857

Concord, October 13,
1857.

Dear Caroline,

You will never write me again, I have been so ungrateful, I who value every line & word from you, or about you. Perhaps tis my too much writing in youth that makes it so repulsive now in these old days. What to tell you now that I have begun, you that are in the land of wine & oil, of us in the land of meal? Italy cannot excel the banks of glory which sun & mist paint in these very days on the forest by lake & river. But the Muses are as reticent, as nature is flamboyant, & no fire-eyed child has yet been born: Tis strange that the relations of your old friends here remain unchanged to the world of letters & society. I mean, that those who held of the imagination, & believed that the necessities of the New World would presently evoke the Mystic Power, & we should not pass away without hearing the Choral Hymns of a new Age & adequate to nature, still find colleges & books as cramp & sterile as ever, & our discontent keeps us in the selfsame suspicious relation to beauties & elegant society. We are all the worse that you, & those who are like you, if any such there be, as there are not,—but persons of positive quality, & capacious of beauty,—desert us, & abdicate their power at home. Why not a mind as wise & deep & subtle as your Browning, with his trained talent? Why can we not breed a lyric man as exquisite as Tennyson; or such a Burke-like *longanimity* as E. Browning (whom you mention in interesting positions, but do not describe to me—)? Our wild Whitman, with real inspiration but choked by Titanic abdomen, & Delia Bacon, with genius, but mad, & clinging like a tortoise to English soil, are the sole producers that America has yielded in ten years. Is all this granite & forest & prairie & superfoetation of millions to no richer result? If I were writing to any other than you, I should render my wonted homage to the gods for my two gossips, Alcott & Henry T., whose existence I impute to America for righteousness, though they miss the fame of your praise. Charles Newcomb, too, proves the rich possibilities in the soil, though his result is zero. So does Ellery But who cares? As soon as we walk out of doors, Nature transcends all poets so far, that a little more or less skill in whistling is of no account. Out of doors, we lose the lust of performance, and are content to pass silent, & see others pass silent, into the depths of a Universe so resonant & beaming. But you will dispense with my whims, which you know, for a few grains of history. There is nothing very marked in our neighborhood, which keeps its old routinary trot. I suffered Anna Ward—I am sorry for it to go again, without so much as a note to you, & she could have carried the books you ask for, & the pretty copy in red & gold of my "English Traits," which has slept in my drawer for you.

Our club is an agreeable innovation, holding Sam G. W.; Agassiz, Pierce, Lowell, Longfellow, Dana, Whipple, Dwight, Hoar, Motley, & Holmes, & dining once a month;[58] Agassiz is my chief gain from it,—I have seen him to very good purpose during the last year. Ellery comes to Concord occasionally, & hides for a fortnight in a chamber of his house, which is rented to Sanborn He will dine & walk with me a few times, & suddenly disappears for months again. I think he never writes. He loves dearly to hear

---

58. *Emerson's fellow members of the social Saturday Club are Samuel Gray Ward, Louis Agassiz, Benjamin Peirce, James Russell Lowell, Henry Wadsworth Longfellow, Richard Henry Dana, Jr., Edwin Percy Whipple, John Sullivan Dwight, Ebenezer Rockwood Hoar (Elizabeth's brother), John Lothrop Motley, and Oliver Wendell Holmes.*

any scrap of news of you, if he can get it without asking for it, & will plot to elicit it, affecting supreme indifference.

To William Emerson, May 27, 1859

Concord
Friday Evening
May 27, 1859

Dear William

Mrs Reuben Hoar has just come from Littleton to tell me that Bulkeley died this morning, at 7 o'clock. I am not sure that I sent you any details of his illness in the end of the winter. He had, about the end of February, a sort of fit, which Dr Bartlett, as well as the Littleton physician, thought apoplectic, though of short duration, and after that was feeble & lost flesh. I went to see him, & sent Doctor Bartlett afterwards with Lidian; & Ellen & Edward have visited him lately But he had now got out of doors again, & resumed work a little, & yesterday was abroad, appearing comfortable. This morning he did not come down at his usual hour, Mr H. spoke with him once & again, and Mrs Hoar went to call him, and asked him if he would not come down to breakfast. He appeared surprised to know that it was past the hour, but would not come down; and when she went up again, he was speechless, & soon dead. It seems that only on Wednesday he was dressing himself to come to Concord to visit us, as has always been his practice on "Election Day," but Mr Hoar thought him not quite strong enough & dissuaded him. I am very sorry tonight that I have not seen him again in this week, or the last, as I had hoped to do. It seems, he said, this morning, to Mr Hoar, that he thanked him & Mrs H. for their kindness to him. (Mrs Hoar arrived at our house, when I was in the village, & waited long to see me, and I only met her, on my return, already setting forth on her way back. She had given Lidian her account of his last days. I have agreed with her, that I will send the sexton to Littleton, early on Sunday morning, to bring the body hither, & that the funeral shall take place on Sunday P.M. at 4 o'clock from this house. Mr & Mrs Hoar signify their wish to attend it. They have been very kind & tender to him, especially through all this illness.

It is very sorrowful, but the sorrow is in the life & not in the death. In the last few years he has never seemed to enjoy life, and I am very happy to hear of this singular piece of sanity, this premonition of approaching death which led to the thanking Mr Hoar.

On consideration of the short time, I have not thought it necessary to telegraph you; as indeed there was scarcely time before our office was shut. You would not easily arrive at the funeral, if it were praticable at so sudden a call. I will write you again presently

Affectionately,
Waldo E

I ought to have said that Dr Bartlett, when he visited him, said, there was congestion of the brain, & that it might end in apoplexy, or, more probably, in idiocy. The event agrees with his belief.—

To James Russell Lowell, July 13, 1859

Concord
13 July 1859

My dear Lowell,

I have threatened you from time to time with springing on you the subscription paper of what Mr Ward's clerk calls a little magniloquently the Alcott Fund, I dare not say, prophetically It was set on foot more than two years ago, & took its first shape as I think in a conversation between Longfellow & me at Longfellow's house, when I was describing the genius & the wants of the man, & querying whether some moderate annuity might not be gathered for him, from his friends. Longfellow said, Every body shall give him one day: he would give him a poem, fifty dollars; I should give him a lecture's value; Whipple, Parker, Phillips, should give as much: and your name was relied on by both of us for a poem also. I proceeded at once to obtain such promises as I could and, as his nearest neighbor, led the subscription. Theodore Parker promised his part, Starr King, Whipple, Phillips, Woodman, Thomas Davis of Providence. Mr Apthorp said, he could obtain me certain names, & I was told of friends at New Bedford, & Hingham; so that I began to hope for an annuity of $100. But the Kansas claim drained some of our friends, & others failed us from other reasons, so that my real issue is now, as follows; T. Davis $100, R. W. E. $100. T. S. King 50. H. W. Longfellow 50. W. Phillips 50 H. Woodman 50. Mr & Mrs S. Cheney 50. F. Beck 40. C. F. Hovey $10. H D Thoreau $1.00 One or two promises more I still confide in, particularly of a Mr Locke, who told me he had great expectations before him, & who is much Mr A's friend. The money collected is in Sam. G. Ward's hands, & draws interest;—& Ward also intimated his good-will to add to it. If now you are not dangerously drawn upon by the wants, that always go in swarms, & if you believe, as I, that among the things that go to make up the world, there must be one Capuchin or divine mendicant, & that Alcott is he,—then you shall, at your own time, send your gift for him to S. G. Ward.

Mr Alcott knows that some such fruit was forming, but that he was never to hold it in his hands, & only bite an annual berry—

Yours faithfully,
R. W. Emerson.

James R. Lowell.

To James Russell Lowell, October *c.* 15? 1859

Private)
Concord
October 1859

Dear Lowell,

Just before your note, Bartlett came here, with a double purpose; in both points a friendly one, so far as I was concerned: 1. he wished to justify himself for his suspicions formerly expressed touching P[hillips]. S[ampson] & Co. by telling me of a fraud which they had committed on him, & which he had just detected by examining their books in the hands of the assignees, and which certainly was gross enough: and, 2. he wished to advise me to make Little & Brown my publishers.

I judge by your note that he had not conversed with you. I wish he had, for I think all his informations of some importance to you; but especially for my sake, because I should like your opinion on his showing of the advantage of publishing by L. & B.

It is very easy for me to fall into the hands of Ticknor & Co., whom you recommend; the gravitation is plainly that way. It will require will, which I hate to exert, to go elsewhere. So, if you see him, say I told you he advised me to go to L. & B. & please ask him why? I ought to decide tomorrow, today, this hour perhaps, for the sake of having a printers devil to spur the sides of my lazy intent. I only wish to know if you will say Ticknor, in full view of L. & B.

I send you a poem for the December Atlantic, in despair of having presentable prose,—which both of us would prefer. But do not let the Magazine stop. I will really work for it, rather, & so will we all.

> *Ever yours,*
> *R. W. Emerson.*

Mr Lowell.
I hope to mend the poem in printing.

To Ticknor and Fields, October 24, 1859

> *Concord*
> *Oct. 24, 1859.*

Messrs Ticknor & Fields.
Gentlemen,

You expressed to me, a few days ago, through Mr Ticknor, your wish to become the publishers of my books. The proposition was very agreeable to me, &, at Mr Ticknor's request, I will set down the few principal points which I wish to be considered in the agreement.

The six works in which I hold copyright as author, & of which Phillips, Sampson, & Co were, until recently, the publishers, are;

1. Essays, Vol. I.
2. Essays, Vol. II.
3. Miscellanies.
4. Poems.
5. Representative Men.
6. English Traits

Of these books I own the stereotype plates. I wish to deposit these with a printer, and whenever, from time to time, Ticknor & Fields think it expedient to publish an edition of any or all of them Mr. E. will give a written order for the printing of so many copies. And no copies shall be taken from the plates without such written order from him.

Ticknor & Fields shall pay for printing, paper, & binding, & shall sell the books.

And shall pay Mr E, 20 percent on the retail price of each book, on the day of publication.

Mr E. shall relinquish this copyright on all copies sent gratuitously to authors & Editors.

Mr E. proposes to put into the hands of Messrs Ticknor & Fields a new work, entitled "Conduct of Life," for publication, to which work the same terms shall apply.*

These are all the points that occur to me, of importance; and I shall be glad to have your opinion concerning them.

Respectfully
R. W. *Emerson*

Messrs Ticknor & Fields.

*In regard to a new work I am content if Ticknor & Fields *wish* it, that for the *first* payment of copyright after its issue, it shall be six months after the day of publication. But subsequent payments on it shall follow the rule stated above.

To Stephen G. Benedict, December 13, 1859

Concord, 13 Decr.
1859.

Dear Sir,

You shall hold me engaged to you for 8th February. I see you write me *Revd.*, to which I have no title. Do not advertise me so.

Respectfully,
R. W. *Emerson*

Lafayette Indiana
5 February, 1860

Dear Lidian,

Ellen says you wish for letters: tis a surprising anachronism—be sure,—that you should fancy that an old gentleman plodding through this prairie mud, on such dingy errands, too, should be capable of letters. They are for idle young people, & from such. Praise rather my good manners which would save your wearisome details, & turn them on Ellen, who is willing & ought to learn them. She is a darling of a correspondent too, & has kept me in letters at each step of my march. I have had a much easier western trip thus far, than ever before, partly owing to the fine weather, which has been almost unbroken. My foot, which admires railroad cars, rewards their rest by strength & almost friskiness, on each arrival. I walk much without a cane. I fear shall not even reach home on the 21 or 22d, as I have designed; as it will probably cost me a day or two to repair a failure of mine at Zanesville, and I must write today to Cambridgeport where I am due on 21st to pray for release. I hope all goes as well at home as usual, & with yourself—I have not yet been able to obtain Darwin's book which I had depended on as a road book You must read it,—"Darwin on Species." It has not arrived in these dark lands. I shall send Ellen money from Chicago. Dear love to my darlings!

Waldo E

To Moncure Daniel Conway, June 6, 1860

Concord, 6 June, 1860

My dear Sir,

When I shrink sometimes on the thought of your expectations & my abysmal non-performance, I try to assure myself that I never dared to make any exact promises, but only good intentions, to crystallize into act at a long day. Still whatever prudence or diffidence I may have used, I confess, my dulness & incapacity at work has far exceeded any experience or any fear I had of it. It has cost me more time lately to do nothing, in many attempts to arrange & finish old MSS. for printing, than ever I think before to do what I could best. For the scrap of paper that I was to send you, after Philadelphia,—Dr Furness, when he came here, told me, I was not to go. Then I kept it to put into what will not admit anything peaceably, my "Religion" chapter, which has a very tender stomach, on which nothing will lie They say, the ostrich hatches her egg by standing off & looking at it, and that is my present secret of authorship. Not to do quite nothing for you, I long ago rolled up & addressed to you an ancient MS. Lecture called "Domestic Life," & long ago you may be sure, familiar to Lyceums, but never printed except in newspaper reports. But I feared you would feel bound to print it, though I should have justified you if you had not printed a page.

For the question you now send me, all this is the answer. I have nothing to say of Parker.[59] I know well what a calamity is the loss of his courage & patriotism to the country; but of his mind & genius, few are less accurately informed than I. It is for you & Sanborn & many excellent young men who stood in age & sensibility hearers & judges of all his discourse & action—for you to weigh & report. I have just written to his Society who have asked me to speak with Phillips, on the funeral occasion, that I must come to hear, not to speak; (though I shall not refuse to say a few words in honor.) My relations to him are quite accidental & our differences of method & working such as really required & honored all his catholicism & magnanimity to forgive in me. So I shall not write you an Essay: nor shall I in this mood, whilst I am hunted by printers (who do not nobly forgive as you do,) hope for reformation. But can you not, will not come to Boston & speak to this occasion of eulogies of Parker?

Yours, with very kind regards,
R. W. Emerson

Mr Conway.

---

59. *Theodore Parker had died in Italy, on 10 May.*

To George Bancroft, January 1, 1861

> *Concord*
> *1 January 1861*

My dear Bancroft,

You have wonderful magnanimity. You send me a noble History which I sit & read from time to time, and thank you silently whenever I read, that you have made that difficult road so easy & inspiring to me who could not else enter it & I render you no account of my satisfaction, waiting till I have mastered the whole; &, meantime, I send you my little book of notes & fragments [*The Conduct of Life*], & you send me instant thanks & ever praise. And now you open wide to me again, as ever, that house-door, which I have ever found it a privilege to enter, a place where genius & persistent kindness dwell. Well, in response to this beneficent mind, I send you my hearty thanks. I shall just pass through New York next week staying I hope long enough to see your faces in Twenty First street, if I am fortunate in my moment of arrival. With kindest affectionate remembrances to Mrs Bancroft

> *Yours faithfully*
> *R. W. Emerson*

Mr Bancroft.

To Josiah Phillips Quincy, January 23 and 25, 1861

> *Concord, 23 Jany. 1861*

My dear Sir,

My letter comes very tardily to tell you what good gifts you sent me in your MSS. & in your letter. They found me very busy with sundry tasks, before a journey, from which I have just returned. But I carried my treasures with me, for such they are. I delight in talent, as in the arts it has made—but "that strain I heard was of a higher mood," & gives me a better joy and opens a future. I share very heartily, whilst I read, the austere & religious sentiment which prevades the poem, the scorn of mean living, the aspiration, & the worship of truth. Perhaps *religion* is yet too strong a word,—perhaps the character has not yet arrived so high, has not cleared itself to that, but is resolutely dealing with low enemies & dangers, listening to itself, & cheered haughtily by comparing itself with these. Yet this heroism & stern self communion is a germ of all grandeur, & we shall see the heights & celestial flowerings, in due time.

25th I had written thus far, when a friend arrived here from New York, who puts all *aside* where he comes,—has taken all hours whilst here, gone to Boston with me, & still interferes a little with the earlier visions. I am glad no printer has yet touched these sheets. Time enough for him by & by: But I owe many delicious hours to unpublished records of mind & heart. Their virginity charms, & perhaps I should not read them if printed. If my 'farm' were nearer to yours, I should try to show you one or two such, long since confided to me, & which your poem & letter again & again suggest & refresh in mind. The author of one of them, if he is what he was, I think you should certainly know. But though I wish this poem to lie in manuscript for a time, I heartily approve your design of continuing it & making it a canvas for new colors & lines, as new experiences shall require. I have or shall have many little matters of literary criticism to add, if it were going earlier to the public. But its privacy & soliloquy deeply please & content me now. Not to keep this late note any longer, I must reserve what I have to say to your letter.

With kindest regards,
R. W. Emerson

Josiah P. Quincy.

To Edith Emerson, April 20, 1861

Dear Edith

You have heard that our village was all alive yesterday with the departure of our braves.[60] Judge Hoar made a speech to them at the Depot, Mr Reynolds made a prayer in the ring the cannon which was close by us making musical beats every minute to his prayer. And when the whistle of the train was

---

60. *The forty-seven men of the Concord regiment had marched off to war.*

heard, & George Prescott (the commander) who was an image of manly beauty, ordered his men to march, his wife stopped him & put down his sword to kiss him, & grief & pride ruled the hour. All the families were there. They left Concord 45 men, but on the way recruits implored to join them, &, when they reached Boston, they were 64.—

Papa

To Henry David Thoreau, May 11, 1861

Concord, Massts
11 May, 1861.

My dear Thoreau,

I give you a little list of names of good men whom you may chance to see on your road. If you come into the neighborhood of any of these, I pray you to send this note to them, by way of introduction, praying them, from me, not to let you pass by, without salutation, & any aid & comfort they can administer to an invalid traveller, but one so dear & valued by me & all good Americans.

Yours faithfully,
R. W. Emerson

Henry D. Thoreau.

To James Elliot Cabot, August 4, 1861

Concord
Augt. 4, 1861

My dear Cabot,

I was very glad yesterday to hear from you, & on such high matters. The war,—though from such despicable beginnings, has assumed such huge proportions that it threatens to engulf us all—no pre-occupation can exclude it, & no hermitage hide us—And yet, gulf as it is, the war with its defeats & uncertainties is immensely better than what we lately called the integrity of the Republic, as amputation is better than cancer. I think we are all agreed in this, and find it out by wondering why we are so pleased, though so beaten & so poor. No matter how low down, if not in false position. If the abundance of heaven only sends us a fair share of light & conscience, we shall redeem America for all its sinful years since the century began. At first sight, it looked only as a war of manners, showing that the southerner who owes to climate & slavery his suave, cool, & picturesque manners, is so impatient of ours, that he must fight us off. And we all admired them until a long experience only varying from bad to worse has shown us, I think finally, what a noxious reptile the green & gold thing was. Who was the French Madame who said of Talleyrand, "How can one help loving him he is so vicious?" But these spit such unmistakeable venom, that I think we are *desillusionnés* once for all. There is such frank confession in all they do, that they can have no secrets hereafter for us. Their detestation of Massachusetts is a chemical description of their substance, & if a state more lawful, honest, & cultivated were known to them, they would transfer to it this detestation. This *spiegato carattere*[61] of our adversary makes our part & duty so easy. Their perversity is still forcing us into better position than we had taken. Their crimes force us into virtues to antagonize them and we are driven into principles by their abnegation of them. Ah if we dared think that our people would be simply good enough to take & hold this advantage to the end!—But there is no end to the views the crisis suggests, & day by day. You see I have only been following my own lead, without prying into your subtle hints of ulterior political effects. But one thing I hope,—that 'scholar' & 'hermit' will no longer be exempts, neither by the country's permission nor their own, from the public duty. The functionaries, as you rightly say, have failed. The statesmen are all at fault. The good heart & mind, out of all private corners, should speak & save.

I had a letter lately from Mrs Tappan, who encloses a patriotic plan of Virginia politics, written by her husband, & really important, had it been earlier offered. I think it anticipated by what New Virginia has done. Thanks for the account of the Scandinavian books, which I shall look for at once. Josiah P. Quincy has just now come to see me. If you have opportunity I hope you will meet him. His instincts are the best. In the "Anti-Slavery

---

61. *"The showing of character."*

Standard," he writes lately papers signed with a star *. With new thanks for your letter,

> *Yours faithfully,*
> *R. W. Emerson*

We must all go to the next Club. Is there not a special agreement?

To Moncure Daniel Conway and Ellen Dana Conway, October 6, 1861

> *Concord*
> *6 October, 1861*

My dear Sir & my dear Lady,

I have your note, & give you joy of the happy event you announce to me in the birth of your son. Who is rich or happy but the parent of a son? Life is all surface until we have children; then it is deep & solid. You would think me a child again, if I should tell you how much joy I have owed, & daily owe, to my children, & you have already known the early chapters of this experience, in your own house. My best thanks are due to you both, for the great good will you shew me in thinking of my name for the boy. If there is room for choice still,—I hesitate a good deal at allowing a rusty old name eaten with Heaven knows how much time & fate, to be flung hazardously on this new adventurer in his snow white robes. I have never encountered such a risk out of my own house, &, for the boy's sake, if there be time, must dissuade. But I shall watch the career of this young American with special interest, born as he is under stars & omens so extraordinary, & opening the gates of a new fairer age. With all hopes, & all thanks, & with affectionate sympathies from my wife.

> *Yours ever,*
> *R. W. Emerson.*

My wife declares that name or no name her spoon shall go.

To Blanche Smith Clough, January 14, 1862

Concord, 14 January,
1862.

My dear Mrs Clough,

I had already heard the heavy news first from Mr Norton, when the last steamer brought me your letter, which was a great relief & comfort to me. The details, which usually aggravate, in this case, lighten the load, for your husband seems to have spent his last months as his earlier ones in chosen places, & with happy friends; and I like well to learn that his love of verses returned & clung to him to the last. He interested me more than any other companion, when I first knew him, in 1848, by his rare freedom & manliness, whilst not the less at home in his Oxford element. I remember we met cordially on his high appreciation of Wordsworth, & his own frank entertainment of any good thought; & this intellectuality,—in my limited acquaintance in London, seemed so little English,—that I wrote home to my friends that I had found in London the best American. The rare talent shown in his poems delighted me all the more for the surprise, for, when these came to me in America, I had seen nothing from his pen beyond a little brochure in prose, printed at Oxford. His visit to America was too short a pleasure, and I grieved at his departure as the loss to us of a needed element. *Now* I lament that I have not kept up an active communication with him in so many years. I had never doubted his health, & had assured myself that he was a sure ally in all the future, and a power that was only augmenting by its reserves & delays. I must think so still in spite of his disappearance from his place.

Certainly his poetry should all be collected, and all the old, & I hope, a good deal of new, carefully printed here. I am sure that all our best readers are its friends. It was deeply gratifying to my friend Miss Hoar,—her brief acquaintance with him & yourself, and she receives with the warmest sympathy all the incidents that so rapidly followed her visit. My wife, too, has the kindest remembrances of her few days' guest & cherished poet. And I am not without hope that, in one land or the other, I may some day see you, or, at least, that my children may meet yours. You will do me a welcome kindness if in any manner you can make me useful to you.

Yours, with affectionate respect,
R. W. Emerson.

Mrs Blanche Clough.

Concord
21 April, 1862.

My dear Sir,

I owe you hearty thanks for your valued letter,[62] received three days ago, & which nothing but the cares of sending away my son to California have prevented me from instantly acknowledging. The interesting incidents you relate bear out your inference. It is cheering to see the common sense of mankind justified when the facts so long concealed are shown in daylight to observers whom it is not possible to deceive. The testimony of the soldiers is not likely to be invalidated. Nobody will attempt to gainsay your experience. And though the southern people have never seen their own state, (as the Turks say, "Fate makes that a man shall not believe his own eyes.") Yet I think that looking at the same things in your presence, they may possibly begin to see the same thing.

I am glad to have this weighty testimony on behalf of the negro. My fear is that he needs every advantage, & at the strongest is not strong enough for his salvation from the cupidity of the white races. Poor Irish, rich planter, & planter's poor tenant, all all alike his enemies. His best hope lies in his proved faculty to make himself useful & indispensable in hot climates: & when the odds of ten to one are taken off, that is to say, when New York & Massachusetts are not made by false law to help Carolina & Georgia to keep him on the ground, I doubt not he will be able to get to his feet & insist on wages for his work.

I must esteem it a consoling benefit of the war, that in your Army the northern people go personally to the South, & see for themselves, & our brave soldiers will not only vindicate the Government, but come back Americans & not provincialists, no longer at the mercy of southerners & south sympathizers for the facts, but eye-witnesses & judges of their social

---

62. *From a camp near Edinburgh, Virginia, Colonel Gordon wrote on 8 April 1862, that he had just read Emerson's paper on "American Civilization." He says "What I hear from slaves may not be uninteresting to you—I find no exception to their manifestations of joy at sight of our columns.—The blacks are our faithful friends and as against the rebels of the south—they can be trusted—I could sir fill my sheets with sad stories and criminal outrages narrated by this unoffending people . . ." [Tilton]*

life & its workings, &, I hope, at last re-constructers of an honest world there.

Thanking you once more for this record of your manly feeling and sympathy, which in my eyes gives a new glory to your honored name & camp & campaign, & not omitting to say, what you already know that all we who sit at home here hold you & your brothers affectionately as our benefactors in the past & in the future, I remain, with kindest regards & best hope for your successes, Yours

R. W. Emerson

Colonel Gordon
George H. Gordon
2nd Mass
Commander 3rd Brigade

To Henry Wilson, August 11, 1862 [63]

Concord
11 August, 1862.

Hon. Henry Wilson.
Dear Sir,

Allow me to make you acquainted with my brother, William Emerson, Esq. of New York who wishes to consult you in reference to placing his son in the U.S. Army. He, the son, is at present serving as a private in the Seventh Regiment of New York, having left the junior class in Harvard University to enlist, on the rally of three months ago. Of this young man I can say, that, in my opinion, any military man would pick him out in his college as possessing rare qualifications for a soldier, in his sense & spirit, in the gymnastic training of his body, & in his settled purpose of going to the war. I may add that he possessed great personal popularity among his contemporaries at college. If I could send this young man to you, I should not need to send any word of recommendation. If you could give his father any good counsel as to the best

---

63. *This letter is first published here, from the collection of the editor.*

mode of putting him into the army in the best manner, I confide that it will
be not only a favor to the young man & his friends, but a public benefit also.

With high regard,
R. W. Emerson

To William Henry Seward, January 12, 1863

Concord ⎱ *Jan. 10*
Masstts. ⎰ *1863*

Dear Sir,

Mr Walt Whitman, of New York, writes me, that he wishes to obtain
employment in the public service in Washington, & has made, or is about
making some application to yourself.

Permit me to say that he is known to me as a man of strong original
genius, combining, with marked eccentricities, great powers & valuable traits
of character: a self-relying, large-hearted man, much beloved by his friends;
entirely patriotic & benevolent in his theory, tastes, & practice. If his writings
are in certain points open to criticism, they yet show extraordinary power, &
are more deeply American, democratic, & in the interest of political liberty,
than those of any other poet. He is indeed a child of the people, & their
champion.

A man of his talents & dispositions will quickly make himself useful. and,
if the Government has work that he can do, I think it may easily find, that it
has called to its side more valuable aid than it bargained for.

With great respect,
Your obedient servant,
R. W. Emerson

Hon. William H. Seward.
    Secretary of State.

To Matilda Ashurst Biggs, April 8, 1863

Concord—
April 8, 1863

My dear Mrs Biggs,

I send you hearty thanks,—though so late,—for your prized letter, which arrived when I was absent on a long journey in our Western States. I read it with joy on my return. I wished to write instantly, as I ought. But my absence had provided me with a crowd of duties on my coming home, and I waited days & weeks and—But I did not love less the probity & honor which prompted this protest against what appears the governing opinion in England,—nor could I expect less from you. It looks so easy & inevitable to be just & noble when we see good people, that we cannot account for any others. Your beautiful house at Leicester, & the beautiful & excellent people in it, shine in my memory out of such a rearground of years! I wish to see the mother again, & the beautiful children once more. All that I heard of you—in the short interview I had with your father,—or from others—has been happy. I remember that Mr Biggs in Leicester questioned me on the point—why good & cultivated men in America avoided politics (for so he had heard) & let them fall into bad hands? He will find in our calamities today the justification of his warning—Our sky is very dark but the feeling is very general in the Union that bad as the war is it is far safer & better than the foregoing peace. Our best ground of hope now is in the healthy sentiment which appears in reasonable people all over the country, accepting sacrifices, but meaning riddance from slavery, & from Southern domination. I fear this sentiment is not yet represented by our government or its agents in Europe, but it is sporadic in the country. Indeed the governments of both England & America are far in the rear of their best constituencies. in England, as shown in the resolution with which the government shuts its eyes to the building of ships of war in your ports to attack the Republic,—now in this spasm to throw off slavery. This unlooked for attitude of England is our gravest foreign disadvantage—But I have gone quite too far into these painful politics whose gloom is only to be relieved by the largest considerations. I rejoice in so many assurances of sound heart & clear perception as come to us from excellent persons in England,—among which I rank your letter chiefly;—and the significant sympathy of the Manchester workmen, which I wish had been better met. I beg you to present my kindest remembrances to Mr Biggs, & to the young people of your house though they be 14 or 15 years older than they arc in my memory. I dare hope that when better days soon come I shall yet see inmate or friend of your house here in mine. May it be so!

Your affectionate servant,
R. W. Emerson.

To Benjamin and Susan Morgan Rodman, June 17, 1863

Concord
17 June, 1863

My dear friends,

I have waited a week since I heard the heavy news from Port Hudson,—fearing to disturb you,—but do not like to wait longer. I believe I have read every syllable which the journals contain of William's heroic behavior & death at the head of his regiment, & with entire sympathy for, &, I fear, too true knowledge of the desolation the tidings will have brought to your house, however consoled by the cordial testimony which the Army sends home of the love & honor which attached to him in life & in death. I had kept up by frequent inquiries some knowledge of his whereabouts, & read the New Orleans correspondence with hope of quite happier news.——But this sacrifice which he has finished, I am sure, could not be a surprise to his thoughts, nor to yours. The soldier & the soldier's father & mother must have rehearsed this dread contingency to themselves quite too often, not to know its face when it arrives.—And yet there can be no sufficient preparation.

His life, so fair & amiable from the childhood which I remember,—his manly form & qualities, promised a solid character & fortune. I dread to think how the change will darken your house,—hitherto the home of every friendly influence. Neither perhaps can any considerations of duty to country & mankind for a long time reconcile to this devastation in the family. And yet who dare say, amid all the greatness the war has called out, in the privatest & obscurest, as well as in eminent persons, that these calamities do not suddenly teach selfrenouncement, & raise us to the force they require. I am sure your son's own devotion will arm you to surrender him.

I think daily that there are crises which demand nations, as well as those which claim the sacrifice of single lives. Ours perhaps is one,—and that one whole generation might well consent to perish, if, by their fall, political liberty & clean & just life could be made sure to the generations that follow. As you suffer, all of us may suffer, before we shall have an honest peace.—I have seen Mrs Anna Lowell, not long since, (whom I believe Mrs Rodman knows,) mother of Capt. James J. Lowell who fell on the peninsula,—and found in her not so much grief, as devotion of herself & all her family to the public service. My kindest remembrances & best thought to both your daughters. Susan at home will miss her brother most, & love him best.—

One of these days, I shall seek an opportunity of learning all you know & think in these hours.

Very affectionately yours,
R. W. Emerson

To Mr & Mrs Rodman.

To George Bancroft, September 28, 1863

Concord
28 Sept. 1863

Dear Bancroft,

I am glad you plant pears. Under fair conditions, they give an ample return to labor & patience: and the strictest causationist will yet find the most agreeable surprises in his success. The multitude of experiments has weeded out of the lists all the doubtful claimants: And I give you, with much confidence, a list of fifteen which fill the season well, if not best, in Massachusetts. I have placed them pretty nearly in the order of their ripening. With kindest regards to Mrs Bancroft, & all in your household, from all in this,

Yours affectionately,
R. W. Emerson

George Bancroft.

To James Elliot Cabot, December 29, 1863

Concord
29 Decr. 1863

Dear Cabot,

I have borrowed of Miss Thoreau a volume of her brother's MSS.[64]—taken almost at random from those I have read,—to send you: it will be as good a specimen probably as any. You will find the handwriting hard to read at first, with abbreviations,—*appy* for apparently, *mts* for mountains, &c, but I got through several volumes with ever mounting estimation, though I have postponed further readings for the present. I need not say to you, that Miss Thoreau values these books religiously, and I have assured her they would be perfectly safe in your hands. I am delighted to have you see one, and perhaps you will suggest what can be done with them.

Ever yours,
R. W. Emerson

J. E. Cabot.

To Alexander Bliss, March 14, 1864

Concord
14 March 1864

My dear Sir,

I have been unable until today to find any presentable Scrap of Margaret Fuller's writing.[65] I have spent a great deal of time in the search, & at last, only this morning, discovered the pasteboard box in which her letters were

---

64. *Thoreau had died on 6 May 1862.*
65. *Bliss was collecting manuscripts for reproduction in* Autograph Leaves of Our Country's Authors *(1864), which he edited with John Pendleton Kennedy for sale at the Baltimore Fair for wounded soldiers. Emerson's response suggests the ease with which manuscripts were dispersed to good causes or to people who merely wished to have a sample.*

contained. But on looking over the contents, I have not found a single paper suitable for your purpose. Her letters are all private & confiding, and I have found no detached poems. I am therefore only able to send you two or three insignificant notes, which may serve the purpose of showing her handwriting, if you think proper. The one marked (1) I send, simply because it has a signature, which you can cut out; if you wish, & annex to either (2), or (3), if you like to use one of them.

I have not fared much better with Thoreau's mss.; but I send you a loose sheet of his containing characteristic lines; & have annexed to the paper an autograph signature cut from a letter.

I do not now remember which two pieces I sent you of my own verse. One of them I am pretty sure might be safely called "Worship." "This is he who felled by foes" The other————? I have written a great number of these sad verses within a few months.

It grieves me to serve you so ill in a cause so good, & for your interest in which I, with the country, am gratefully yours

R W Emerson

Col. A. Bliss.

You shall lithograph or otherwise use either of Margaret Fuller's letters, if you wish.

To George Bancroft, April 6, 1864

Concord
April 6 1864

My dear Bancroft,

Our "Saturday Club" in Boston send you by me today their invitation to a Shakspeare dinner. Be greatly good & come! They are good men, known to you, & they eagerly desire your presence. The Club counts about twenty. Agassiz, Longfellow, Sumner, Hawthorne, Pierce, Dana, Judge Hoar, Motley, (far away),—Lowell & the rest. Whittier we mean to bring, & some best scholars & men at home. But it will be a patriotism to your native state, to your once adopted city, and a cordial pleasure to some good men here, if you will leave your beautiful house, & come spend this day in Massachusetts.

The whole party may make 35 or 40. Let the admired & beloved lady in your house, who is with best reason revered by all in this—back my suit, & speed you on. I dare not suggest that she also should come with you now, for the snow lies before my eyes, & the north wind blows unfitly. But you shall make good report to her of Boston & of Concord & dispose her heart to the north again. Send word that you will come.

> *Your affectionate servant*
> *R. W. Emerson*

George Bancroft, Esq.

To Ticknor and Fields, May 13, 1864

> *Concord*
> *May 13, 1864—*

Messrs Ticknor & Fields.
Gentlemen,

I decide to accept your proposition as far as the 1st & 2d series of my "Essays" are concerned, & you shall if you please proceed to print an edition of 3000 copies in "blue & gold"[66] on the terms proposed in your note of May 7th. I shall rely on you to carry out in a special contract the further provisions for the more exact protection of my copyright, which were suggested in my recent conversation with Mr Fields.

I have been looking over the books with a view to correction, & will send you presently a short list of *errata*.

> *Respectfully*
> *R. W. Emerson*

Messrs Ticknor & Fields.

---

66. Essays First and Second Series *was published on 6 April 1865 in the "Blue and Gold Edition," so-called for the blue cloth with gold stamping in which volumes were bound.*

To Sophia Peabody Hawthorne, July 11, 1864

Concord
July 11

Dear Mrs Hawthorne,

Guests & visiters prevented me from writing you, last evening, to thank you for your note, & to say how much pleasure it gives me that you find succor & refreshment in sources so pure & lofty.[67] The very selection of his images proves Behmen poet as well as saint, yet a saint first, & poet through sanctity. It is the true though severe test to put the Teacher to,—to try if his solitary lessons meet our case. And for these thoughts & experiences of of which you speak, their very confines & approaches lift us out of the world.

I have twice lately proposed to see you, & once was on my way, and unexpectedly prevented. I have had my own pain in the loss of your husband. He was always a mine of hope to me, and I promised myself a rich future in achieving at some day, when we should both be less engaged to tyrannical studies & habitudes, an unreserved intercourse with him. I thought I could well wait his time & mine for what was so well worth waiting.

And as he always appeared to me superior to his own performances, I counted this yet untold force an insurance of a long life. Though sternly disappointed in the manner & working, I do not hold the guarantee less real.—But I must use an early hour to come & see you to say more.

R. W. Emerson

Mrs Sophia Hawthorne.

---

67. Nathaniel Hawthorne had died on 19 May 1864.

Concord
7 December 1864

Dear Sumner,

I learn that James Russell Lowell desires to go abroad, & would like to be employed in the public service. I am concerned to hear it; for I think him happily placed now. He is a fortune to the College & might revive things more dead than the "N[orth] A[merican] Review" It seems he is out of health, is too hard worked, & holds an estate by his father's will, which is only expensive. I am sorry for the necessity, whatever its cause. But if he wishes to go in the public service, the Government ought to appreciate his great & rare merits. No literary man in the country suggests the presence of so much power as he; with a talent, too, that reaches all classes. Add to this, that he is a person of excellent address, with social & convivial gifts; a man of great spirit, with plenty of resistance in him, if need be. His thorough knowledge of the European languages adds to his competency for such duty. His wide popularity as a writer would assure the sanction of the best part of the nation to an important appointment, & would conciliate those to whom he should be sent. I am sorry I did not know this wish of his in time to have had a little conference with you on the point; for there is very much to be said on his behalf. In whatever changes may occur in our representation abroad, if Massachusetts shall have any claims, I trust so old & able a champion for the best policy as Lowell, will be remembered. He is one of those few who are entitled to have all they want.

Ever yours faithfully,
R. W. Emerson

To Louis Agassiz, December 13, 1864

Concord
Dec. 13, 1864

Dear Agassiz,

I pray you have no fear that I did or can say any word unfriendly to you or to the Museum,—for both of which blessings—the cause & the effect—I daily thank Heaven, May you both increase & multiply for ages! I cannot defend my lectures,—they are prone to be clumsy & hurried botches,—still less answer for any report,—which I never dare read.—but I can tell you the amount of my chiding. I vented some of the old grudge I owe the College now for 45 years, for the cruel waste of two years of College time on Mathematics without any attempt to adapt by skilful tutors or by private instruction these tasks to the capacity of slow learners. I still remember the useless pains I took, & my serious recourse to my tutor for aid, which he did not know how to give me. And now I see, today, the same indiscriminate imposing of mathematics on all students, during two years,—ear or no ear, you shall all learn music,—to the waste of time & health of a large part of every class. It is both natural & laudable in each professor to magnify his department, & to seek to make it the first in the world, if he can. But, of course, this tendency must be corrected by securing in the Constitution of the College a power in the Head (whether singular or plural) of co-ordinating all the parts. Else, important departments will be overlaid, as, in Oxford & in Harvard, Natural History was until now. Now it looks as if Natural History would obtain in time to come the like predominance as Maths have here or Greek at Oxford It will not grieve me if it should, for we are all curious of Nature but not of Algebra. But the necessity of check on the instructors in the Head of the College, I am sure you will agree with me is indispensable.—You will see that my allusion to Natural History is only incidental to my statement of my grievance—But I have made my letter ridiculously long, and pray you to remember that you have brought it on your own head. I do not know that I ever attempted before, an explanation of any speech. Always with entire regard, yours,

R. W. Emerson

Louis Agassiz.

To James Bradley Thayer, December 16, 1864

Concord
16 Dec Friday

My dear Mr Thayer

If you have the ear of the "Daily Advertiser," & can without inconvenience, I wish you would ask the Editor to omit any report of my Lectures. The fault of the reports is doubtless owing to the lecture itself which lacks any method, or any that is easily apprehensible, but it distresses me a little to read them & more that others should. Of course to any general notice I have no objection but much to the rendering of sentences. And I should take it as a great kindness if it were omitted. But it is not worth giving you any trouble. Mr Slack I believe made some such request & told me it was all settled but it is not all ended.

Yours always,
R W Emerson

J. B. Thayer, Esq.

To Charles Sumner, December 19, 1864

Concord
19 Decr 1864

Dear Sumner,

I tried the other night to engage Longfellow, Lowell, Holmes, & Curtis, to talk over the affair of the "National Academy," with me, at the Union Club. Mr Dana declined to entertain the subject altogether, alleging age as his excuse. To my regret, Longfellow did not come at last; Curtis, too, was unable to come; so that Lowell, Holmes, & I were the whole committee. We agreed that the existence of such a Society was inevitable; that the existence of an Academy of Science would inevitably draw after it the attempt to establish this; and, therefore, it would be prudent to accept the offered form under such good auspices as it now brings from your hands: prudent,— because if the present nominees are not the best, yet, by accepting it, we are likely to defend it from falling into worse. We agreed on the general objects of such a society; as, for the conservation of the English language; a constituted jury to which questions of taste & fitness in literature, might be carried: a jury to sit upon abnormal anomalous pretentions to genius, such as puzzle the public mind now & then. Custodians of sense & elegance—these colleagues are to be,—in literature. They would be the college of experts, to which the Government might sometimes wish to refer questions touching Education, or historic forms or facts. They would perhaps suggest to the Government the establishment of prizes for literary competition. Certain aesthetic & moral advantages did not fail to appear, as the matter was more considered. What recommended to us a cordial sympathy with the proposition, was, the belief shared by us & we believe by the community, that, we are at an important point of national history, & one from which very great expansion of thought & moral & practical activity in all kinds is likely to follow; &, that organizations hitherto sterile may easily hereafter come to be of great scope & utility.

The objections which were raised in our conversation were

1. the obvious one of want of a national centre for an Academy, such as Paris & London furnish in France & in England. We agreed, however, that the only proper centre this Academy could have is Washington, and we found many considerations to fortify this opinion.

2. The want of provision in the Bill for any compensation to the members for their expense in attendance on the meetings of the Academy,—which omission, or rather forbiddal, in the Bill, threatens to make full sessions of the Academy impossible, in a country of such geographic distances as ours. An allowance for mileage will probably be found indispensable to its successful operation.

3. We see difficulties in the Union of two classes of such unlike bias & objects as Scholars and Artists, in one Academy; for example, in the first election of officers & of members that may occur, I want Gibbon, & Dwight wants Paganini. But probably we might soon fall on a fair proportion of candidates to each, according to the numerical strength of each class. But, really, for all practical purpose, these classes must sit & act as separate sections.

We all agreed that the simple meeting of an Academy under the inspiration of national aims, would tend to quicken the power & ennoble the aims of all the members.

I think this is a fair sketch of the points that appeared in our half hour's conversation. I am sorry to have been so late in getting this little result, but have been unusually occupied since I saw you, & could not well bring together a company which I hoped would be larger. I infer, however, that the heat will rapidly accumulate at future conferences.

Tell me if you wish something more precise.

Ever yours,
R. W. Emerson

Hon. Charles Sumner.

To Louisa Kenson Perkins, January 13, 1865

Delavan House
Albany, 13 Jan.y 1865

Dear Mrs Perkins,

I enclose $10, the sum you so kindly lent me, with my best thanks; but am still vexed with clouding your pure hospitality by your sympathy for such an absurd mishap.

In the bare chance that the wallet should be picked up by an honest finder, I add, what I believe I told you, that there was no name,—it was a common purplish one, containing the uncounted bills which Mr Wicker had just given me, & perhaps $25 or 28 more, two or three bills being of the Concord Mass. bank; some postage stamps, & a blank cheque of the Atlantic Bank, Boston. I do not think of any other means of identification, & I am quite sure none will be wanted. But I am sorry I did not say to you, that I had rather lose it than have it advertised in any manner.

I recollect your house & its inhabitants with great pleasure; & I hope I may see you again. If you are in my neighborhood, it will give me great pleasure to show you my household. One of these days Willie will come to see me on his way to Cambridge, I hope, if Cambridge mends its faults, & deserves the best boys. But the boys of this day, as I told you, seem to me to have a proud future before them.

Yours, with kindest regard,
R. W. Emerson

Mrs J. G. Perkins.

TO JAMES THOMAS FIELDS, FEBRUARY 26, 1865

Concord
26 February

My dear Sir,

I have read the proofs of the new chapter "closely," as you requested, and I am confirmed in my opinion that it should appear as it is. The matter is excellent, & if the manner of statement is too frank for our customs, it will only recommend it the more serious readers. The shortness of the piece will defend it from prominency to those to whom it may be distasteful, veiled as it is by such a roll of other letters on all subjects. I hoped to have seen you yesterday. I am running away again tomorrow, but shall be at home on Wednesday, Ever yours,

R W Emerson

Mr Fields.

TO JOHN MURRAY FORBES, MARCH 13, 1865

Concord
March 13, 1865.

My dear friend,

I cannot allow these young lovers[68] to have all the letters to write or read. If they have the largest stake in their affair, we seniors have a real part, and if an ever diminishing part, we do not value it less. The surprise of Williams visit, when I learned the result, was deeply gratifying to me. In a manly character like his, a tenderness so true & lasting tempers the soldier & endears the man. His manners, so far as I have seen him, are faultless,—manners & speech so modest & sensible, & with such correct opinions,—whilst some turn now & then suggests the soldier quite ready for action. Indeed I found

---

68. *William Hathaway Forbes had become engaged to Emerson's daughter Edith on 4 March 1865; they would marry on 3 October.*

myself measuring him, & very curious to see his behavior with his men, & to watch such a perfect engine at work. You can judge I am rejoiced to give my little country girl into the hands of this brave protector, & shall rest at peace on her account henceforward. I hope she may know how to deserve her felicity. But I confide much in her. She does not please in advance as much as she merits, but can sometimes surprise old friends who tho't they knew her well, with deeper & better traits. She is humble, which is the basis of nobility. But I must not add another word, except to send affectionate salutations to Mrs Forbes, to Alice, to William & Edith & to the juniors also Malcolm & Sarah if they remember me

Yours faithfully,
R. W. Emerson

J. M. Forbes.

To James Russell Lowell, September 17, 1865

Concord
17 September, 1865.

Dear Lowell,

I send you warm thanks, if late, for the admirable Ode. I shall always be sorry that I did not hear it. The eighth Strophe, with its passion & its vision, was made to be spoken. The technical skill shown throughout is masterly, & yet subordinated by the high thought & sentiment of the piece, which make me glad & proud of it as a national poem. When you shall collect your recent poems in a book, I hope you will drop from this the one or two needless reminders of Tennyson, & I shall affirm with joy, against any possible previous speeches of my own to you, that your eminent success with the comic muse has in no wise hindered you from the command of all the resources of the noble & serious goddess.

Ever yours with great regard,
R. W. Emerson

James Russell Lowell.

TO THOMAS CARLYLE, MAY 16, 1866

Concord
16 May 1866

My dear Carlyle,

I have just been shown a private letter from Moncure Conway to one of his friends here, giving some tidings of your sad return to an empty home.[69] We had the first news last week. And so it is. The stroke long-threatened has fallen at last, in the mildest form to its victim, & relieved to you by long & repeated reprieves. I must think her fortunate also in this gentle departure, as she had been in her serene & honored career. We would not for ourselves count covetously the descending steps, after we have passed the top of the mount, or grudge to spare some of the days of decay. And you will have the peace of knowing her safe, & no longer a victim. I have found myself recalling an old verse which one utters to the parting soul,—

"For thou hast passed all change of human life,
    And not again to thee shall beauty die."

It is thirty three years in July, I believe, since I first saw her, & her conversation & faultless manners gave assurance of a good & happy future. As I have not witnessed any decline, I can hardly believe in any, & still recall vividly the the youthful wife & her blithe account of her letters & homages from Goethe, & the details she gave of her intended visit to Weimar, & its disappointment. Her goodness to me & to my friends was ever perfect, & all Americans have agreed in her praise. Elizabeth Hoar remembers her with entire sympathy & regard.

I could heartily wish to see you for an hour in these lonely days. Your friends, I know, will approach you as tenderly as friends can; and I can believe that labor,—all whose precious secrets you know,—will prove a consoler,—though it cannot quite avail,—for she was the rest that rewarded labor. It is good that you are strong, & built for endurance. Nor will you shun to consult the aweful oracles which in these hours of tenderness are sometimes vouchsafed. If to any, to you.

I rejoice that she stayed to enjoy the knowledge of your good day at

---

69. *Jane Welsh Carlyle had died on 19 April 1866.*

Edinburgh, which is a leaf we would not spare from your book of life. It was a right manly speech to be so made, & is a voucher of unbroken strength— and the surroundings, as I learn, were all the happiest,—with no hint of change. I pray you bear in mind your own counsels. Long years you must still achieve, and, I hope, neither grief nor weariness will let you "join the dim choir of the bards that have been," until you have written the book I wish & wait for,—the sincerest confessions of your best hours. My wife prays to be remembered to you with sympathy & affection.

Ever yours faithfully,
R. W. Emerson

Thomas Carlyle, Esq.

To Wendell Phillips, September 23, 1866

Concord
23 September 1866

My dear Sir,

I hear with great interest that your friends believe that your District will elect you to Congress, & that you will perhaps yield your objections & go there. I heartily hope both statements are true, or that you will speedily make them true. With your extraordinary adaptation by genius, by training, & by the experience of success, I do not know how you can hesitate, (now that the Constitution has come to your terms,) when the Country formally asks you to do that for it which you have ever been ready to volunteer. When the people say, 'We have learned at last that your words are true, & your counsels sound—Come & guide us'—not to go would imply doubt on your part of their practicability. You enter the canvass with one advantage, to lose the election would damage a political man, but cannot hurt you. Then if it were not for the extreme need at this hour of character & counsel at Washington, I should look beyond, & say,—if this design is carried into full effect, it fortifies every good step taken, & ripens good hopes, not here only, but in England, in Italy, in Protestant & liberal Germany.

But though these are animating lights in the wonderful picture of the time, the American questions will not let you sleep, or refuse to answer them, or find time yet for any others. So I rest & rejoice in the belief, that when some what so essentially belonging to you comes to you, you will receive it.

> *With affectionate regard*
> *R. W. Emerson*

Wendell Phillips, Esq

To Seneca M. Dorr, February 25, 1867

> *Tremont House*
> *Chicago, 25 Feby. 1867*

My dear Sir,

Your letter, dated I think weeks ago, was forwarded to me by my son from Concord, but shared more than the delays by the snow-storms on account of my own erratic tour; &, though I had it some days ago, I have not been until now in condition to bring up the arrears of my correspondence. Neither is it a letter quite easy to answer. The booksellers appear to have made up their minds to refuse to print all new poetry except at the sole risk of the author. I have not been able to induce my friend Mr Fields to insert in the "Atlantic" some poems intrusted to me by several writers, each of which poems I read with pleasure, & thought better than poems which are printed there. And last summer, I sent him MS volume from a new poet in New York which I thought to have extraordinary claims,—but which he did not hesitate to decline. I have not fared much better with my own private venture. At his own instance long ago, I began in the autumn to collect my own scattered verses not hitherto published in a book, & added of quite unpublished verses about half the volume & when it was all in type about the 1 December. he said he was sorry but it would be madness to print it for New Year's for all his western correspondents had written to him, "Send us no new book, least of all poetry." So it was put aside, with the chance of better times in April. I have quite ceased therefore to recommend to him any new adventure in this kind. And he is the only publisher with whom I have any particular acquaintance,—I may almost say, any acquaintance at all. But he, like other booksellers, may easily mistake. In fact they were all agreeably surprised by the large & facile sale that all the new books, including poetry, found last

Christmas: It was quite as large as in former years. In these circumstances, I know not what to advise. In regard to the terms to be made, I have a very limited experience. Phillips & Sampson published for me, for many years. In each instance, I paid for the printing, & owned the stereotype plates. They took all the books, &, on the issuing of each edition of any book, that is, in advance, paid me 20 per cent on the retail price of all they printed. Of course, they issued, after the first edition, small editions, say 250 copies, or only so many copies as they judged would easily sell.

Ticknor & Fields, after the dissolution of Phillips & Co, took my books on the same contract. Where the author does not choose to own his plates, they pay a less rate; in the case of Mr Thoreau's books, they pay I think 12 per cent, more often 10.

I beg you to say to Mrs Dorr, with my affectionate regards, that I think she will yet sympathize with me in a kind of surly pleasure that I find in these resistances which it is good practice to overcome & establish our right to find our predestined readers in spite of the bookseller.

With great regard
R W Emerson

S. M. Dorr, Esq

P. S. I add a few lines which I might say to a publisher.

I have read with much interest a number of Mrs Dorr's Poems. They are written with an elegance which shows much practice & easy command of lyric metres & expression; but much more than that, with great tenderness & humanity. It is long since I have seen them, but a poem, which, I think, was entitled "Outgrown," was a favorable example of her truth to life & living characters. And I think all the pieces I read had the warmth & vivacity which belong to poems growing out of the writer's personal observation & experience,—a merit which good readers are sure to appreciate.

R. W. Emerson

Concord 1867

TO ABBY ADAMS, SEPTEMBER 22, 1867

Concord—
September 22, 1867.

Mrs Abel Adams,
My dear friend,

I received, two days ago, a note from Mr Ingersoll Bowditch, announcing that he was or would presently be ready to pay me the bequest which Mr Adams had given me in his Will,[70] and also those which he has given to each of my children. If I had been sure that you were at home, I should have instantly come to your house, to say to you, for myself & for them, how much I rejoice in these proofs of his persistent kindness & care for me & mine. He intimated, at one of the last times when I saw him, such a purpose. I told him that his great goodness in charging himself with Edward's education at Cambridge, should have relieved him of any further care of my interests; for that was a solid & enduring benefit, that had made him very dear to us all; and, besides, I had given him, first & last, a good deal of trouble, in his counsels & anxieties about my different pieces of property which he had looked after with the same faithfulness & final success he brought to his own. But he has chosen to carry his loving purpose into full effect, as his habit was. We can not love him better than we did, but it is certain that in this house, when the ear heareth of him then it shall bless him. My debts to him, however, are much older than these I have named; for, from the first day when I saw him in 1828, until you left Boston for Brookline, your house was always one of my homes, & long my only home. His hospitality would make any house beautiful, but he had also a talent for making abundance of comfort wherever he was, & seeing that his guests shared it. He seemed so built for long life & useful power, that it is painful to me that he should not fill his full term;—more sad, that disease should have clouded his last years. But perhaps our own eyes,—yours and mine,— shall soon see through these shadows.

Edith has been spending a fortnight with us, & has just gone home with her husband & child. Ellen & Edward are at Naushon, for a few days more.

---

70. *Abel Adams, Emerson's lifelong friend and financial advisor, had died on 9 July 1867.*

I do not yet know whether you are travelling, or at home. As soon as I have
passed the 1 October, which is a task-day for me, I mean to come & see for
myself how it is with you & your household. My wife, who admired your
husband, is fully sensible of this new mark of his hand to her children & to
me. She sends you her blessing & her sympathy. Kindest remembrance to
Abby, & to Mrs Larkin. Affectionately yours,

> *R. W. Emerson*

To Samuel Longfellow, January 28, 1868?

> *Concord,*
> *28 January,*

Dear Mr Longfellow,

Mr Potter writes me, that if I, who am to read a discourse before I know not
well what Society, in Cambridge, on Thursday evening,—should want any
direction or aid there, I may apply to you. I hope he is authorized to say so
much, so I shall be to ask it. There are two things—each of some importance
to me, first, that my manuscript should be well lighted for my old eyes; for I
sometimes find immoveable gas burners two or three feet from the desk: &
secondly, I desire not to be reported. I am to read a lecture "on "Immortality,"
long since written, but not yet finished, & which I hope in some good day
to mend, &, in some sort, complete. And it did not occur to me, at first,
that, at Cambridge, it would run that risk of what is falsely called a verbatim
report. But I have lately been much annoyed by those scribes. There are parts
of my lecture which I should wish to omit, if they come,—and indeed all of
it. If you know that this enemy is there, & if you know how to dissuade or
smother him, you will remove my only regret at having accepted the invitation, & greatly oblige

> *Yours, with great regard,*
> *R. W. Emerson*

Rev. S. Longfellow.

To Emma Lazarus, February 24, 1868

Concord
24 February 1868

My dear Miss Lazarus,

I have so happy recollections of the conversation at Mr Ward's, that I am glad to have them confirmed by the possession of your book & letter. The poems have important merits, & I observe that my poet gains in skill as the poems multiply, & she may at last confidently say, I have mastered the obstructions, I have learned the rules: henceforth I command the instrument, & now, every new thought & new emotion shall make the keys eloquent to my own & to every gentle ear. Few know what treasure that conquest brings,—what independence & royalty. Grief, passion, disaster are only materials of Art, & I see a light under the feet of Fate herself.—Perhaps I like best the poems in Manuscript. Some of those in the book are too youthful, & some words & some rhymes inadmissible. "Elfrida" & "Bertha" are carefully finished, & well told stories, but tragic & painful,—which I think a fault. You will count me whimsical, but I would never willingly begin a story with a sad end. Compensation for tragedy must be made in extraordinary power of thought, or grand strokes of poetry. But you shall instantly defy me, & send me a heartbreaking tale, so rich in fancy, so noble in sentiment that I shall prefer it to all the prosperities of time. I am so glad that you have kept your word to write to so ancient a critic, that I regret the more that you should have had to wait so long for a reply. But I was absent from home when your book arrived, & only now have found & read it.

Yours with all kind regards,
R. W. Emerson

Miss Emma Lazarus.

Concord, 14 April,
1868.

My dear Miss Lazarus,

You are very kind to write again, & it is good in these cold misplaced days to see your letters on my old desk. I shall not lose my faith in the return of spring. It is the more kind that you risk the wasting of time on such a shut-up dilatory correspondent. But on poetry there is so much to say, that I know not where to begin, & really wish to reply by a treatise of thirty sheets. I should like to be appointed your professor, you being required to attend the whole term. I should be very stern & exigeant, & insist on large readings & writings, & from haughty points of view. For a true lover of poetry must fly wide for his game, &, though the spirit of poetry is universal & is nearest, yet the successes of poets are scattered in all times & nations, & only in single passages, or single lines, or even words; nay, the best are sometimes in writers of prose. But I did not mean to begin my inaugural discourse on this note; but only sat down to say that I find I am coming to New York in the beginning of next week, & I rely on your giving me an hour, & on your being docile, & concealing all your impatience of your tutor, nay, on your inspiring him by telling him your own results.

In which good hope,

I rest yours faithfully,
R. W. Emerson

Miss Lazarus.

TO ANNA C. GREEN, JUNE 30, 1868

Concord
June 30, 1868

Dear Miss Green,

I fear you have thought me a sad cynic to have utterly neglected the letter which ought plainly to have fixed my attention & found an answer at once.

But my correspondence is large,—larger than I can meet as it requires, & I at almost all times indisposed to write any letter that is not indispensable. Tis only at intervals that I dare take up my sheaves of letters to see what has been neglected. And tonight I have alighted on yours which I must have read on its first arrival without recalling the person of its author. I now believe that you must be the young lady who, with Miss Tryon, represented the Society which invited me to Pulteney, & who with her gave me that pleasant drive to the quarries in your neighborhood. I hope I am not mistaken—for if it be not as I suppose,—I am at sea again. But for the verses which you sent me, & which I have just been reading. They are well chosen & give me as you meant they should a good guess at your style & quality of your work: clearly indicate a certain good degree attained in power of expression, & the specimens together show the variety & range of the thought. It is much to have got so far, & you cannot easily stop there, but will attempt new steps & heights in these pleasant experiments. I think one is to be congratulated on every degree of success in this kind, because it opens such a new world of resource & to which every experience glad or sad contributes new means & occasion. But it is quite another question whether it is to be made a profession,—whether one may dare leave all other things behind, & write. And I should say, this cannot be determined by cold election. If our thoughts come in such wealth & with such heat that we have no choice, but must watch & obey & live for them, the question is answered for us But for the most part the writing talent only adds to culture & to resources, & lifts society here in America, but the creative power is & remains rare. I should say to you, write whenever you can, & be thankful; read Milton & Shakspeare a good deal from time to time to see if your own lines are growing more cheerful & wise; And with whatever success you obtain, you will be sure of that one,—that all your writing educates to a better insight & enjoyment of the good minds & of Nature. I do not know whether to send back the verses you have confided to me or not.

With great regard,
R W Emerson

Miss Anna C. Green.

New York,
Sunday P M
September 13, 1868

Dear Lidian,

I came this morning to this house a little after 8 o'clock and found Haven &
Susie at breakfast. They said their father had had a better night than usual, &
was more comfortable today. I went up into his chamber, & found him much
altered in face & in speech, but entirely intelligent, &, though speaking with
difficulty, yet we talked of various things & persons for half an hour; then I
left him, & then returned again. At my next visit to his chamber, he was
asleep; &, at dinner, at one o'clock, Haven left Charles to preside, whilst he
sat with his father. Presently he called up Charles, & soon after came to tell
me that he thought all was over. I went up & found him quite insensible,
one or two groans escaped him, but his pulse soon ceased. Haven said when
they two lifted him to the bed, he said—"Goodbye."

It was all a sad surprise to me. I am glad to have come, if it was the last
day. He did not expect to see me. The boys have been excellent sons, & I tell
Charles that he can never reproach himself.

Their father told them he did not wish any funeral ceremonies to be
performed in New York & wished his body to be carried to Concord, & they
will proceed at once to obey him. The warm weather allows no delay, & I
suppose it will go on Monday night, & arrive at our house for a funeral on
Tuesday.

You must not go to Cohasset on Tuesday; & Charles & Haven do not
wish that Edward should be kept from Naushon, or recalled if gone: but if at
home I think he will wish to stay. Ellen must ask Mr Farrar to open the tomb
for Tuesday, & ask Mr Reynolds if he will be so good as to attend the funeral
at our house.

Affectionately
R W Emerson

Haven & Charles have just decided on conference with Dr Stone to have the
body sealed tonight in a lead coffin & they depart with it in the 8 o'clock train
tomorrow morning I shall go with them. Of course the coffin can not be

opened in Concord. Tell Mr Farrar this. Charles sends a notice to the B. Daily Advertiser announcing the funeral at 12.15 on Tuesday.

To James Bradley Thayer, November 22, 1868

Concord
Sunday Evening Novr

My dear Mr Thayer,

William Forbes came to me the other day with a pleasing project that I should have a private class of young men, his friends or acquaintances, for readings of poetry or prose, & conversation; & I should give what form to the project I would. He could not have devised anything that would flatter me so successfully. O certainly, bright young men & young women, either or both, met on any ground of culture delight me, & always provoke what faculty I have. Yes, I would think of it, & tell him,—if he persisted, & found any good will to it,—what I should like to attempt. I have now last night, a note from him intimating that he has talked of it with you, & that I should send you some scheme of a basis.

To meet this request as nearly as I now can, I will say, that I fancy that, like every old scholar, I have points of rest & emphasis in literature. I know what books I have found unforgetable, & what passages in books. It will be most agreeable to me to indicate such. I should like, in poetry, especially, to mark certain authors & certain passages which I prize, & to state on what grounds I prize them; & to distinguish good poetry from what passes for good. I believe I might secure proper consideration for some remote & unfrequented sources. If the class would bear it, I have something to say on Oriental poetry, which poetry seems to me important, & yet not studied hitherto except as language,—for language as a part of paleontology.

So in History, I should have my valued selections. Even of Natural Science something would need to be said, & of the future it is opening. And even of American biography, I think at this moment of much that would fall fitly in a class, that would be quite unparliamentary in a book or a public lecture.

I think this is the whole of my outline,—Readings of poetry; Readings of passages of prose; with my own commentary, & with special regard to making opportunity of conversation.

Perhaps it will be found impossible to add ladies to the class, on account of the hours chosen. It will be equally agreeable to me to come in the afternoon or the evening. Only one condition is important to me, namely, that no person shall be coaxed to come. If it is found, as may easily happen, that those on whom you reckoned are pre-occupied,—you must drop the plan at once, or postpone it to a better day.

With very kind regards,
Always yours,
R. W. Emerson

James B. Thayer, Esq
    P.S.

    Let me say that my wife & I are resting in a perfect assurance that Ellen & Edith, one or both, have conveyed to you & Sophy our invitation for Thanksgiving day, at 2.30 P. M. Our little friends the children, & their guardian are surely counted in. R. W. E.

To Emma Lazarus, July 9, 1869

Concord—
July 9, 1869.

My dear Miss Lazarus,

I ought long ago to have taken a decided part either to work out my criticism on your poems—as I doubted not at first to do,—or to have sent them back, & committed them to your own. But I still believed that my preoccupations were temporary, & the freedom would presently return—which does not return. I think I have never had so many tasks as in the last twelvemonth, and just now some revolutions at Cambridge have embarrassed me more than ever with time-taking duties, so that—added to the old ones—my rainbow leisures are thrust far forward quite or almost out of sight. For Admetus, I had fully intended to use your consent & carry it to Mr Fields for the "Atlantic." But on reading it over carefully, I found that what had so strongly impressed me on the first reading was the dignity & pathos of the story as you have told it, which still charms me. But the execution in details is not equal to this merit or to the need. You permit feeble lines & feeble words. Thus you write words which you can never have spoken. Please now to articulate the word "smileless,"—which you have used twice at no long interval. You must cut out all the lines & words you can spare & thus add force I have kept the poem so long that you will have forgotten it much, & will read it with fresh eyes. The dialogue of Hyperion & the Fates is not good enough. Cut down every thing that does not delight you to the least possible. I have marked a few heedless words. "Doubt" does not "ravage" nor be "revenged"

But I hate to pick & spy, & only wish to insist that, after reading Shakspeare for fifteen minutes, you shall read in this MS. a page or two to see what you can spare.

My present thought being that it would not be fair to yourself to offer it to the Atlantic until after your careful revision.

For the Masque,—I had it in mind when I first brought it home to indicate some capital scraps of pastoral poetry in Ben Jonson, to show you what a realism those English brains attained when gazing at flowers & pheasants.

I think the best pastoral is Shakspeare's "Winter's Tale." You will think it cheap to say these proverbs. Who could n't conjure with Shakspeare's name?

And now that I may pour out all my vitriol at once, I will add that I received the poem on Thoreau, but that I do not think it cost you any day-dawn, or midnight oil. But the poem to the *Heroes* keeps all its value.

On the whole, in this cynicism of mine, & on this suggestion of yours, I decide to inclose the two Manuscripts to you by mail today, & I am not without hope that I may find an opportunity to talk with you about them when you have forgiven me my bilious mood. Your friend,

R W Emerson

Miss E. Lazarus.

To ———, july 21, 1869

Concord,
July 21, 1869

Dear Sir:

I am sorry to be wanting to kind expectation, but in these days I find so much work that cannot be set aside laid out for me that I am forced to decline all new tasks that are not imperative. So I must beg you to say to the

Essex County Woman's Suffrage Association, that while I think their political
claim founded in equity, and though perhaps it does not yet appear to any
what precise form in practice it will and ought to take, yet the seriousness
and thoughtfulness with which it is urged seem to me to mark an important
step in civilization.

Respectfully,
R. W. Emerson.

TO JAMES FREEMAN CLARKE, MAY 3, 1870

Concord
3 May 1870

Dr J. F. Clarke.
My dear Sir,

I hoped to have found you at the Meeting of the Academical Committee at
Mr Adams's house the other day. Mr A. summoned us with a hope to receive
reports & to notify the sub committees that the visitations must be made
during the now current month of May.

The sub-committee on Modern Languages consists of yourself Mr Perkins & me. Mr P. has wished to resign: I have begged him to persist in trying
to serve & he will I think remain I wish to entreat you to take up the task
with him I shall not be able to go for an hour to any class during this month.
I have three lectures each week to read at Cambridge, & their preparation
over occupies all my time. After I had accepted this work my publishers
pressed me with proposals that I should revise my six books & prepare a new
edition for last October and a collection of unprinted papers for January.
Both of these tasks took much more time than was counted for at first, and
my new book was not published until March. Then much that had been
neglected in correspondence & affairs remained to be done & though I begun
as soon as I could to think how I could work properly on Philosophical Lectures the 26th April found me in a most unprepared state. And in my beginnings I have doubts if continuance is practicable. At all events, I must think of
nothing else & hence this appeal to your goodness to join Mr Perkins & lead
the work. I can take my part in seeing the Examination papers later.

I throw myself on your goodness.

R. W. Emerson

To Theodore Roosevelt, Sr., January 11, 1871

Concord, Mass.,
January 11, 1871

My Dear Sir:

I cannot come to New York, but I heartily join you in your joy at the series of events which within a few years have redeemed the fortunes of Italy. I am perhaps less acquainted than others around you with the details of the history, but one thing is plain, that for a long period the government of Italy has been a proverb for misrule. It was foreign—broken into small principalities, standing only on military possession—and odious to the subjects. It is now *one;* native, constitutional, and welcome to the people; and the recent abandonment of Rome by the French troops, and the vote of the Roman people to accept the government of King Victor Emmanuel instead of the anomalous and distasteful temporal power of the Pope, completes the emancipation. In America it is a principle of our government to abstain from the interference with European States. That is a political, but no wise social rule. Italy has an exceptional attraction for all nations. A visit to it is a point of education—a necessity of culture. Its history was for a long time the history of the world. It was for ages the centre and source of the highest civilization, and it was the calamity of mankind that the genius of the nation, to which all nations owed theirs, should be oppressed and in part extinguished.

I rejoice with you in the new days, with their auspicious omens. There is a new spirit in the world—an aim at better education, better natural and social science, and a pure religion, and we behold with more assurance the regeneration of Italy. With entire good-will and trust,

Yours,
R. W. Emerson.

To Caroline Sturgis Tappan, November 4, 1871

Concord
4 November 1871

Dear Caroline,

Mr Sanborn & I have combined to publish Ellery Channing's poem "The Wanderer," for the author's benefit. You shall not have so much as a Presentation Copy sent you, but must buy one at one dollar & persuade all your neighbors to buy one. I can send you if shall find it, as you may, to have some great merits,—any number of copies in paper covers at 50 cents. If you know that Tom Ward & Edward carry a little party every August to camp out for a week on Monadnoc, & that Ellery manages,—if they please or not, to find himself there at the same time, you will have some key to the dramatis personae. But the poem contains admirable things which, with all his perverseness, he has not been able to spoil.

Ever Yours,
R. W. Emerson

The "Hermit" very truly paints an eccentric naval officer who built a lodge some years ago at Walden Pond, & managed to spend the winter there.

To George Bancroft, December 17, 1871

Concord
17 Decr 1871

My dear Mr Bancroft,

I wish to re-introduce my son Edward to you. He was your guest with his mother at New York more than twenty years ago, & was very kindly treated. I believe he is as harmless now as then; & knows more; but wishing to know very much more he comes to Berlin, & seeks your protection. He carries with him the salutations & the affection of his mother to Mrs Bancroft, & my own also to her & to yourself.

R. W. Emerson

Hon. George Bancroft.

Concord
5 February 1872

My dear Muir,[71]

Here lie your significant Cedar flowers on my table, & in another letter; & I will procrastinate no longer. That singular disease of deferring, which kills all my designs, has left a pair of books brought home to send to you months & months ago, still covering their inches on my cabinet, & the letter & letters which should have accompanied to utter my thanks & lively remembrance, are either unwritten or lost,—so I will send this *peccavi,* as a sign of remorse. I have been far from unthankful,—I have everywhere testified to my friends, who should also be yours, my happiness in finding you,—the right man in the right place,—in your mountain tabernacle,—& have expected when your guardian angel would pronounce that your probation & sequestration in the solitudes & snows had reached their term, & you were to bring your ripe fruits so rare & precious into waiting Society. I trust you have also had, ere this, your own signals from the upper powers. I know that Society in the lump, admired at a distance, shrinks & dissolves, when approached, into impracticable or uninteresting individuals; but always with a reserve of a few unspoiled good men, who really give it its halo in the distance. And there are drawbacks also to Solitude, who is a sublime mistress, but an intolerable wife. So I pray you to bring to an early close your absolute contracts with any yet unvisited glaciers or volcanoes, roll up your drawings, herbariums & poems, & come to the Atlantic coast. Here in Cambridge Dr. Gray is at home, & Agassiz will doubtless be, after a month or two, returned from Terra del Fuego,—perhaps through St Francisco,—or you can come with him. At all events, on your arrival, which I assume as certain, you must find your way to this village, & my house. & when you are tired of our dwarf surroundings, I will show you better people.

With kindest regards yours,
R. W. Emerson

---

71. *Emerson had met Muir during his trip to California in the spring of 1871.*

John Muir.
    I send 2 vols. of Collected Essays by Book-post.

To Ednah Dow Cheney, March 25, 1872

Concord
25 March '72

Dear Mrs Cheney,

I shall come with pleasure to Woman's Club next Monday Evening but wish to say that I will not be reported. and I have the impression that I have seen lately in the newspapers that one of those violators, a reporter, had crept into your sacred assembly also. Now I gladly read to friends any paper that I have at the moment under my hands, in the hope that whilst it may interest them, it helps me to see its faults & wants, & am disgusted if Paul Pry is there, & prints his parody of it in a newspaper. So please to secure my safety if any such danger exist. I should not write this if I had not been surprised lately with this vexation in most unexpected quarters.

With great regard, yours,
R. W. Emerson

    Mrs Ednah Cheney.

To James Thomas Fields, April 12, 1872

Concord, 12 Apr. '72

My dear Fields,

I entreat you to find the correspondent of the N. Y. Tribune L. C. M. (a lady, I suspect it is,) who reports Miss Vaughan's, & Henry James's lectures, in Boston, in the "*Weekly Tribune*" of Wednesday, 10th April, & adjure her or him, as he or she values honesty & honor, not to report any word of what Mr Emerson may read or say or do at his coming Conversations. Tell the dangerous person, that Mr E. accepted this task proffered to him by private friends on the assurance that the audience would be composed of his usual circle of private friends, & that he should be protected from any report: that a report is so distasteful to him that it would seriously embarrass & perhaps cripple or silence much that he proposes to communicate; and if the individual has bought tickets these shall gladly be refunded. & with thanks & great honor of your friend,

R. W. Emerson

James T. Fields, Esq.

TO JAMES ELLIOT CABOT, JULY 26, 1872

Concord
26 July, '72

My dear Cabot

Thanks for your kind note & brave offer to lend me your household gods. But our little village holds us fast till we can see what can be done with the house & whether it cannot be re-built in a few months.[72] Meantime, I am getting my books into the Court-House which now belongs to the Insurance Company, & has room to spare, & we live with my cousin Miss Ripley at the Manse. A fire is a rude experience to an old housekeeper, but was alleviated by the tenderness with which every thing that could be saved was cared for by friends & neighbors.

---

72. *The* Boston Daily Advertiser, *25 July 1872: "A few hours after daybreak yesterday morning the people of the usually quiet town of Concord were startled by . . . a large conflagration . . . which subsequently proved to be the burning of the residence of Ralph Waldo Emerson. The fire was first observed by persons passing by . . . the library and all the furniture of the house were saved [by firemen and citizens]. The house was almost totally destroyed, except the walls of the lower floor . . . In the attic were a number of books and valuable manuscripts belonging to the late William Emerson of New York some of which were badly damaged and others destroyed. It is supposed that the fire originated in a defective flue, that it caught on Tuesday morning and has been smouldering ever since. The value of the house was estimated at $5000, and was insured . . . for $2500." [Rusk]*

With affectionate remembrances to Mrs Cabot & to the young people,
Yours,

R. W. Emerson

J. Elliot Cabot, Esq.

To J. C. Sanborn, July 29, 1872 [73]

Concord, July 29, 1872.

Dear Sir—I desire to express to you, and through you to the engineers and members of the Fire Department of this town, the sincere thanks of myself and each one of my family for the able, hearty and in great measure successful exertions in our behalf in resisting and extinguishing the fire which threatened to destroy my house on Wednesday morning last. We owe it to your efficient labor and skill that so large a part of the building was saved, and let me say that we owe it to your families and a great number of generous volunteers that almost all the furniture, clothing, and especially the books and papers contained in the house were saved and removed with tender care. I hope to have the opportunity of thanking, sooner or later, every one of our benefactors in person.

Yours, most gratefully,
R. W. Emerson.

To J. C. Sanborn, chief-engineer Concord Fire Department.

---

73. *Because no manuscript exists for this letter, the text printed here is that of the 1872 newspaper printing, which is styled with large and small capitals in the date and signature lines.*

To LeBaron Russell, August 16, 1872

Concord, Aug. 16, 1872.

My dear LeBaron:

I have wondered and melted over your letter and its accompaniments till it is high time that I should reply to it, if I can. My misfortunes, as I have lived so far in this world, have been so few that I have never needed to ask direct aid of the host of good men and women who have cheered my life, though many a gift has come to me. And this late calamity, however rude and devastating, soon began to look more wonderful in its salvages than in its ruins, so that I can hardly feel any right to this munificent endowment with which you, and my other friends through you, have astonished me.[74] But I cannot read your letter or think of its message without delight, that my companions and friends bear me so noble a good-will, nor without some new aspirations in the old heart toward a better deserving. Judge Hoar has, up to this time, withheld from me the names of my benefactors, but you may be sure that I shall not rest till I have learned them, every one, to repeat to myself at night and at morning.

Your affectionate friend and debtor,
R. W. Emerson.

Dr. LeBaron Russell.

To Ebenezer Rockwood Hoar, August 20, 1872

Aug 20./72.—

My dear Judge,

I have carried for days a note in my pocket written in Concord to you, but not finished, being myself an imbecile most of the time, & distracted with the multiplicity of nothings I am pretending to do. The note was not

---

74. *Emerson's friends raised $10,000 to help him rebuild his house and take care of other expenses.*

finished & has hid itself, but its main end was answered by your note containing the list so precious & so surprising of my benefactors. It cannot be read with dry eyes nor pronounced with articulate voice. Names of dear & noble friends, names also of high repute with me, but on whom I had no known claim; names too that carried one back many years, as they were of friends of friends of mine more than of me, & thus I seemed to be drawing on the virtues of the departed. Indeed I ought to be in high health to meet such a call on heart & mind, & not the thoughtless invalid that I happen to be at present. So you must try to believe that I am not insensible to this extraordinary deed of you & the other angels in behalf of

> *Yours affectionately.*
> *R. W. Emerson.*

To George Barrell Emerson, August 31, 1872

> *Naushon, Mass.,*
> *Aug. 31, 1872.*

My dear George:—

If there be one person whom I have from my first acquaintance with him held in unbroken honor, it is yourself. Little time as four or five years appears to us now, at the day when I first saw you it was serious and impressive,— you just graduated at college; I just leaving school to enter a Freshman. All the years since have not quite availed to span that gulf to my imagination. But I know not the person who has more invariably been to me the object of respect and love. You speak to my delight of your relations to my brothers, William, Edward, and Charles, but you do not seem to recognize my wide, and in some respects, unfortunate difference of temperament from them all, as being solitary from my youth, wishing always to be social, but by nature and habit always driven to solitude as the only home and workshop for me, I delight in seeing and watching good manners, and yours as of the best, and I believe it is my very respect for them that makes my visits short to those who have them, that I may not mar the grace. So I wish you to banish from your mind, once for all, any dream that I do not know and honor and love you as a friend and benefactor to me and mine, as well as to society. My children three all well know my regard for you and yours, and I believe Edith and

Edward have both made their calls at my instance at your house, but with the mischance of not finding you or Mrs. Emerson at home. You will have heard of our recent misfortune in the burning of my house. It is fast being rebuilt, and the wonderful kindness of many friends, it appears, will make it better than before. William R. Emerson has volunteered his active aid in mending its form. I shall not feel that it is quite complete until you come into it.

Yours affectionately always,
R. W. Emerson.

George B. Emerson, Esq.

To Lidian Emerson, Ooctober 31 and November 2, 1872

Steamer Wyoming,[75]
October 31, 1872

Dear Lidian,

Our floor & table tip a good deal, & perhaps our pens will refuse a straight line: but we are recovering our own personality, & mean to remember our relations. On the whole, the sea has been merciful, & for myself I have not had a sick hour. Ellen has not been so stout, but has found the steamer a far better floor than her beloved barque Fredonia. We have a quite amiable ship's company, & no social difficulties. Tis now our eighth day & we are promised, perhaps flatteringly, to reach our port on Sunday. We run about 260 or 270 miles per day. My well known orthodoxy, you will be glad to know, is walled round by whole families of missionaries, & I heard two sermons, & the English service, & many hymns on Sunday. But the liberal ocean sings louder, & makes us all of one church. Our ladies are very amiable & keep us civil. You will have heard from Edith & Will of our auspicious departure from Boston & from New York. I do not think that any travellers have departed under such galaxy of gifts & kindness. You will be waiting to hear

---

75. *Emerson and his daughter Ellen were travelling to Britain, Europe, and Egypt while the family home was being rebuilt.*

of our plans or schemes, but though Ellen is such an eager organizer, the next months are hardly sketched yet, & Edward doubtless will have much to say. The very peculiarity of our adventure is that it offers such liberty of choice for the next months, & my rainbow of Athens & of Egypt grew more realizable in New York, on learning that many American travellers were abroad with the same design. Meantime I trust that George Bradford has succeeded in finding you a good home in Boston for your visit, which, if not found, you must supplement by the Parker House, which, if less agreeable, is yet always certain & secure. For your affairs, Will is the king of men & the best of bankers, & will, I know, serve you wherever Edith can not. When have you known me write so long a letter? If the voyage permits, perhaps it will have a postscript.

Affectionately
R. W. E.

November 2d.

We have finished our 2680 miles today noon, & are now land-bound, having passed Cape Clear,—are to coast along the Irish shore all day tomorrow, & reach Liverpool at evening. Ellen has, I think, acquired a saintly reputation on board, by cherishing, blanketing, & coaxing the sick, tucking them up in her own chair,—which itself has proved a precious piece of furniture at sea, tell Edith. Our plans are still somewhat loose, but will crystalize as soon as we reach Liverpool, London, & Edward.

To Lidian Emerson, January 21? and May 11? 1873

Thebes Jan 73

Dear Lidian,

We enjoy heartily this watery journey, & have spent the last two days in the colossal temples on the two sides of the river here. Every day is clear & hot, the sky rich, the shores lined with palm groves, the birds innumerable, the ibis, the penguin, the hawk & the eagle, with vast flights of geese & ducks & flocks of little birds of sparrow size who fly in a rolling globe, whirl round & return again every minute. The crocodile is promised to us a little higher up the river but not yet seen. The Nile has daily the appearance of a long lake whose end we are always fast approaching, but the shores separate as we come to them opening new lakes of which we choose the broadest. Egypt is nothing but a long strip of land lined with a rocky desert on either side, & the river brings down each year the mud from the unknown regions in the South to give these wretched ribbon strips three harvests instead of one. The people are negroes in color, & often in the whole head & face, but are called Arabs, speak Arabic, and have excellent forms. The men at work in the fields or at the little aqueducts all along the shores are naked, with a rag tied round their loins: the women wear some kind of blue or black sheet about them, but the forms of the men are admirable, & their walk & action perfect.

Alas, dear Lidian, since the above lines were scratched, a long idleness—say incapacity to write any thing has held me;—not a line in my diary, not any syllable that I remember unless a word or two to the bankers, or unavoidable billets in reply to notes of invitation here or there has been written. You have been good & forgiving, & have sent me welcome letters, & must try to believe that this rest or absolute indolence was unavoidable & medicinal. Ellen has been a good angel here as always, & so acknowledged & received wherever we have gone—Skilful in business, perfect in temper, a welcome guest in every house we have entered, so that I have not needed to put off my solitary & silent ways. Then she has written letters by day & by night in steamboats & in trains so that there was no need for me to fight my dumb daemon.

Here we are at last on Scottish, yesterday, & today on English ground, at Keswick; & promising tomorrow to reach Manchester; &, on Wednesday, Liverpool, where our Steamer awaits us. I hope we shall both bring home better health.—Ellen certainly is no longer lame, but needs to be checked from overdoing continually. She makes friends everywhere, & all the more they must be prevented from drawing on her limited strength.

We have heard gladly of your comfort & good deeds in the long exclusion from home, & soon, I trust, we shall meet with renewed strength & unbroken faith in the heart as in the house. Your affectionate

R. W. E.

To Annie Adams Fields, December 8, 1873

Concord 8 Decr

My dear Mrs Fields,

Your wishes ought to be commands but my nerves shook at this invitation from you to this haughty anniversary.[76] I go nowhere, I speak never, I stay at home partly from benevolence to the friends who have had the indiscretion to invite me to their homes and I hope to keep this innocent rule until I shall succeed in accomplishing some petty stints of promised work which still baffle me. So forgive & pity me. Your new note tells a pitiful incident, not easy to meet with sweetness. I have never heard from the proposers. Why should they not come without conditions & each patriot speak for him- or her-self. My wife & daughter send their thanks for your kind invitation which they must not accept on account of the wickedness of your penitent but persisting disobeyer & friend,

R. W. Emerson

Mrs. Annie Fields

To William Dean Howells, March 14, 1874

Concord
14 March

Dear Sir,

I must not attempt the paper you propose though I should like well to do it & for the Atlantic, but my habit of writing is so irregular in these days, & I have so much incomplete work that I must not make new promises.

Yours,
R. W Emerson

W D Howells Esq

---

76. *The anniversary of the Boston Tea Party.*

452   To Lee and Shepard, March? 15? 1874

I learn with interest that you are preparing to publish a complete collection of Mr. Sumner's writings and speeches. They will be the history of the Republic in the last twenty-five years, as told by a brave, perfectly honest, and well-instructed man, with large social culture, and relations to all eminent persons. Few public men have left records more important,—none more blameless. Mr. Sumner's large ability, his careful education, his industry, his early dedication to public affairs, his power of exhaustive statement, and his pure character,—qualities rarely combined in one man,—have been the strength and pride of the Republic. In Massachusetts, the patriotism of his constituents has treated him with exceptional regard. The ordinary complaisances expected of a candidate have not been required of him, it being known that his service was one of incessant labor, and that he had small leisure to plead his own cause, and less to nurse his private interests. There will be the more need of the careful publication in a permanent form of these vindications of political liberty and morality.

I hope that Mr. Sumner's contributions to some literary journals will not be omitted in your collection.

To W. Robertson Herkless, Thomas S. Blyth, and P. Hartley Waddell, Jr., March 18, 1874

Concord Masstts.
18 March 1874

Gentlemen,

I received, a few days since, your letter of the 17th February, inviting me to allow my name to be proposed as one of the candidates for the Lord Rectorship of the University of Glasgow.[77]

I confess to a surprise that reached almost to incredulity, which the careful reading of your letter changed into a respect & gratitude to the kind and noble feeling with which you & the young gentlemen whom you represent

---

77. *Emerson eventually lost the election to Benjamin Disraeli.*

have honored me. Dr Stirling's letter, which came to me with yours, added its confirmation & the friendliest details to your own. At first, I thought the proposition so novel, & so unlikely to be sustained by the whole body of the matriculated students, that I must not think of it as other than a kindest compliment of a few friends,—& very precious to me as such, but only to be respectfully declined. On thinking it over, I find that it is for you & not for me to judge of the probabilities of the election, & that you, & not I, must decide whether these are such as to justify you in actually proposing my name to the electors. If you persist, you are at liberty to propose my name, &, if elected, I shall certainly endeavour to meet your wishes, & those of the University, as to the time & the duties which the office shall require. With this letter I shall send to Boston my affirmative reply by the Ocean Telegraph, as requested by Dr Stirling.

> *Yours, with very kind*
> *regards,*
> *R. W. Emerson*

Messieurs
    W R Herkless, President.
    T. S. Blyth Secretaries
    P. H. Wadell, Jr.

TO HENRY JAMES, SR., NOVEMBER 3, 1874

> *Concord*
> *Tuesday 3 November*

My dear James,

No, once & forever No, to your marvelous proposal of putting me or even my name into that mud.[78] I told you that I avoided the reading after the first

---

78. *The intrepid James had prepared the publication of a pamphlet to be given the title "What is Morality? Base or Superstructure? Being a Letter to Ralph Waldo Emerson Suggested by the recent events" of the Beecher-Tilton sexual scandal. James proposes to allude to the scandal at the start in a quotation from a recent discussion at Emerson's house. [Tilton]*

days broaching of the odious paragraphs & columns of the scandal & have kept until this a dear hope that the whole wretched story may yet prove to be a filthy plot. I never talk of it at home, much less abroad & wonder that I expressed any more to you than to shudder at the chance of one lump of the mud proving to be his. I beseech you not to name me with it. I have met the man repeatedly at distant intervals in many years sometimes in railroads sometimes at private houses, & admired his bold rustic talk, & rejoiced in his friendly trust. Perhaps I spoke to you of my latest meeting perhaps a year ago in Boston, when he changed his course, & walked down a street & across the Common with me to express a limited sympathy with my ways of thinking, & a purpose of spending a day with me at home. I dare hope that this was the true Beecher, & that the visit is yet to be. I beseech you let us all three keep our sanity & not touch this newspaper delirium. Affectionately yours,

R. W. Emerson

Henry James.
    I have been imprisoned by printer's work, & household events, that I could not write before.

To William Henry Furness, February 10, 1875

Concord, Feb., 10, '75

My dear friend,

Oldest friend of all,—old as Mrs Whitwell's school, & remembered still with that red & white handerchief which charmed me with its cats & rats of pre-historic art, & later with your own native genius with pencil & pen, up & upward from Latin School & Mr Webb's noonday's writing, to Harvard,—you my only Maecenas, & I your adoring critic, & so on & onward, but always the same—a small mutual admiration society of two,—which we seem to have founded in Summer street, and never quite forgotten despite the 300 miles tyrannical miles between Philad. & Concord—well what shall I say in my defence of my stolid silence at which you hint. Why, only this,—that while you have, I believe, some months advance of me in age, the gods have given you some draught of their perennial cup & withheld the same from me. I have for the last two years, I believe, written nothing in my once diurnal manuscripts & never a letter that I could omit (inclusive too of some that I ought not omit) and this applies to none more than yours. Now comes your new letter with all your affectionate memories & presence fresh as roses. I had received an invitation from Mr Childs, (who had sent me for years his monthly papers, until they ended though I have never seen him) with large invitation to his house, & with some deliberation I said Yes, & wrote him so, in spite of my almost uniform practice of choosing the hotel when I read lectures, for the reason that my lecture is never finished, but always needs a superfinal attention. Then came your letter, & I must obey it. My daughter Ellen who goes always with my antiquity insists that *we* shall, and I must write *no* to Mr Childs. So you & Mrs Furness receive our affectionate thanks for the welcome you have sent us. My love to Sam Bradford, if you meet him.

> *Your affectionate*
> *R. W. Emerson*

W. H. Furness.
My Wife—too much an invalid, sends you her kindest regards.

To Frederick Beck, July 7, 1875

Concord, July 7th, 75

My dear Mr Beck,

I cannot tell you what mortification I suffered last night, on my return from my prolonged journey, with my daughter, in the New Hampshire mountains when my wife informed me that I had failed of my engagement to you!

I had promised to give the retiring class of the New Hampton N. H. Academy their annual lecture on the evening before their Commencement. I knew little of the School except that it was not far from the Mountain region, and my daughter Ellen, who always goes with me when I travel entered heartily into the project of the journey which would lead us to the Notch to the Flume Agiocochook & Franconia, &c. none of which points she had seen. Then I write seldom in these days & a lecture was to be prepared not too old nor too dull Then it slowly was discovered that the day 30 June was

the very day of the Harvard Commencement & of the elections wherein I
had special interest in certain candidates Phi Beta too must be sacrificed It
was too late to repent we must go & went. The N. H Academy or College
held us also on the day following which was their Commencement. We must
speak there too, & badly. But we managed to reach Plymouth that night
climbed the hills & gathered strawberries the next morning on the hills &
reached the Flume House before night. I had seen nothing of the local
wonders for forty years they were far better than I remembered, &, day &
night were too charming to think of aught else we reached Fabian's the next
night but the rain would not let us behold the Profile Rock as we passed it,
nor hear the voices of the Echo Lake as we passed it, and even those of
Fabian's—which I well remembered in my youth—were now recusant to the
horn blower whom we persuaded to go out & wake them. Thence to
Crawford's; thence, the next day, to Wolfborough, &c &c & I never remembered my engagement for 4th July, till my wife at home last night scared me
with my broken faith. I shall come to you quickly to ask forgiveness, & a
new day. Yours penitently,

R. W. Emerson

To William Hathaway Forbes, April 29, 1876?

Concord, April 29.

Dear Will,

I hope for Edith's & all the children's sakes, & your own, & also for mine,
that you have got safely home. And for one of these person's sake I write to
say that when you have leisure to call on Mr Osgood one or two things
should be considered.

Of all my preceding books the plates from which they are printed belong
to me, & when any new edition is wanted Osgood writes to me to ask an
order on the printer to give him so many copies—say 100 or 250,—& sends
me a cheque covering my claim on that number. Of *Parnassus* three editions
have been printed, but thus far I have had no written record of the number
of copies in each edition. Of course, the expenses of the book would exhaust
probably all these editions, but we ought to know at each printing how many

are printed, & how the account stands. This book too is printed, I believe, in the same building in which his book store stands—as they have commonly gone only to the farther end of their store to bring me any information I wanted concerning the book, or proofs for examination. This arrangement prevents me from going to the printer to learn if his account agrees with mine, as I could do, (though I never did,) with the Cambridge house of Welsh and Bigelow who hold the plates of all my other books.

Another point. Osgood & Co. have never sent me the corrected copy of the *Contract* (is it?) between us for Parnassus. I forgot to ask for it when I have been there. I think I will not add a third little point that occurs, but ask forgiveness only for these.

> *Yours affectionately*
> *R. W. Emerson*

William H. Forbes, Esq.

To Harrison Gray Otis Blake, December 7, 1876

Concord, December 7, '76

My dear Sir,

I recieved your letter & should have immediately acknowledged it, but waited to go to the Library, & see the Treasure before it is sent. The two boxes containing Henry's Manuscripts are in perfect condition as they came,—and the third containing his surveys. It grieved me to think that they had remained so long so near, & I had never found time to read the books,—ever expecting that the booksellers would come to me to demand in behalf of the public new volumes. I can well understand that he should vex tender persons by his conversation, but his books, I confide, must & will find a multitude of readers. Did I not understand you that you were preparing your own notes of his life & genius?

> *With kind regards & good hope,*
> *R. Waldo Emerson*

H. G. O. Blake, Esq.

To George Stewart, Jr., January 22, 1877

Concord Masstts
22 January 1877

Dear Sir,

I have to thank you for the very friendly notice of myself which I find in Belford's Monthly Magazine, which I ought to have acknowledged some days ago. The tone of it is courtly & kind, & suggests that the writer is no stranger to Boston & its scholars. In one or two hints he seems to me to have been mis-informed. The only pain he gives me is in his estimate of Thoreau, whom he underrates. Thoreau was a superior genius. I read his books & manuscripts always with new surprise at the range of his topics & the novelty & depth of his thought. A man of large reading, of quick perception, of great practical courage & ability,—who grew greater every day, &, had his short life been prolonged would have found few equals to the power & wealth of his mind. By the death recently, in Bangor, Maine, of his sister, Miss Sophia Thoreau, his Manuscripts (which fill a large trunk,) have been bequeathed to H. G. O. Blake, Esq, of Worcester, Masstts, one of his best friends, & who, I doubt not, will devote himself to the care & the publication of some of these treasures.

When your journeys lead you to Boston, it would give me pleasure to have a card from you of your address. With kind regards,

R. W. Emerson

Mr George Stewart, Jr.

To Ellen Emerson, March 10, 1879

Concord
10 March

Dear Ellen,

If there be any assurance that I should attempt to do the work. which Sampson, Low, & Co. of London, persist in asking—now in a new letter;— it is absolutely necessary that you should come home & tell me what hints &

what resources Mr Cabot & you have found in my workshop possible to this
end.[79] I hate to draw one day from Edith your heart & hands, & I wish that
I had absoluted at first the English proposal. But as I have made no reply, I
must make a trial of at least one day to find a possible sheet to send them, &
if not finding the same, to write my regrets. I am aware that Mr Cabot has
marked on one role, "Sampson, Lowe, & Co" So give my blessing to Edith
and my joy in her new joy, & entreat her to let you come to me, if only for
one day.

Your loving Papa

To James Herbert Morse, April 16, 1879

Concord, Masstts
April 16,

Dear Sir,

I have recieved your letter arriving this morning and not the foregoing one of
which it speaks. I grieve not to obey your kind invitation. I am not in
condition to make visits or take any part in conversation. Old age has rushed
on me in the last year & tied my tongue & hid my memory, & thus made it
a duty to stay at home. I regret it the more that Mr Frothingham has strong
claim on me, not only on his own, but on his father's side, who was a noble
friend to my youth. I rejoice that after so long & faithful labors in the
church, he has this well-earned rest & enjoy before him. With great regret
that I must send no better reply,

R. Waldo Emerson

---

79. *Ellen Emerson and James Elliot Cabot mined Emerson's journals and prepared the*
"General Introduction" to The Hundred Greatest Men *(1879) to meet this obligation.*

460   To William Henry Furness, August? 20? 1880?

Ellen asks me what message I wish to send to you. I tell her immortal love, &
the gladness that though you count more months than I you have not &
shall not like me lose the names, when you wish to call them, of your
contemporary or antecedent friends & teachers.

Ralph Waldo E.

Index